Over the Rim of the World

FREYA STARK
Selected Letters

Also by Freya Stark
published by John Murray

THE VALLEYS OF THE ASSASSINS
THE SOUTHERN GATES OF ARABIA
SEEN IN THE HADHRAMAUT
A WINTER IN ARABIA
BAGHDAD SKETCHES
LETTERS FROM SYRIA
EAST IS WEST
PERSEUS IN THE WIND
IONIA
THE LYCIAN SHORE
ALEXANDER'S PATH
RIDING TO THE TIGRIS
ROME ON THE EUPHRATES
THE JOURNEY'S ECHO
THE ZODIAC ARCH
THE MINARET OF DJAM
A PEAK IN DARIEN

Autobiographies
TRAVELLER'S PRELUDE
BEYOND EUPHRATES
THE COAST OF INCENSE
DUST IN THE LION'S PAW

Letters
Eight-volume edition
published by Michael Russell (Publishing) Ltd

Over the Rim of the World

FREYA STARK
Selected Letters

Edited by
CAROLINE MOOREHEAD
Foreword by
PATRICK LEIGH FERMOR

JOHN MURRAY
in association with
MICHAEL RUSSELL

Letters © Freya Stark, 1936–1988
Editorial © Caroline Moorehead, 1988

First published in 1988
by John Murray (Publishers) Ltd
50 Albemarle Street, London W1X 4BD
in association with
Michael Russell (Publishing) Ltd

British Library Cataloguing in Publication
Over the rim of the world
Stark, Freya, *1893*–
Selected letters
I. Moorehead, Caroline, *1944*–
826′.912
ISBN 0–7195–4619–2

Typeset by Inforum Ltd, Portsmouth
Printed and bound in Great Britain by
Richard Clay Ltd, Bungay, Suffolk

Contents

Foreword

Sprung from an earlier generation, Dame Freya Stark has escaped the decay of literacy which has smitten the rest of us. Most of these letters were written haphazard from wild places – perhaps while animals were being loaded at an oasis or during shelter from a blizzard in the Taurus – and then published as they stood. Yet there is indeed something unusual in the lucidity of her style, its balance and smooth flow. In writing as in speech her sentences always fall on their feet with a light, spontaneous and unfaltering aptness.

Most of her correspondents are friends of long standing. The list is increased by newcomers now and then, thinned from time to time by deeply felt losses, like those of Sir Sydney Cockerell, Berenson, Austin, Harrison, Victor Cunard and Field-Marshal Wavell, and the mood of the letters is affectionate, charming and informal, all of them marked by a certain unmistakable *tenue*. Those written during her journeys, and especially the ones addressed to her old friend and publisher John Murray, make up a kind of serial diary posted at random stages for fear of loss. The others, until her recent move to simpler quarters, are chiefly from her house in Asolo, where the cypresses of her terrace command the Venetian champaign from a ledge on the Dolomite foothills. This Palladian neighbourhood, with its Veronese frescoes, its Giorgione altars and echoes of Browning, has been her home for almost a century and it is here that the itineraries were plotted, the ancient authors pored over, the languages studied in advance and the books written when she got back; and today she is certainly the most celebrated and honoured inhabitant of that beautiful arcaded town since Catarina Cornaro, dethroned in Cyprus, set up her court there in 1489.

It only takes a few pages for the reader to become utterly absorbed by the places and people Dame Freya describes, by the delights and the mishaps and above all the personality of the letter-writer herself. Inevitably, one takes down those of her books which cover the same regions as the letters – perhaps *The Lycian Shore, Alexander's Path* or *Rome on the Euphrates* – and then plunges into them with new pleasure. They in turn illuminate the *Letters*: the two form an intricate counterpoint. For these books alone she read Herodotus, Isocrates, Xenophon, Arrian, Plutarch, Polybius, Cicero, Seneca, Tacitus, Suetonius, Strabo, Pliny, Lucan, Diodorus Siculus, Frontinus, Dio Cassius, Marcus Aurelius, Ammianus Marcellinus, Synesius and Procopius, and then the church fathers, as well as studying later travellers down to Spratt, Fellows, Leake, Robert Byron and Bean. There are moments of protest. 'Pliny's so boring', she bursts out. 'Cicero insufferable, Julian an appalling prig, even Catullus jeers at a man *for being poor!* What a relief to turn to Polybius, who was Greek. I would like to have married him.' When Asia Minor journeys loomed she learnt Turkish, and brushed up her Arabic too; and the language duly fluttered down from the air when it was needed, undamaged by a decade of disuse; and her Persian carried her safely *communicada* through Afghanistan and Iran. She attended classes at the Academie Julian during her sixties and was soon backing up her accomplished photography with deft and lively sketches.

Dame Freya's visible baggage, by contrast – a lesson from mountain-climbing as a girl – was light and wieldy. It had to be. The Xanthus valley and its enigmatic tombs, the slopes of Mount Climax, the giant tumbled fragments, the theatres and the overgrown temples and the Hellenistic stadia where the mouldings run their halting and endless egg-and-dart races were as tough going still as they had been a century before, and the terminal unjeepability of the mountain tracks often meant many days in the saddle. Among the Hakkiari Kurds, somewhere on the watershed between the Khabur and the Kizi, a girth breaks and she and her pony topple over 'forming a sort of Bernini group'. At nightfall she settles into her grim and sometimes hellish quarters with stoic humour and finds comfort where she can: 'The Turks are less tiring than the Arabs because they are silent by nature – and of course not so amusing but easier at the end of a long day'. Now and then there is an obstructive *kaimakam* or a thick-headed police officer, but the villages, devoted to *Freya Khanum* by now, invariably back her up and foil them. In the rush-lit evenings she ploughs through the *Illiad* in Turkish: 'Not a very useful language for every day, except in times of massacre.'

Sometimes moments of distress and contemporary tragedy cut clean across her tracing of ancient dramas. Dame Freya calls to mind the Arab lands as she knew them first, when the strong, the wise, the just and the good seemed to be entrusted with their destinies, when our faith with them was still unbroken; and a sigh is just audible from the page. And more than a sigh at desolate Trebizond, when in a moment of bleak isolation in July 1958, she learns of the revolution in Iraq and the massacre of the young King, the Regent and Nuri-as-Said, the Nestor of the youthful state: all of them closely bound to her and with more to follow: 'It makes seven of my friends murdered, and Nuri I can't bear to think of, and the little King with his thoughts of marriage, his new palace and his care for his country'.

Her return to Baghdad, the scene of her earliest Arabian appren-
ticeship, is very moving. (She and Gertrude Bell had missed each other
by a few years; there is an opening here for a Plutarchian comparison.)
Among the enduring ruins of the old world, the scattered new buildings
collapsing from jerry-building and lack of maintenance defy every
traditional law of eastern light and shade: one 'should never look out
direct on a landscape, but have an interval of cool shadow, like the
eyelash to the eye'. She avoids the effendi-world. It is the Bedouin and
the mountain people that she loves, the barbarian fringe and the nomads:
we follow her step by step.

Every now and then she breaks away, takes the ship and sits up late
talking to friends on a Greek island, moves on to Guardi-like festivals in
Venetian palaces, attends a ball at the Castle of Duino, listens to *The
Barber of Seville* at the Vienna Opera, stays in Paris with her exact
contemporary, Lady Diana Cooper – 'five days dashing between Chanel
and the Bibliothèque Nationale' – picks up threads in London – 'sat next
to Alec Guinness, who says Shakespeare should never be acted again till all
the modern methods are forgotten and that Cleopatra should be acted by
a boy'. There are sojourns at Cliveden and Houghton and a long spell in
Devon, where she had lived as a child; then back to her desk above the
winding Brenta and her library with its eighty-seven yards of books,
including her own not inconsiderable total, as well as her letters. Some of
them, in 1976, are to Paul Scott. This new friendship was based on her
discerning of and early admiration for *The Raj Quartet*; but it was soon to
be broken off by death. She thinks of a return to Cairo – 'just to let the
lumbago sniff the desert air'.

Her cogitations on events are shrewd and striking, deeply thought
out, often at odds with political fashion; marked by loyalty and by pity.
They are urbanely set down, indignant with the government now and
then – 'surely they wouldn't have lied in Parliament before 1914?' –
especially when infirmity of purpose and shuffling expediency seem
particularly damaging or flagrant; and the general decline of everything
else brings moments of despair which she passes over quickly. She reacts
with courage and stoicism to the passage of time and lets a quiet
philosophical, open-eyed optimism take care of her own destiny. All
these things, and the themes that I have already outlined, turn her
correspondence into the most coherent, impressive and stimulating
body of letters it is possible to imagine.

Books have been written about Dame Freya by friends and one of her
many godchildren: *A Tower in the Wall* and *Rivers of Time* with many of
her original photographs by Alexander Maitland (Blackwood, 1983),

Freya Stark by Caroline Moorehead (Viking, 1985) and *Traveller Through Time* by Malise Ruthven (Viking, 1986). They are an accompaniment to these letters and they reconstruct the thread of her life beginning with her birth in Paris where her parents – both of them painters and one a musician as well – had a large studio near the Luxembourg Gardens. Her childhood and growing-up in Asolo and Piedmont alternated with the tors and heather of Dartmoor, where she and her sister ran wild and had fun dressing up and – a wise precaution, as we have seen – learning how to fall off their ponies, while their father, leaving his easel, followed the Mid-Devon hounds. Prosperity was tempered with lean years. Her early education was rather haphazard – helped later on by an accomplished governess and, later still, by the guidance of the brilliant scholar W.P. Ker, whom she adored. He was one of the older people who saw how unusual she was and helped to shape her life. But – as it is with most brilliant people – private curiosity was her main guide. A dangerous accident, then nursing on the Italian Front at the time of Caporetto, an unhappy love affair and, penultimately, the study of Arabic, were her stepping-stones. Then everything began to change.

What was it that dissolved all the barriers? Mastery of the languages, certainly: strangers were automatically half disarmed; good manners, a quiet pitch of voice and a touch of formality evoke a kindred answer; and even on the barbarian fringe, charm, sympathy and interest in other people worked wonders. The fact that she was a woman, travelling with no retinue but a guide of their own people, prompted chivalrous admiration among these wild folk. She knew their speech and their ways and, apart from everything else, guests in these regions are sacred, even though blood-feuds may be reciprocally depopulating the two nearest canyons. Very occasionally things looked bad. She was, after all, a giaour, a *feringhi* and a Nazarene. What was she up to? Surrounded in a remote spot by wild-eyed Islamic zealots, she would say with some ceremony, '*We are people of the Book*!', seeming, between finger and thumb, to hold up an invisible volume, wherein it is written that Islam and Christendom spring from a common stem. The mention of the *kitab* was like a talisman: Isa and Mariam dimly took shape in their minds alongside Ibrahim, Musa, Harun and Mohammed and, after a pause, the seated greybeards round the nargilah would wag their agals and kef-fiyehs in concert, and the danger was past.

Travelling in Uzbekistan a few years ago, heading for Bokhara, Samarkand and Tashkent – and, at seventy-four, a tourist for the first time – she was alerted, when they touched down at Khiva, by the sudden closeness of the Oxus. Only sixteen miles! But access was forbidden and the Soviet official, an almost Chinese-looking Uzbek, was inflexible. (No good slipping him a shilling, like Wilde with the surly Café Royal doorman: 'There my man! An Alsop for Cerberus.') He was too exalted for silver, too moral for gold. But memory was an ally, and her luck held: she discovered he spoke English and that he pined for English books. And poetry too? Yes: *But why did she want to go to Oxus? Sohrab and Rustum* provided the answer. She moved a step forward. 'And night came down over the solemn waste', she murmured, and her kind blue eyes must have become mesmeric:

> And the two gazing hosts and that sole
>   pair,
> And darkened all; and a cold fog that
>   night
> Crept from the Oxus. Soon a hum arose
> As of a great assembly loosed, and fires
> Began to twinkle through the fog; for now
> Both armies mov'd to camp and took their
>   meal . . .
> But the majestic river floated on;
> Out of the mist and hum of that low land,
> Into the frosty starlight, and there mov'd,
> Rejoicing, through the hush'd Chorasmian
>   waste
> Under the solitary moon.

The nearly Chinese features were rapt. It was Open Sesame. The Oxus was hers.

P.L.F.
Kardamyli, May 1988.

This introduction is based on an article, 'A Delight in Wild Places', *Times Literary Supplement*, 1983.

For Lucy

O heart of insatiable longing,
What spell, what enchantment allures thee
Over the rim of the world
With the sails of the sea-going ships?

Bliss Carman's SAPPHO

Introduction

By temperament and the customs of her time, Freya Stark was a diarist. Keeping a regular, well-written and clearly thought-out log of her life was for her a completely natural thing to do. In fact, she kept no diary: she wrote letters instead. And these letters, begun in her childhood in the early years of the century and going on into her nineties, are like the entries in a continuous notebook, added to day by day.

There are, of course, enquiries about illness or new jobs, terms of affection, personal remarks; but the core of virtually every letter is a narrative, a bringing up to date of her own life, a series of observations about what she is seeing or doing, or about a book she has just read, or a new person she has been introduced to. They are the letters not only of a traveller, describing journeys day by day, but of a writer interested in literature, politics, history, philosophy, her contemporaries and their dress, behaviour and oddities. And she believed that she was being realistic, not self-important, when, arguing in the early 1970s for the publication of at least six volumes of her letters, she wrote: 'The interest or main line is . . . in the almost Tolstoyan development of a human being in extraordinary family relationships'.

Freya's earliest letters are addressed to her mother Flora, whom she called 'Biri'. They are loving, but on occasion firm. Flora remained her main correspondent right up until the late 1930s, when Freya began to make close friends who rapidly turned into close correspondents. Even then, she continued to write regularly to her mother, sometimes daily, referring from time to time to her letters as a 'diary', and reminding Flora to be sure to keep them. They became the notes that later made their way into her travel books and into the four volumes of her autobiography. There are many fewer, but in some ways more affectionate, letters to her father, to whom she wrote as 'Pips'.

Though in time Freya was to make good women friends – Pamela Hore-Ruthven (later Cooper), Sybil, Marchioness of Cholmondeley, Dulcie Deuchar – it was to her men friends that Freya really preferred to write, letters that were often almost essays, and also funny, engaging and perspicacious. She wrote with exceptional ease.

Apart from her mother, her closest and longest-lasting correspondence has been with her publisher, Jock Murray, whom she met in 1933 when she was in London not long after the publication in Baghdad of her first book, *Baghdad Sketches*. After her mother's death, it was to Murray that she addressed the diary of her life, as well as her anxieties and insecurities – and at times reproaches. In the late 1930s and early 1940s, possibly the happiest years of her life, Freya met and became friends with Sir Sydney Cockerell, General Wavell (later Field-Marshal Earl), Sir Kinahan Cornwallis and Bernard Berenson. To all of these, until their deaths, she wrote constantly. There was something about these men, something to do with the admiration she felt for them as well as the fondness, that conjured up the best in her writing. Her letters to her husband, Stewart Perowne, during the brief years of their marriage, also show to what extent Freya saw letters as a natural component of any intimate relationship. To everyone she wrote remarkably about what she noted on her travels; but she was also a shrewd observer of human behaviour; and she wrote well, often touchingly, about herself.

Not only are the letters full of detail: they are also very numerous. It was not unusual for Freya, when settled anywhere, to write five or six in a day. These were the serious letters, three or four pages long, almost invariably on thin blue airmail paper, the handwriting looped and rather foreign looking but legible except when, short of space, she ran the last few sentences up and down the margins. She wrote in ink. Other, shorter messages went on postcards.

When Freya began to assemble her letters in the late 1960s, writing to all those with whom she had ever corresponded to see what they had kept, and drawing on the copies that in the later years she took to keeping, she found herself with close to two million words. In the eight-volume edition of her letters, published by Michael Russell between 1974 and 1982, these were reduced to about a million. This single volume consists of a selection from the original letters, plus a small number of previously unpublished letters, which have come to light only recently, and were very kindly sent to me by their recipients or their heirs. They include letters to: Lady Drower, Gerald de Gaury, Jane Boulenger, Pamela Cooper, Sir Harry Luke, Malise Ruthven, Edward Hodgkin and Jock Murray.

Because I wanted to include as much of what is best in as many letters as possible, individual letters have been cut. There are no marks to show where this has been done, so that the flow of words is not broken; but nothing of importance has been left out.

*   *   *

Freya Stark was born in Paris, on 31 January 1893, in a studio on the Rue Denfert Rochereau. She was early, and nothing was ready: Robert, her father, took Herbert Young, a student friend, to buy clothes for the baby

2

at the Galleries Lafayette. The nomadic spirit of her first days continued. The family was constantly on the move: to Genoa to visit one grand-mother, to Devon to visit another, to Italy for long visits.

Robert and Flora, Freya's mother, were cousins and both were painters. Up until Freya's birth, Flora had been studying at Julien's atelier, and had won a medal for a picture in the Salon. It was not a happy marriage. Freya's earliest years were spent in Chagford in Devon where her father built, one after the other, a series of houses along the edge of Dartmoor and created round them marvellous gardens. Flora, tall and very pretty, had her roots in Tuscany, where her grandmother had presided over a Florentine salon of the Brownings, Thackerays and Trollopes. She found the moors bleak and isolated and her husband, who loved the countryside, taciturn. Freya and her younger sister Vera had governesses, but remained wild, little educated and with few companions.

By 1901 Flora was restless. She took the two girls to a house in a village in the foothills of the Dolomites called Asolo, a place of narrow colon-naded streets, once the summer resort of Venetian merchants. The Starks knew the village well as it was here that Herbert Young had settled in a gatehouse in the village walls, and where Robert Browning's son Pen had bought and restored three houses. Herbert Young was much attached to the two children.

In 1903 came another move, this time to Dronero, a grey and cobbled town in Piedmont, where a new friend of Flora's, Count Mario di Roascio, a short, round young man with dipping moustaches whom the girls disliked intensely, had started a carpet business. Flora rented a house of his called La Mal Pensà, while Robert stayed behind in Chagford. He paid visits to Italy and one summer took them to Le Touquet.

There was never much money. The girls learnt French and embroid-ery from the nuns at the Sacré Coeur convent and tried to ignore the apparent involvement between Mario and Flora and the scandal that soon surrounded it. Vera was timid and passive; Freya self-reliant and somewhat censorious. She had discovered books: Dumas, Plato, Mil-ton, Spenser, Hazlitt; and she was teaching herself Latin. It was an essential discovery. One afternoon in Mario's new carpet factory, standing by the vast looms, her long hair was caught up in one of the steel shafts and she was carried round, her feet hitting the wall as she was dragged by. When she was pulled free, half her scalp was found to have been torn away. She spent the next four months in hospital, patched up by the newly invented skin grafts, which left her forever slightly disfigured down one side of her face and always conscious of the effect of her appearance on other people.

3

In 1908, Freya went to stay with Harry Jeyes, assistant editor of the *Standard*, and his wife Vera in London. It was there that she met W.P. Ker, later Professor of Poetry at Oxford, whose lectures on English Literature at London University she attended and who became her adopted godfather. These visits to London delighted her, particularly once she began a degree course at Bedford College, though she worried constantly about being unattractive and that her fellow students might find her too formal and foreign in manner. She was happiest listening to W.P. Ker, or talking socialism with a new friend, Dorothy Varwell, on Dartmoor, and racing her pony across the moors.

Family life provided little pleasure: Robert had sold his last Dartmoor house and gone to Canada to start a new life farming, and Mario cast gloom over Dronero. It took Freya a long time to notice that Mario was courting her, but when she did she backed sharply away. Three years later, in 1913, he married Vera, who was received into the Roman Catholic Church. Despite promising to move, Flora continued to live in the house with them. It was a bitter and unsettled place, which gave her the incentive to make a life of her own.

PUBLISHER'S NOTE

The first six volumes of the eight-volume edition of Freya Stark *Letters*, published by Michael Russell (Publishing) Ltd in 1974–82, were edited by Lucy Moorehead; after her death the later two volumes were edited by her daughter Caroline Moorehead.

1

1914 war, Caporetto, farming at L'Arma, mountaineering with W.P. Ker, learning Arabic

On 31 January 1914, Freya was twenty-one. She spoke English with a slight foreign accent and had completed much of an Honours Degree in History at London University. She could ride, dance, embroider, construe Latin, speak perfect Italian and adequate French and German and was, according to friends, 'a very funny little thing', with home-made dresses worn too long because her mother insisted that long clothes suited short people better than short ones. From her father she believed that she had inherited 'a feeling of almost physical discomfort in the face of any lie'; from her mother, vitality.

When war broke out she decided to abandon the university and left for Bologna to train as a nurse at the clinic of St Ursula. She became engaged to a bacteriologist called Guido Ruata, but this lasted only a year. Freya caught typhoid which turned into pleurisy and then pneumonia and she very nearly died.

Returning to London, she worked in the Censor's Office, reading soldiers' letters in French, German and Italian, waiting to continue her training as a nurse, after which, in the autumn of 1917, she joined G.M. Trevelyan's ambulance unit near Gorizia, retreating with the wounded when the Austrians broke through at Caporetto.

FLORA STARK

1 February 1914

My dear my own Mother,

I feel I have had so much more than I deserve, and now I am quite bewildered and overpowered. It is so good to feel that one is loved – the only real riches in the world, and I am very happy in that. I think my soul came to me quite suddenly, when I was about eleven years old, and all at once I realised how precious you were to me – since then have we not been growing nearer and nearer? When we go to the next world I hope St Peter will not know which is which.

Here are some of my birthday flowers as a remembrance.

FREYA

My darling Biri,

I hope you will have received the wire and not be thinking of me at the bottom of the Channel. The journey was quite good considering. At Modane I was brought into an office with three spectacled Frenchmen in a row all asking questions, so that I felt like Mr Winkle in the witness box; their looks finally however melted to benevolence, and I was allowed to go, with many bows.

I travelled to Havre with two girls from Salonika, doctors, who were in uniform, and one had her hair cut and was so like a boy one couldn't possibly have told the difference if it hadn't been for her skirt. There was also a charming elderly naval officer going on leave: he told us that in the fog a day before, a German submarine got itself entangled in the Havre *reticolati* and came to the surface right in the Havre waters, and went off gaily before anyone could catch it. He said these submarines were 'great sports' and 'awfully cheeky', and spoke of them with evident affection!

There was a tremendous crowd at Havre and we were all herded together and standing for over an hour with a lot of French who always try to get on by sharpness of their elbows. The Tommies kept wonderful order: it was so nice to see the dear boys. They look so huge after the French. It was a great joy suddenly to hear one of them call out 'ladies first' and open a way for us: we went proudly past the disgusted French people!

The passport room has two long tables with a row of civilians and soldiers, and a soldier at the bottom to keep guard: and we were cross-examined by them all one after another and our life-history looked up in a file. After that we went to the customs – all looked after by women, and then on board. The charming officer had asked if he could do anything for me and I asked him to find me a berth: but for him I should have had to sleep on deck, and it was bitterly cold!

At about midnight, all the lights were put out, and we started going at a tremendous rate with quite a heavy sea, as the water was coming in at one of the upper portholes. But I slept beautifully and enjoyed it, and only woke in time to have a good breakfast before reaching Southampton.

I found dear Viva [Jeyes][1] at Waterloo, and it was lovely to be driving again through London; but also rather sad.

---

1 Viva Jeyes was a family friend of long standing.

Here they expect the war to go till June! Who knows?

Your
FREYA

FLORA STARK

11 Grove End Rd. 29 September 1916

My own Biri,

What nonsense you talk to me! Do you really think that I could have any happiness at all left if you get ill? I feel that it doesn't matter what one does or what happens so long as we bear it properly and do not lose our sense of proportion or throw up the sponge and be miserable just because we are one of a few millions who are going through a bad time. I am so afraid now you are alone you let yourself go to be unhappy, my dearest, when there is no reason: you will see that everything will come all right in time, and then you will have wasted years in a kind of misunderstanding of the meaning of things. I do believe that our lives are in God's hands and he guides them as he wishes, and it is bad not to accept it with faith in the ultimate good, and not to take things cheerfully as far as may be: and then you will feel a tranquillity, just as anyone has found who has met sorrow and accepted it for what it is. So buck up, and don't let us be downhearted!

FREYA

FLORA STARK

11 Grove End Rd. 19 October 1916

My darling Biri,

I have been typing for the last two days at the Canadian Red Cross, making out lists of 'missing'; such a sad work. I typed steadily, lists of names, and all practically belonging to September. It is very tiring, also because of shifty offices, with artificial light, and no glimpses of the hills: only a little whiff of petrol, from one's motor bus! It seems I am a most satisfactory clerk however, and I hope I shall get some work that isn't too deadly.

It is so strange mixing up with all these girls whose life is all in these rabbit burrows: they seem to talk of nothing but young men, and hats, but are very amiable and ready to be nice, and not much different from the college girl.

Viva came yesterday and took me out to lunch: we tried the Carlton Grill Room, and couldn't find a table, and only with difficulty got in at the Criterion: it is all crowded with officers on leave, and they look so nice. One feels quite 'undressed' without an officer belonging to one!

I think we may be going to St. Margaret's for the week end, and hope to see some Zepps or Taubes[1] over there. The searchlights are so wonderful these misty nights, like great animals shooting their heads out of the darkness, and feeling about for something to fasten on.

Your own
FREYA

FLORA STARK

11 Grove End Rd. 16 November 1916

My own darling Biri,

We had your letters yesterday. I am glad Miss Smith told you of the event,[2] and Viva is writing for my picture: the other presents I hope he will keep. I am sending his rings back of course.

We both feel that this explains a great deal; if there was an earlier tie he may have had a difficult choice to make, or perhaps he came again under her influence while I was away: these things happen, and I believe the more one knows the less is one inclined to blame. Certainly I feel it puts him in a better light, and explains much that was dark to me.

I am very glad for his sake that he should have married: I believe she is a very nice woman and clever, and quite young. I should like to know more about her if you happen to hear. Of course I feel he should have been more straightforward and told me the real reason, which I would have understood and accepted: but even there, it is possible that there were very good reasons why he could not tell.

Anyway that is done with, and I would not worry any more about it if I were you, Biri. I do believe that a sense of proportion is the most important thing one needs, and sometimes I feel that yours is rather wobbly: please don't become intense, or get a religious craze, or chronic melancholia. Dorothy[3] told me yesterday that you were the sort of person to head a 'Movement', and I have been alarmed ever since.

Your
FREYA

1 The German bomber aeroplane.
2 Guido Ruata had broken off the engagement to Freya and married a musician. Freya was to remember the time as 'a short and perfect happiness . . . when every trivial moment lives as if in a halo of its own'.
3 Dorothy Varwell, whose family lived at Thornworthy, the neighbouring estate on Dartmoor to Ford Park, one of the houses built by Robert Stark.

FLORA STARK

My own Biri,

I have only two hours of free time in the day, and have wasted three quarters of the precious time by not having energy to fetch my paper to write. But my poor legs. They feel so tired. I am only just realising what a wonderful experience St. Orsola was, where I had all the interesting things to do and none of the drudgery. Here it takes a lifetime to reach that stage, and all my brilliancy in bandaging, giving anaesthetics, etc. . . . is of no use. I'll tell you the timetable – one is called at 6.30 – breakfast 7.15 – then cleaning the wards, sweeping, dusting, brushing their hairs, etc. till 9 – then one gets the luncheons – then one clears them, then the doctors come and there is a scurry till 12.30 – then the real lunch – then a short respite while we eat – more sweeping (the wards are swept four times a day), washing of various things, then teas to be prepared, and then they have to be got ready for bed. It is usually but not always all done by 8.30 – and by that time I go about like an automaton.

The etiquette is very strict, and the Matron is a small goddess whose smile and frown settles everything for us in this world and the next. Luckily she is very pleasant and kindly with a twinkle in her eye. After the Matron comes Sister, amiable but uncertain, with not a very good accent, and a nose with an inquiring and rather complaining look down which the spectacles seem constantly on the point of sliding. They have all been very nice to me, though evidently not thinking much of my muscles – but I do hope to be able to manage the work. Tomorrow I have the afternoon off, and am longing to see Viva again, and be in a place where everything is done for one, no fetching and carrying, and one pours tea out of a silver tea pot and feels like a lady.

I am hoping this training may get me out to Italy and near you, my own mother: – that is what I long and long for.

Being in hospital brings back so much to me, and the first day I could hardly bear it; this is so different, with none of the glamour of my wonderful time in Bologna. In spite of all I am so thankful to have had that, which nothing can ever take away.

You hardly ever write to me, Biri. I have sent at least four since your last.

FREYA

Hornsey Cottage Hospital. 19 April 1917

My darling Biri,

Yesterday I was again allowed in to an operation – also a serious one – and I thought it was never going to end. The intense heat, and the smell of ether, and the standing still with nothing to do, make me feel intensely sleepy, so that there always comes a stage when I ask myself 'Is it sleepiness, or am I going to faint?' It goes off after a time, and never bothers me while I have anything to do. I was left on guard by the patient while she woke up, and she started kicking about so violently I thought she would fall off the bed. You can't think how useful a few extra inches would be to me here.

I feel limp sometimes – but have lost the wretched feeling of inertia that hung over me so long. So long as one doesn't feel tired right into one's bones it doesn't matter. Oh, won't it be lovely when we get a real holiday, with no war in the background.

Your own
FREYA

11 Grove End Rd. 11 May 1917

My darling Biri,

I can't realise how it is that I have let a week go by without writing; but suddenly, when I just seemed to have arrived at Thornworthy, I found I had to come back to town post-haste, and six days had already gone by. It was so beautiful down there – hot sunny days, with a little sudden wind that came round corners and seemed to spring up out of the earth. We were out all day: I had one ride all alone when Dot and Pud were in Exeter, and went exploring up over Assacombe, and a good gallop home by Fernworthy.

I also looked at the plantation and arranged for the sale of a little timber which is rotting there at present: Mr Varwell is going to manage it for me, and if there is anything from it I'll put it in War Loan for Pips. I didn't manage to go over my little plot, but looked at it with great satisfaction across the stream: there is a mysterious pleasure in owning a scrap of earth, far greater than that of any other possession. I wonder why.[1]

I was called back from the moor by a note from Mrs Trevelyan, who wished to see me, so I went down in fear and trembling yesterday. Mrs Trevelyan is an attractive little woman; enthusiastic, but not intense –

1 Freya later gave the plot to John R. Murray, her godson.

not a society woman, and I should think very practical. She thought it would be possible to arrange for me to go out some time in June; then I would have to wait, perhaps a fortnight, perhaps two or three months; but I would have to join up when called upon. As far as the work goes, of course I couldn't do anything better or more useful, and I should be glad personally too to be within easier reach of you. So I would go on with it unless you have any reasons against it.

The hospital isn't near the fighting line (worse luck!) and there are twenty nurses under the charge of a Sister and Matron, so one is well looked after. I thought that if the fact of me nursing would shock people [in Dronero], you might say that I am to do housework, that the nursing is done by older and more experienced women. I'm afraid that is more or less true, as the Sister does all the interesting jobs.

But if you would prefer me not to go, I shall try and get out of it. But I do so want to come out and see you again, my dearest.

Don't make me keep away from Italy without good reason. I think I ought to volunteer for nursing: there is such a shortage now, and it really seems to suit me.

Your own
FREYA

FLORA STARK

11 Grove End Rd. 5 June 1917

My darling Biri,

I am working nearly every morning at the British Museum. I struggle with the bad Latin of an 11th century chronicle written close to the Mont Cenis – Monte delle Ceneri – and very fascinating. There is a great deal of material, all picturesque and not very reliable, but the difficulty is to reach a point when one has read enough and can begin to write. Yesterday as I was ferreting about in one of the catalogues, a very very old gentleman came up to me, and said pathetically: 'I wish I were young.'

The dear Professor[1] is always dear, but he has too many goddaughters. A new one every time, and he produces them without the rudiments of tact. He asked us to tea Friday previous to a Carducci lecture, and of course I thought we were to be the two and only, as it were: but there was another anaemic-looking girl (she was pretty really, but I didn't like her) and it spoilt it all. I believe she thought me just as much in the way.

Ever so much love. I do hope to see you soon.

Your
FREYA

1 W.P. Ker.

11 Grove End Rd. 8 June 1917

My own darling,

Boris Godunov was very interesting: not difficult music: very decorative and picturesque, with no 'art shades' in it, and some wonderfully fine marches. Beecham is doing it, at Drury Lane, and in English – which we thought rather a pity. We were amused by the audience in the intervals; the boxes were very well filled – the Duchess of Marlborough, who looks snake-like and pre-Raphaelite; and Lady Randolph Churchill, who was behaving very badly and seized on the hat on the girl next her and clapped it on the unruffled brilliantine of the poor young man at her side.

Arnold Ward[1] has got together a good many people in Parliament to propose an amendment to the Woman Suffrage clauses, suggesting that the bill should be passed but not made effective till six months after the war, when a referendum is to be taken from the women to ascertain their wishes, and then a men's referendum whose decision would be final. I feel sure that if the referendum were to include all classes of women it would be anti-suffrage by a great majority: but it is to include only those who would vote under the provisions of the bill: and that result is more doubtful.

Yesterday morning I met Arnold Ward, who is a huge, heavy man with rather sleepy observant eyes and a brusque manner. He thinks of what is being said to him and not of the person saying it, and is therefore not very popular in the House; but I liked him very much. His sister Mrs Trevelyan has rather the same sort of manner. He has managed this business very well indeed.

In the afternoon there was a meeting of all the influential people in a Committee room of the House of Commons, and Viva gave me a ticket. I felt most awe-inspired going along the dark corridors, with the members standing about in little groups, and a great air of business and antiquity about it all. Viva introduced me to Mrs Humphry Ward, who received us rather with the manner of an empress: a little too much so I thought: but she does give one rather the impression of one of England's monuments.

Mrs Trevelyan has just written that they are over-staffed at Gorizia for the moment; it is too vexing. But she is going to try and let me have a letter saying that they will give me the first vacancy. Meanwhile it's very

---

1 Son of Mrs Humphry Ward, and Member of Parliament.

trying to be hanging at the end of a string with nothing doing. I did get an offer for Salonika, but I suppose you would have a fit at the mere mention?

Your own
FREYA

FLORA STARK
Villa Trento [near Udine]. 4 September 1917
My darling Mother,

I am here quite safely and happily, after a long night's sleep and no work till tomorrow, so I am just looking about today and putting away my things. It is the most lovely place, one of the old Venetian villas with the two statues at the entrance and hill and *vigna* behind; just a few cypresses on the brow of the hill to show the old aristocratic country – and the beautiful opal distances of the Veneto.

The sound of the guns comes through the sunlight and seems to beat on one's heart with the thought of all those men. I went out with two of the nurses yesterday and watched it all in the sunset time, beautiful rolling country, rising gradually to the barrier of the rocks; – well worth fighting for – 'Evviva l'Italia!'

By the time one gets to Venice one notices the difference in the type of officers; because all those *embusqués* of Turin are gone, and you find the people who are doing the real work. One of the first impressions was really sad. Between Udine and here my carriage filled up with a party of young lieutenants rejoining their various regiments after leave and they started talking about things in general and life in the towns they had left; of the carelessness and heartlessness about the war – and the attitude of the women! One can only hope that they chanced on the very worst entourage, but really the bitterness and their absolute *scoraggiamento* about it all hurt one to listen to – so much so that I had to look out of the window as I found myself almost crying. I hope no Englishman can talk like that of our women. When one thinks of their life out here, and that all the sweetness it has comes from the people they have left at home, one sickens to think how these wretched people can spoil it and take away the one thing that can give them courage and hope.

It was so nice to arrive at last, and everyone has been kind to me. There are quite a number of people altogether; we have supper out of doors, in front of the house, with the road and its constant stream of lorries just beyond. Nearly all the wounded [censored] . . . I am told there is not

13

very much theatre work as only the essential operations are done here – the rest sent back to the rear.

Mind you let me hear often.

Your own
FREYA

Villa Trento. 9 September 1917

Darling B,

I can't tell you about things here, except that I like the work and hope to get on all right with it. One loses touch with the outside world and I haven't seen a paper all these days; the last was the fall of Riga and one just hates the news and is glad to plod on at something that holds all one's thoughts and gives a tangible result of good. I have been sad these days because Viva tells me Prof. Ker's godson was killed; what poor wrecks we shall all be by the end of it all.

There are a lovely lot of books here, if one has the energy to read. At present I am really happy with Theocritus; the beautiful hot landscape is all round one as one reads and is all so far-away and peaceful; one wonders why anybody ever wishes for anything except to lie in the sun and watch a few sheep, and have the gift of *singing*. It is also interesting to find the origin of so many later things, like Lycidas and Spenser and Ronsard – only this was actual life and rings quite true and genuine; – it might be the life of the shepherds at La Gardetta if our climate were different.

Am writing this in bed. I have a lovely painted room, shared with four other V.A.D.s. You would love this house and to be let loose to furnish it properly; – it is the regular Venetian villa on a small scale, and would make the most ideal place, only Count Trento – to whom it belongs – doesn't seem to have troubled much about it. I expect all he cares about is the *vigna*. We have to be very careful in my ward; if the disinfectant falls through the very slight board and plaster arrangement of the floor to the wine vats below, a whole barrel of this year's *vendemmia* may be done for!

Your
FREYA

Villa Trento. 8 October 1917

Darling B,

It is the funniest place here; every sort of person all jumbled up

14

together, from the mechanics, who are paid, and not 'gentlemen', to the drivers, and Mr Trevelyan's set. The girls are all very nice, except two rather common ones who spoil things by flirting all the time. What the Italians think of us I don't know. We have the utmost liberty till 10.30 at night, when we are supposed to be in our rooms. In the summer nights one is invited out on the hills by whichever of the men one happens to know, and it is quite embarrassing to stumble over all those *têtes à tête* dotted over the hillside. As a matter of fact it is very pleasant just because they are very nice girls and we are all much annoyed with the two who are not so. The only real trial was the one I worked with, now on holiday, a journalist and artist of uncertain age, kittenish manner, dyed hair, *fearful* snob and says clever and peculiarly illnatured things.

Before the Inspecting Lady came here to reorganise, the V.A.D.s and men used to sleep out of doors dotted about promiscuously round the house; it was perfectly all right, but think of the feelings of the Italians! Now the V.A.D.s sleep on one side of the moat, more or less hidden by tents, and the men on the other. We also eat more or less at separate tables, though we invite whom we like to our table, and all sit together when dining out of doors.

I haven't any young men friends. The only one who asks me for the regulation moonlight walk is away now; there is no danger anyway, as Mr Trevelyan is the only really fascinating person besides Geoffrey Young, whom I have not spoken to. But I know quite a lot just sufficiently to pass the time of day, and have already been presented with one Australian and one Italian helmet as trophies.

I am not to give you any military news. When you see reports of artillery action on the Faiti, Ternovo, or Bainsizza, you know we can look on at them and see the huge black clouds of the shells. The English have a record here; they go nearer the front than any Italian car of the Red Cross, and Trevvy is anxious this should be kept up; that explains our heavy casualties lately. The dangerous piece is up the S. Gabriele, where the road is hidden from the enemy behind a precipice of rock; they can't see who goes along, but have the range and shell the place constantly. (When the road is open, they usually don't fire on the Red Cross.) I am told it is the most exciting feeling to rush along an open road, where nothing else dare show itself, flying a huge red cross and trusting the enemy will not fire. There is one station where one can see the road from a balcony and watch the cars racing by and count those that are hit, and the men do this and see how many are smashed, and then have to go and race along there themselves. A trying thing at first too are the Austrian searchlights that suddenly illuminate and make one conspicuous when all round is black as night – and you may be jammed in a row of lorries and unable to move. The searchlights are extraordinarily powerful; I was sitting on the hill when the one from behind the Carso (Austrian) fell upon me in a belt of light about three or four yards wide – a most uncomfortable feeling.

Your
FREYA

FLORA STARK

Villa Trento. 23 October 1917

My own darling,

It was lovely to get a letter from you, after so long. It seems to me that you live in a whirl of gaieties, I hear nothing but parties: I expect to find you a wreck by the time I come home.

We were inspected the other day by the Lt Colonel of our army corps, such a pleasant energetic-looking man: Dr Brock told him I lived in Piedmont when they came to our ward, and he spoke Piedmontese and I answered . . . very badly, but he seemed much pleased; and he was most flattering to Sister about the ward. It is really very pretty now; all the men have red winter bed-jackets and look nice against the whitewashed walls and rafters: it is also comparatively peaceful, as our carabinier has stopped using such awful language.

One of the men here, just come from an out-station, plays Chopin and Schumann and all the things I love, and it is such a treat and luxury: I had the lounge all to myself yesterday while the evening was coming on, and just lay on a sofa and listened in the half dark, and outside the cypresses grew deeper and deeper against a clear wonderful sky, just flushed with the hidden sun. I shall never be afraid of death, not even for the people I love – one thinks of it so often out here.

Your own
FREYA

During the battle of Caporetto Freya's hospital unit was the last to leave. She was one of the nurses who retreated with the Second Army through Udine, Codroipo and finally to Padua. She returned to Dronero, and finished the war nursing in a hospital in Turin.

In the early summer of 1918, Robert Stark returned for a visit to Italy from Canada. Freya and he decided to buy a house away from Piedmont, Flora's often difficult relationship with Vera not having improved during the years of war. They found what they wanted at La Mortola on the French–Italian border, a cottage with four rooms, a vineyard, and two and a half acres of land separated from the sea by a railway line. It was called L'Arma.

The plan was to provide a home for Freya and her mother, to which Vera could from time to time bring her children; but it had to be made to pay. Freya's next seven years were spent between L'Arma, where she grew and sold fruit, carnations, stocks and wine, and went climbing, particularly with W.P. Ker; London, where she studied Arabic; and Asolo, where she stayed with Herbert Young. She was often ill and had several operations.

ROBERT STARK

L'Arma. 2 November 1920

Dearest Pips,

I believe I haven't written to you for ages, since the *vendemmia* last month; it has all been a rush ever since. I wish I had been with you for the camping. I should love to be out with you looking for bears and climbing.

I sold the grapes for 2,500 francs clear and have about a thousand worth of wine now fermenting in the *cantina*: there is white and red – the pale pink you like, and a few bottles of raisin wine, specially good, which will be kept for when you come. I am writing your name on the bottle. It is great fun making it, and deciding how long it is to ferment.

Altogether I am quite pleased with the first year of this little place. It has given four percent on what it has cost altogether, land, building and all. Don't you think that is quite good? The grapes were the best in the neighbourhood, huge yellow bunches, a joy to behold, looking as if the sun lived inside them. Now I have a patch of strawberries and a lot of peas and some artichokes to attend to, and am planting lots of potatoes to sell about Easter time. And I have a *man*! He is quite young, just married, and wants to settle in life. I have taken him for one year as a labourer, with the promise of giving him an extra share of whatever profits there may be: and by the end of that time one will know how things develop over here. I will not have to slave away like last year I hope, but will do some of the work also so as not to be in any danger of dispossession by Bolshevists.

They have been pretty bad here and in the big towns things are more or less at a standstill: in Turin the workers (so called) took hold of the factories, filled them with machine guns, and there were killed and wounded every day. And prices are getting higher and higher: I sometimes don't know what to do for housekeeping: it is a blessing to have vegetables and milk of one's own. We are all going back more and more to old patriarchal ways of living and it is not a bad way either.

The building is not yet done: there seems to be no end, and the various saints whose feasts have to be kept are endless. We have had over a

17

month of rain, torrents and hurricane, with huge waves over the promontory, and mud to wade in whenever one goes out. Professor Ker came in September, and now Viva and Mr Bale,[1] and it is very disgusting to give them this sort of weather.

The *Literary Times* come at intervals and are very welcome; they are the only way I keep a little in touch with what goes on in literature. I have been reading Borrow – *Romany* and *Lavengro* – and enjoying every word; that is the way to talk of travels! That and Jane Austen have been my two authors lately.

Have you got enough warm things to get through the winter? I hope you will keep a sharp look-out for that pneumonia and not let it come again; do be careful dear old Pips. I should like to know you take all precautions.

Lots and lots of love from

Your
FREYA

FLORA STARK

11 Grove End Rd. 21 October 1921

My darling B,

I went to Finsbury Square this morning with Viva to see Sir Denison Ross,[2] who was most amiable, tripping about with his round tummy and bulgy eyes and lively manner, in a room hung with Chinese inscriptions and Arabic MSS on the tables. He was in a great hurry, but seemed well impressed by my grammar, which I took with me. I told him I could stay only till Xmas and wanted coaching, and he went out and came back in two twinks saying 'You will have four hours a week here, two with a young Englishman, and two with an Arab from Mesopotamia!' Imagine my joyous feelings – so joyous that I forgot to ask the fee. I begin on Nov. 1st so as to have a free week first for Pips. I think I should get on fast.

Lots of love dearest B, from

Your
FREYA

1 Edwin Bale had married Viva Jeyes' mother. He was a director of Cassell's.
2 Director of the School of Oriental Studies and Professor of Persian at London University 1916–37.

FLORA STARK

My dearest B,

I have got such a pretty toque – jade green taffeta, very close fitting with frills of the same round it: looks nice with the black coat and only 30/–; and another for 10/– because it was a little knocked about, made of coppery-brown little ribbons shot with gold.

Pips arrived on Saturday last, looking very well, and has been busy ever since getting his apples in to the Crystal Palace exhibition. If he gets a prize I will make him buy a new suit: otherwise no hope! He has got a new burberry and a cap, and that is all – having only £15 balance at the bank. It is hard on me, as I feel we *must* ask Viva and ought to ask Dot and Maurice to a theatre, and I will have to pay the tickets and that means about £2. I do so dislike being poor. When you see Pips do let him understand – without rubbing it in however – what a hard struggle it has all been.

Your loving
FREYA

ROBERT STARK

L'Arma. 7 May 1923

Dearest Pips,

I heard from Mama that she wrote to you about my difficulties and am vexed that you should have been worried about that. Prof. Ker lent me the amount to cover my deficit last winter and he does not want it back in a hurry, and I shall save up gradually for it; I think I shall be able to do so now – especially as I have discovered a new and most exciting way of making money . . . smuggling Old Masters across the border! I really have done this: a Sienese primitive 5 ft x 3, a most lovely Madonna on wood. My picture dealer friend came to spend two days here and spoke of his difficulty; I said airily (not knowing the size of the wretched thing) that I could easily get it through for him; and he said 'If you do I will give you £100 commission.' So the thing was brought here one evening and I spent a sleepless night wondering how to manage. I thought of a boat and using it as flooring with the face down. Then however some Scotch very respectable neighbours were leaving, with innocence and virtue written large all over them. So we got a cart which happened to fit the Madonna exactly; I bribed the nice girl by all her feelings of friendship and the prospect of a new leather bag – and we put the picture face down without even a piece of paper round it; we piled the luggage on top; and draped our scarves over the bits of gold frame that *would* show; then she and I

19

ascended the cart; the parents walked behind. We stopped at the douane; the little *guardia* strolled out, shook hands, we offered to show him our luggage, but he was all amiability and hoped we should have a good voyage and return. We passed the French douane at a trot, and I have just received my commission now. Isn't that a thrilling story from real life? I do think however that I earned my commission, because it was a most awful moment and the night after I kept waking up in a panic.

It is so late, I must go to sleep. I am working rather hard between Arabic and garden.

Lots of love dear Pips.

FREYA

ROBERT STARK

L'Arma. 30 May 1923

Dearest Pips,

It is beautiful weather now, warm and gorgeous and lovely to bathe, only I don't seem to be up to it and so shall wait till August. We are going to get away to the mountains at Macugnaga for a month and that will be fine. Mama has not been at all well, with *gout* of all things! but she is better now. I am doing Arabic hard for my first exam, do not get enough time at it to hope for much success. Some day you will hear of me in the deserts of Arabia discovering buried cities.

Goodbye till next letter dearest Pips. I wish you were here sitting under the olive tree.

Your loving
FREYA

ROBERT STARK

Macugnaga. Mid-July 1923

Dearest Pips,

We are just here for three weeks, and I am having a thorough good rest. I had three weeks in London working very hard and got through an Arabic exam at London University: I did it on the chance, having had only five months (and interrupted) instead of a year to work at it, but my lecturer informs me that I have a talent for grammar, and was so pleased that he is going to let me take a diploma without going to attend the courses in London. This is very pleasing and makes things easy for me. The result of my exam was the offer of a teaching job in Egypt, but I did not think it worth while to accept unless something really too good to miss comes along. I have been reading up Mohammedan history and

20

finding it very interesting; quite a new world opening out – and I am so glad to have brain-work that can be done away by myself in the country.

Here are Prof. Ker and his two goddaughters, Olivia and Poldores [MacCunn],[1] and Viva is over the hills at Zermatt. I am thinking of crossing over the glacier to see her and, if I feel fit, of doing something amusing like the Matterhorn before restoring myself to my family.

We had great luck to arrive before they cut the hay, so the place is covered with flowers, red and yellow lilies, fields of campanula and wild pink, and the rhododendron still out near the glacier. But it is very hot and stuffy and thunderstorms breaking themselves against M. Rosa, and the Prof. does not care for much climbing any longer so that we feel rather like horses on a curb. We had one good walk up to 3,000 metres and looked over to the Jungfrau and the Dom and Eichhorn. Monte Rosa itself is one of the most beautiful shaped mountains there could be, with all her crests and glaciers pouring down.[2]

Your
FREYA

ROBERT STARK

Rome. 13 April 1924

Dearest Pips,

A very happy birthday to you. I cannot wish you anything nicer than to spend the next one here in this wonderful place: I am revelling in it, only retiring now and then in a state of exhaustion from seeing too many beautiful things.

Biancheris,[3] whom I expect you remember, are here and one of them is in the Foreign Office and getting us all sorts of privileges such as a window on the 24th to see Mussolini opening Parliament, and permits into the Vatican, and an audience with the Pope which I am rather terrified of: I am told one may only speak when spoken to, so I can't talk to him about Macugnaga nor tell him that I mean to do his own pet climb up Monte Rosa this summer.

I am doing some work – going four times a week to read Arabic: the lady professor says I have a remarkable talent for Oriental language and compare favourably with a Monsignore who has been learning for five

---

1 Poldores MacCunn was a doctor.
2 On July 23, at the start of what was to be a climb of Pizzo Bianco, 'W.P. [Ker] gave a little sudden cry and died'. Freya sat with him for seven hours, while the guide went for help. She missed him greatly, for friends were already of exceptional importance to her.
3 Neighbours from L'Arma.

21

years and gets no further. Prof. Browne, who is the great Cambridge Orientalist, came over to lunch before we left and has invited me to stay there, and will probably discover a teacher for me sooner or later along the Riviera.

Elections here were a great fascist triumph – and the trams and houses are all fluttering with flags. The black-shirts and all the pageantry look extraordinarily in the right place here with all the columns and arches of Imperial Rome. We saw Mussolini talking to the assembled Romans in Piazza Colonna, from the balcony of the Palazzo Chigi: it was really impressive, with flags and the crowd below, and the column of M. Aurelius standing very tall in the half light and Mussolini himself in profile against the pale spring evening sky. The crowd was amiable but nearly killed me all the same, it was such a squash.

When you write, tell me where you used to live in Rome and what your special haunts were. Love to you dearest Pips, lots of it always, from

FREYA

ROBERT STARK

Macugnaga. 29 July 1924

Dearest Pips,

I have been and done it – that is to say I have been up to the tops of M. Rosa from this side, which is the most difficult and has only been done once before by a woman. We left the hut at midnight and crossed the 'Canalone': it was exciting because the night began with clouds and if it got worse we would have had to return across the Canalone, which is only safe from avalanches for a very few hours when the heights are frozen. However the moon came out and shone wonderfully as we zigzagged up the glacier, cutting steps sometimes in hard snow, sometimes in clear blue ice, with big chasms of ice hanging over us in fantastic shapes – a wonderful sight. We were caught by the sunlight on the last slope and reached the rocks at eight in the morning. I went with a Belgian climber and two guides, neither he nor I in very good training (as I am supposed to be living on milk and eggs and quietness!) – and we were very tired by twelve when we reached the top – twelve hours' climb with very little rest. Then we saw the whole of Switzerland clear, in a keen wind, every peak showing as if cut in steel. I would have been fit for the return down the glacier, but my companion was feeling the height (4,630 metres) and could hardly get along, so we walked along the crest to the Capanna Margherita, which we reached about 4 p.m.; it is the highest Alpine hut and I found that I could neither eat nor sleep from the beating of my heart. The wind howled all night and it was cold and we wondered why we had come. At two in the morning we got up in thick mist and came down over an easy glacier the other side, across two passes back to Macugnaga, another twelve hours' good walking – and neither of us apparently any the worse, to the amazement of my doctor-friend Poldores who says that my constitution is an insult to the medical profession. The truth is that the high air is like champagne to me. I feel I could do anything in it. I am so pleased to have succeeded, as I have wanted to climb that peak for three years. Now I have been very good, leading a quiet life and taking milk for all I am worth, and am much better than when I came up.

We go back to L'Arma on 31st – just as well, as the weather is breaking and anyhow I couldn't stand sitting down in the valley much longer. This hotel is full of the noisiest Milanese, the only pleasant people to talk to are the guides.

Tanti baci dearest Pips,

Your
FREYA

ROBERT STARK

Ospedale Mauriziano, Aosta. 25 January 1925

Dearest Pips,

You will be surprised with this address, but by the time this letter goes, I shall be well through an operation and on the way to spending a busy February here getting over it. The good doctor from S. Remo came to the conclusion that it was better to cut away the ulcerated piece of my intestine, rather than face another six months of diet on my sofa with a chance of a relapse if ever I do anything energetic afterwards. We have come here because there is a particularly good surgeon whom he knows, and I expect that by the end of the week the ordeal will be over. I shall have to take things fairly easy this year, and then I hope be as strong as ever again, as the cause of the trouble will have been removed.

Your own
FREYA

ROBERT STARK

Asolo. 1 June 1925

Dearest Pips,

There is lots of news: first of all my exciting summer plan, which consists of a five-roomed chalet in the Cadore (San Vito near Cortina) where Viva is inviting me for the summer. I shall stay till the autumn, under the care of my doctor who has a villa there, and in the hope of getting back the strength which so far is making a poor show: I wish it was a matter of letting one's hair grow, like Samson.

Vera came up to see me for three days from Milan. It was very nice after such a long time (without husband) – and we just sat about like old times here. She was looking very well, and enjoyed it too very much. We have been reading Trevelyan's last book, on Manin and the defence of Venice in 1849: it is a magnificent story and well told. That, and learning Venetian embroidery are my two occupations, and then people drop in.

Mrs Beach is starting a weaving factory[1] of silks: it is just beginning with two work people and one apprentice and we are all taking an interest in its proceedings. They make beautiful silk. That, and Mme Casale's embroidery school, will make Asolo quite an 'arts and crafts' sort of place, but as yet no sign of the crankiness that seems to accompany such.

Lots of love
FREYA

ROBERT STARK

S. Vito. 22 July 1925

Dearest Pips,

This is a short note, just to tell you that the doctor has finally come, and put me to bed for a week to be under observation. I think you would rather know the state of things though I am not telling Mama. There is still some trouble and I am afraid it will be a long affair, though he is quite cheerful about a complete cure in the end. I am afraid it will mean a good while still on my back, living on milk. It is depressing: I have not had a good meal for fourteen months and long to lead a real life again, but what can one do? He tried to cheer me by saying it was neither a tumour nor tuberculosis! I will be here all August for certain and probably September, and then see how things go. Viva has been such a brick: she has been housekeeping and nursing me, and has not let me spend any money, which was a blessing considering my denuded state – and makes it possible for me to see this year through without any more borrowing: so you need not worry about that.

My darling Pips, I am afraid this letter will worry you. It is nothing fatal however: and I have every hope of being my own self again before I am quite middle-aged.

Your own loving
FREYA

1 Lucy Beach's Tessoria Asolana, later run by Flora Stark.

FLORA STARK

11 Grove End Rd. 10 December 1925

Dearest B,

I went to see Mrs Trevelyan at the B. Italian League which seems to have turned to a nest of anti-fascist refugees. I shall be going to one of their meetings and will know more about it, but as far as I can see there is very little sympathy here for the present state of Italy. I think the chief reason, or anyhow one of them, has been the sort of person who supports the fascists here – all the Die-hards and the *Morning Post* and ultra-conservatives so that anyone even moderately liberal is thrown into the opposite camp. I spend my time trying to persuade people that the same names do signify different things in different countries, but what is the force of mere reason against sentiment.

I shall stick to my Arabic, and spend next winter here and get my diploma in 1927 and go out: they say I am quite good at it and only need a year's study now.

Your own
FREYA

FLORA STARK

Varazze. Friday [July 1926]

Dearest B,

Vera is seriously ill. She has the best doctor in Genova to look after her and two nurses, but I must stay here till she is through the wood for she clings to me and I feel I can give her more strength than anybody else.

The trouble is, besides her heart, a uricaemia which has now started; also trouble in the liver. It seems she had a miscarriage and this developed after. I have not yet seen either her or the doctor so merely send this news at second hand and will hope to write more definitely tomorrow morning.

Your own
FREYA

ROBERT STARK

L'Arma. 2 October 1926

My darling Pips,

I have very sad news. I wish I could be with you, to have you in my arms and tell you. Dear little Vera died, quite peacefully and without pain, early on Thursday morning. Mama was with her, and she was very happy: no fear, only the thought of getting better and coming away with us to rest. She was very weak, but the crisis seemed over: the new centres

25

of infection were getting smaller, and we hoped to pull her through in spite of all – and then the infection developed just under the heart, and nothing could be done. God bless her, and us too dear Pips. My whole heart is with you – if only I could be near to help you bear this sorrow. Darling, darling Pips, you know how near I really am. I love you so very much. Mama has just come and is very exhausted but all right. She went to Dronero and will write to you. Everyone was so devoted and grieved – all the poor people, and country people, even from far away in the mountains, came down.

Our one comfort is that nothing different could have been done to avoid this. She had the most careful and best treatment and doctors from the first – but it was blood-poisoning and nothing could help.

My dear, I will write again.

Your loving
FREYA

ROBERT STARK

L'Arma. 18 June 1927

Dearest Pips,

I have had such an awful time getting in to the house and mopping up the tenant's mess that I can't remember when I last wrote to you; the cool sequestered way of life seems as far off as ever. Now however we are fairly straight and only two really serious problems impending – first the water supply, which has vanished and shows no sign of reappearing: I have had to build a new cistern, and may fill it if only the wind blows hard enough and makes my wheel go round: and secondly the fascists, who are becoming insufferable, looting everyone on their beat and arresting or beating anyone who protests. The lot we had before were all right, but these are the kind to show up despotism in its worst form. They come lolling on my garden seat, have carried off my little St Christopher and front door bell, and spend the night eating the fruit in anybody's property: one peasant remonstrated, and twelve of them lay in wait and beat him one dark night – and no one dares speak. If there are any troubles, this countryside will rise against them like one man. If I catch them eating my peaches I shall go down with my little pistol in one hand and British passport in the other.

I have just finished Lawrence's book and wish I could afford to buy and send it you. It is good reading, especially in blowing up of the desert railway. Who knows but I may be in that country some time next winter: I am trying hard to save up enough and have got hold of a Syrian Quaker who is going to find me cheap lodging in an Arab village where I shall meet no Europeans. These Quakers are at a place called Brumana, 23 km from Beirut – in Mt Lebanon. I think if I can scrape together £80 or so, I could manage three months out there. I do feel I must get out before I become too old.

I must stop. There is a stream of people always wanting something or other. Ever so much love from

Your
FREYA

2

First experiences of the Middle East, to father in Canada, harems

---

In November 1927 Freya left for her first trip to the East. She was thirty-four, unmarried, which gave her a 'miserable sense of being a failure', and not well off, though her income had at last risen to £300 a year, through a characteristic bit of gambling on the Stock Exchange. Her health was still poor, but she had decided that she would rather die than endure the life of an invalid. Her father was back in Canada, running his fruit farm; Flora was in Asolo, working with the silk factory. In February 1926 Herbert Young had written to Freya offering to leave her his house in Asolo. 'When first I saw you, you were crawling about on the floor of my studio, an inarticulate infant, and I know you love the place.' The house became known as Villa Freia.

There was little now to keep her in Europe. 'It was like the prince's story in an Arabian tale', she wrote, many years later, 'who shot his arrow farther than he knew and then went out to find it. I had prepared for this journey during many years.'

ROBERT STARK

Fiume. 20 November 1927

Dearest Pips,

This is the first stage, and we have been stuck here since seven o'clock yesterday morning because of twenty-two truck loads of Hungarian sugar that cannot be loaded in the rain. The boat – *Abbazia* – is only 3,000 tons I believe, and her decks very black with age, and only six passengers (1st class) so far – so that it is rather a family party, except for the fact that one Austrian, one German, one Turinese, two Irish and myself cannot talk in one language.

It was bitterly cold in Venice: and Mama was late, so that we came in our gondola through the small canals and out against the Banchina di S. Basegio in the dark and saw the *Abbazia* towering above, spitting smoke and steam, and making me and my luggage feel very small and forlorn. At night she ploughs through the sea in pitch darkness, so that one doesn't know where the deck ends and the sea begins, except for a tiny headlight far up in the air: so I have kept indoors so far, and will wait for a starlit night to go on deck.

28

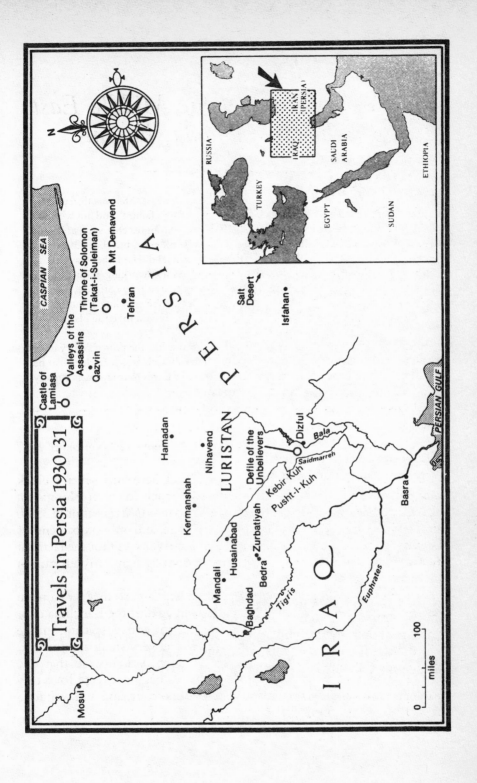

Travels in Persia 1930-31

CASPIAN SEA

Castle of
Lamiasa

Valleys of the
Assassins
Qazvin

Throne of Solomon
(Takat-i-Suleiman)
▲ Mt Demavend

Tehran

P E R S I A

Salt
Desert

Isfahan

Hamadan

Nihavend

Kermanshah

LURISTAN

Defile of the
Unbelievers
Saidmarreh

Dizful
Bala

Kebir Kuh
Pusht-i-Kuh

Mandali
Husainabad
Bedra Zurbatiyah

Baghdad

Tigris

I R A Q

Euphrates

Basra

PERSIAN GULF

Mosul

0   100
         miles

RUSSIA

TURKEY

EGYPT

SUDAN

ETHIOPIA

IRAQ IRAN
(PERSIA)

SAUDI
ARABIA

Will post this in Serbia tomorrow.

Your own
FREYA

VENETIA BUDDICOM[1]

Brumana. 14 December 1927

My dearest Venetia,

I have taken my map and a compass out this morning, and sat under a pine tree looking at Lebanon, and thinking of you. Brumana is a glorious village, a long ridge of neat stone houses with red hillside and pines and stones running straight down to Beirut and the sea. Even from here one can see where the civilised fringe ends and we should get into lovely country inhabited by jackals and Druses.

Goodness knows how much of this impossible colloquial Arabic I shall be able to manage by the spring. I have a charming young Syrian professor every day, and a beautifully clean lodging with excellent food – and kind landlady with nothing to complain of except the most acute cold. It is all right while the sun shines, but then there is an interval of absolute numbness till I reach my nice warm room.

When I came here (four days ago) Mlle Audi[2] rather appalled me by telling me that there was 'quite a lot of society in Brumana: Bible classes, Y.W.C.A., and reunions for reading and improving one's mind': so far however this terrible vista has not been filled in as far as I am concerned, except for a Quaker service on Sunday, all in Arabic, and Arabic words to some familiar hymn tune; all which I found most improving, though not in the manner intended.

Ever your
FREYA

VENETIA BUDDICOM

Brumana. 4 January 1928

Dearest Venetia,

I have just been taking a rest from perpetual Arabic, looking into Graves' book on Lawrence. Save us from our friends! I begin to feel the man almost unbearable. This attitude of continually saying 'I would like to be modest if only I could' is ridiculous and probably not at all true to the poor man. If only I can get to Baghdad, I have a letter to Mr Woolley[3]

1 Venetia Buddicom's parents had a villa at Bordighera, near La Mortola.
2 Her landlady, Mlle Rose Audi.
3 Archaeologist, the excavator of Carchemish and Ur.

who worked with him on the Euphrates and should be full of interesting information. I see with pleasure that it took four years in the country to teach him Arabic: it makes me feel less painfully stupid. I now begin to follow the drift of conversations and to attempt ambitious subjects like Doughty's Arabian travels in my efforts with Miss Audi at lunch. There is plenty of practice: every afternoon we pay a lengthy call (about two hours) and sit on a divan talking gossip interspersed with one of the sixteen formulas of politeness which I have collected so far. After a while a large tray is brought in with all sorts of delicious sweetmeats, wine, tea; we take a little of each – (fearfully bad for my inside) – and say 'May this continue' as we put down the cup: and the hosts say 'May your life also continue', and then we leave. I believe there is no feeling of class in this country at all: you are divided by religions, and as you see nothing practically of any religion but your own, you never have the unpleasant feeling of being surrounded by people who are hostile and yet bound to mix up their lives with yours.

I am very popular here – the one and only person who has ever come to learn Arabic *for pleasure*.

Your loving
FREYA

MARGARET JOURDAIN[1]

Brumana. 14 January 1928

My dear Margaret,

The East is getting a firm grip. What it is I don't know: not beauty, not poetry, none of the usual things. This place is a grand scene with all the details neglected. Of course it is not the genuine Orient, only the semi-European fringe full of French ideas second-hand and second-rate, and European clothes and furniture peculiarly unadapted to the casual Eastern silhouette. And yet I feel I want to spend years at it – not here, but further inland, where I hope to go as soon as I get enough Arabic for the absolutely necessary amount of conversation.

The village is kind, at least the Christian part, for we all live in separate compartments and have little to do with such people as Druse, or Greek Orthodox, though we may live next door. My landlady speaks of the Druses as Napoleon used to be spoken of to naughty children in England.

I find the people just as human here as anywhere else: and one great

---

1 A new London friend, 'Margaret Jourdain, with her quiet biting sparkle of wit I was devoted to'.

interest in such a different civilisation is that it gives you a sudden fresh view of your own; the nearest in fact to getting out of the world and examining it as an object. The only people I don't care to study are the uncivilised. Here it is too much, not too little, civilisation that is the trouble. That, and an incapacity for forgetting. Mlle Audi talks of iniquities of Druse governors two hundred years ago as if they had just happened. It is amazing to see all the primitive feelings coming through the refined convent breeding.

Your affectionate
FREYA

VIVA JEYES

Brumana. 30 January 1928

Darling Viva,

I have never been anywhere where it is more fun to have clothes: everyone is so interested in them, and if I put on a fresh hat on Sunday mornings, it is with the agreeable certainty that it is going to give pleasure to the whole congregation.

When there is anything new, the etiquette is to show it to all your visitors. Today we paid a morning call to some people near by and were shown, first, the new coat and shawl sent from sons in America; and next, the new w.c. We went in procession, husband, wife, daughter, son-in-law, and the chain was pulled with solemn pride – only no waterworks followed. I rummaged among my adjectives for something suitable, and finally brought out 'healthy' with what I consider creditable discrimination.

Did you know that camels in the evening bring bad luck? Eight of them came padding past our door at dusk as we came up the steps; rolling along like waves in the half light. They have a very soft footfall, as if they were treading on dust. I don't think it is only my romantic mind that clothes them with mystery. Mlle told me of the ill omen and was reluctant even to pause and watch as they rolled by.

She told me today how she watched the Allies entering Beirut from her little balcony up here. There were two 'fregates', or three (she can't remember): one was British, and the other French. The French flew an enormous flag, and the British waited to let her pass first into the harbour, right up against the quay: and Mlle, looking through her glasses, realised that it was to be France in Syria after all.

Your loving
FREYA

DOROTHY WALLER [VARWELL]

Brumana. 12 February 1928

Dearest Dot,

What I find trying in a country which you do not understand and where you cannot speak, is that you can never be *yourself*. You are English, or Christian, or Protestant, or anything but your individual *you*: and whatever you say or do is fitted to the label and burdened with whatever misdeeds (or good deeds) your predecessors may have committed. And then of course your sentences, intended with just the shade of meaning you desire, come out shorn of all accessories, quite useless for anything except the mere procuring of bread and butter. How glad I shall be when I feel that the country is really *mine*, not the mere panorama to the stranger. Meanwhile the world is open.

Your loving

FREYA

FLORA STARK

House of Khalil 'Aid, Damascus. 15 March 1928

Darling B,

I haven't been out yet, but the East has been coming home to me quite busily. Imagine one of those little backyards in Venice as the entrance to my home. You climb up rather rickety stairs, through the lower litter of garments, saucepans, old shoes and flower-pots, to a pleasant room with seven windows; where, unless you are extremely careful, everyone can see you while you dress. I really think the bed is all right: I have found nothing alive anyway: in fact what I complain of is that everything smells as if it were dead. The children's clothes were bundled out of my room, and various necessities like jugs, towels, mirror, rug, brought in at intervals while I sat rather dismal on the bed. That has a lovely yellow quilt and two long hard bolsters. I do manage to get hot water in the morning. But there are so many smells.

I had breakfast with the family this morning and felt how much I am still fettered to the lusts of the flesh. We sat round the primus stove beside the washing-up bucket, and I tried to anchor my mind on the fact that nothing much besides old age can happen to the inside of a boiled egg.

The landlady is pretty and looks tired. Her name is Rose: she is at this moment blacking her eyes at my mirror; and she uses my powder, which I do so dislike. If she did not wear incredibly sloppy European clothes she would be quite ornamental. There is no particular sort of privacy here, except that the men are out of the way most of the time. It will be splendid for my Arabic, and I believe I can stand it. The best of it is a roof to walk on and look at the other roofs, and the minarets and the red hills. The desert comes close: just red rock, not a shimmer of grass on it; the cultivated land washes up to it like a wave and stops as suddenly. It gives one the feeling of being in prison.

Later

I have been out with Sitt Rose, and discovered a European side to the town, tramlines, avenues and shops: it is what they are proud of, of course.

I found Mr P, the Vice-Consul, in that district. He was evidently very pleased to have a new English person to talk to, but I did not like him very much. He has invited me to dinner, and to go walking, but I hardly think I shall do so. He does not know a single Syrian here. He thinks it impossible I should stay in my native lodging, but says there is no alternative except hotels.

I am so glad of letters. I have been feeling a little depressed.

Your most loving
FREYA

FLORA STARK

Damascus. 21 March 1928

Darling B,

The older lady has just been in to tell me tactfully that Moslems are not to be trusted. 'Even if a Moslem smells like musk, do not put him into your pocket' was what she said.

Yesterday I was asked if I was Arabic. It was only on the strength of two words, but imagine my joy.

Your own
FREYA

FLORA STARK

Damascus. 1 April 1928

Darling B,

I had tea at the Mission yesterday, but did not go for a walk as intended, feeling too ill. I do find those ladies too suffocating. Even the young ones seem to have all natural interest in life and buoyancy taken out of them and think of nothing but their own narrow little bit of path of righteousness.

To feel, and think, and learn – learn always: surely that is being alive and young in the real sense. And most people seem to *want* to stagnate when they reach middle age. I hope I shall not become so, resenting ideas that are not my ideas, and seeing the world with all its changes and growth as a series of congealed formulas.

Your loving

FREYA

PENELOPE KER[1]

Damascus. 7 April 1928

Dearest Pen,

Yesterday was a wonderful day: for I discovered the Desert!

One must not believe people when they tell you things. They told me I could not see desert unless I went to Palmyra which is too far this time. I looked at the map, however, and decided on a lonely ruin marked where the Damascus streams lose themselves in lakes, and the villages end. Nothing beyond but names of hills and water-places and the road trailing away south to the lands beyond Jordan. My Moslem friends came with me bringing their guns, which we had to hide whenever police came in sight. The pretty sister wears a black veil over her face, but she throws it back in the country.

Such a road! It was sandy and smooth at first, running through avenues of walnut just coming into leaf, and the green corn on either hand. Then we began to wade streams, water well up to the axles: then on to banks at absurd angles. We began to meet Beduin: their black tents were dotted here and there. The country got poorer, the corn thin and uneven, the trees stopped. For some time there would still be a clump of shade by the villages – then nothing – just the mud walls baked yellow sloping up one of the strange solitary little hills that rise out of all this country like dolphins' backs.

We were taken along a road that melted into invisibility, then found ourselves on hard sand, thorns and desert rushes brushing against the wheels. The country looked white like chalk here, all gentle lines and travelling shadows; and, half lost in distance, a glimmer of snow from Hermon, and the Damascus hills.

And then the wonder happened! Camels appeared on our left hand: first a few here and there, then more and more, till the whole herd came browsing along, five hundred or more. I got out and went among them to photograph. The two Beduin leaders, dressed gorgeously, perched high up and swinging slowly with the movement of their beasts, shouted

1 Sister of W.P. Ker.

35

out to me, but the Beduin Arabic is beyond me. I can't tell you what a wonderful sight it was: as if one were suddenly in the very morning of the world among the people of Abraham or Jacob. The great gentle creatures came browsing and moving and pausing, rolling gently over the landscape like a brown wave just a little browner than the desert that carried it. Their huge legs rose up all round me like columns; the foals were frisking about; the herdsmen rode here and there. I stood in a kind of ecstasy among them. It seemed as if they were not so much moving as flowing along, with something indescribably fresh and peaceful and free about it all, as if the struggle of all these thousands of years had never been, since first they started wandering. I never imagined that my first sight of the desert would come with such a shock of beauty and enslave me right away.

Love to you both always from

FREYA

In June, after a three-week journey in Egypt with Venetia Buddicom 'crowded . . . with every sort of adventure except being taken prisoners', Freya returned to Asolo. She was planning to visit her father, who had had a stroke, and left to cross the Atlantic for British Columbia in the autumn, after an unhappy summer with her mother and arguments with Mario, her brother-in-law, over money.

MR EDMUNDS[1]

L'Arma. 7 September 1928

Dear Mr Edmunds,

I am very grateful for your letter – more than I can say by just saying thank you. It is what can be most helpful. I shall try and answer as well as I can. It is difficult for me to get things put into words unless they deal with images of people or objects.

That I have confidence in you is very certain. I would not otherwise have told you about these problems at all – which so far I had kept to myself. I don't think I am unreasonable enough to dislike a theory because of the person who holds it: but I know that I accept ideas more easily if they come from people I like. I mean that I know, quite independently of you or anyone else, that your way is in the direction in which I want to go. If the fact of your being a friend makes it a little easier to follow, is there any harm? I suppose you mean that one should not take one's ideas ready-made from anyone? I think I would never do that,

1 A disciple of Rudolph Steiner.

for on the whole I respect ideas more than people: but when it is connected with a person, it becomes much more valid to me, and easier in that way. Even when I read a book, it is usually with the thought of someone who would enjoy it also.

I agree most completely with all you say about the goal to make for; I have long felt that there is a Purpose for us, and that if one could know it, recognise it I mean and be convinced, the whole of life would fall into a proper proportion and would become independent of circumstances. So far I have felt that the other plane is there and that our greater teachers have lived in it. But the roads they went seemed to me not our roads – or at any rate not for most of us, because it meant shutting oneself practically out of life. There must be a way, not of renouncing, but of accepting the world and transmitting it to its greater possibilities. I don't think I could renounce this beautiful world: I love it all, from the frills on my tea gown to the Alps, and I love everything that is living on it, just because it is alive. I feel it is part of me too. One cannot say all this is vanity and scrap it. There must be a way of *interpreting* it all. I think you can. If you can I shall be very deeply grateful. I explain myself so badly. It is not the goal I am in doubt about: it is the way of getting there – as if our life were the pebble which is to be turned to gold. We have it in our hand and we know what we want to make of it: it is the instrument, the alchemist's recipe, that is missing. To get control of one's will and thought and feelings seems the proper – indeed the only way: to become conscious, in fact. If you start me on the exercises I will try what I can do and tell you.

FREYA STARK

FLORA STARK

Dronero. 19 September 1928

Dearest B,

I have just got your letter and must answer at once, for there are two things I really need to make clear. One is that I do not grouse in the sense of worrying over the past, *except as regards the future*: I should not have bothered to mention that the business with Mario ought to have been settled this year, except that I am anxious not to find it going on next.

The second point is that one can't change one's nature 'entirely', you say. One can hardly change it *at all*, and not without a degree of ruthless honesty which is most exceptional. So that the best thing to do is to see that one's life runs so that one's nature does good and not harm, don't you think? In other words, it is infinitely preferable that you should make scarves which you do well and enjoy doing rather than do

37

housework and p.g.'s which you dislike and consequently do remarkably badly. What one does badly is no good to anyone. And if I could
know that you were doing your own jobs well, I could really face my
own lot with a far larger share of strength.

The children are still a problem. I don't quite know what will happen
but can do very little about it. Mario of course wants me to stay here; but
then I feel I should be doing just as you if you took housekeeping at
L'Arma: I should be forcing myself and so lose all usefulness really. And
it is children and not grownups that they need. They are all well and
jolly. Please do not waste emotion, canalise it to whatever your object
may be in the future. You have the luck to be doing the work you like. It
is not basking in the sun, and still it is a *great luck* and worth sticking to. I
have not yet got it, for I have to do all the jobs I don't like in between and
shall not reach my own work until I am about forty: I do, however, hope
to reach it eventually, if there is anything of me left.

Ever so much love dear B,

Your

FREYA

HERBERT YOUNG

Creston. 4 November 1928

Dearest Herbert,

I was glad to arrive, with a vile cold produced by the meeting of hot
radiator air and the icy current off the window panes – but now I have
had two nights' rest and am spending a lazy day indoors with the big
stove going, and two puppy dogs lying about like woolly mats, Pips'
gun in the corner by the door, and all the genuine atmosphere of the Wild
West – except that I haven't got to cook the dinner. It is a cosy little log
hut, four rooms and a veranda, and we look downhill to the roofs of the
barns and stable, and little three-roomed hut where Tom and Alice[1] now
sleep – all cedar-wood slats, very neat in the landscape – and then across a
low undulation of cleared land, brown and yellow stubbles, with patches
of forest here and there, to the wide valley: they call it the 'Flats' and the
mist lies there in the evening, and the Selkirk range comes out of it
steeply, with the sunset straight behind it, for we face due west. There is
a little powdering of snow fallen last night on the tops, and a filmy grey
sky drifting over the blue, and smoke from various fires going up in long
streamers. Pips himself came to meet me at the station: he is very stiff and
cannot raise his arms much, but he can walk quite well, and it was lovely
to see him, looking as if all these years he had been busily growing more

1 Tom and Alice Leaman had worked for the Starks in Devonshire and later went out with Freya's father to settle
in Canada.

and more a bit of the landscape; at a few yards distance his dear old clothes would just melt into it invisibly. He has a few books (nearly all I sent at various times) and a gramophone, a bath, a stove, and some Chippendale chairs he picked up from a man who was leaving, and a geranium in a tin on the window; and these are all the luxuries – except the telephone, which seems very out of the picture, but is indispensable.

The village is hidden behind the hill and has two shops. There are seven or eight neighbouring ranches visible from our window, and nearly every one belongs to a different nationality – Swede, French, German, English – they are all mixed, and Nature is such a big enemy that all the rest become insignificant.

There is really no means of describing the immensity of this great lovely country. This is comparatively inhabited, and Montreal is a very fine city, with handsome buildings. It is all beautifully organised so as to rest the jaded city-mind and avoid unnecessary trouble. Then your train starts and soon you are out in the endless flat stretches of woods and lakes, solitary as anything you can imagine. The train slips along for two days, and it is always the same: the long stretches of water where the ice is now forming at the edge: the thick pines and white birches, and here and there a sandy road with perhaps two lonely little square boxes of three or four rooms, or some shanty by the water's edge with a canoe drawn up for the winter. People get lost in these woods and can never find the way out again. They go to shoot moose, or fish in the lakes. The monotony of it adds extraordinarily to the sense of remoteness and of the valiancy of men's efforts who live here and make the land habitable.

After these two days we reached Winnipeg and the prairie, and came through what might have been a desert sunset over the rolling yellow stubble land. Here there is never a tree: it seems they can hardly live through the gales that sweep from the north and east. The towns are springing up like mushrooms, and more hideous than one can easily imagine: and the people seem a hard prosperous lot, with a dollar-lined smugness beginning to spread itself over the rugged pioneering virtues. While they are fighting to tear a living out of the unknown, these people have something very attractive, free and self-reliant and keen: but when it gets money and comfort, it is not so pleasant any longer.

Your loving
FREYA

HERBERT YOUNG

Creston. 3 December 1928

Dearest Herbert,
This is exactly timed by your letter and Mama's, so that it *should* arrive

on Xmas Day. We shall be thinking of you, and wishing for that magic carpet – at least I shall – for though I like the interest and excitement of a new and empty country, I do feel myself *European* to the very bottom of my heart: or at any rate I feel that I belong to the Old World – partly because of the climate of the New, which is twenty-two below freezing this morning, and twenty-six below zero just a little east of us. Yesterday I came home just about supper time with the big planet of the moment (whatever it may be) shining like a bonfire over the western range, and a cold green sky: the road hard with wide frozen ruts of solid ice: and it was so cold that I had no sensations at all below the knees.

I am so depressed, having tried to write a second article – which has been born as flat as a pancake: which just shows that I am not really meant by Destiny for an author.

A long kiss to you.

Your
FREYA

HERBERT YOUNG

Creston. 14 December 1928

My dearest Herbert,

It is very kind to write, for one does feel *very* far away out here, partly because, with the exception of Pips, there is absolutely no one with whom to talk of anything but apples – except Canadian politics, which seem to be rather messy.

I must describe a dance in the Wild West to you. It is really rather fun. Imagine a cold clear night, Orion swinging up over the pines: the mud frozen hard, and me with overshoes and a flashlight, all warm in furs except where an icy zone encircles my silk stockings, making my lonely way through the wood to the Parish Hall. It is not more than half a mile away, all built of pine planks and cedar, and already very cosy with a roaring stove and red paper streamers down the windows: two gasoline lamps buzzing from the ceiling, and the orchestra tuning up. Mrs Lister, the wife of our provincial M.P., runs the orchestra; she has thin ankles, and a short white skirt, and striped blazer coat, and carries on with immense verve till any hour of the morning. The piano-player's husband is said to have swindled his uncle out of a coppermine just above us on the hill. And a fair young man with a blue shirt and intellectual fore-head plays the banjo and also owns the garage here. We slowly begin to collect, sitting ourselves in one long row. We all wear home-made dresses and pink stockings, and really look very pretty especially when the colour we bring in from the outside has stopped interfering with what we so carefully applied before starting. The young men don't come up unless they happen to know you, so that your social status can be gauged by the darkness of the coat or the amount of polish which has been given to the shoes that come up to dance with you. No sitting and flirting in corners: it would be difficult anyway in a bare square room. I was then taken to sup with the orchestra and acted umpire while the drum and the lady pianist played dice with the sugar lumps. It was very like the proper Wild West out of the movies looking through the smoke and the gasoline lamps to the young women with their shingled curls and the young men in the tartan shirts. At two we broke up, and packed ourselves back into furs and galoshes and snowshoes. Some kind person offered to see me home, but they all have to get up early, so I resisted and came by myself through the snowy stillness of the pinewood – very lovely.

I manage to do my Arabic every day. Have also started shooting with a small rifle – great fun but not easy. It seems strange that half my time here is up.

Your
FREYA

HERBERT YOUNG

Creston. 6 January 1929

Dearest Herbert,

I feel it quite hard to write, for I shall now be leaving in little over three weeks and it already seems as if the unsettled feeling of departure were beginning.

I am re-reading Gertrude Bell's *Syria*, and comparing her route with ours. She however travelled with three baggage mules, two tents, and three servants: so I consider we were the more adventurous. She also says that the water in the J[ebel] Druse is 'undrinkable by European standards', so I suppose our standard cannot be European: or perhaps an Italian education has hardened us?

Your loving
FREYA

Freya was determined to return to the Middle East. She left once again for Brumana in the autumn of 1929, then went on to spend the winter in Baghdad, where the British community, centred around the handsome High Commission overlooking the river, found her a most disconcerting addition. She was very precise and sometimes steely in manner, and determinedly eccentric, wearing Arab dresses for dinner parties and living, out of financial necessity, with a shoemaker's family. She had not expected, she wrote, to find the British residents so 'hen-like' nor so full of 'froth and foam', though it was the men, rather than their wives, who were disapproving of her.

'The East affected me, on this second arrival', she wrote later, 'with a rapture such as I have never known except on my rediscovery of the Alps after the first World War.' She was now looking for a subject to give her travels a purpose.

ROBERT STARK

Villa Freia. 25 May 1929

Dearest Pips,

I myself am just now busy trying to turn my diary of Druses into a light sort of travel article: will see what happens.

I also have a good subject for the winter, if only it hasn't been exhaustively done already, and that is to combine a sort of history with travel notes to the fortresses of the Assassins, who were the followers of the Old Man of the Mountains, and had a series of castles between Aleppo and the Persian borders. I am very vague about it all, but am trying to find out some more before going out. It seems to me rather promising: although it may all have been done by some thoroughgoing German already.

Love from all here

FREYA

FLORA STARK

Rihàne, nr Damascus. 22 October 1929

Darling B,

I am sitting in a room furnished with rows of chairs in mother-of-pearl inlay, and an immense tall wardrobe of the same, which glitters at one in the morning when one wakes. It is a sort of country house with farm attached, at one corner of the village. We came in a ramshackle car; Mme Azm and the two girls and I had quantities of bundles. It was lovely to get away to life in the country, with the owners looking after their land and the wives attending to the household chores. Delicious things made of walnuts in grape preserve – the grapes boiled and mixed with flour into a paste and rolled round the walnuts. The aunt is quite young, about twenty-four I should say, immensely fat and rosy, with bobbed hair, and all sorts of evening dresses which she has been wearing for us. She lives here with her mother-in-law, an old lady with long nose and a sort of nondescript gown of white and blue stripes, who smokes most of the time. The harem consists of two rooms on either side of the *dar*, or raised loggia open on one side on to a delightful courtyard. On the other side are the kitchen and dining-room, with two maids with checked cotton veils over their heads and pink frilled trousers, running round. We can

42

get out into the stables, but are careful to call out before doing so and ask if there is a man about. I am getting to feel quite ashamed of my unveiled condition, and turn my back with the rest when we pass a peasant on the road. The girls and the young wife are inclined to be careless about these matters, but the uncle, Najib Effendi, keeps them up to the mark. To come home and find six women and two maids all waiting to be pleasant must be a delightful feeling and is I am sure responsible for that sort of assured and reposeful dignity which the Moslem has. From the feminine standpoint, the life is easy enough too: I think our Western strenuousness and sense of responsibility would be very hard on them at first. There is a sort of privacy with no privacy, for all the women wander about in all the rooms, so that even if one wanted to read or study it would be very difficult.

This is now my fourth day, and I feel quite accustomed to the harem, though not inclined for a lifetime of it. There is a deadly boredom about it. The way of passing time is not really more monotonous than the way most of the girls at Dronero, say, spend their time; and the talk – clothes, gossip, relatives, food – is exactly the same. The only difference is one of possibilities – someone very strongminded *can* get out of the rut at Dronero; here, I don't see how they could.

They are all amiable to me though we talk little, my Arabic being really very inadequate. In the evenings and afternoons the Effendi spreads his carpet in the *dar* and intones the Koran in a beautiful voice: the two older ladies, their heads swathed in white, spread their carpets behind him and pray in silence holding their two hands palm upwards for the blessing from heaven. I would like to watch and listen, instead of having to go on playing dice close beside them with the young people who seem never to pray at all.

You would be surprised to see me now, as I am writing with the eternal gramophone and the ladies sewing, and my eyes are – according to them – much beautified with a long black streak underneath them. Soon I shall go and have a bath. It is all wonderfully clean and nice in its own way. It is only the communal life I find difficult.

Tomorrow we return to Damascus, and I must get all ready to leave at six the next morning.

Your own
FREYA

VENETIA BUDDICOM

The Zia Hotel, Baghdad. October 1929

Dearest Venetia,

It is very remarkable – here I am in Baghdad. I sometimes wonder how it comes about. It is a long flat city in a flat land, and all you see as you come from the west is a fringe of palms and a mosque. The bridge of boats is not nearly as beautiful as it sounds, and there is a faintly English flavour of the 'High Street' about the one tarred road which runs down the length of the town. But the *people* are there; and I shall be very happy I do believe. That is after all the real interest: the people here are of all fascinating sorts – the beautiful ones being Kurds. Never have I seen more fine-looking men, so agile and strong with legs bare to the thigh and red turbans, and long hair under, and a wild aquiline handsomeness that is quite intoxicating and I only wish I could paint it.

The Christian ladies appear to go about in the lovely silk wraps which have vanished from Damascus, and the Moslems wear their *'abeias* in a clumsy way over the top of their head with a black veil. I got here very tired and did nothing yesterday but write to a man who is recommended by my friend in Damascus. I hope he may come to help me to a room and am waiting to see before going visiting among British and being told not to.

I am now here with only £10 till November 15th, but feel optimistic enough for anything.

Your
FREYA

ROBERT STARK
11/186 Amara Quarter, Baghdad. 14 November 1929
Dearest Pips,

I have just got into my house. A lady at dinner last night asked me if it is 'fit for an Englishwoman to live in', and I'm sure I don't know, but it looks quite nice once you climb through my dank little well and up the incredible steepness of the stairs (of which only the narrowness keeps you from falling down headlong every time, so that you are like Pickwick's cab horse, supported by the shafts). I have also got an Armenian maid coming tomorrow and a nice boy in the meanwhile.

A tragedy has just taken everyone by surprise: the Prime Minister, who seemed quite happy when sitting next Mrs Drower[1] at dinner on Tuesday, came home from the club on Wednesday night and shot himself dead through the heart. He was the most if not only honest man in the cabinet, and comparatively a friend to the British. He wrote a letter to his son, a boy of nineteen now studying engineering in Birmingham,

1 Wife of legal adviser to the Iraq Ministry of Justice 1922–46.

and went out on to a veranda over the river, and shot himself, his wife holding his arm and begging him to shoot her instead, and his daughter looking on. It was just that these filthy politics were too much for him and he was so badgered by every party that he could stand it no longer. Mrs Drower and I watched the funeral as it passed our window: there was a huge crowd, very silent, but no hostility visible.

I am just reflecting what an awful place one of these flat-roofed towns must be in times of massacres. There is no way of defending your house, for anyone can walk over from the next roof and find himself at once and with no barrier in the heart of your house. I have put a pot of paint just in anyone's way coming down from the roof to my bedroom, and if a cat comes along and overturns it in the middle of the night I shall get a most awful fright for nothing.

Your own
FREYA

VENETIA BUDDICOM

Baghdad. 24 November 1929

Dearest Venetia,

The greengrocer who lives opposite in a little open booth sold me his black and white headcloth to cover my tea table when I gave a party, and came the other day to say that a wealthy Moslem was anxious to give me lessons on Arabic and to read English with me – all for love: at least I hope not that but anyway not for money. He was described as middle-aged with a family, which turns out to be thirty-five, pleasant, plump and grizzled. He doesn't seem to care much about the English, but sits for two hours chatting Arabic and going through the newspaper with me, and has now suggested a visit to one of the Shammar chiefs up the Tigris. I don't think it is really essential, but it seemed to me it would look better to ask for a chaperone, but I must say that the presence of even the most understanding and charming official person seems to cast a shadow.

I am not to be here long, in this house I mean. All the ghosts of all its inhabitants arise and smell during the night till I can hardly breathe and I am looking for something less poisonous; though otherwise I do enjoy being in this disreputable quarter. One day it is a fortune teller coming up, you pass your hand on a mirror and then she looks and sees what is not, with a plausible air: yesterday a small street fight and the night before a death with rows of black hooded women crouching in the dim courtyard and shrieking their barbarous grief. The street is not more than two yards across. All the refuse is thrown there and collected on

45

donkeys early in the morning so that the atmosphere is slowly degenerating through the day. The trouble is with the houses however, every family living over its own cistern where the accumulated filth of ages oozes up through the brick and makes for the parchment faces and sunken eyes and, I am sure, the jaundiced fanaticism which distinguish the townspeople here. In the night you hear sharp whistles at intervals, and that is the police – but whether the whistle is meant to startle the householder or the thief I haven't yet fathomed. Anyway a smart Iraqi in uniform came with a big book and got nearly a rupee out of me for the nightly protection.

Your
FREYA

VIVA JEYES

Baghdad. [end] November 1929

Dear Viva,

My new house belongs to Michael the Shoemaker from Mosul and his wife and two dear little boys, and my room has five big windows on the river and a wide balcony in front and the sun after just peeping in of a morning goes round and shines in at the opposite window for an hour or two before setting. Not all the panes are quite entire, but Mrs Longrigg the wife of the financial adviser has sent me four lovely heavy woollen rugs which I have hung up today. The Longriggs[1] and Sturges[2] live just a few houses further up so that I am now not only healthily but even respectably situated. I only hope this may not discourage the Arabs. Communications are supposed to be easy. The first day we went down to the riverside and shouted out to the boats which are supposed to act as buses: 'Oh father of the boats hear us,' but the father of the motor wasn't taking any notice and I had to run along the river bank and cross by the Maud bridge of boats. Down the river bank southwards are flat mud hovels where the peasants live: a little pale maid in her dark blue gown and with her slim little figure and silent barefoot walk comes every morning with a bottle of milk. She has a gold circle with turquoise and little gold dice hanging from it sticking in the nostril and her name is Jamila.

On Tuesday I had tea with a Syrian girl educated at Columbia University, and now teaching here, and then met one of the local editors, and an Armenian who is translating Lawrence (and doesn't think very

1 Brigadier S.H. Longrigg spent twenty-five years in the Middle East. In 1929 he was receiver of revenues in Iraq 'though they all say there aren't any'.
2 Mr and Mrs Sturges, 'friends from the first', with a little house near the Embassy.

highly of him). These were all particularly anti-English. It seems a dreadful pity. My hostess said to me rather pathetically, 'We should so much like to be allowed to love the English, if they did not always make us feel they were snubbing us.' On the other hand not more than about two people in a thousand can find any interest in *really* mixing with the natives. So what is the way out? It is all a wonderful drama, and I love to be watching it, but it is a heartbreaking job to those who have given their best years to it and see it not only unrecognised but with every prospect of being annulled very soon.

Your loving
FREYA

FLORA STARK

Baghdad. 17 December 1929

Darling B,

What a blessing that Paradise isn't run by our Civil Service, or so few of us would get in. It seems that I have put my foot in it most *dreadfully* by accepting the mu'allim's invitation for the Beduin Sheikh. I am surrounded by a kind of frost, and Mrs Drower tells me that all the men disapprove of me. It makes me feel like a kind of pariah from my own kind, and awfully disgusted, because after all I really have done nothing and, beyond wishing to talk as much Arabic as I can, and regretting that we can't be less superior and more polite, I am not even pro-native, certainly as much of an imperialist as any of the people here. But Mrs Sturges told me today that one *can't* be friends with the natives and British both; and so what is to be done? It seems to me an almost unbelievable idiocy, and I shall have to put up with being out of it all and getting on steadily with my grammar, and I suppose it is good for one's character. Mrs Kerr[1] gave out at the last moment and told me that Lionel Smith[2] didn't want her to go with me; so I should have had to go alone, if dear Mrs Drower hadn't come nobly up to the scratch: she hasn't yet told Teddy that she is coming. It is only for one night, with a tame Sheikh who is a friend of most of the people here – so this fuss is too ridiculous. The Sheikh came today to call, looking so nice with his flowing *'abba* and fine head, so infinitely better and more dignified than these degenerate townsfolk who have lost their own virtues and not taken ours. And it was a joy to listen to the good Arabic of the tents. We are to go on Friday, and the Sheikh Habib has gone on to see that the falcons are being starved

1 'The nice American head' of the big school for girls in Baghdad.
2 Adviser to the Iraqi Ministry of Education 1923–30.

so that they may be ready to hunt for us. It will be great fun, and we will pay the Devil when we come home. I have written a note to Lionel Smith asking if he is really responsible and whether it is I or the Beduin who are bad for Mrs Kerr (in a polite way). I reminded him that even a dog is allowed one bite before being suppressed: and I really haven't yet had my bite.

Mrs Sturges would have loved to come and hunt with the Sheikh, but Mr S said he thought 'it would be cold for her' with the tones of an iceberg. She now wants to come and study in school with me, but I bet that will be squashed before the first lesson even starts. The truth is that the people here don't want any English in the land except themselves: they feel responsible, and yet can't actually order you about if you are an independent traveller. In fact it really *is* that attitude of *A Passage to India*, though I would never have believed it before, and it does make one rather sad.

Your own
FREYA

3

Winter in Baghdad, the Assassins' castles, learning Persian, Takht-i-Suleiman, Teheran, the Lurs

During one of her visits to London, Freya had read von Hammer-Purgstall's account of how the Assassins, a branch of the Ismaili Moslems, had ruled by murder throughout the Near East, under the Old Man of the Mountain, who dominated them with hashish ('hashashin' = hashish-takers or assassins). Though the details of this exotic legend were later dismissed by scholars, the castle of Alamut in the Elburz mountains south of the Caspian remained a fascinating place, for it had been the Assassins' headquarters until its destruction by the Mongols in 1256. Freya spent part of the winter in Baghdad, learning Persian, and in April 1930 she settled in Hamadan for a month to practise her conversation, planning her first expedition on her own to the castle of Alamut.

VENETIA BUDDICOM

Baghdad. 6 January 1930

My dearest Venetia,

Thank you my dear for thinking of my Xmas with all your troubles, and with so much insight into my weakness for unlawful extravagance. I shall be able to indulge in a silk dressing *'abeia*, and not feel that I am doing anything criminal. I am rather hard up just now having just invested in a Persian master, who is teaching me Persian in Arabic, which is good for both. Persian seems very easy by comparison, but if it goes on doing so is of course to be seen. The object is to go up to the ancient (now vanished) castle of the Assassins in one of the valleys between Kazvin and the Black Sea. The Oriental Secretary to the H.C. [Capt. Vyvyan Holt],[1] who is a really first-rate young man, full of understanding, is going to procure a lorry to take me cheaply to the foothills, and then (in about three or four months) my Persian is supposed to carry me on. It is really heart-breaking that you are not to be in all this. But if all goes well (and given that I can manage it, for I really don't quite know how to do the finance), I think this will be a preliminary visit, and some day soon we must go and perhaps settle awhile in a

1 Exceptional Arabist, traveller and lover of the desert.

village there or in the Kurdish hills in Rowenduz, which is a hill town between two gorges and all the ranges of the Turkish border.

My dear, you can't imagine what a place this is for taking an interest in other people's affairs, nor what a mutual shock my first contact with proper conventional civil service society has caused. No one else (respectable) appears ever to have settled in a shoemaker's home on the banks of the Tigris, nor has anyone succeeded in living in Baghdad on two rupees a day. One lady has asked me if I am not 'lowering the prestige of British womanhood' by sitting in school among the Iraqi girls. Today on my way there I had to be carried across a puddle on the back of a Kurdish porter, which I am sure would have shocked the ladies of the Alwiyah suburb into fits. For a time, except for one or two people who were really very nice all through, I felt rather like an outcast; the men nearly all disapproved and looked on uneasily if their wives were nice to me – apparently expecting something explosive to happen every second. The East must have rather a distorting effect on people's perspectives. I feel that there was something to be said for the poor bull in the china shop, whose most innocent and natural movements all seemed to cause a smash.

Today the Tigris is like a small sea, the waves all going upstream and the east wind and rain beating like hurricanes – turning the palm trees nearly inside out.

I can't tell you how often I wish for you out here. How pleasant it would be to sit here together in my quite warm room with the Tigris flapping its waves below, and maps and plans to make and life in general to talk about. The more I see of people, how set they are apt to get, and dead to all the moving things and the meaning of things, the more I feel how good it is to have one's friends near to talk to.

My dearest love always,

Your
FREYA

ROBERT STARK

Baghdad. 10 January 1930

Darling Pips,

Such a good adventure to tell you this week, and I am sitting up to do so, having just come home from it safe and sound. I have been inside the Kadhimain Mosque, which is so holy that Christians are not allowed even to touch the threshold, and would in fact be killed if found inside. But I wore a black veil over my face and a black *'abba* over my head, covering me all up, and black shoes that looked as un-English as I could find – and so dressed up went from here with two native Syrian Christians, also got up. We did the dressing in their house and sent the servants to get a taxi so that the driver shouldn't know, and then we sped along the four miles to Kadhimain about 7 p.m. with a row of dim lamps either side the road all the way to the holy city. Our friends there are a Shi'a doctor's family, and we couldn't find the house: we got into the bazaar and had to make ourselves conspicuous by asking. The bazaar is a Rembrantesque sort of place at night, full of shadows. We found the house at last and then all sallied forth, the doctor leading, a servant and lantern ahead to light up the various sloughs and drains of the road, the brother Kerim behind, and we in true female Eastern fashion trailing at intervals as best we could. I was very anxious not to let the wretched veil slip off my head.

We got through a dark gate into the enormous quadrangle of the mosque, like a great piazza, with groups here and there, and a few lamps lighting the mosaic portico, and the gold and mirrored lunettes of the sanctuary in the middle. The stars, very bright, overhead; and one had a great feeling of space. No Western note here. It was a weird feeling to know that really one's life depended on not being recognised; and still weirder to see people looking straight at one and to remind oneself that they couldn't possibly see through the black veil. We went up to the door of the sanctuary – our host exchanging greetings with various Sayids in flowing robes and green or white turbans. At the gate we took off our shoes and a man with a stick poked it into the toe and lifted the impure object to one side. The marble was very cold to stand on. 'You are people of the house,' said a misguided Mullah to our host, and took us into the shrine himself with the proper prayers: he stood at the front great gate and prayed in the beautiful half singing voice to which they are trained, an invocation to Muhammad and Ali, and then – with 'God is great' – we stepped back into a mirrored place: then through another great curtain into the holy of holies, the tomb of the two Imams. It didn't seem very large, and the whole centre is filled by the two tombs whose carved wood can be seen dimly through the glass, and the iron grating, and then the enormous silver grill with bands of silver texts perpendicular around it, all polished by the hands of the faithful who press round, pressing their hands and bodies against it and kissing it. The atmosphere of the place was extraordinary. Such intensity of passion. A woman sobbing beside me, kissing the silver grating again and again; people crouching on the ground with their heads against it; old Sheiks immovable there, with their hands upturned, their faces rapt, their eyelids lowered, lost to all sensation. And the strongest impression was that of these passionate

51

hands, pressing their way round the four sides of the great square tomb – Kerim murmured to me not to move off but to go round also, which I did, my hand along the thick bars but not kissing, being a Presbyterian. When we reached the third side, we stopped, and our Mullah again chanted a prayer. Muhammad, Ali, Musa the holy Imam: I did not catch it all, but the sound was extraordinarily moving. On the fourth side, an old Mullah was offering candles for the obtaining of all one's desires: very like Italy really, except for the intensity of the whole thing and the fact of course that these people would not hesitate a minute to do you in.

I am just home now at ten and wondering whether this is going to get me into trouble when it gets known. I believe one or two Englishwomen have been in before, but not many, and I know the official attitude will not be very cordial.

Do write soon. I think Baghdad will find me for another three months anyway.

Your own
FREYA

PENELOPE KER

Baghdad. 25 January 1930

My darling Pen,

This morning I had a rather sad experience. I was taken to call on Queen 'Ali, the wife of the deposed King of Hejaz. She is kept in a big house lower down on the river, and the house and its yard, with a rear exit to visit her in-laws at King Faisal's palace, is all the range of these poor ladies' lives. We banged on the door, and at last a little black boy with a red gown and turban came running along, opened the door and let us into a yard. A big board, like a scoring board for cricket, was just about six feet inside the door, so that even when open no one could look into the courtyard. If the house caught fire, all those females inside would be burned. A beautiful white saluki came bounding down the steps to meet us. But the house was old and squalid, with its earthern filter for water in one corner and the painted porticoes of light blue wooden pillars picked out with yellow. Upstairs, we went into a long room all upholstered with embossed yellow velvet and purple curtains and large enlargements of royal photos on the walls – Faisal, and Hussein, 'Ali, and his son the young Emir who is learning to play tennis in a British school in Alexandria while his mother lives this life of ten centuries ago here. A lady-in-waiting with untidy hair and shabby old flannel coat entertained us, till Her Majesty came in, in a little green ready-made house dress, very simple, with bobbed hair and the most unhappy eyes you ever saw. She is still quite young and had been used to a pleasanter life in Constantinople (where she belongs) and even in Mecca: people hate to visit her for she hardly speaks or even answers, but sits in her yellow chair on the opposite side of the room with her fierce unhappy eyes and rather pale plain little face, saying 'ay' to all efforts that are made to entertain her. Today she was more talkative than usual, and at times looked quite pretty and gentle when she smiled. The black slaves came in with very heavy steps because they had been made to put on high-heeled shoes, and gave us coffee out of black and gold cups, and we then came away feeling saddened in the lovely sunshine. A man outside, who sat in the mud skewering a huge fish to roast over a fire on the ground, was a much happier sight.

Your
FREYA

CAR KER[1]

Mosul. 17 March 1930

Dearest Car,

Now I am up in Mosul and spring just beginning with a tang of the north in it: no palms here but peach blossom, and pear trees just bursting into fat little bunches, and rolling shallow green hills like downs, with strips of ploughed land: and far away, the Kurdistan snows and the Turkish ranges. And the streets and bazaars are cobbled with stones like a proper northern town, and have every sort of mountaineer and plains-man swaggering about in them.

I spent a lovely peaceful morning yesterday in what was once Nineveh – a low very wide saucer of downs and wheatland, with a shallow wave hiding it like a rim where the old ramparts lie buried. There is nothing much to see, only this consciousness of great peace over what was once so tumultuous.

[continued] 20 March 1930

Mrs Drower and I are now well out in the desert, a marvellous grassy world – and we are staying with the chief Sheikh of the Shammar. We have a big tent to ourselves with white mattresses and purple cushions spread in it, and all the tents of the Sheikh's family and slaves spread around, with horses, donkeys, camels, and small foals and children all out enjoying the short delicious season. I can't tell you what a sense of peace and loveliness it is: the women sit out with their tents open on the sunny or shady side according to the time of day, and show us their old

1 Another sister of W.P. Ker.

53

barbaric jewels and magic beads. Some bring children, or cure serpent bites, or if they touch a man's cloak, will make him instantly love you: and one, which was offered me as a present yesterday, is to be rolled on the carpet and any woman you happen to dislike is brushed out of existence on the instant; this is called the 'carpet stone'.

Many of these Shammar come from far away south and have a good deal of negro mixture. We are guests and they are charming to us: one has a wonderful feeling of safety and protection within the limits of the tribe: the fierce thick furry dogs roam about the outskirts ready to attack wolves or strangers. In the middle of our camp there is a little grassy rise: one can look out thence to the Kurdish snows, and the Sinjar hills and French border, with other mounds rising as if from a green sea – and the grass full of flowers.

Your loving
FREYA

PENELOPE KER

Hôtel de France, Hamadan. 20 April 1930

Dearest Pen,

This is being written in a garden with little streams running through it, and a square tank in the middle, and blossoming trees all round; and I am really more surprised at being here than I can tell you – surprised at its being I myself, if you know the feeling. We are 6,000 feet up, and the snowy ridge behind, half hidden by the poplar trees, goes up to a gentle peak of 13,000. Hamadan, with a tumbling stream and low untidy little mudbrick houses slopes down into the plain, very shallow, and brown as yet: and the Kurdish hills are on the farther edge, blue and distant. There are wild tulips, yellow, and white and very dark purple violets in the hills, and wild daffodils and hyacinths and Crown Imperial, but I can't go to look for them because I fell off a horse in Baghdad, and strained a muscle; hoping to be well next week however, and then I shall walk and walk and rejoice in the feeling of turf and a hillside under my feet again.

It was wonderful coming up from Baghdad. I was not sorry to leave, as the dust storms were just beginning and I had left my own nice room and spent three days on a sofa in the hotel feeling *degraded* into a tourist.

I wish you could see my Persian teacher. He looks just like the circus clown with a hennaed beard added – and badly put on too, for it sticks right out; and his absurd frock coat and peaked cap, which is the modern polite costume in Persia, give him the most low-down musical comedy appearance you can imagine. We had some difficulty in fixing a time. I suggested the morning, and he said 'Would 5.30 suit you?' He promises that I shall be able to speak in a month's time and I am going to work at it as hard as I can: at present I can just ask my way and get things from the servants, that is all.

We are going out today to look at Esther's tomb. Avicenna also was buried here, and old Assyrian seals and things are found in the ground. I never get over the fascination of the *age* of all these lands – back and back, and we never come to the beginning, but find still older traces of old and tired civilisations. The earliest bits of pottery, which they find among the flint instruments long before metals were known, are decorated so beautifully that they must have ages of practice behind them. Of course there must be marvellous buried treasures in this country, only it is very hard to get permission to dig here.

There is no one in this hotel except passing motorists; yesterday it was the ex-Shah of Afghanistan and his family, only as it merely looked like an ordinary fat man sitting in the garden, I did not look at him with any attention.

Your
FREYA

FLORA STARK

Hamadan. 6 May 1930

Darling B,

Don't know why but I am so very depressed this evening – feeling so old, and as if my whole life were wasted and now it were too late to do anything with it: such an uphill work, with so much less health and strength and power than most and already half way through and nothing done. And as if what I *do* do were not worth doing: no one seems to think it is, but just wonder at me and are sorry for me if they are nice, and disapprove if they are not. To be just middle-aged with no particular charm or beauty and no position is a dreary business. In fact I feel as if I had been going uphill all the time to nowhere in particular, and – like poor Venetia – most dreadfully lonely, envying all these women with their nice clean husbands whose tradition is their tradition, and their nice flaxen children who will carry it on in the same simple and steady way. And though it *is* my tradition too, no one thinks it is, because of a silly difference of form and speech and fashion – so that I feel as if I *had* no people of my own. If only I could eventually find some work that would make me feel settled and interested. I hope it may be: but no one seems to want women very much – and I don't quite know that I am fit for anything but philanthropy, and that would not really thrill me. Well, I

55

think it must be because no one any longer makes love to me except when they are drunk.

I feel that I really may end by doing something; only it is not a thing that can be hurried. But in three years' time I could know enough Persian, Turkish, Kurdish, and Arabic to get about, and I believe I would be the only English woman in the Near East to do so: and then something amusing is bound to turn up. As it is, another six months here will give me Persian: it is most comforting to find how easy these languages are after Arabic. It is merely a matter of learning the words. If only I had a better memory it would be such a blessing.

Dearest love to you both.

FREYA

ROBERT STARK

Gd. Hotel (so called), Kazvin. 13 May 1930

Dearest Pips,

The adventure is starting: it is all being set going and now promises well: a Bahai letter I have is to a doctor who owns several of the villages en route. I have already separated myself from civilisation by leaving all my respectable clothes behind and am here with only my tent, bed, and saddle-bags full of woollies and things. The tragedy is that my boots rub: I am going to get some of the native things with cotton tops and soles made of linen in close layers put on perpendicularly, and then cut to the required thickness and kept together by camel's hide. If I can, I will bring you out a pair: I'm sure you would like them.

I got a seat in a native car for four tomans yesterday: 12/- for 216 kilometres isn't bad is it? It took us eight and a half hours over great plains bordered with bare hills, and then another great plain – till one thought it would go on for ever and ever. In all this distance there is not a single town, and not many villages: just the road, and perhaps twenty to thirty cars and lorries in the course of the day. One or two strings of carts on their squat wheels and bodies like the Ark, with the driver sitting on bright carpets high up above the horses. The whole desert was full of flowers.

At 12.30 we reached a big village and stopped for lunch. I pooled mine with the family behind: someone provided a carpet and we sat in the shade of baby poplars. The men bought hardboiled eggs from an old peasant squatting there with a basket and it was very pleasant. Two beautifully groomed Englishmen in a lovely car whizzed past, but luckily did not think of looking at our native group, far less imagine a British female there, so I was spared the look of pained surprise. The family is travelling back to Resht with an elderly mother, who still wore the old-fashioned costume – enormous black bloomers sewn into black stockings of the same stuff and gathered into voluminous gathers at the ankle. Once inside them you must feel as if you were in a sort of cage. I always keep my Persian grammar handy, so I now fill in the 'waits' by learning new words and can bear the uncertainties of travel with much more philosophy.

A horrid new street leads all down the length of Kazvin: a doctor has been given carte blanche by the Shah and has laid out the whole place in boulevards and electric lights: the roads are cut quite ruthlessly (the Shah told him he could cut the Royal Hand off if it happened to be in the way) and no compensation is given: and the Persians are all fearfully pleased. Perhaps one would be if one were a Persian: there seems nothing for it but to be European and so the sooner they do it the better from their own point of view: but it doesn't make it attractive for travelling.

Your own
FREYA

VENETIA BUDDICOM

Kazvin. 14 May 1930

Dearest V,

There is an agreeable atmosphere here of native provincial life, very like a small Italian or French town. The hotel owner is an old Parsee turned Bahai with a shrewd face and a twinkle, and not above a glass of whisky with his guests – the remains of the Fire worship no doubt. His son is still a devotee of the ancient Persian history which belongs to the Parsees. Then there are a few Russians who spend all day here talking and talking so that you would think they were trying to imitate their own novels.

I wandered all over the bazaars this morning in that labyrinth of faded splendours, which the business of Kazvin today can hardly fill, and watched the little pale-faced boys knotting their carpets with incredible speed. One could pick up heaps of treasures if one had money and time: all Persia is crazy for modernity and selling its old stuff, and there it all is, treasures here and there among the rubbish: but one ought to know a great deal. I hardened my heart however, as I am so broke that I have to borrow off a kind Armenian here and shall be on the verge of bankruptcy till I get back and trust to Providence that some money may have turned up.

For anything except serious business the people are charming. But I have come to the conclusion that to put off doing troublesome things is really a much more serious fault than it looks: I think it means a fundamental lack of will-power – for you will notice that *no* nation which has this defect will ever get on: it means that it hasn't got the backbone to make itself do something it doesn't like, and of course there is no hope for it. I certainly like the Arab best so far as I have seen.

Love dear Venetia from

FREYA

FLORA STARK

Zavarak. 19 May 1930

Dearest B,

I haven't been able to write and such a lot to tell. We got to Shutur Khan, where the Doctor's brother lives, in the afternoon the day before yesterday, and found he had gone off for the day. However they showed us into a room with nice carpets, and in time the laird arrived, a man with a nice face of a gentleman rather rusted over by the country. We sat on the veranda outside, looking from our little valley into the big valley running below. At the head of the valley, where a black mountain closes it, the great rock of the Assassins' castle is plainly visible though two hours' mule ride off.

We slept the night, and presently – before supper – had a visit from the one police officer whom here we simply call 'The Government'. 'Are you going to take tea with The Government?' The Government was rather a nice little Persian with an enormous district all to himself: 15,000 souls who all quarrel, he says, and says his hair is going grey. He was exercised over me, only I am now an expert with hostile police. However the little man was much too polite to make it really obvious that he suspected when I obviously took it for granted that he didn't, and kept telling him how charming the police in Kazvin and Hamadan are. I couldn't find out anything about the Assassins, but we started next morning, leaving the sunk bed of the stream and coming out on a wide grassy platform tilted southward. The castle rock is always in sight and as you come near you see what a magnificent position it was: romantic isn't the word. It holds the whole enormous fortified valley, overlooking it from one end to the other over the lower ranges, across the tilted pasture-desert to the snowy range of Elburz and his brother peaks.

The Syalan pass leads down to it, and the only other outlet except the bottle-neck we came through leads down the valley below it, so that an enemy would have to climb uphill through weary open spaces before even reaching within range of the castle.

When we reached Qasir Khan, we found ourselves expected. Someone comes nearly every year – and one woman and an old Assassin with aquiline nose and hennaed little pointed beard knew all about it and appeared with a samovar and two helpmates with spades. Then we went up a desolate stony valley tilted up the hillside with the great rock on our right. It is a huge mass, with the hillside hollowed out behind, and when you get to the neck at the back of the cliff, you look down the other tilted valley on the other side of the rock and see Elburz gleaming across with slabs of grey rock in the foreground. We zigzagged up to the rock and saw what was left: a bit of buttress and wall and tunnel cut through the skeleton of rock which runs along the length of the whole thing – evidently just a completion of the natural defences. There are two rooms cut in the rock below, but inaccessible: at least they all begged me not to go, and to say the truth I funked it, not having very reliable footwear and a fearful drop if one slipped. But I do not regret the cowardice, for I believe there is a tank down there where seven black dogs breathing fire sit and guard the treasure. We reached Shutur Khan in the afternoon and found The Government waiting with the laird in a little room with one chair and table and two carpets on which we sat down and talked.

Then I had really a great stroke of luck. A rather unprepossessing unshaven gentleman came in to call, with the Pahlevi hat which looks very wrong here, and after salaam and all half rising, and all sitting down, and then all rising again to the newcomer and making little murmured polite inquiries, and settling down again to collect ourselves again after the disturbance, we began to talk about the castle. The new arrival had seen us yesterday at Badasht: Badasht, he says, is corrupted from Baghdasht which means a desert garden: and where there is a great stone in the river bed just below this place he says that there is an old building high up on the cliffs above: that there are seven reservoirs one below the other, and the remains of ancient chains which once carried a water conduit across the Shahrud valley. 'There should be a garden somewhere,' said I, 'for it is written that Hassan-i-Sabah kept a garden hidden in the fortresses here.' 'Oh, that must be up in such and such a place,' says this wonderful man. And he explained that in coming over a pass right at the back – exactly in the position one would expect, too – and about 11,000 feet up, he had been surprised to see fruit trees growing on a space of ground about three to six acres as far as I could make out and far above the level of any cultivation now. The place is yet deep under snow and will not be clear for another two months – but it is a thrilling thought isn't it? I got so excited I felt my fingers *trembling*. Ever since I went up to the castle and indeed came into the valley I have felt there must be a good deal in the old legend (as there usually is). People told me

59

that there is no sign of the garden by the castle now, but the very meaning of the legend points to the fact that the garden was somewhere else, far out of the ordinary way: and this barren valley which looks like a desert until you come on some patch of incredible greenness and fertility is exactly the place where such a little paradise could be made.

It has been a wonderful time altogether, and I can now *see* how the story of the Assassins really was; can see their life here in the valley and the devotion of their people, and the remoteness from all the world: and the comparative wellbeing which there still is, though it has to be practically independent from all outside.

Dear love,
FREYA

FLORA STARK

Garmrud. 20 May 1930

Darling B,

This village is 7,500 feet, and I have just been up and down again to 10,250 – and seen the whole valley below from end to end, a green winding streak between its red hills, to where the western castle of Badasht must be above the cliffs that close the other outlet.

I have had a proper bit of Alpine climbing up real rock, holding on with my hands and looking sheer down, and without the moral support of a rope, and my native givas not yet familiar and apt to slip on their heels from under me. Having now again lost the trail of my only Englishwoman – and in fact of any English at all, for only one European is remembered to have climbed up to Nevisar, and that before this generation – I have been setting the standard and the next lady will have to be some climber.

You can see that the place is absolutely closed. I sat up there for an hour, finding the points of the compass, getting the names of the hills sorted, and trying in vain to disentangle the absolute wrongness of my map, which has actually got the Elburz *range* in the wrong valley. However, I have got about half a dozen new mountains and two really important villages in the pass that figures as uninhabited in the maps.

Here I am staying at 'Aziz's house. Such a pretty wife, and knows it too, and gave him a terrific rating for staying away so long. It is so pleasant to be welcomed by the whole village: all the relatives and friends coming in – and three ladies sitting round me while I washed which I could have done without but it gave them so much more pleasure than my own discomfort that it didn't seem kind to interfere with it.

There was a bit of old worship when we left the castle: 'Aziz told me one must salaam to Elburz, whenever one leaves the sight of him.

Your own
FREYA

FLORA STARK

Nr. Khurramabad. 23 May 1930

Dearest B,

It is a most extraordinary sight to come out on to the Caspian after all the forest – all yesterday afternoon and six hours today riding through it, lovely in the lower parts like some lonely bit of Pyrenees with its rushing streams and enormously tall trees. One leaves the big river, the two Hizars they are, which have joined their waters and rush down foaming together: one crosses a small col which the Emir Sipahsalar paved with boulders before he was asked by the government to commit suicide: then one crosses the Valmirud – a broad slow stream in a big bed: up another steep, short col – and there is the Caspian, and between you and it a landscape that has walked out of a lacquered tray: a flat landscape shining like a dull mirror with endless little sub-divisions of rice plots divided by tiny mud barriers: islands of green trees, oranges and pomegranates in flower, rise all among these water plots, and every island has a few houses under enormous beehive roofs of rice thatching. Little observ-atories on four pillars, under a dome of thatching, stand about in the water, and beyond it all is a pale streak of sea without shadows that also might come out of a Japanese print. Blue dragonflies, with the outer half of their wings velvety black, dart about doing their little best with the mosquitoes: but, of course, this is a perfect trap for malaria and even the poorest house has a veranda which you climb to by a ladder and are supposed to be out of their way. I am sitting on one now, after lunch, and the centre of an interested row of onlookers who look very much more Russian than Persian, with darker eyes, and pretty oval faces, and a generally softer expression. Their language is quite incomprehensible – and especially today because my cold is so bad that I could scarcely understand English if there were any to be heard within fifty miles.

My coming has evidently been heralded by the muleteers who went ahead, for I was greeted with looks of expectant surprise by all we met. It is quite a shock when you are jogging along amiably absent-minded to see people meeting you suddenly petrified with surprise.

I believe these people used to be very wild and a man who is now political officer in Fars was kept a year or so as a prisoner tied to a tree: at least that is what Captain Holt told me, and said I should get to know him as he is as mad as me. Anyway they seem friendly enough now.

I am waiting to know whether or no a motor is going to take me to Resht or not this evening. I had been hearing so long of Tunakabun as the centre of all things here, and was thinking of it as a kind of metropolis where civilisation, films and chairs were flourishing. What it is, is a peaceful little village with a market twice a week where people from Resht spread awnings and all sorts of bright cottons, buttons, beads, elastic, and such European oddments for the rice growers round to buy. It would be a charming spot with its green gardens and the row of wooden slopes rising to snow behind, if it were not a perfect death-trap for malaria; I dose myself with quinine which may explain why I feel so peculiar – but I shall be glad to get away to a drier country.

Resht. 26 May 1930

I had just got so far when a motor car finally turned up. Two in fact; one which had been ordered from Shahzavar came along, but with the intention of taking me only half-way and then stopping: so we took the other one, which had a charming chauffeur like a Mujik with an enormous beard. The first car wanted to be paid for coming so far, but even the easy benevolence of the Doctor came to the conclusion that a car which comes to take you to a place where you haven't asked to go, needn't be paid. To make all sure we appealed to a village Elder with a red hennaed beard: and the verdict being in favour, started off without more ado. Most affectionate farewells. I felt I was leaving quite a familiar place: having sat under the orange trees, drinking tea in the Emir's garden: and spent the morning with a little procession of Bahai notables behind me, visiting the bazaar (and buying a silk bedcover which I regret, for the sum would have just prevented me from being impecunious now): and having visited the school, which is a lonely old dilapidation in a garden with a tank and big trees where the little boys read out short moral stories in high sing-song voices.

It was now about seven o'clock, and I had discovered that it would be another four hours at least to Resht, and was not too pleased when it turned out that the fat chauffeur was taking me alone through the Caspian jungle. It did seem very lonely: the forest here reaches almost to the water's edge; the sea lay very quiet and dull with a last light in it; and this road drifted along through sand or gravel, with not a soul on it. Luckily the chauffeur was a really good man and not fond of talking: his only remark was as we came to a particularly shadowy bit under the trees, that there used to be a lot of robbers here. We met a woodcutter or two trudging home: a horseman now and then: and about one car an hour coming the opposite way. Here and there were clearings for rice fields. We punctured conveniently in one of these clearings – and the chauffeur turned out really capable and put it right quickly. After that I saw no more of the country; we went through like a dream, and it was extraordinarily like England – the green hedges, and trees, and thatched roofs. Only the little towns with their bazaars still busy looked foreign enough – shoemakers and tailors stitching away at ten o'clock at night round a big lantern, and the tea-shops handing round their little glasses. About 10.30 we waded up to the footboards through the first branch of the Safid Rud which I had crossed a week before near Chala; when we got across, a man in a little hut sounded a gong, and by the time we reached the second branch the ferry was waiting and a posse of men ready to get us across. It was so like a dream. I could not help wondering all the time how I came to be there on the edge of the Caspian in the middle of the night. A little after eleven, I got to Resht and asked for the Grand Hotel – having been told this name by the A's: it was a mistake, however, of theirs, for the Savoy is the one to go to, and the Grand is an awful little place with nothing clean except its notice board. I was too exhausted to care much however.

Next day I decided to go and call on the Consul – whether I knew him or not. We went and looked at maps: he had done some exploring himself – farther east – and, by the time I was going, he asked me to stay to dinner and rang up Mr Ward the bank manager. Dinner with candles and silver: and the two men so friendly. They discussed Valerian and the Persian wars, very agreeably remote – and by the time Mr Ward took me back to my disgusting hotel and asked me next time to stay at his house, I was feeling much refreshed.

Later, Kazvin. 27 May 1930

After refusing to go from Resht at 5 p.m. I thought I was fairly safe to travel by daylight, leaving at nine-thirty. The motor turned out to be one of these lorries with a wire grill like a menagerie behind where the passengers sit on whatever the freight may be: rice done up in straw bales it was. I sat in front, rather dubiously – but there was nothing for it – and I was only paying about 8/- for 110 miles, so I couldn't be particular. It was only after a couple of hours, noticing what a very small impression we seemed to make on the map, that I began to ask if it was really only a six-hour drive and if I would be in Kazvin by four. 'Oh, no, not four: possibly by eight *inshallah*.' Then the wheel broke down: they said nothing was the matter with it, but went on tinkering for a long time. The seat had no springs and an abyss behind just in the small of one's back where the jolts come: I wondered how I could bear it, as eight o'clock was an endless way off. The wind was blowing huge curtains of dust all up the wide valley: the tumbled hills stretched away beyond eyesight, and our poor old ramshackle lorry, puffing and smelling horribly, crawled along the little dips and rises in the most exasperating way.

My temper was long ago ruined inwardly, but I was hoping I could keep it in outward control: the one thing that never pays in the East is to lose one's temper: it doesn't anywhere but especially here. When seven o'clock came and they said cheerfully that if God willed we might arrive in another three hours, I did lose it however. I had had no lunch, not having any money and not wanting to borrow off the chauffeur. It really did seem the last straw after all the fatigues of my real trip, and then when it was eight o'clock, and already dark, and the wind like ice over the pass, we all had to wait for half an hour shivering while one of the passengers in the menagerie cage behind got out to smoke a pipe of opium. These people were putting up quite cheerfully with all the discomforts, and the chauffeur even suggested not wearing his greatcoat because it was being used to support my back: so I recovered as best I could, and finally at 11 p.m., after thirteen and a half hours in that unspeakable lorry, arrived in Kazvin.

Dear love to you.

FREYA

Freya spent the rest of 1930 in Europe and paid a visit to Canada to see her father. She had shown her Alamut records to Arthur Hinks, Secretary of the Royal Geographical Society, and was encouraged to study surveying before setting out for Baghdad again and returning to the Alamut. These were her first, and pleasurable, encounters with the world of professional geographers.

On this second journey she drew up maps of the region, discovered a third and as yet unidentified Assassin castle, and set off to look for some Bronze Age figurines she had been told came from a little-explored corner of Luristan. She travelled alone, and as the first European woman in these parts, was a figure of constant curiosity and speculation.

FLORA STARK

11 Grove End Rd. 14 February 1931

Darling B,

My [map-making] lessons at the R.G.S. get on. A charming old man, Mr Reeves, who is very keen to push me on, says I am 'quite as good at it as Gertrude Bell'. I think it must be my hard work at C. Hobbs' book which has given him this illusion. Anyway I shall have the rudiments of the business I hope.

A fearful shock when I went in yesterday. The Secretary, a charming young woman, came with a MS which is to appear next month – an account by Major Edmonds[1] of *his* visit to Alamut; he says that I have 'adequately described it', but ends by demolishing me over something etymological I never meant to say. Really the life in the public eye is very trying: I think I shall leave scientific papers alone in future. I have written a little explanation and may get them to put it in. It is fun really though absurd, my learning not being of the sort that should be taken seriously. But if they want to argue, why they shall – and I shall tell Major E what I think of him when I see him.

Love
FREYA

FLORA STARK

11 Grove End Rd. 18 February 1931

Dearest B,

I am just home, tired, but having much enjoyed my visit [to the Lawrences].[2] They were so kind to me – especially Sir Henry, who likes me I believe and is going to have a whole twelve hours of my society when he comes up on Friday week. Lunch at his club, and then we are going to the India Office to look into a file about the Agha Khan's ancestry and his descent from the Assassins, on which his revenues depended: the documents are there, and only the Initiate can get at them, so I shall go as Sir Henry's secretary. Then dinner and theatre: I think I shall find it very hard to remain conversationable all that time and fear we shall both be exhausted. He is a charming man to talk to, full of a dry humour which flashes out suddenly in a quiet way. Lady Lawrence is very delicate and an invalid, but she is rather nice all the same and artistic: her sketches have a lot of feeling, and she talks very pleasantly but in a vague way, and begins stories which hover about aimlessly till she resigns them into the capable hands of Henry who sits chafing inwardly but outwardly calm under this mismanagement and immediately takes them in hand. It is wonderful how a strong character makes itself felt, without speech or any apparent *action*: just by *being*.

Yesterday they took me to a League of Nations Union lunch to hear Mr [Philip] Noel-Baker[3] speak: he is secretary to [Arthur] Henderson, a clever quick young man, and very able speaker: says something for the Labour people that they can get this type of man. What he actually said

1 FS had first met Major Edmonds in Baghdad in 1929, when he was Adviser to the Ministry of the Interior. He was an authority on the Kurds.
2 Sir Henry Lawrence was a fourth generation of Lawrences in India, former acting Governor of Bombay.
3 Labour politician and lifelong worker for disarmament. Won the Nobel Peace Prize in 1959.

was not so startling: the need for 'international' instead of 'national' fiscal policies: which of course is obvious, but no nearer for that.

My little note in reply to Major Edmonds is to be published with his article for the R.G.S. for March: so now the deed is done.

Your

FREYA

FLORA STARK

Baghdad. 26 June 1931

Darling B,

It was much nicer than a party this morning. The A.H.C. took me out all alone with the A.D.C. and cooked scrambled eggs in his launch down the river. So peaceful and pleasant and beautiful. I had an awful problem wondering what to wear: as it happened, riding breeches were right and all was well. We floated down stream between the low green banks, all still cool and early, watching turquoise jays (rollers) flying in and out of the sand banks. The A.H.C. is an impatient man (probably working two jobs in this heat) and the A.D.C. depressed, with nose a little pink from the fact that he never gets any rest: he told me the sorrows of A.D.C.'s as we rode home – for after we landed, we rode down stream to the lovely palm glades and fig trees and orchards where I used to ride last year.

Captain Holt looked in yesterday to tell me that the Persian quarantine is quite impossible and that I must fly, and that anyone might have known that one would be ill coming here in the heat – 'but that of course is what you say you like'. I am so sorry to be enabling him to say 'I told you so' in this way. However I am much better today and will be perfectly all right in Mrs Sturges' nice house, and will fly to Hamadan and so avoid quarantine.

I do realise why people's tempers go in this heat: it all is extraordinarily trying: I was reduced to getting up at five, doing all the indispensable things while it was comparatively cool, and then lying down again: but now that I am better exercise is really necessary and the only way of keeping fit.

Your own

FREYA

FLORA STARK

Hamadan. 18 July 1931

Darling B,

I have been depressed this week not feeling very well – still effects of Baghdad heat, and also feeling that I am getting so plain which is *very* depressing: I always find it takes people about a month to overcome their first impression of my plainness. Also Capt Holt was so cross and snubby the last evening, and I feel if only I were a *little* prettier and younger it would make all the difference with him: as it is I think he is just going on miserably by himself, making such a hash of things.

I shall be leaving here end of July for Kazvin, then Alamut and Teheran where I hope to arrive sometime in September. The Secretary of the R.G.S., Mr Hinks, is really extraordinarily kind: he has just sent me a note of introduction to the First Secretary of our Legation, saying that I am a serious student who avoids publicity and that they can *safely* give me any assistance. I feel very pleased with this description. Really everyone now is ready to help – it is just marvellous what my one little Alamut trip last year seems to have done.

Your own
FREYA

FLORA STARK

Kazvin. 3 August 1931

Darling B,

I suppose the adventure has started, though it does not feel like it yet, and 'Aziz[1] is not here but only *expected* which in Persia is a dubious word. I left Hamadan at 9 p.m. and it was rather lovely going through moonlight with the barren open ridges very soft and dim on the horizon. The Public Prosecutor who sat with two friends at the back of the car offered me a rug which I refused in my ignorance.

We kept on breaking down and it was very cold, so that I was glad enough when daylight came and showed us to be on the great plateau of Kazvin. I gave the three travellers bread and they gave me tea: and the Public Prosecutor invited me to call in Teheran, he being a philologist and possessor of rare books, with M.R.A.S. printed on his card, which is Member Royal Asiatic Society. He had a nice face in spite of lots of gold teeth and little shaving, and the long, narrow fingers you think only exist in Elizabethan pictures but which one sees quite often in Persia.

I went to bed here and stayed there and feel a bit better today, and received a visit from Mr Sookias and the doctor, very charming – only my Persian is really inadequate. He tells me of the castle of Lamiasar in Rudbar which, if really *it*, is very important being one of the Assassin castles mentioned in the chronicles and not yet identified. So I shall go and look, if only 'Aziz will turn up. I am going to be short of money

---

1 Aziz had been FS's guide on her Persian journey in 1930.

again I believe, but Mr Summerhayes says he will come to the rescue anywhere where there is a telegraph office to send to.

I had lunch with the doctor and landlord, who took my volume of Sa'di and started reading verses with great enthusiasm, not shared by the rest: he is an irascible impulsive little man with an eye to business, so the poetry was rather pleasant to discover.

Very hot here, and mosquitoes and sandflies and noise. Nothing but a quilt on one's bed so that one is either suffocated or bitten. And the water supposed to be unsafe.

6 August 1931

Still here: one does learn to be patient in Persia – everyone so amiable and full of kindness, but nothing gets *done*. 'Aziz hasn't turned up, but I hope another *charvardar* will appear by tomorrow.

I had a nice morning in the bazaar with the doctor's son who is going to be a chemist: first we went and bought a rope and a little blue and white cotton saddle-bag to keep tea and sugar in; then we got six handkerchiefs of green and blue striped silks, and six towels woven in Yezd at 7½d. each (not very good cotton). Then a knife, a lantern and a mirror; then a *lihaf*, which is a dark blue cotton quilt, for 4s. 7½d.: then almonds, raisins, tea from Lahijan that 'smells like attar'; candles, matches, and seven cones of sugar; then a little purse for cash and a porous water-jug and earthenware mug. All this took two hours and was very amusing. The ropes come from Isfahan: each place has its own industry.

I do wish I could be off now. The bank man and his wife invited me to tea; it is funny, but my wanderings seem to be a test of most people's social status and some always disapprove: the wife told me that for *her* part she liked looking after husband and children (quite nicely): 'I have neither one nor the other,' I explained humbly: I couldn't after all look after anyone else's.

7 August 1931

I hope I really am off this time. Ismail – sent by 'Aziz – turned up looking more dilapidated even than I remembered him: I have bought him a safety razor for when we part. He has tied up all my things in saddle-bags so I hope we shall really start tomorrow dawn.

I am just looking at some Persian pigs in the yard: they are fiercer than any domestic pig I have ever seen except the kind near Perugia. They are running amok among the cars.

I have bought two knives, two purses, a little trumpet, two dolls, and

400 doses of quinine (as presents), five tins of biscuits and six of ovomaltine – so ought to be all right.

Your
FREYA

FLORA STARK

Siahdasht, in the Shahrud Valley. 9 August 1931

Darling B,

By the time you get this I shall either have or not have malaria, so I may as well tell you I am being bitten for all I am worth here in the gardens round the rice fields: all this country is a perfect trap in summer and I shall be glad to get out as quickly as possible . . . but meanwhile I am practically certain I have got my castle. I was feeling rather despondent having nothing but one doubtful mention of a name not marked in any map in a district of about 10,000 inhabitants: but luck is with me. We left Kazvin only two hours later than arranged, and got in the heat of the morning to Rashtigan where we found a shady place under plane and willow trees beside a shrivelled stream – the long range of the northern passes very red and bare above, with the heaps of the village corn arranged on the threshing floors and the landscape for a background: very fine in its barren way. Then, resisting Ismail, I waited till three to start on again and we climbed the pass. It has no view to the south and nothing of the glory of Chala, but when one has walked along the ridge thinking nothing is going to happen any longer, the northern landscape, the Shahrud valley and hill-wall of Rudbar, the long saw-like edge of Syalan peaks and Takht-i-Suleiman in the far east, all suddenly burst on you. A high wind was blowing: my compass bearings seem to be no use at all; but I took them, and as it was late already and the mules threatening to stamp on my instruments, I sent Ismail ahead to an inn which was supposed to be just below, to order pilau etc. . . . By the time I had finished it was dusk, the landscape looked very immense, and Ismail was far out of sight below. As I ran down to catch up, feeling very much alone there, I saw three men with reaping hooks in their hands leaping down to intercept me. A reaping hook looks horrid in the hands of people whose intentions you don't know. However I went up and said salaam, and asked whether the blessed inn was far away: and they were most friendly: told me the inn was only open by day and nothing in it, and took me to their little village plumb down below, a little Kurdish colony settled there from Shiraz 100 years ago owing to some domestic trouble. And on the way, when I mentioned my castle of Lamiasar, they showed it me across the valley a day's journey off, and undoubtedly *it* – only one letter in the name altered. It seems very lucky, as I believe it is carrying out a theory of mine, and I feel almost certain it has not been identified by anyone else so far. And as we discussed old castles in the evening I asked about another which also is not known, and have got a vague indication I am going to follow up, though it means two more days with the mosquitoes.

Imamzadeh,[1] *Zeinabar. 11 August 1931*

I will not be sending this till long after the trouble is over so may as well tell you that I *know* I have dysentery and may have malaria: it is inconvenient as it is out of reach of anyone, a small *Imamzadeh* looking out across the valley from a lovely little nest of fields and fruit trees to the absolute barrenness of the Rudbar hills. It is above the mosquitoes, and the village is someway off, and altogether a peaceful place to be ill in. I am only disquieted by the fact that my dysentery vaccine seems to be only half the first dose prescribed and the emetine has got lost: however, I have yoghourt and hope for the best, though it is rather depressing. I fear I am getting too old for this sort of thing, alas – or too much of a crock anyway.

The castle was a marvellous find. I hope I may not die before writing about it, for it *was* the missing castle, and it is a grand place, covering the slanting top of a hill (about 1,200 by 400 feet) surrounded by cliffs, with battlements still left here and there, and a passage built down to the river about 800 feet below.

14 August 1931

Cannot write much but am better. I found the emetine and am injecting it. Temperature nearly normal. All very fatiguing. The people are kind in a rather harpyish sort of way: they come in groups and squat by my bed for medicines.

Shutur Khan. 16 August 1931

I am having malaria now, but the worst of the dysentery is over – and Providence intervened at last and discovered a doctor five hours' ride away taking his summer holiday. He says he will put me right in six days' time, and has injected quinine, camphor, emetine, and given powders: I hope it will be all right.

When Ismail came from Kazvin to my hermitage he brought the

---

1 A shrine dedicated to an Imam.

doctor's prescription and a letter of remonstrance, rather hopeless as movement is the *most* fatal of all the fatal things in dysentery. Anyway I had managed to stop the most acute symptoms and I knew I was never going to get well in that nest of mosquitoes down near the river, and I made my mind up to risk the ride, get a car from Kazvin and reach Teheran hospital. When my mules were already heading for Kazvin, I saw the mountains so lovely and serene and alluring, that I turned the mules' heads round and decided to trust to the hills. I can't tell you what an awful journey it was, on white of egg and brandy, though nice to be in the air again and I got a photo I particularly wanted of the lower way into Alamut. We didn't go over the ridge thank God but waded up the defile – an impressive way in through the tortuous cliffs, the river winding in among them like a yellow snake. Very soon I began to think less and less of the landscape, those hot red reaches seemed endless. I took rests at intervals, lying down flat, one in a lovely meadow under big walnuts at Shahristan where the people were winnowing their harvest under the trees. I also took no bearings except two that were really indispensable. When we reached Shutur Khan I *couldn't* have gone further. It was nice to be welcomed: even before the village an old man living on a little platform on four poles to get away from mosquitoes, beside his melon patch, came out to greet me and invite me to a melon. And the ladies here and the Arbab [Squire] himself were as cordial as could be, and gave me hot water to wash in (my first proper wash this past week) and let me get to bed. The dysentery seems really to have got steadily better in spite of all: the greater height here must have done the trick.

Your
FREYA

FLORA STARK
Darijan Valley just under Takht-i-Suleiman. 27 August 1931
Darling B,
   Just breaking camp – my second night out above the villages, and very wonderful – a high corrie enclosed on three sides; a great drop to the river below whose noise comes up with the wind intermittently like the noise of a train: absolutely no other sound except a little shriek of bats; and the moonlight spreading slowly like a fan first in the sky behind Takht-i-Suleiman, then down the walls of our amphitheatre and across the valley on to Narghiz and Syalan and Salambar. It was very cold. This place is over 10,000 feet and the col we are climbing is about 14,000 feet. I have renounced the climbing of Solomon's throne: the mules can get no

nearer than eight hours away, and I cannot do it – but am sorry. I may get a more accessible mountain further east.

It is a wonderful feeling to be here where the map puts only little trees (which don't exist) and to be plotting out my camp every night and marking the passes as I cross.

Evening

Have got over the pass. Our camp was beautiful, but cold by morning – nothing to what this is going to be. We came down from the pass alongside a long couloir of snow. This is over 10,000, the pass about 14,000 feet – marvellous view: all new ridges eastward, with pleasant dark patches of jungle and smooth white mist from the sea.

I was exhausted. It was four hours from our high camp, like a wall, so that the mules had great difficulty. I just couldn't go uphill because my heart is still so feeble: did it slowly and resting, and riding whenever possible regardless of cruelty to animals. It was worse because 'Aziz would get on to the other mule whenever I did – and is much heavier.

They all tried sardine today, with much hesitation, as one kind of fish is forbidden and one couldn't tell through the tomato sauce. I have only four boxes, but it was so *delicious* to have something not rice or sour milk.

Your
FREYA

FLORA STARK

2 p.m. 2 September 1931

Darling B,

I am writing from a nice camp, near the source of the Chalus river, about 8,700 feet up: the shepherds have left a little semicircular wall against a cliff and our camp and fire is inside that. The tops are hidden by mist – which is getting to be a serious question, as it is no use going up hills if you are wrapped in a blanket of cloud. We saw nothing but a ghostly whiteness all the way from Bijeno to Delir this morning: gentians, wild snapdragon, iris-leaves here again, and sempervivum and violet leaves among the cracks in the rock: the gentians seem widespread at anything over 8,000 feet.

The population of Delir just went off its head when it saw me. First a group of children appeared, looked, burst into tears, and fled as fast as they could: then women gathered, till it was a regular flood, with men interspersed, the women looking very rakish with their coronets all lopsided under their headshawls. The roofs got crowded; about a hundred came behind me, it was like a race meeting – and the more polished and energetic of the men got busy shooing the nearest away from time to time when I threatened to be submerged. They were quite friendly, but very excited.

If one is not a Moslem, it is as well to know all about the faith in these valleys: the people are friendly but quite fanatical.

We have a nice man to go with us and show the way. He has longish black hair and a long-handled axe and a nice smile: I hope he will not prove a villain. An old trapper has just been sitting here, telling me how he traps sables in winter: about 20/- to 40/- a skin: I wish I could buy some now.

Later

Sitting in our little shelter – the gun and instruments on a ledge of the cliff, and the pilau cooking in the pot. The river making its noise and a sky clear at last with little clouds floating and a crisp of mist poking its nose up the valley.

'Aziz is singing – an awful noise. I sang yesterday to my hosts who were enchanted: an unsuspected accomplishment.

Dearest love,

Your

FREYA

FLORA STARK

Dohtar Qal'a. 8 September 1931

Darling B,

We are up by the pass to the plain – really near the end, about time, as I have to pick lice out of my clothes and my hands are all skinned by the sun. But the view from here is so beautiful, one forgets all the rest. Takht-i-Suleiman is high up in the sky about fifteen miles away, with a deep valley and six ranges between, all rising gradually up to him as if it were a crowd carrying him on their shoulders. He is the only one with snow running down his side. Tomorrow from the pass I shall take my last bearings, and hope that they may turn out *probable*, when I come to work them out. I don't think I have got any result of any moment from my tour; but it has been wonderful practice and I have done useful though unobtrusive work if my bearings come right, for I will have got the geography of the top of this valley complete and the names and position of Takht-i-Suleiman and his group – all of which were completely wrong and their names not mentioned. It is a tiny piece of work, but I hope it will be good all the same. It will not be a lecture at the

73

R.G.S.: a terrible fate pursues my photos – my three *best* films all spoilt: I nearly wept. We had a wearisome day – after leaving the pleasant leafiness of Joistan, we came up the Shahrud, and went for over five hours up that hot dreary valley without meeting a village – and finally reached the end of the valley where the river comes down from two valleys. There was a short cut to our castle, but I insisted to go the long way (so as to get my places correct). The two men are beautifully docile. . . 'Your wish' is all they say, with their hand on their breast. The result was we had a very cold night on the hillside, about 9,500 feet up with an icy wind at dusk, and nothing much to eat only raw eggs, cold mast, and cold rice and almonds: a little hot tea and a fire of dung picked up on the mule track made us happier – and it was very beautiful.

We had a two-hour walk this morning up to the famous castle [Dohtar Qal'a], which is only a little five-sided fort with a tower to guard the pass, but has at least the merit of not being entirely underground. Instead of going on as we should, to get to Teheran tomorrow, I let myself be deluded into a two-hour expedition to see a water reservoir: it turned out to be much farther, down a precipitous exhausting hillside, and was only a disgusting cave with bad stalactites. We crawled in through a hole and got wet, and I hate caves anyway: by the time we got back, Teheran tomorrow was done for, so I stayed here and trotted off with the old man who keeps the tea-shop to see a graveyard in a lovely neck of the hills.

The people only stay to gather their harvest and in less than a month the pass will be shut for the winter. At Parachan they told me they are imprisoned for three months: if they get sick they die, if they run out of anything they do without. They shut themselves in with their cattle and wait till the snow melts.

It is now cold again: and getting dark. I must go in with the little family of muleteers in the dark little house.

Dearest love,

Your
FREYA

CHARLES KER[1]

British Legation, Teheran. 22 September 1931

Dearest Mr Ker,

I feel I ought to have written before, but have been incapable of any effort since I came here a week ago – feeling more tired every day, but otherwise well.

---

1 Brother of W.P. Ker.

I found sad news here: my father died at the end of last month: the telegram is all I have so far, but a letter of his was here, written a month before and very happy – so I hope it was a swift and peaceful passage. I cannot feel sad for him, for we so feared long illness and incapacity for him, but sad for myself, for he was a most dear friend and companion and I feel I ought to have been there – there is too much parting in this world.

I don't know what I shall have to do: whether to go out at once or if possible to wait till the end of winter. And then I don't know what I shall do with that land, or whether I shall have anything else at all to live by, as things are going in our country. Have just heard now of the collapse of the gold standard. But you must have quite enough of this sort of thing, and I will tell you rather about the Persian hills.

I heard of a really good castle, and found it with battlements and cisterns and a covered way down to the river, on a magnificent crag in the Shahrud Valley, but so unhealthy that though I hurried as much as possible I was stricken with dysentery and nearly died, and then complicated things by developing malaria. A Persian doctor was discovered and in a week 'though pale and weak' I was able to sit on my mule and get up into the higher mountains round the Throne of Solomon, which is 15,500 or 16,000 feet high. It was wonderful to see the moonlight flooding those great slopes and hear nothing but the wind far below – I could not walk much: one pass was nearly 15,000 feet and too steep to ride, and I had great difficulty and felt like the people on Mount Kamet, with a darkness coming down over my eyes, very unpleasant. My two muleteers were so devoted; they sat me up on my mule whenever it was barely possible, and we got to the top somehow, and there saw the Vision of Demavend streaked with snow, across ranges and ranges, and the sea mists far below lying on the jungle.

The Military Attaché here has got my map. I hope it will be made use of. Unfortunately I had no aneroid beyond 10,000 feet so that all the high points are rather vague, but anyway it is a better map than the one now in use which put in about 30 × 15 miles of country *twice over*, enough to bewilder any traveller.

Love to all at Cliveden Crescent, but especially to your dear self.

FREYA

FLORA STARK

Tusirkhan. 6 October 1931

Darling B,

This will be a surprise – it is to me. I meant to go quietly in a motor car, but a chance of a letter to a chief Lur was *too* much temptation and I am off to try and see where the bronzes are dug and to get photos and a skull. I think it can be managed if I dodge the police, and really the chief obstacle is my own feebleness. Mr Summerhayes found me a *charvardar* called Hajji and two very lean horses who must be real optimists for I can see no other reason for their continued enthusiasm in trotting with a pack over stones. We chose Hajji out of two others because of a charming smile minus one tooth; hope he lives up to it.

We went up by Ganj Nameh and saw the cuneiform inscriptions – fresh as if cut yesterday. Mr S sent his man in gold braid behind me – a funny mixture with my equipage.

We went up a 10,000 feet pass – very mild after my other ones: but then a long afternoon dipping into one shallow basin after another – a lovely fertile busy peaceful country, with no hard white roads: just blue figures digging or ploughing: the stubble strewn in the fields, the green autumn wheat sprouting, villages in vines and groves, and the long shallow bare ridges going away on every side to the horizon, all tawny. It has been twenty-two miles at least and I can hardly move, besides having a cold. But a chicken is cooking.

Your
FREYA

FLORA STARK

Alishtar. 12 October 1931

Darling B,

I have discovered something. The plains of Alishtar and Khava, where I have spent four days, are *not* the site of the Luristan bronzes. All the things I have found are at very *earliest* Sassanian: the bronzes come from the hills – I shall have great difficulty in getting at them but hope to succeed. Another thing I believe is that the horse, whose origin is so mysterious, was *not* originally found here: none of the bronzes have horses, though cows, goats, and sheep figure largely and of course the horses were used as one can see by all their bronze bits: but I believe they were an importation which did not find its way into the very stylised art of Luristan.

I had a good night last night after standing in a cellar downstairs with an open door into the yard and being soused with boiling water by the little girl who talks English.

They sow lots of opium here, but do not smoke it. My guide from Nihavend wasn't wanted by the other man from Qal'a Kafrash because

76

'an opium smoker is unlucky'. This year they are sowing cotton; and there is rice, and much corn: hardly any trees, though the governor's fort is in a grove of apricots and there seems nothing to prevent their doing well. But the Lurs have only begun to live here in winter in houses these last three years; they used to move south to the jungle, and do not like the Government's efforts at settling them and making them build houses.

Dear love,

Your
FREYA

FLORA STARK
Dilfan, Abdul Khan. 14 October 1931

Darling B,

I have got well into the country and am sitting in the black tents while the tribe is digging for a nice new grave with a skull, for which I have promised three tomans.

We were delayed by having to wait for the Chief of Police. They made up their minds that I must be accompanied: a blow: but the Chief Nail Sardari Khan is a nice man whom I thought I could manage. We went riding up the pass, very stony: policeman with gun ahead and a man in an '*abba*: the Sardar next (I made a friend of him by insisting on his going first) with another blue policeman and gun behind: then a man on a very smart saddle with a kettle in a red handkerchief tied on to it; then the Scribe in black spectacles with a large account book under his arm; then us three, and a Lur in a badly fitting European coat and Pahlevi hat whom at first I did not recognise for the handsome wild man with long locks I had photographed the day before.

I stayed behind in a stony bit and joined the caravan again, and passed two Lurs with very black looks coming down with donkeys: they said something I did not understand – their caps had just been taken and torn up by my policemen. They are trying to enforce European clothes all over this country.

16 October 1931

This morning we left the Khava plain and Chavari, which is the north-west of it (and where there are Ali-Ilahi fire-eaters) – and went west into Duliskan which belongs to the Ittiwand Lurs. We were soon very friendly haggling over bronzes. The bronzes however are not found at all in this plain – they all come from the mysterious and forbidden Ittivend country of Sari Kashti. I bought two bracelets, a belt, a little animal pendant and baby waterpot pendant (very unusual), a knife, three

77

pots, two earrings, and a collar and about six foot bangles for 15/- or so: gave quinine to a sick woman, and left with great friendliness.

Meanwhile my archaeological news is I believe very useful – for it appears that the horses and men are buried in *separate* graves: if I can only get to the place and *see* one I shall have achieved something – perhaps loot another skull.

I wish I could describe to you the beauty of colour here: the sky pink now, the land with a pink light beneath its faded yellow of grass or stubble – the glorious openness, these plains like great shallow bowls with jagged rims lifted to the sky. There are no particular places to put on the map, but the lands of this and that tribe, one does not know (though they do) where one ends and the other begins. And next year they will be wearing Pahlevi hats. Already Abd Ali did not dare to come to Harsin because they would tear up his overcoat. The white felt coats are forbidden. And soon the first car will appear on the new motor road which now travels along with such pleasant loneliness.

Darling love, dear B,

Your Lurish
FREYA

FLORA STARK

Ittivend Lurs. 18 October 1931

Darling B,

It is very disappointing – a grave is not forthcoming: the only way would be to stay here about a month and pay for a lot of digging. I hope I have found out something worth while, but not nearly what I hoped, and even if the skull is good I fear it is not the right sort of skull.

We did not have a very good night. Hajji in abject terror: he came up as I was lying down to sleep to beg me to sleep lightly – that we were surrounded by thieves. I thought that as there was no way of escape, if one had to have one's throat cut it would be nice to have it done in one's sleep, but I was visited by insects and only woke with a gentle light of dawn on the mountains and all my belongings still safe around me.

The people were quite friendly by the time our supper came and we had all been sitting in a circle round the fire and talking about suttee, and astronomy, religion, the British Constitution, and antiques – a most elevated conversation I thought to take place outside the pale of civilisation. As a matter of fact the Lurs seem much more men of the world than the people of Elburz.

Just now two gipsy women have passed. They are pointed out to me as outcasts who eat pig and will not even touch a cock, and they look distinctly Indian. They are scattered all over this country down to the sea.

I can hardly understand anything the Lurish women say. They came to look at me yesterday, and refused to believe that I was a woman, to dare to come among them. 'She is more than man,' said Hajji with really pathetic conviction. He does not dare to say that he is afraid, having been teased since Nihavend.

Your
FREYA

c/o Mrs Hoyland, Kermanshah. 21 October 1931

Darling B,

I must tell you my last day's ride from Luristan. I had quite a good night with the Kakavands, though the tent came down in the midst (a horse stepping on the ropes): and there was a lot of noise. The horses eat straw, maize, and corn when oats are scarce. But the Lurs love them, and treat them like people and when a horse dies they say to its owner: 'But you are in health', and condole with him just as they do for the death of a relation.

We rode away on very friendly terms and the Kadkhuda's son rode with us to the next camp to sell a plate he had there. Keram went along telling me stories. First of all about our night among the Ittivend which really was more dangerous than I had realised as one of the guests there was an Ittivend whose brother Keram had killed. Keram did not feel happy about it and asked him to be removed to some other place for the night. He got up and left, and the disturbance at night was not his doing, but was a woman creeping up to steal from my luggage. Keram told me that the Lurs pride themselves on their stealing: when they were conquered two years ago and the Persian general was camping with 1,800 men at Tudaru where I had slept, the Lurs crept in at night and stole his gun and all his clothes. In spite of the guards, they got in again the night after and took his blanket off him and got away just as he woke up.

I was sorry to part with Keram. He had a charming twinkling smile, and was quite fearless, and a real connoisseur in raiding. I gave him my old fur coat and my watch to take to the police Sardar who apparently expressed a liking for it (shows how convenient it is to travel with only 3s. 6d. watches) – and we parted on the col with Harsin and its gardens below and the downs and peaks of Luristan behind me.

Your
FREYA

4

Working on the Baghdad Times, thoughts on marriage and the single life, treasure hunt in Luristan, London and the 'ghastly business of publicity'

Freya now settled in Baghdad, moving eventually into a small house near the Embassy lent to her by the Sturgeses. The British community had been impressed by her solitary travels. At a dinner at the Residency, she found herself seated opposite an Archdeacon, a distinct mark of social approval. She had a Turkish servant who prepared a small dinner party for four every Friday and made close friendships among those settled and working in Iraq. Some, like Sir Kinahan Cornwallis, Adviser to the Ministry of Interior of the Iraq government (and later Ambassador in Baghdad), Gerald de Gaury, the Middle Eastern soldier-diplomat, and Captain Vyvyan Holt, who had replaced Gertrude Bell as political adviser, were to become regular correspondents until their deaths.

In the spring of 1932 Freya, who had been putting together her first book, *Baghdad Sketches*, and writing pieces for the *Cornhill, The Times*, the *Illustrated London News* and the *Spectator*, was asked by its editor, Duncan Cameron, to start work on the *Baghdad Times*.

LIONEL SMITH

Baghdad. 5 November 1931

Dear Lionel,

It felt very homelike to reach Baghdad again. I am not an 'outcast' this year it seems, and everyone is being nice to me. I stayed with the Drowers while settling in, and went and called on the Queen (who has cut her hair and wears short sleeves) and had tea with Sayid Ja'far[1] at Kadhimain and dined with the Youngs[2] when they had an Indian conjuror to entertain King Ali, who looked quite pale when the conjuror began to breathe out fire and smoke from his mouth.

Yours ever,
FREYA STARK

---

1 Mayor of Kadhimain.
2 Major Hubert Young was Counsellor to the Ambassador in Baghdad.

Baghdad. 4 December 1931

My dearest Venetia,

I am just off now to see my map: it is being done by the R.A.F. here and to be sent to the Survey of India: I feel it is like the Day of Judgement: one's mistakes being recorded into a permanent form.

I have a fear this may be my last year in the East. All my money, except £80 a year or so, seems to be in Brazilian loans. I don't know what will happen. But it is no good to worry. And meanwhile I feel that these last three years have been thoroughly well spent: that is always a satisfaction.

I am learning Russian: I don't think it will go very far – it is a brute of a language – but I think the most interesting just now. Perhaps we may travel there together and see what it really is?

Your
FREYA

c/o Y.M.C.A., Baghdad. 20 February 1932

My dearest Venetia,

I have been and am going on with a harassed time, with more to do than I can cope with. For one thing I am ill with some internal thing which means x-rays and next week in hospital: I hope no more. Then I have taken on a dull mechanical job on the local paper, which means eight hours a day at least for a time. The Russian lessons in the evenings – and all my writing to get in somehow.

By the end of the summer I hope my book will come out. I hope it will be readable. It will be called *Baghdad Sketches*, and printed here by the *Baghdad Times*: I have no share in it till 500 copies are sold, so that I don't expect to get very rich on it.

I feel rather like the Prodigal now that I am to leave my native lodgings: the High Commissioner's wife pressed my hand and said, 'I am so glad we are rescuing you from going native'. Everyone beams upon me as if I were a brand from the burning – as if I had ever been 'going native', but such is the human being's slavery to labels.

The other day I drove to the border and looked at the snowy ranges of the Persian hills. On the other side is Luristan. No impossibility in getting across I do believe – only this miserable want of money. But by autumn I hope to do it, and also to be perhaps fitter in health than I am now.

The spring seems here at last. Orchards full of apricot and apple blossom. It makes me sad, I don't know why – perhaps because the spring makes one feel the fragility of life so much more. I feel I have wasted so many years just in learning how to live, and now the machinery is all a bit worn and creaky and all the beautiful new gloss gone off it.

Such amusing things happen in this country. If you go to the Prime Minister's wife's receptions you meet the lady who monopolises all the brothels of Baghdad: apparently she keeps the Prime Minister in motor cars and his wife in diamonds. A League of Nations commission on the white slave traffic is here just now, but I don't imagine this will figure in their report.

Your

FREYA

FLORA STARK

Baghdad. 26 February 1932

Darling B,

I have begun work – and today my first day on my own – and my editor, Mr Cameron, says he notices 'a great difference' and will 'begin' me at £20 a month – and extra for any little things of my own I find time for. Now if only my health will stick it, I can make a decent living and get fun out of it too later on. Just now I am still a bit thin and weak and so plain.

CH[1] is furious with me: you will be tired of hearing this: all because I won't go home. He can't bear the thought of my going to an office every day, says that it's mere obstinacy, quite ridiculous.

Your

FREYA

FLORA STARK

South of Kuwait. 20 March 1932

Darling B,

It is so lovely out here and I am feeling better and better in the good light desert air. The Dicksons (he is British Agent at Kuwait) brought us to their camp: two white double tents and one Beduin one, very gay with white and black and yellow woven patterns and tasselled saddlebags – looking out on to the low desert ridges where the sand shows through bushes of 'arfaj' which will be full of little yellow daisy flowers in a day or two, but are still just brown prickliness at present.

We came on to Kuwait, a little desert town on the Persian Gulf – about

1 Captain Vyvyan Holt.

70,000 inhabitants and still so unwesternised that gramophones have only just been permitted and the Agent's whisky is imported as 'lemonade'. There is a long sea front on to the bluest sea, and every kind of boat for pearl fishing – lovely old shapes with carved flat sterns, and built with wood from Malabar.

We got delayed by a sort of cloud burst and had to go round a great sheet of shallow water pouring across the desert at a tremendous speed.

I have bought four Arab woman's dresses – black, orange, dark red, and stripe. They are very becoming as tea-gowns and I hope you will approve. Also fifty-two rupees of jewellery of rather barbaric gold – a clasp, two turquoise rings, three things for brooches, and about fifty small irregular pearls. The pearl industry is at a low ebb – if one had lots of money, now is the time to buy.

We had one day to potter in the bazaars. It is a charming place, washed with the desert sun and air, and with a wall with round towers enclosing it, and great open empty spaces everywhere. It is an independent place, under its sheikh, and is just now being blockaded by Ibn Saud who had sixteen raiders over the border last night and carried off five Kuwaitis. This is miles out in the desert – the Nejd border quite near. There are only a few Beduin tents and sheep and camels. We have all been on a camel this morning, a very pleasant hypnotising swaying motion, not unlike my mule on a pack saddle.

I do wish I could jump off from here into the middle of Arabia. It is good to be on the very edge. The desert has its extraordinary fascination, quite inexplicable – the emptiness and the buoyant air.

The Youngs are charming to be out with: so pleasant and pleased with little things like beetles or sunsets or food. Lunch here – must stop. A green kettle just brought to wash our hands for the meal.

Your
FREYA

FLORA STARK
Baghdad. 2 April 1932

Darling B,

Mr Cameron has just asked me up today. He discovered one of my adjectives in a Reuter telegram. It said that the money from death duties was less than had been expected owing to the abnormally low mortality in millionaires. I thought 'abnormally' a poor sort of adjective and substituted 'regrettably low mortality of millionaires'. I was so sorry to be found out before it was published.

I have been writing reports and things, and think I ought to make about £25 a month altogether: and my work does not now take more than four hours' hard work. A lot of time is wasted going to and fro, and a good deal more resting after meals – which I find makes my tummy much better.

Dear love,

FREYA

VENETIA BUDDICOM

Baghdad. 26 April 1932

Dearest Venetia,

I know how you feel.[1] I lost my little niece years ago, nursing her mostly myself, and cannot think of it even now without a tight feeling at the heart. It seems a terrible waste: and yet now I do believe it does not matter, any more than it matters whether the drops of water in the river are out in the sunshine or swallowed down in the current below: all are moving to whatever is our mysterious goal – of that I feel more and more sure. I think I would like to have been born a little later: we are to discover so much in the next few hundred years. Your talk about marriage and what we lonely ones miss was making me think of it. I used to feel that I had missed the real reason of life by not marrying, and was out of the stream in a backwater as it were. But now I feel this is not so. I think the human being is just coming to that point where sex is no longer the only means of progress – as it has been so far: we are just stepping along into a wider world, and need not feel lonely, except in the way that pioneers are lonely. Life is easier for married people: but I think it ought to be if anything richer for us, so long as we take it with full hands and not with the inferiority sense which has often ruined the lives of spinsters. Don't you think this is so? Anyway it is a comfort to know that all the greatest thinkers are with us; I think there is not one who considers marriage as a necessity to the fullness of life – though personally I would like to be married, having a fatal devotion to *habit* in my affections, so that I hate to be torn away from the people around me.

Oh my dear, I *hope* to get home this year. But do read the financial papers and remember that nearly all my income is either in South or North America. I am now living on my own efforts, and dare not give it up till I know I have something else to live on. When we are old and grey shall we settle together, half at Penbedw and half at Asolo? I think it

1 Venetia Buddicom's nephew Robin had died.

would be fun. And we will have time to talk all the talks we are missing now.

This climate is most trying. The dust storms *fiendish*, and lay me low instantly with a bad throat. And – you will be horrified – I am to lecture to about fifty men on Saturday. I go sick with fear at the thought alone. It will be a dismal failure.

It begins to get hot – but cold at nights – lovely when there is no dust. I am going to remove from the Y.M.C.A., being bent on a house nearer my work. I like this institution, with all done for me, and all sorts of amusing freaks wandering through at meals, but it is too hard walking to and fro more than two miles to my office.

My very dear love.

Your
FREYA

FLORA STARK

c/o Mrs Sturges, Baghdad. 27 May 1932

Darling B,

Well now I have just been doing some real journalism. We have this war going on and nothing but the meagrest news and *The Times* in London clamouring to hear about it. I had a happy thought and suggested going up into the enemy country and getting news there, but Mr Cameron was not bold enough for this and said if I went it must be officially: so I asked the A.V.M. (Ludlow Hewitt) and of course could get nothing satisfactory: CH said it was a 'monstrous' suggestion. But then he suggested I might get leave to look at all the despatches and get an article that way – and that is what I have now got leave to do. The A.V.M. most kind: will let me copy the maps and get the news, and may even get some photos taken of the actual fighting area – and he says he will give me the bits of 'local colour' himself. To get first hand help from the British Commander of Operations is no bad start for a journalist, is it?

Mr Cameron says he would like me to stay on permanently. He says the paper is much improved. I do feel rather pleased to feel that my first effort gives me a chance of £240 a year or more in these hard times.

Your
FREYA

FLORA STARK

Baghdad. 7 July 1932

Darling B,

Such a *hectic* time getting the second article off for *The Times*.

Meanwhile comments on the last article are pouring in – *Times, Manchester Guardian*, a *furious* letter (which I really rather agree with) on behalf of the poor Kurds. It feels very funny reading it and thinking that I set the ball going.

I am now busy with prostitutes. It appears that the Colonial Office classes Prostitutes and Artistes under one category – and the municipality here has made a law for having all the cabaret artists medically examined at intervals. This leads to great abuses as it gives too much power to these native doctors – and is unpleasant to think of with European women (though I don't think most of them are very far off the Colonial Office definition).

Still, an A.D.C. in the R.A.F. here is very much interested in one of these ladies and says he will kick the medical officers downstairs – and would I get something about it in the paper. So we had an interview this morning and hope something may be done.

I prefer messing about with military matters.

Your
FREYA

FLORA STARK

Baghdad. 29 July 1932

Darling B,

Eric Maxwell[1] is going to take me to Persia for a week on Thursday, all being well. It will be nice, and Eric very pleasant to go with. He is teaching me to drive. I forgot which was the brake and a Beduin seemed unable to realise this fact, so got gently pushed along. He didn't mind, but turned to smile apologetically and seemed rather pleased than otherwise to see Eric and me overcome with laughter. It is great fun, only I do find it hard to think of three things at once.

I think I have found a good site in Mazanderan. Am looking into it for the first time and it all seems to fit with the references and may be quite an important historical discovery. One never knows. Anyway I have done a tiny bit of real work: I mean finding something new, not just other people's sayings and ideas *rechauffés*.

Dear love to Herbert. How nice it would be to sit in the garden now.

Your own
FREYA

1 A judge in Baghdad.

Baghdad. 8 September 1932

Darling B,

Most exciting thing has happened. I am on the track of a hidden treasure. Don't please mention to *anyone* for a few months.

One of the Intelligence people here came up to me, said he heard I was leaving for Persia, and would I like to go with a young man who wanted a reliable English person to help him get this treasure which is hidden in twenty chests in a cleft in the mountains. They had a map in the family which he came upon as a boy and showed to a school friend of his: the friend's father seized on it and now refuses to give it up, but the boy has a copy. His family was a big tribal one and the tribes are still loyal to him, and one day a Kurd came to him and told him how he had come upon this treasure while taking refuge in a cavern from a storm. It seems and sounds quite genuine, though fantastic. It is worth going to look anyway, and sounds too alluring for this prosaic century.

Captain de Gaury back from Jerusalem looking very fit. Came to see me first day he arrived and told all about the rebel Ibn Rifada. They were horribly massacred, his head was impaled on a spear, and the few survivors, nearly starved, crossed into Palestine where Captain de Gaury saw them arrive.

I have got £8 for my Tunis article – all going in carpets.

If I get the treasure, you will come to Rhodes next spring?

Your
FREYA

Baghdad. 9 September 1932

Darling B,

This letter is not to be posted till I return, so as to spare you unnecessary qualms – but I must put it all down now before I forget.

I have just had a visit from the owner of the treasure, an engaging youth who is however getting more and more into a funk. He was implicated in the last Lurish rebellion at Deh Bala, and is doomed if the police once catch him. He finds that everyone knows that he is going, and is afraid: but tells me that he will go separately by himself and *meet* me there. He is only twenty, but with a nervous determined face that makes him older: a very determined little man, not too open. He knew an old man who would have been able to get us safely through the intervening tribes (between the frontier and his own people) but the old man refuses to take *me* because he says he has just done his pilgrimage and he might accidentally touch my cloak or something and be polluted and all his trouble for nothing. But the young man will give me letters and guides. I decide tomorrow.

Meanwhile Captain Hare, a nice young man from the Indian Army who is here to study Arabic, came this morning and tells me he has found out that the young man is arranging to smuggle things out of the country *now* on his own and has a box ready with a few daggers, etc., for which he has been offered 25,000 rupees: he is giving £100 to have it taken across the border.

I have come to the conclusion that the guide I took is not trustworthy. He has come four times asking for money – first to buy new clothes. I gave him £1 and he is now resplendent in a stiff Persian coat of grey cotton sticking out all round. Then he wanted more for his aged parent and for the rent and to buy corn – and begged me several times to take 'many bank notes' to buy antiques. So I thought this was not a healthy frame of mind for one's only supporter in the hills and am going to send him off tomorrow.

CH brought me a lovely yellow switch to flick flies off my horses as a parting gift – and we had tea together.

The treasure hunt is planning out nicely. Even CH seems grudgingly to acquiesce and admits its charms. I have the map of the place – a valley – a big rock; three pistachio trees in front – and the cavern behind it. Only skull and cross bones missing. It is fine isn't it to come upon this in 1932?

Love to you both.

Your own
FREYA

Lovely to think I shall be coming back to new clothes.

Later

Captain Hare, Abdul Kerim, the owner of the treasure, and I have just finished a long two hour conference. He brought the man who is to take me to the hills, a dear old man with ears like an elephant's sticking out under his turban and eyes pulled up a little at the corners so that he might be a benevolent mandarin. He seems just the right sort and I feel very happy with him. His name is Shah Riza.

Abdul Kerim is not coming with me. I go on alone on Tuesday. He is embroiled with the enemy, who have told the C.I.D. not to give him his passport. Our friends are to get the passport for him and then he is to pretend to go off to Syria and double back for Luristan and join me. The enemy threaten to report to the police if he goes without them – so it looks like war. If he does not join me, I am to try to see the cave with the twenty boxes on my own. He drew me the map.

What is happening to the stuff in Baghdad seems very vague: and he does not appear to be telling the truth: anyway there seems no harm in going on with the business so far.

Your own
FREYA

FLORA STARK

Bedrah. 16 September 1932

Darling B,

If there is one thing more exhausting than the other, it is the waiting which always precedes these expeditions. This is my *third* day here: I hope we start tomorrow. There is nothing to do but to wait, learn a few Lurish words, and read *The Pilgrim's Progress* which luckily I brought.

I paid a call on the authorities this afternoon: all very cordial and pleasant except the Judge, who never looked in my direction and was heard to say 'Allah' when I left. I have told the people here to murmur to him that I knew the Drowers, so as to make him feel unhappy. The others were all pleasant and say there should be no trouble in getting over the border: but I shall try to get through incognito all the same in my Kurdish dress, so as to avoid being shepherded all over the country later.

We came back, my old guide and I, about two miles along the desert edge, with a tiresome wind, which has been knocking the dates down these three days, worrying us – while he beguiled the way with stories and told me that Alexander the Great said: 'If there were five men like me the world would know no trouble.' But his friend said: 'If there were *two* people whose hearts are as one, they would do with the world as they like.'

Your own
FREYA

FLORA STARK

Baghdad. 9 October 1932

Darling B,

I have just got back and had a bath, and send this off at once. The reply from Teheran came at last (after four days) to say that 'with the perfection of courtesy and honour' I was to be escorted the nearest way to the border. I feared as much. I begged for a little less 'honour' and only

89

one policeman escort, but they insisted on four: a sergeant and three men. Whenever I got off to walk a little they all four got off and walked too, the sergeant ten steps behind me with his gun; and it took us four days to ride back across the hills.

They were very nice policemen and it was a lovely country and most enjoyable if it hadn't been just the opposite direction to what I wanted to go in. However being so well guarded no one asked about my skull at the frontier, and I hope to have got *some* interesting information though nothing to what might so easily have been – and me on the edge of it all.

It was the fault of the treasure. I hung about waiting for my accomplice (and knowing he wouldn't keep his promise). I can't remember if I told you about how I went to the place, recognised the valley, but the actual spot was indistinguishable among a hundred others alike. I could not go alone, as it is not a safe place, so had two tribesmen and a policeman, and had to slip away from them after their lunch: all managed successfully, and I had a bag round me under my skirt, and torch and candle all ready. If the wretched man had come we could have brought lots of it away – but no one can possibly find it without. Will let you know developments later.

Your own
FREYA

FLORA STARK
Baghdad. 17 October 1932
Darling B,

Am now waiting every day anxiously for the arrival of *clothes*; do long for them with genuine *hunger*. All Baghdad is to be filled this winter with young and lovely débutantes – about half a dozen so I shall not have a look in: but still it will be nice to have clothes all the same.

Yesterday at tea I met Sir Aurel Stein, the great explorer,[1] a charming little old man of seventy, as keen as a needle, and as obstinate – and with a misleading benevolent smile. Very interesting to talk to. I don't think he approved of my expedition, and he told Gerald de Gaury, whom he met today, that it was a great pity to waste time over Luristan bronzes – which are quite late – and only hoped I had not spoilt his chances in Eastern Persia. I of course feel terribly pleased at being considered *able* to spoil anyone's chances, and de G. came along much amused at these archaeological preoccupations.

1 Traveller and archaeologist in Central Asia, India and Persia; at this time conducting archaeological explorations in southern Persia.

He comes two times a week for Italian and it is very pleasant; he is a charming interesting man and tells me all the gossip. I shall sit in my little study this winter and just lead a quiet life, seeing the friends who take the trouble to come to me.

Your
FREYA

FLORA STARK

Baghdad. 1 November 1932

Darling B,

The treasure story is getting too wildly improbable. It seems now that the man sent to rescue me and the six sent to murder me met out there and had a scrimmage out near the site; the six were caught by the tribe, and had their heels put into a wood fire till they confessed – an unpleasant affair – and are now home again in Baghdad. Whether to believe it all, or how much of it, I don't know. Anyway I hope I am clear of them for good.

Your
FREYA

VENETIA BUDDICOM

Baghdad. 10 December 1932

Darling Venetia,

Your letter came yesterday, rousing my conscience which had already been murmuring that I had neglected you. But I had to get through *ninety* letters and cards before tomorrow – all now *off* I am glad to say. And this I suppose will be my Christmas letter to you, with dearest, most dearest wishes. It is good to think that somehow or other there is every chance of seeing you in 1933. I feel I have been a long while now a wanderer, and that I have earned a good rest.

I am reading the life of Lord Carnock by his son Harold Nicolson – a fine and serious piece of writing and one which gives a good understanding of all that period of politics preceding the war. I can just manage one or two books of a concrete kind now and then – but not philosophy – for I have no time to *think* about them. Your leisure is good in that: to have little time to read and much to think is not at all bad – one does too much the other way when one is well and strong, and crams in more than one can digest. I called this morning on the very charming little wife of the German minister, Frau Grobba, and told her I was preparing all these hobbies of mine, languages, etc. . . ., to make my old age amusing, as I would then I hoped have time to assimilate them: she seemed to think this quite eccentric, though it appears good enough sense to me.

Your loving
FREYA

VENETIA BUDDICOM

Baghdad. 9 February 1933

Dearest Venetia,

We are more or less marooned, and all letters and passengers stuck in mud in the desert. It is amusing to see American globe-trotters arrive here, accustomed to having the elements under command and amenable to timetables, and furious at being kept for days beyond their time by the mere potency of Mud.

I finish work here at the end of the month and then go to stay for a week with friends at Nasariyah and thence to Ur and Warka, and I also hope for a week at Kirkuk to see the oil fields. There are a thousand and one things I should like to do, but they can't be fitted in and must just be left.

Sir Hubert Young's book is out, *The Independent Arab* – good and amusing though not great. We spend our time creating a magnificent *average* type of Englishman, the finest instrument in this world: which we then fritter away because we have little *super average* to use him: none of our education sets out to produce great men.

Dearest love,

FREYA

Freya left Baghdad in the spring of 1933, having trained someone to take over her job on the *Baghdad Times*. She had been in the East for over two years and was emerging as a rather considerable figure, well versed in Arab matters. She was trying to save money, so she took a seat on a lorry from Baghdad to Amman, and from then on by train across the desert to Ma'an, Petra and Jerusalem. She reached Asolo to hear that she had been awarded the Back Grant by the RGS for her travels in Luristan. A London season brought further honours – the Burton medal of the Royal Asiatic Society – new geographer friends and her first contract with the publisher John Murray for *The Valley of the Assassins*. One new friend was Sir Sydney Cockerell, director of the Fitzwilliam Museum in Cambridge, who wrote in his diary that he had met 'a nice Miss Stark, who has travelled alone in Persia and is going out again'. Cockerell was a great admirer of female charm and courage. Until his death in 1962, at the age of ninety-four, they were fond friends.

A surgeon had told Freya that an operation to her damaged scalp would lessen the pain from a nerve and that 'by removing some of the scar, my appearance would be greatly improved', something she continued to mind about intensely. In order to keep what little money she had, for a journey she was planning to South Arabia, she went into a public ward.

VENETIA BUDDICOM

Villa Freia, 24 April 1933

Dearest Venetia,

Your letter was waiting here in a great pile, and I have been saving my first clear moment to write. It takes a little time to settle down after such a time away, and I have not yet succeeded in getting the matter of clothes going, and am going about hoping the weather may soon become suitable for what I have with me.

I found all well here and it is a luxury to sit still at home, and have room to put all one's things, and generally to be civilised again. And I found a nice review of my book in the R.G.S., and a grant to be made to me for exploration: I know nothing about it yet, but hope it may enable me to go to Yemen next. It has had the surprising effect of inspiring a note from *Who's Who* with a questionnaire: I don't mind telling them my private life, all except my age, which I think is quite unsuitable for the general public to know. What do you suggest as Recreations? And where, if anywhere, was I Educated? And what is my Career?

I have got to try and finish two articles, and to get on with my neglected Russian. I can just get about with it and talked to a lady from the Crimea on board ship. I came third class, and made up for discomfort by learning a lot about Zionism – and realising how much Communism is gaining ground in Central Europe. Do you think we shall live to see the end of Capitalism?

Your loving
FREYA

VENETIA BUDDICOM

Villa Freia. 5 May 1933

Dearest Venetia,

I have broken it to Mama, and all seems easy – and I think I could get to you for a fortnight somewhere about June 20th. Do you mind if we just *sit* at Penbedw and do nothing – with perhaps a small excursion now and then to look over moors? How *lovely* it is to think of.

I ought to be writing. All day long I ought to be writing, but my soul loathes the very thought of it. Two friends from Dartmoor are coming out next week, and then time will be scarce – and also it is so tempting now to sit and watch the roses coming out in the garden.

I have been reading *When William Came*, a sad fierce little book by Saki written before the war by a man who believes in being ready to fight. It is a picture of England under German rule, very fair and not over-drawn. I always know when I read this sort of thing that in spite of reasonable pacifist convictions as far as general theory goes, I really do prefer the people who fight.

I have been asked for an interview by the *Daily Mail*. I feel this is preposterous.

Your
FREYA

FLORA STARK

London. 22 June 1933

Dearest B,

I must send you a scrap, though I am being literally rushed off my feet. I had no idea what a ghastly business Publicity is – beginning with the terrible ankles they give me in the *Daily Sketch*, and then the flood of the lowest kind of newspaper writing for interviews. However, a nice publisher came and *offered* himself to me, and I am to fall back on him if Mr Murray fails.

I find I am not at all good at being a celebrity, and feel very shrinking: Viva, with her usual insight, says it is 'put on' – but of course it is not: one feels one is being turned into someone not oneself, and it is very uncomfortable.

The formal presentation was a fearful ordeal.[1] I had to stand in front of about 100 people and listen while such nice things were being said: then go up and receive my diploma, and make my little speech. Viva thought I would stop half way, but she does not know what stern stuff I am made of: I went on to the bitter end in a quavering voice, and am told it sounded quite right with just the suitable nuance of diffidence. And next night I had to speak on the wireless. A charming young man rang up and said, 'Hullo I am the B.B.C.' I said, 'Oh,' being quite at sea. 'Have you ever heard of this institution?' said he. And then he inveigled me down: I spent a hectic afternoon getting the speech together: and was finally left in a little cabin and told to 'talk naturally': the current was switched on: a nice red-headed young man read the day's news, introduced me, and then motioned me into a chair and I began. It felt dreadful, but not quite

1 The Back Grant by the RGS.

as bad as facing an audience, and I am told it sounded quite good. They pay £1.1s. a minute.

Your own
FREYA

FLORA STARK

c/o Mrs Guest [London]. 12 July 1933

Darling B,

First I must tell you the Great News. Murray is going to publish my book on Persia. It is marvellous. I went yesterday and met Sir John,[1] very nice though deaf: and also Lord Gorell, the new *Cornhill* editor. So I hope my literary career is started now on a fair basis. *Two* other publishers have asked to see any long work by me: that makes *four* willing publishers.

I am in such a vortex – parties all day long. Yesterday the most lovely Beethoven by a fine player called Lamont all to ourselves in a drawing room. Dr Munthe[2] of *S. Michele* was there: a tiresome old man I thought; I can't bear people who set out to be sweet and gentle.

The Guests[3] are such dears – and I am *so* happy, and enjoy being made a fuss of. *Such* a difference. They are giving me a party today – and before that I go to the House of Commons with Lady Iveagh.[4] Tomorrow a cocktail party at young Mr Murray's. It is all great fun.

Your
FREYA

VENETIA BUDDICOM

L'Arma. 22 August 1933

Dearest Venetia,

My friend Captain de Gaury has just left. He came here off and on after bouts of fashionable grandeur in the great world of Cannes, etc. and found us I think very dowdy. He bore it nicely however and painted a fresco of St George over our gateway which looks very fine. But the inferiority complex occasioned in me by his unspoken comparisons must have sunk deep, because I dreamed the other night that he was telling me, rather apologetically, that it is no longer *fashionable* to smile. 'What can I do?' said I in my dream. 'I can't *help* smiling.' 'Well,' he said, 'of course

---

1 Sir John Murray, uncle of Jock Murray and head of the publishing firm.
2 Dr Axel Munthe, author of *The Story of San Michele*.
3 Rhuvon Guest, 'a fine Arabic scholar and one of the dearest, most generous and unselfish of human beings'.
4 Wife of 2nd Earl Iveagh, née Lady Gwendolen Onslow.

. . . if you must . . . but perhaps you could smile *very* slightly . . . not as much as you do.'

I have just read *The English: Are They Human?*, an amusing and subtle study, attributing our inhumanity to the public school. I wonder what all the muddle is going to end in. I think we shall soon have to relinquish our contempt for intelligence and do something in the way of *thinking*.

Your loving
FREYA

FLORA STARK

L'Arma. 28 August 1933

Darling B,

Mr Sykes's[1] visit was quite a success and he was an engaging young man, very pleasant to talk to, and I gave him useful information – though when he asked me whether there was a 'lot of homosexuality in Luristan', I could not help saying that really I could not be expected, with the best will in the world, to be an authority on that point. The modern frankness is really amusing.

Your
FREYA

SIR JOHN MURRAY

Villa Freia. 13 October 1933

Dear Sir John,

Thank you for your note about my MS. I am so sorry it still needs revision. If Mr Murray could send it me as soon as possible and mark the parts that can be deleted or altered, I will try to do it at once.

I think that a rather loose construction and certain amount of repetition is unavoidable and rather desirable in a book about desultory travel, because one *must* give the impression of leisureliness and the varied and timeless monotony of that sort of life; and that is why the nineteenth-century travellers are generally so much pleasanter to read than the modern ones. But of course one should not be dull, and I will do whatever I can if Mr Murray can tell me where he finds that the thing drags.

I want to do it as soon as I can – or you may have to send the proofs to S Arabia.

Yours sincerely,
FREYA STARK

1 Christopher Sykes, the author, had been Hon. Attaché in Teheran 1930–1.

London. 26 November 1933

Dearest B,

My lecture on Wednesday is very near. I don't know it, and feel more and more sick when I think about it. It should take just fifty-five minutes. Last night I was wakeful and thought I might as well read it, and it sent me to sleep before I was half-way through – so what will it do to the audience? The slides seem good however, and Mr Murray is so delighted with my photos that he has allowed me twenty-four instead of sixteen pages of illustration. He is taking infinite trouble over the book and is so enthusiastic about it. We hope it may be ready by April. It is to be red and grey with a picturesque general map, with mountains, castles, etc. and all fancies inside the covers and repeated on the outer cover.

I was welcomed with open arms at the Oriental school, Professor Gibb[1] and Minorsky both *so* friendly and helpful and even Sir Denison Ross[2] now notices my existence and is to be my chairman on Wednesday, Lord Allenby being away. I am going to take four lessons in Sabaean script so that I may be ready if S Arabia is possible.

Sir Percy Cox,[3] to whom I spoke for a minute at the R.G.S., wrote me a note after to say he would like a chat – and today I had tea with Mrs Ness, an explorer who is also a most beautiful Society Lady with white hair arranged like E.B. Browning – so pretty. She is making me lecture at the Forum, and she was so nice, and had nice people – a soldier nephew and a Colonel somebody or other who talked to me about their travels. The great thing about being a Traveller is that everyone tells you the amusing things *they* have done! It is quite reasonable, as they know that one can understand and sympathise and I find it *much* better than being expected to talk myself.

Your own
FREYA

St Andrew's Hospital. 9 January 1934

Darling B,

All going well but they have decided to wait another fortnight or so for the next operation, as they hope then to do it all and want me as strong as possible. I am still bothered with headaches and can't get my

1 Orientalist and Professor of Arabic at the Universities of London and Oxford.
2 Former High Commissioner in Baghdad.
3 Major General Sir Percy Cox was President of the RGS 1933–6.

nerves located: if it tickles I have to rub in quite a different place and can't yet discover *where*: it is very difficult but I suppose they will all get accustomed to their new homes soon.

I am glad I am not in a private ward. They all have biblical names and the one now vacant is called 'The Agony of the Garden'.

Your
FREYA

SYDNEY COCKERELL[1]

St Andrew's Hospital. 22 January 1934

Dear Mr Cockerell,

I cannot call you by your proper title, because I don't know the names your initials stand for – but I *do* want to write all the same to say how nice it was to see your picture in the *Illustrated London News* the other day and to read of the recognition given to your work. I think that one of the greatest tributes to people's real character is when all their friends are pleased when the world appreciates them, and I am sure that *hosts* of people will have seen this news with pleasure.

Yours very sincerely,
FREYA STARK

VENETIA BUDDICOM

St Andrew's Hospital. 23 January 1934

Dearest Venetia,

When you get this you will know all is well, as I am leaving it to be posted when I am safe back in bed some time this evening. I am suddenly so much better that I hope they may do quite a lot – though not all, alas. They have shaved *all* my hair off again: so discouraging for the poor little roots, which had grown quite a lot.

I quite agree with all you say about peace and internationalism – but how are we going to keep people individual? In towns it seems impossible. I feel that my ideas are changing rapidly in one way as I lie here and see the masses at close quarters – eleven of them in the other beds, ranging from what I take to be a charlady to a lady-typist. Not *one* of them with a *personal* idea in her head; not one of them *vitally* interested in anything that is not material and tangible; not one of them using her leisure to do anything but read the most appalling rubbish and look at

---

1 Sydney Cockerell (knighted 1934) had been secretary to William Morris and the Kelmscott Press, was literary executor of Wilfrid Scawen Blunt, William Morris and Thomas Hardy, and Director of the Fitzwilliam Museum at Cambridge.

cinemas and shops. I begin to feel that the only thing to do with such people is to train them: other nations at least have started *physical* training which these women get nothing of. When one thinks that leisure is increasing all the time, and this appalling misuse is being made of it – it is really depressing. And how can one ever get clear thinking when the government has to consider these masses who *never* think. That is at the root of the whole question – and I imagine it will soon be so obviously acute a question that something will be done to cure us of being ruled only by thoughts that can be understood by people who *never think*. Nothing can be done *practically* (or very little) until it is watered down to this level: how can we expect to get any honest idea translated into national and, far less, international action?

Your
FREYA

FLORA STARK

London. 20 April 1934

Dearest B,

I have been neglecting you, but I have been *inhumanly* busy, and even in the evenings had to do things till the last possible moment.

I have found a charming dressmaker – a Russian refugee, very fascinating and temperamental, who tells one exactly what one *ought* to wear and insists on a dark brown wool with beige gloves for my party: brown straw hat and most adorable shoes from M. Pinet, who now quite knows he has to give me £5 pairs at £2.10s.

The party is getting more and more imposing: Peter Fleming, Rose Macaulay, H.C. Armstrong (who wrote *Grey Wolf*, the Mustafa Kemal biography), Sir Denison Ross, Sir William Goodenough.[1] I have asked the Guests, some other Baghdad people, Venetia, and Sir Henry Lawrence, the Minister to Ibn Saud, and the Allenbys. It seems strange that I should be inviting the Conqueror of Jerusalem to a party given for me in the old Murray house. I feel inadequate in these social efforts.

After that I go to Nancy Lambton's[2] home at Newmarket for the weekend – also *very* frightening, as they are all smart racing people and not a bit my sort.

I went to R.G.S. and said goodbye to Sir Percy Cox who asked me to keep in touch and said I have 'the gift of writing'.

Your
FREYA

1 Admiral Sir William Goodenough was President of the RGS 1930–2.
2 Daughter of Hon George Lambton, the leading racehorse trainer.

VENETIA BUDDICOM

Villa Freia. 29 July 1934

My dearest Venetia,

To read the papers makes one quite sick and here one cannot help feeling that the horror over poor little Dollfuss[1] is largely mixed with eagerness over the excellent excuse for waving flags on the Brenner. I hope the British idea of civilisation will win through in the end: the more I see of other nations the more I feel that ours is the only one that is ever actuated by any remotely decent motive at all.

I have done nothing this week but pore over Arab maps and am worn out by it in this hot steamy summer weather. Also a feeling of loneliness. Also the worry of contemplating Mama's finance which, however, I hope to get settled on a very small but more or less trustworthy basis before I leave. Also the lecture which hangs like a millstone. How *lovely* it would be if one could gather medals without lectures, roses without thorns.

The map of Arabia is very exciting. There is no doubt that the south-west corner is practically *full* of things to discover. It is rather trying that three English people have just gone and vanished into space there.

A horrid reviewer says I have the 'nose of an explorer': he means to be kind, but *how* misguided, and regrettably true.

Your most loving
FREYA

VENETIA BUDDICOM

Villa Freia. 5 August 1934

Dearest Venetia,

I may get over to London by the beginning of the month: there is an Arabic MS in the British Museum, an old geographer who gives the Arab trade routes. I ought to see it if I can and will have to get someone to help me decipher the script (which would take me *months* single-handed). So I shall get to London as early as October if I can.

I have just heard that I am getting excellent introductions (native) for South Arabia. I hope this venture will end in some result. The more I study it the more exciting it appears. If only the British authorities will keep gentle and quiet and not interfere. No one has been anywhere *near*

1 The Austrian Chancellor had been murdered by the Nazis.

where I want to get, as far as I know, and there must be masses of old ruins strewn all over the countryside.

Your
FREYA

VENETIA BUDDICOM

Villa Freia. 2 September 1934

Dearest Venetia,

We have disgusting weather, cold and rainy like autumn, and I am depressed at the thought of going to Dronero this week. I have just finished 760 pages of the dullest Arabic historian, and feel quite exhausted by the effort: there is something nauseating in reading so many murders all at once.

Meanwhile I have received six letters of introduction from the Sultan of Mukalla – with crimson coats of arms that ought to open every door wide. They say that I am a Lady of the Aristocracy and must be given two servants and two sepoys: this will have to be toned down to be useful: I shall take up poverty as a religious principle; there is nothing like making a virtue of necessity.

Your
FREYA

5

Aden frankincense and myrrh, by dhow to Mukalla and the Hadhramaut, tribal conflicts, heart failure, return to the Hadhramaut and archaeology, London and hats

---

In December 1934, Freya left for her first travels in South Arabia. 'I wanted space, distance, history and danger,' she explained later, 'and I was interested in the living world.' She spent a few weeks in Aden studying the Arabic of the south, then, with thirteen packages and letters of introduction to the sultans in the Hadhramaut, she set sail for Mukalla in a small coasting vessel, before turning inland through still wild country to the then almost unknown towns of the interior.

Her journey would not have been possible before. Until the previous year the Hadhramaut had been at war, split between two reigning dynasties. Late in 1934, Harold Ingrams, Political Officer in the Aden Protectorate, had ridden out with his wife Doreen on camels, on a mission to conciliate the many warring tribes, which became known as 'Ingrams' Peace'.

VENETIA BUDDICOM

Aden. 23 December 1934

Dearest Venetia,

I can't begin to tell you everything. The chief news is that my journey promises quite well – that I am just in time, as everyone is now going to the Hadhramaut, but no one has yet been to Shabwa, and everyone here is ready to help. I have been adopted so to speak by M Besse:[1] he is French and came as a young man to Hodeida: has made fortunes, and become a great merchant, spreading his influence over Asia, Africa and Europe: and kept alive to all other sides of life – a wonderful person in fact, who lets life play upon him as if he were an instrument responsive to its variations.

His daughter took me into their storehouse of frankincense and

---

1 Anton Besse, millionaire colleague of Rimbaud, at that time king of the Red Sea traffic. He founded St Antony's College, Oxford.

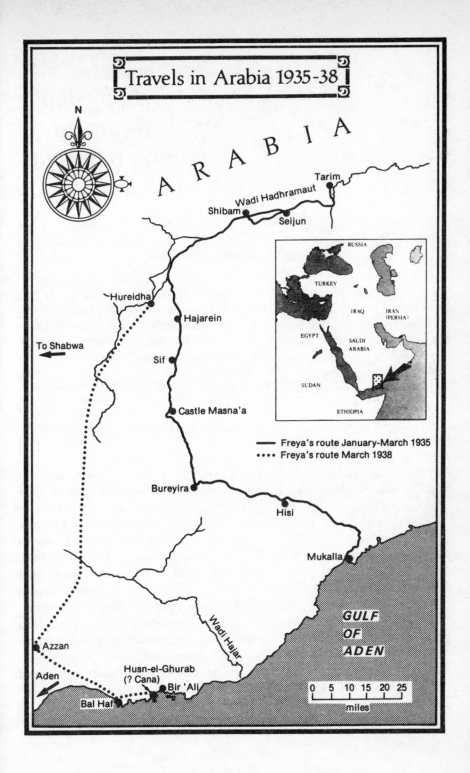

Travels in Arabia 1935-38

N

ARABIA

Tarim

Wadi Hadhramaut

Shibam

Seijun

Hureidha

Hajarein

To Shabwa

Sif

Castle Masna'a

—— Freya's route January-March 1935
···· Freya's route March 1938

Bureyira

Hisi

Mukalla

Wadi Hajar

GULF
OF
ADEN

Azzan

Aden

Husn-el-Ghurab
(? Cana)

Bir 'Ali

Bal Haf

0 5 10 15 20 25
miles

RUSSIA

TURKEY

IRAQ

IRAN
(PERSIA)

EGYPT

SAUDI
ARABIA

SUDAN

ETHIOPIA

myrrh. Doesn't that mere statement thrill you? An old Jew, with a curly short beard and little curly ringlets on his cheeks, all dusty from the powdered spices, showed us round. The myrrh is dark and sweet and parti-coloured browns like very old amber; the best frankincense is very pale yellow, almost white – called *samr*: the storehouse was piled with great stacks of it in sacks. The whole trade depends now, as it has for so many ages that no one can count them, on the wind. When the monsoon blows the little dhows cannot land, and so they wait till this season, and now begin to arrive in little fleets from all the incense bays along the coast.

You can have no idea of what a sunset is in Aden. Imagine one half of the sky a luminous green. I can't tell you how luminous, like green water when you are in it and looking through it to the sun: and this green shoots up fanlike in rays towards the other half of sky where night is lying already, deep blue. Above the sea along the horizon are pink ripples of cloud; the sea heaves with the sweep of the coast past the mouth of Aden bay, with flat lights on it as it catches the west. And half-bathed in the light, half-black in their own volcanic shadows, the rocks of Aden stand up like Dolomites, so jagged and old. M Besse took me for a long walk over these jagged ridges; they are all lava, spongy and unsafe; we came down to the sea where the beach is undercut and a coating of barnacle shells makes the edge quite delicate pink: here the launch met us and we came back towards the sunset, and the full moon came up behind the great natural rampart of Aden. There is a feeling of gigantic and naked force about it all – and one thinks what it was when these hills were boiling out their stream of fire, hissing them into the sea – and wonders at anything so fragile as man living on these ancient desolations.

Your
FREYA

JOHN GREY MURRAY

Aden. 1 January 1935

My dear John,

I hope to leave on the 15th and take about a month getting to Shabwa. It appears to be still inviolate though two people have got to the very gates. I have now got all my belongings packed into five small tin boxes and two saddle bags, and I have the names of the tribes and the man to go to for guides. I have been and still am in a small flat in the native town of Aden trying to get the colloquial Arabic but I am going to spend the last few days at the Residency in orthodox fashion.

Yours ever,
FREYA STARK

Off Bir Ali on South Arabian coast. 15 January 1935

Darling B,

We sailed at 2 a.m. on Monday morning. I had a last rush up the hill with M Besse and looked on Aden Crater, its straight rows of houses pink, blue, grey, and cream-coloured in the arms of the volcano – then dined quietly at the Residency. Colonel Lake came before dinner and we arranged the best policy for the route I am to take: when I get to his borders I will write and ask the Imam's permission to enter, and meanwhile Sir Bernard[1] is writing a personal friendly letter to Raghib Pasha, his wazir (who looks a charming old man). I think that everything that could be thought of has been done, and no one in the world could have thought of so many things as M Besse. He and Meryem took me over with the A.D.C. at the pier and we went in the launch to M Besse's ships in harbour: I was left on the *Amin* – we were for Mukalla, stopping on the way there at Bir Ali to see about a dhow which went aground.

I was so sad to leave the dear Besses. What they have been to me is quite impossible to say. I went to sleep and woke up with the lights of Aden slipping by: the sea was horrid: we had deluges of rain in the morning, and the wind was in the wrong direction. Everyone was ill next day, including the Chief and Second Officer and the Engineer: this morning I feel none too grand, but got up as we slowed down to see the Arabian coast. We cast anchor about seven, and there were the hills, bare and not very exciting, with sandy flats and knolls between them and the sea, and little scrubby plants. We are east of Bir Ali, near where the dhow foundered: her cargo is lying shining in the sun on a little sandy rise – and the Arabs were all on the look-out, waving black mantles to us from the roof of their little square white fort. A wild-looking lot with ancient silver-worked guns were waiting on the beach. When we were carried to land they shook hands, polite but much on guard. The Sultan was not there – we must go back to Bir Ali for him. I took snapshots while they discussed, and admired the terrific curve of the dagger in a young barbarian's waistband.

This is a rather pleasant landscape in the sun; a flattish plain of scrub and sand; no sign of cultivation or habitation except the white watch tower and the piled up wrecked cargo on the shore. The Sultan at Bir Ali must have seen us passing: he has sent a messenger and is hurrying here on a camel: so we are waiting and that is why I can write (still feeling rather sick).

Your
FREYA

1 Sir Bernard Reilly was Resident and C-in-C, Aden, 1931–7; Governor and C-in-C, 1937–40.

Mukalla. 17 January 1935

Dearest Venetia,

It is a rather nice feeling that I am just now the only European for at least 200 miles either way along this coast and goodness knows how many miles northward. Anyway here I am a guest of the Sultan, in a white guest house near the palace which faces the sea west of the town. I am provided with all *confort moderne*, a little dingy after being used by various guests and not being cleaned up in between: but the water flows, the bath will be dusted out by this evening, a tribesman black as ebony with a fierce little beard and fierce expression (partly smallpox) has been asked for a duster, and an old Prophet from Khoreiba comes in in the morning with a red and white turban, and red plaid thrown over his shoulder, draws up a chair, and asks me what I would like for lunch. The guests who come here have servants of their own so that I am a novelty, but this is the second day and they are settling down to it; I hope I may get off without hindrance. A woman alone has also never been seen in Mukalla and there may be difficulty.

The Captain considers all the inhabitants cannibals and looked down with a face of pity and concern as I was being lowered into a most friendly boat with the Sultan's agent and M Besse's Indian agent ready to receive me. This morning early the little ship departed; I got a note with 'God bless you' from the Captain, and now I feel my anchor is really up and the journey begins.

The view from my window meanwhile is as romantic as you can imagine: a sweep of bay, a patch of white sand dunes huddled against the rock by the monsoon, and hills and hills and hills: the sunset catches the ripples of the bay and loses itself among those ranges: a little straw village in the foreground with a small white mosque and square minaret like a village church in England: then three heaps of dried fish which the camels eat; then the camping place of caravans, on the sand and the colour of sand; fifty or sixty camels always there and always one long string leaving or arriving: always when you look at the sea you see some naked figure striding down to the water, beautifully made, his curly hair tied with a band round the forehead, his skin a dark ebony brown: the way these people move is simply a delight to watch. The tribesmen come down with nothing but a loincloth, a bracelet over one elbow, a wisp of wool tied for luck under one or both knees, and a smearing of indigo which is supposed to keep them warm. Their daggers are very fine and I must get them.

Stray people come walking into my drawing room to call on me. It is a gorgeous place, with two Venetian mirrors, two sofas, and eight chairs, five tables and an equestrian bronze: there is a pleasant verandah in front and a little white corner at the back – and the lovely view interrupted on the east by the new palace which is only bearable by moonlight.

Soon there will be an esplanade: now there is only one long market street and a sort of obstacle course among boulders by the sea along which a car can make her way. The chauffeur, an Afghan called Afzal Khan, tells me there are twenty-five or thirty cars here, but one does not see them. He took me for a drive this morning to the east of the town where sharks are dried on a headland (the most appalling smell) and sent to Aden: thence M Besse sends them to China.

Love from
FREYA

FLORA STARK

Mukalla. 21 January 1935

Darling B,

It is three o'clock, and all my luggage has gone trotting away on the four donkeys. I shall follow by car in an hour or so and meet it up the valley. At the last the Government has insisted on giving me a Somali soldier of the Bodyguard. I think it was because I gave a ring to old Ali Hakim – they think that I must be somebody after all, and I feel sorry not to be left alone with my Beduin. They are almost incomprehensible but I shall pick up their language fairly soon.

Everyone has been very kind here, and I believe I am quite popular in spite of the strangeness of my behaviour. I gave five rupees for the prisoners: this is a proper object of charity, and far better I am sure than showering pennies on the wretched little street boys merely because they are a pest.

Your
FREYA

FLORA STARK

Sarab on the Jol. 25 January 1935

Dearest B,

I have just been looking sadly over my instruments – they are not in a satisfactory state: rolling off the donkey did no good to the aneroid and it has got its needle stuck to the roof so that it has to be coaxed to a place that does not stick before anything can be done with it. The compass also has five air bubbles in it and sticks: the rangefinder and clinometer I haven't tackled yet and I think I shall have very little chance of doing anything with them – but one might do quite a lot here getting the names of the wadis and where they join up; I have collected a few.

We had a good evening last night in one of these little square buildings put up by philanthropists as shelter; they stand all alone in the stony wilderness with a rock hole for rainwater near them, and are real refuges on the cold highland. There were ten of us round the fire, and fellow travellers, one little boy from a cave in the wadi below. The bags were arranged in a semi-circle behind us against the wind, the rice was bubbling in the pot, and two young men had just finished greasing their legs and thighs with our table oil (which they say is very restful) when Sa'id said he saw a shadow moving. Sa'id II had his gun behind him resting on a saddle bag and with a sack over it against the damp, and he swung round in no time, his nice shiny legs one on each side of my luggage and the gun cocked. We were asked to go on conversing, and I tried to describe ice and snow in England – but no more sign of the shadow until after I had gone to bed, and they discovered that a halter was missing.

Today we continue to ride over this upland: I love it, and like to see the wadis dropping down as it were at my feet: the earth opens and a valley is born, and Sa'id tells me where it goes to sea.

I am having a little struggle with them now as they all want to hurry me on and I *won't* and they are all sitting very bored and wondering how long I shall be (and I haven't slept at all yet).

Dearest love,

FREYA

FLORA STARK

Masna'a in Du'an. 27 January 1935

Dearest B,

I am sitting in the Government House at Masna'a in Wadi Du'an, and a kind man is just chasing away all the female inhabitants and children, and leaving only a comparatively harmless half-dozen.

This is the most surprising place to come upon suddenly: it must have been incredible to the people who came upon it without knowing after riding through more or less desert for six days. I refused to get here late last night and the Bedus were very nice about it – it was all very pleasant, sitting round the fire and eating a very good mixture of flour, sugar and butter, after the rather painful consumption of rice and shark. They were all so friendly and thanked me for eating with them, and the moral peace was worth the physical troubles. I had a pleasant night under the stars, and this morning we trotted the last one and a half hours over the *jol* and suddenly, after seeing the white cairns of the R.A.F. landing ground on our right and two little sand-coloured square forts in the chasm's edge, we came to Wadi Du'an. It is sliced down straight with palm trees, a river of palms in the bottom, square earth fields and white stream bed, and little towns growing out of the soil and the colour in clusters on either edge. We took fifty minutes to climb down. Quite a good path descending into less lively air leaves the Beduin and comes among peasants. The Ingrams have made things easier, though in a way have set a precedent rather trying to me: wherever we go we substitute a money value for the personal value and it means hard work to live this down. I think it is sound to make it one's object that – however rich one may be – what one *is* must count for more than what one *has*: I try to do this, and I think succeeded with my Beduin.

Sa'id took us up to Masna'a, which is the castle of Government, its square buildings higher than the rest and balconies crowded to see us as we came: a shot fired as we climb up; carved doors studded with iron bosses and someone to shake hands at each – there were three, all at different angles: one opens them by chains pulled from above: the wooden locks are ingenious carved arrangements with pegs. It was the entry to a medieval castle. In the divan, three sides were surrounded by men sitting, guns leaning against the wall, all whitewashed. The Governor – Ba Surra – is youngish with a very good-natured face. I drank coffee and then went up through more carved doors and open corners of enclosed street to my apartment, all carpeted, six carved windows with wooden shutters three inches thick, columns, and one wall decoratively furnished with a cupboard.

We all ate out of the dish, before I heard that one of the children has measles: there is no doctor – everything, they say, is done by God. The polite thing to say when informed that someone has died is 'God be thanked'. The ladies all come to call on me: I was then taken to them: a formal affair as one goes round the whole assembly taking each hand and kissing one's own as one does so: the other person does likewise: sometimes the lesser person kisses the top of the other's hand instead.

Your
FREYA

FLORA STARK

Masna'a. 4 February 1935

Darling B,

It was measles as I expected, and I hope the worst is over. I had a high fever all these days, and at last this morning am back to normal.

Everyone has been so kind; Khadija, the Governor's daughter, comes in first thing in the morning, all rustling with bangles and girdles, and provides breakfast. Everybody rather takes it in turns with meals, which has disadvantages as one's efforts at explaining what one would like have usually been directed to the wrong person – the eggs have been hard-boiled instead of being raw, the soup filled with red pepper and chillis (which is hard on a lacerated throat) and little things like the sight of one's hostess taking a lick out of the sugar basin are apt to upset one if one is feeling rather ill anyway. The effort to keep anything clean is very great, and if you could see the general surroundings for half a day you would not find it strange that when I am in Europe I love to be in places where I don't need to think of how and what my food is made of.

Every afternoon the two brother Governors come to see me. They have such nice faces, so alike; they run things here as they like, and the Mukalla Government has very little to say.

The harem sees all the events from its rooms: when we hear a noise, a scream, or anything exciting we rush to the window and look out right over the valley. It must have been very exciting when every little citadel had its own war: the shots are so loud – they flatten themselves out against these cliff walls. One would either become incapable of initiative as are the women, or else break away and do great things like the men – the two effects of living in this sort of cage in the middle of great spaces.

I am longing unspeakably for a wash. *Nothing* can persuade them to give me water till tomorrow – the seventh day; they are kind but firm about it, and I have been so uncomfortable, but find that one doesn't get *much* dirtier after the first two days. Anyway I know all about life in the Middle Ages.

It is not at all true that these people are so very hardy. We have had a hot sea wind and everyone has gone down just like ninepins.

The great amusement of the harem are the children. They can still run in and out, the little girls like thin little butterflies in their yellow hoods and black face veils. The babies are kept to play with, and all suffer from overworked nerves. There is perfect friendly democracy; it is a very nice feeling but makes both cleanliness and privacy impossible: on the other hand it makes saintliness not only possible but frequently almost necessary.

My birthday went in rather a melancholy way as I had fever. It is nice now to be beginning to feel normal again.

Your
FREYA

Seiyun. Evening, 10 February 1935

Darling B,

You needn't worry over me any more. I am safely arrived in Seiyun and lapped in comfort – a bed with mosquito nets, a warm and a cold bathing pool, and everyone ready to look after me. I shall spend a fortnight resting so as to be perfectly fit for Shabwa – which is only three days' journey away anyway.

We drove up the flat sandy valley among the ruin mounds with their dark outlines of stones; passed a little garden city on our right into the open spaces where Wadi 'Amd comes in, where the flatness breaks up again into spiky sandy hummocks which would all be palm gardens but for the feud of two rival families and poisoning of all palm trees by Beduin who poured paraffin over them. One of the families left its native town near the cliff and built a house-fort. We stopped and climbed up to the top and looked at the sloping shooting holes on the terraces. The people are rich hotel keepers in Java, all pleasant and friendly. They told me they had four pairs of field glasses to keep an eye on their enemies, whose village could be shot at 'with a Mauser'. On the whole, however, they said they preferred life in Singapore.

We left this home of peace without stopping for tea, and went in and out of the sand dunes, which gave one all the pleasures of Russian railways in an exhibition with more of reality about it; the Berber chauffeur was very clever, and turned in and out like a snake. We made for the eastern corner of the valley where a dilapidated very old little town, Ajlaniya, stands with a crooked crumbling round tower on a spur: it has only about fifteen to twenty houses now, and *'ilb* trees round in the flat below: the children came running up with the berries which they gave us, called *dīm*. The Beduin powder them into flour and take nothing else by way of provision when they raid up into the north.

After passing Ajlaniya, we turned into the magnificent width of the Hadhramaut valley proper: Ajlaniya is the first village under the Shibam (i.e. Qu'aiti) government after the strip of no man's land we had just been through. I can't describe the feeling of this valley; because it is like nothing else – not a plain, because of that far line of cliffs standing like barricades one behind another; not an island, because of the feeling of being enclosed, so that one is dominated by and not master of the view beyond; not a valley, for the flat bottom is far too wide for that.

We began to come to palms on the southern edge of the valley: the landscape changes because here the water is brought up from wells (at El

Qatn it is only four yards underground): the arrangement of poles, the camels sometimes three abreast or oxen pulling the leather skins from an inclined slope, began to appear everywhere, as conspicuous on the level as windmills in Holland. Fascinating women appeared, like witches, with the high hat and face hidden by the black veil under it; and then one began to see the Shibam dress, a lovely cobalt blue, short in front and long behind, with tight white trousers under. Amid the corn and the palms, with the wells before it on the flat ground, is El Qatn, in a mud wall, all brown except for the white palace of Sultan Ali Ibn Salah and the cream mosque built by his father. Here we stopped. Steps led up to the wooden carved door and people of the Sultan gathered about on them: the Sultan was at the top waiting, tall, with lanky black hair under a tarbush and a pleasant shy boyish expression, with smiling rather deprecating soft eyes.

We had lunch on a gay tablecloth with knives, forks, glasses etc.: Persian pilau, Indian pancakes, Arab soup and boiled mutton; the Sultan, Sayid Hasan and I at one end, and the Sayid and chauffeur at the other. After lunch I was taken through a rabbit warren of dingy inferior little stairs and passages up to a sort of Sister Anne tower room very light and airy where the harem can look out on all that happens below. The pretty but silly little wife, with eyebrows blackened to meet the orange lips, and lovely gold lion bracelets, was not good at conversation. However, all the five children had measles so that made a subject. Then I descended among a crowd of servant maids in the blue gowns, and left for Shibam, which is only forty-five minutes away.

The valley itself is empty, full of sunlight, the ridges of cliff running out into it. It is the feeling of *motionlessness* about them which oppresses one: there is no wave-like movement in their making, no crest, no sense of anything but the gradual grinding away of Time, tearing down their long flat lines. And there in the distance of the valley, in the middle of it, is a little bit of mountain ridge all by itself, like a slice of one of the upper ledges deposited in the valley. The top of it is white, a thin splash as if done by a Titanic brush of whitewash. As we got nearer, its sides showed the same little beehive holes, the same vertical fissures, as the ancient cliff sides. But it wasn't a cliff – it was Shibam, 500 houses all crowded together in a narrow space in the middle of the valley, with a huge graveyard in a hollow beside it. We got near it into bumpy ground with palms and ditches; the long cliffs of the side valleys opened away from it; we saw it through lace tops of palms, the houses rising seven storeys or so, their narrowing white decorated tops giving them a look as if they leant back away from us; a little mosque is clustered in their shadows, squashed up amongst them, its minaret scarce reaching shoulder high, another little white mosque in front, like lace – it is all delicate work of trellis and wave, in mud, white and made smooth and shiny, and then pink with dust.

When all the camels had come out, we took the cobble slope, bumped over the threshold, into a little outer court, through another gate, a steep little square with white minaret and the towering houses overhanging all round, a crowd gathering rapidly – walked along to the house of M Besse's agent, Ba Obaid, welcomed by a nice neat quick little man and taken up little steps and passages to his office where my packet of letters was handed to me. The Governor came in, portly, with a stick, and a hennaed beard round a huge face: no sort of authority. I had to explain that I am making straight for a chemist in Seiyun and will go back and stay in Shibam in a few days. It is always a dreadful mistake to hurry people in the East, and is the best way of taking away any friendly feeling; however they really were all as friendly as can be, and understood the reason for not staying.

We took the quicker desert way along the north bank, the afternoon sun shining on it all in perfect peace. The wide bays and inlets and cliffs were lovely in their light, and one can see why the rich Java merchants come back to this oasis of their childhood, unique in the world. We crossed to the south bank, where Seiyun lies against the cliff, its gardens running back into a side wadi and out into the plain. In its middle is the palace of Sultan Ali, a tower-square painted white and jade green: a few other white houses and delicate white lace-work minaret – but mostly brown: ladies in blue gowns fleeing – the shortness in front and length behind makes them very suitable and picturesque in flight. It is wonderful to be going into towns *purely* Arab – no tourist touch, a world left over and where the West only comes by Arab ways. And with it all the feeling of prosperity, the beautiful green of palm gardens full of birds. We asked around for the keys of 'Izz ed Dīn, the Glory of Religion, my guest house – and finally in and out to a little white pavilion in a garden: a raised court with swimming pool of blue running water: a small warmer pool within walls: all the whitewash gleaming and clear; a sitting room with comfortable sofas: bed with pink mosquito curtains and pink frills to the pillows; windows opening out on to palm gardens full of zinnias and – quite as good a sight – carrots. And here I am.

Your
FREYA

113

Seiyun. 14 February 1935

My dear Stefana,

I am here in Wadi Hadhramaut convalescing from measles and with lots of leisure, as I have nothing to read but Zarathustra, who is magnificent, but not the sort of continuous light reading I rather wish for! So how can I fill in my time better than by writing to you? I wish you were here. You would like the ladies whose faces are painted *bright* yellow with scarlet eyebrows and green patterns on their foreheads: when I woke up after a rather delirious night and saw them bringing in my breakfast, I was always inclined to feel my pulse and see if the fever had really dropped. I luckily succumbed among the kindest people, and spent twelve days getting slowly better before I could ride another two to where a motor met me. Then it was all very easy, as this fantastic Wadi has every modern convenience (even a doctor only he is away in India on holiday): but motors, telephones, ice machines, swimming baths – and all in towns that have not changed since the Middle Ages and very little I imagine since the Queen of Sheba walked about in a blue gown and painted straw hat, and black veil under. The Sultan has put me into his guest house with a charming Meccan who blew up railways with Lawrence to look after me.

I am very much better, and hope to set out on the really difficult bit of travel for Shabwa in ten days or so. There should be no great difficulty; the German who tried to get there apparently told lies and said it was much further than it really is. If I am lucky I hope to get through into Yemen, but that is very uncertain.

You never saw anything so picturesque as these towns. One just has to gasp and wonder if it is real, the fortress – palaces, the beautiful delicate white decorations all carved in mud, and the extraordinary feeling of being shut in by cliffs and desert on every side. It is 8 days camel ride to the sea, and that does not bring you very near anywhere in particular. It was great fun to get my mail when I came up here – such an amusing contrast with all its home gossip.

My love to you dear Stefana.

Yours very affectionately,
FREYA

FLORA STARK

Seiyun. 14 February 1935

Dearest B,

I have been out to call on the Sultan's ladies, such a flower bed of coloured silks in a whitewashed room of the palace. I counted seventy steps up to the roof terrace, and there were more after that in the lower parts. The ladies were all seated round a table and it is a business to know where to begin saluting: one has to go all round shaking hands and kissing one's own hand after; then sit down and begin all over again by asking after each other's health. I got a lot of sympathy for my freckles: 'Poor thing, that is the measles,' they all said. They wore lovely gowns, with every sort of colour worked into them and a lot of Java influence in the silks and embroidery. Their hair all uncovered with hundreds of little plaits and tied in two bows over the ears as one sees cart horses' tails. Their faces were not painted except some red or orange lips: but one of them had very elaborately tattooed hands.

I have been using the bath to develop photos and have got two good rolls; I wish I could get a good lady – but that is quite impossible. I have got some lovely glimpses of the old houses with carved windows and white delicate designs painted on the doors. If only the people knew how lovely the white is on the brown mud. The secret of all our ugliness I have come to the conclusion is just cowardice and laziness – the refusal to make up one's own mind: always take something ready made.

Dear love,

FREYA

VENETIA BUDDICOM

Shibam. 22 February 1935

Dearest Venetia,

I am going tomorrow by car to Huraidha, an old town, and then I come back here and get ready for Shabwa if I am well enough. These measles have been the devil, and I seem unable to get any strength back: the 'elasticity of youth', alas where is it? I began to feel as if Destiny were playing ninepins with me, and only yesterday succeeded (I hope) in stopping a bout of dysentery with emetine. I feel the good desert air may be the best thing and so hope to get off if at all fit. (Also it is getting rapidly hot, 88 in the shade this midday.) I do not like the feeling of being enclosed in cliff walls, even though here the wadi is two to three miles broad.

I have been reading *La Morte d'Arthur* and feeling how absolutely I am living that life so that sometimes I feel as if I were reading pages of my own, the spirit of it is so identical.

I have been very lonely this journey and wished for you often. There are so many things to tell you, it doesn't seem worth beginning. The loveliness of wild doves flocking in the cliffs and their sleepy voices: the

115

little plump goats here, so very dapper, with neat ankles and ridiculous little tails curled up over their backs: they have their udders tied in bags and an amulet round their necks.

Here I am in a charming little bungalow which is always lent to the R.A.F. who now come to a landing ground in Shibam. If the worst comes and I fail of Shabwa, I shall retire here and wait for an aeroplane. It is delightful, the valley all open round it and the skyscrapers of Shibam to the north-west: a little pool of water, pomegranates and palms. What one likes here about the green and growing things is that they are *clean*: I can't tell you what a strain it is always to be bothering about the dirtiness of objects: I almost wish I knew nothing about microbes and put it all down to God as they do. They say that if you smell any scent when you have measles you just die that very day: the scent rushes to your head, and because of the dryness of the air, it expands and bursts.

Dearest love,

Your own
FREYA

P.S. I recommend to you *Zarathustra* – translated from Nietzsche by Common. It is not a book for the weak or sentimental but a great book. I have been fortifying myself with it in moments of weakness. I have come to the conclusion that I am poor in courage really – all I have is a certain obstinacy, but not that serene cheerfulness which one should have to face death if it comes.

VENETIA BUDDICOM

Shibam. 9 March 1935

Dearest Venetia,

I don't know when or what I wrote last. I have been very ill but am better now – heart went and for three nights was on the edge of stopping. In what I thought my last moment I wrote to Aden and don't know what if anything they will do about it. They will think me a nuisance anyway.

You can imagine my sorrow at this illness, my Beduin and all waiting ready. And now a last dramatic touch has added itself to my bitterness – a horrid stunting German who has already written a *cheap* book about this country, is here again, making for *Shabwa*! I am helpless. I think I may be able to go there in ten days or so but not before, and meanwhile he is getting Beduin and all. No one here likes him and everyone is trying to stop him (and I am meanly letting them do so – but he does not deserve any sympathy: he has told such lies all in self-boasting).

I know it is vulgar to want just to *be the first*, but yet it is bitter when one has come so far, and but for this illness I would have been there five days ago. One must learn to be very patient, and thankful to be alive at all as a matter of fact, for I had given up all hope, and would not have lived but for the Afghan chemist. Anyway, Shabwa or no Shabwa, I am glad to think I may yet be seeing you again.

I am being fed on milk and hope to begin to get up in a day or two. So lovely here now and I have a room which can open doors and windows on three sides, according to the sun. A cool breeze comes in; and the sleepy noise of the water pulleys soothes my (very jagged) nerves.

My kind friends here took it upon themselves to wire to Aden from any ship passing Mukalla – to say 'please send aeroplane – Stark.' I fear to think what the R.A.F. will say if they get this!

Dearest love,

FREYA

P.S. I am all right now – no need to worry. Damn the German.

VENETIA BUDDICOM

Shibam. 15 March 1935

Dearest Venetia,

I thought I was better yesterday and that a little walk would improve matters and went and sketched by the old wall; came back for lunch, lay on my terrace reading the *Aeneid* and rather melancholy over the slowness of it all – and suddenly a buzzing came from far away: it crept into my ears so gradually I hardly noticed its strangeness in the desert valley – and four bomber planes came skimming from Tarim, more lovely to my eyes than any aeroplane before. They landed, all the city notables went like a row of ants in flowing gowns to meet them – and finally a doctor came up to me and squashed any hope of Shabwa for a long time. It seems my heart muscle has just stopped work and the rest period of the poor little pump is non-existent. They have all been awfully nice, but I believe they are cursing me in Aden (though after all it isn't the fault of a woman traveller in particular to develop measles). They are carrying me off on a stretcher tomorrow, as it seems I could not possibly do the litter journey to the coast; it is very good of them and I believe against all regulations.

I would have given I don't know what to avoid all this and it will make them much more fussy for ever after – and if it had only happened after

117

Shabwa. It seems incredible that tomorrow night I shall be in an English hospital in Aden.

Ever so much love my dear.

Your
FREYA

FLORA STARK

Aden Hospital. 23 March 1935

Dearest B,

I continue to get on as well as possible: I shall have to spend a good many quiet months without stairs or hills or emotions, but the heart should be as good as ever once it has got over the shock.

The Besses are just back from Abyssinia and rang today. It will be very cheerful to see them. I am suffering *agonies* of boredom as I can neither move nor read nor write much and yet feel quite well. I believe they consider that I have made as little fuss as possible under the circumstances. The Secretary of State telegraphed yesterday to enquire – all in kindness, though every further proof of my deplorable conspicuousness gives me a horrid shock. My only comfort is that Rose Young[1] has been giving much more trouble by crashing among rhinoceros and lions in Africa – but she is a governor's wife, so I suppose she gets a handicap.

25 March 1935

About Beverley Nichols' *Cry Havoc!*: sincere, but the *materialism* of all these modern idealists is so depressing. And so with his pacifism: it is not the horror of war that deters the best of the young men – it is that there is no *cause* to fight for: it is this – the feeling that the sacrifice has been for ignoble ends, that the fine words have been used to cloak unexpressed motives, which takes all consolation from the sacrifice. If one could be a pacifist by *fighting* for peace, would there not then be plenty of young men ready to face the mutilations and horrors which alone Beverley Nichols can think of as the misery of war?

If we had stood resolutely for a *just* peace at Versailles, would we not be stronger now? If we had set our face against the tyranny over Austria? If we were *really* to stand every time for what we think right irrespective of consequence, and kept ourselves armed and ready would it not gradually work for the peace of the world?

Your
FREYA

1 Wife of Hubert Young.

'A feeling of happiness lay over the spring of 1935' Freya wrote many years later in the third volume of her autobiography, *The Coast of Incense*. 'It was partly the peace of renunciation. Shabwa and all other Arabian travel were over for the moment, and life flowed as it does for animals, filled only with what trickles into it from day to day.' She had returned to Asolo on board the steamship *Orontes*, in the ship's hospital, and spent the rest of the spring and summer in Italy, the year of the Italian invasion of Abyssinia which deeply shocked her. She was working on *The Southern Gates of Arabia*, which was published the following May, while she was in London on a social whirl, and at the same time planning another trip back to the Hadhramaut. Another medal came her way: the Mungo Medal of the RGS, which again invited her to lecture.

VENETIA BUDDICOM
Villa Freia. 7 June 1935

Dearest Venetia,

I am busy trying to wrestle with my Arab presents: I have to send about a dozen, and it is a fearful job, first to guess what they would like, next to get the things bought, next to get them up into the Hadhramaut – and each one requires an Arabic letter; it is almost as much of a job as writing my book.

The Abyssinian business[1] makes me sick: if they bring it off I really don't think I can *bear* to live here: it is all very well to shut oneself away from politics, but if one feels that a real crime is being done, it does not seem right to just turn away and think of something else. However, I am doing my little bit by telling everyone who asks me about things that the Abyssinians always mutilate their prisoners, which rather damps the enthusiasm: as a matter of fact almost everyone hates the idea of war here. A Persian proverb is rather prudent at present: 'It is good to know the Truth and to talk about it, but it is better to know the Truth and to talk about palm trees.'

Your loving
FREYA

VENETIA BUDDICOM
Villa Freia. 9 September 1935

My dearest Venetia,

May I spend October with you, more or less? I have to be in London in November – and there is nothing to keep me here, and every reason to get away before I talk too indiscreetly.

1 In 1935 it became evident that Italy was planning to take over Abyssinia and make it part of Italian East Africa. The British and the French, though eager to assist Abyssinia, were also anxious not to anger Italy.

Here one just sits horrified, watching a nation gone mad – all the young that is, who don't remember what we do. The peasants and all the nice and humble people just groan and bear it, – so poor and prices rising. I hope we are not going to be cowards and will lead as we ought to do. What is the good of all our power and wealth if we can't face the responsibility in a crisis when every principle is at stake?

I am reading the *Seven Pillars*. The chapter about the Arab character is very true and finely put.

Your own
FREYA

FLORA STARK

Penbedw. 26 October 1935

Dearest B,

I go to London on November 23rd. The week before that I will be spending with the Methuens,[1] after speaking for the *Sunday Times* on the 15th. I have written out that and the R.G.S. lecture and it has taken all the week. Also choosing out photos – such *masses* of them. Huxley[2] is taking a hundred for his magazine and will give me £50 for three articles, so I shall just have paid for my camera and films.

I have received a really pleasant honour. I am to be made the first honorary member of the Ladies Alpine Club. It is very nice, and I am now waiting to hear from the Secretary.

I got a lovely pair of corsets and look as sylph-like as is possible for nine stone, which is what I weigh at present.

News here is not really better. No one seems able to take it that we *really* mean exactly what we say: the usual mistake of thinking that one says more to mean less,

Lots of love,

FREYA

FLORA STARK

c/o Mrs Rhuvon Guest, Wimbledon. 15 December 1935

Dearest B,

Such a hectic week – not really much done, but I have to rest every minute I can, and that is not enough. The speech tomorrow makes me feel quite ill already and I have learnt all its twenty-five pages by heart. I am to dine first all alone with scores of (most elderly) gentlemen at the

1 Lord Methuen, painter and zoologist, of Corsham Court, Wiltshire.
2 Michael Huxley edited *The Geographical Magazine*.

Hyde Park Hotel: this would be fun, if it were not for what comes after. The party at the Woolleys was fun too, though I don't enjoy being the centre of attraction, but Lady Allenby was charming and the Storrs, too, and I met Lord Curzon's daughter whom I liked and the head of the Air Force and of the Army (who sat next to me at dinner and I liked too). But I am quite unfit for this and get too tired – and the man I most wanted to meet was kept away.

All the country seething and furious over this crisis[1] and Samuel Hoare pretty well done for they say.

Today I lunched with the Goodenoughs – such dears, and the table full of friendly young people besides the great archaeologist Herzfeld, a nice little profound Jew. My dress was much admired at the Woolleys and Sir Ronald Storrs[2] told me I was the most fêted person in London.

Dear love to both of you,

FREYA

JOHN GREY MURRAY

Penbedw. 7 January 1936

My dear Jock,

If there is one thing I really dislike it is this horrid American fashion of dropping away the parts of speech. Please may I have '*A* South Arabian Journey' and not just 'South Arabian Journey'? Apart from my own prejudices, it is a fact that other people have travelled in South Arabia too, and if you take away the *A* you make it sound as if I consider mine the one and only Journey, which will not do. I hope this may be accepted?

I am sending you ever so many chapters – eight in all, so that should make a good beginning: but have you got a *very* intelligent printer, because the corrections seem rather intricate? And do you think he can deal with such things as dots under the 'h's' and 's's' where I have put them, and lines over long vowels, like jōl? I hope he will be very careful with the corrections, because it means fearful agonies of mind to settle them all over again.

Yours,
FREYA

---

1 Sir Samuel Hoare, Foreign Secretary, and Pierre Laval, French Prime Minister, concocted a plan whereby Mussolini was to be conceded even more of Abyssinia than he had occupied. But when the details came out, public indignation in Britain was such that Hoare was forced to resign.
2 Oriental Secretary in Cairo 1908, Governor of Jerusalem 1917, Governor of Cyprus 1926, Governor of North Rhodesia 1932.

57 Beaumont Street, London W1. 13 May 1936

Dear Sir Sydney,

I am in this nursing home for a month, but not too ill to see friends or even to walk about in the Park at a very slow rate – so if you are in London please come and talk to me. They have found the trouble at last – not heart at all: but the heart is a little tired at doing the other people's work for over a year!

Affectionately,

FREYA STARK

FLORA STARK

57 Beaumont Street. 24 May 1936

Dearest B,

I seem to be getting much better at last, so give you this good news first of all. I can walk about a mile along the level, and yesterday drove with Jock to Kenwood. Jock says 1,700 of the book are sold and it is recommended by both Book Guild and Book Society. It comes out on Tuesday. I hope it gets safely out to you.

I have just had to spend £10 on becoming a life member of the Iran Society, made to promote relations with Persia and have a very appreciative letter from the Minister, a nice little man. It is very pleasant sitting here being visited by one's friends. I have had an average of three a day so far and it is like listening to a sea-shell, all the noise of the world coming to one. Lady Iveagh came, looking so handsome, and so nice: she is interested in such vital things it is lovely to talk to her. She will give you my news and is taking two discs for Herbert, though I am sorry you are going so exclusively Brahms.

26 May 1936

This is the great day of the book. Jock has sent an enormous bouquet of sweet peas and roses, and Sir Sydney Cockerell rang up to ask had I seen *The Times*. Quite overwhelming – one *could* not have nicer things than that said – and what pleases me most of all is to be compared to Jane Austen.

I feel rather like a *prima donna* – so many flowers and two enormous jars of bath salts from Vyvyan and the nice little nurses all fluttering about as if I were a celebrity!

The Palestine business[1] looks bad. The public here *at last* begin to

---

1 Proposals by a Royal Commission to partition Palestine and form Jewish and Arab states were bitterly opposed by the Arabs and supported by the Zionists, but had never been implemented.

realise how much Italian propaganda lies beneath. Do you remember my saying last October that the failure of sanctions would mean war with us? Miss Pott told me yesterday that Lord Cromer foresaw this in 1916! – a conflagration which might have been prevented three years ago by decisive preventive measures. And now one can only hope for some Italian collapse to save us from a ghastly war. Thank God we are getting ready for it at last.

Love from

FREYA

FLORA STARK

57 Beaumont Street. 31 May 1936

Darling B,

My book is being so marvellously reviewed that I am quite overcome. I wonder how it all came about. The point is I think that in this welter of matter-of-fact muddles the minds of people are craving for something brave and romantic; cleverness is going out of fashion, and more fundamental values are coming back: and the voices of those who well or ill do stand for simpler and deeper things are coming to be listened to. This pleases me more than the personal success of the book – though it gave me great joy when dear Charles Ker came the other day and said the *Times* review had made him weep! Do you know what he has done – he has given me a credit at a garage for as many cars as I may want, to go out for drives. He has sent me zoo tickets – and he is making me a life member of the R.G.S.! All this is lovely, but more than all the tender thoughtfulness of it.

You will also be glad to hear that I am getting on faster than they expected. The heart man says that there is no doubt I had pneumonia, and the kind that raises no temperature is the worst, so that people rarely recover. I said I probably got over it because there were no doctors around. But I begin to go out a little and got hats with Minnie. Though what is the good of trying to make anyone as fat as I am look nice?

Viva and Harry came yesterday and walked in the Park. Of course the only review Viva talked of was the *Morning Post* which says that 'commonplaces patter from my mind': she said she thought it not so bad as a review. I was amused, as I had made a bet with myself that this would be so, and can now with a clear conscience go and buy a red handbag.

Dearest love,

FREYA

39 Bloomfield Terrace. 12 July 1936

Dearest Venetia,

Did I show you the account I wrote of Italy's effort in Yemen? Mr Keeling[1] has sent it both to *Times* and *Telegraph* and says that *no* Conservative paper will publish anti-Italian stuff now. One would become a cynic if one dealt in politics long. I went to tea with Lady Halifax[2] and got a long talk about Palestine and found her sympathy very much on the right side. She is a clever woman and showed a great deal of knowledge and grasp of essentials. The fact that we are putting every Moslem everywhere against us is the vital point in the case as far as this country is concerned. I am lunching there on Thursday and if I am so lucky as to find Lord Halifax in I hope to hear a little more and use my wee voice too in good cause. If the Arabs will only continue arson and murder long enough, they will gain their point: but what a necessity! I said to Mr Keeling that I was going over to the opposition because of Mr Baldwin's speeches – and he agreed, and said he felt they were absolute invitations to war: so I imagine there is a good deal of discontent in the back benches.

Herbert Young has arrived. It was lovely to see him, as cheerful and well as can be, and delightful with a new flannel suit just got at the Army and Navy Stores – pleasant to see at eighty-five! We shall long be mouldering in our graves, or I at any rate, by that age, but if we did reach it it would be nice to carry it as lightly as that.

I walked in on Jock the other day and found him with Dr Munthe who walked arm in arm with me down Piccadilly. He has a horrid sensual mouth. I don't really like him at all, though he has a superficial sort of charm. He said he met the first person who had not read his book and nearly embraced him. I wonder if that is true. I consider the people who haven't read my book rather incompletely educated. I met Mrs Upham Pope[3] the other day and she told me that the discomforts were so vivid to her mind that she shut the book and never finished it.

This must go. I have been looking through a book of Low's cartoons.[4] Those of 1932–1934 all steadily pacifist, anti-armament etc. . . . it is a revelation and explains the miserable condition we are in now.

Your
FREYA

1 Sir Edward Keeling, Conservative MP for Twickenham 1935–54. After the War, General Manager of the Turkish Petroleum Company.
2 Lord Halifax (as Lord Irwin) had been Viceroy of India 1926–31.
3 Wife of the Director of the American Institute for Iranian Art and Archaeology 1930–52.
4 David Low, influential left-wing cartoonist of the *Evening Standard*.

FLORA STARK

Corsham Court. 24 July 1936

Darling B,

I have had an interesting time these last days, but much too strenuous –
an evening party at the Huxleys',[1] listening to Kathleen Long, a beautiful
pianist – Mozart and Bach, and Schumann sounding rather shallow in
between. I went to the Woolleys' party the same afternoon where
everyone had a title but was otherwise rather dull, and it was curious to
notice the different atmosphere – one just social and the other really
enjoying itself. Ruth Draper was at the Huxleys', and Jelli d'Aranyi (if
that is right)[2] and a most charming old couple, Lady Ottoline and Mr
Philip Morrell, looking just as if they had stepped out of Walpole's
letters. Mr Morrell and I fell in love with each other at sight and talked
about music, poetry, and the eighteenth century, and he told me he hated
books with a lot of nature descriptions in them. I said I did too, but that it
is worse to have to write them. No one there had read my book: I can't
tell you how nice it felt to be happy and friendly and liked without the
assistance of a label. I *know* now that I don't enjoy the limelight: it is not
of course that one is not pleased to have one's efforts made more of than
they deserve, but it is oppressive to be *ticketed*: it is bad enough to feel like
a mechanism expected to work in a certain way and worse when you
know that it simply *doesn't* work that way at all! I can't tell you how
pleasant it was to sit in a corner and watch Ruth Draper being made
much of. She has a very intelligent face which looks as if it had been
sensitive in youth: I should think she must be a good and true friend to
those she likes. She gave me a lift in her car and, as I told her I had never
been able to see her as the theatre was always full, said she would see that
I got in if ever I wrote to her – which I thought awfully nice.

Yesterday I went to Gertrude Caton Thompson[3] to lunch and there
met Lady Rhondda, a far more powerful person with a really beautiful
face, with kind and amused mouth and strong broad forehead and square
hands. She runs *Time and Tide* and tries to raise the standard of literature:
I meant to ask her how much it costs to do so, as I am sure it cannot be a
paying proposition, but we talked of so many different things that I
forgot. She lives with a Miss Bosanquet, who is quite different, fasti-
dious and amusing, and they go very well together, and I have promised
to see them in the autumn and help raise the standard of literature too in
the paper. Gertrude is toying with the idea of digging in the Hadhramaut

1 Juliette and Julian Huxley.
2 Jelli d'Aranyi, Hungarian-born violinist, naturalised British subject.
3 Gertrude Caton Thompson, an archaeologist of some standing, had directed several excavations and had
received awards from both the Royal Geographical Society and the Royal Anthropological Institute.

125

with me: she would be an excellent person and knows as much as anyone about prehistoric flints. She has looked through all my Meshed stones and found two insignificant little obsidian things that are probably the teeth of a saw, and about four or five thousand years old – and interesting enough to be published in the autumn. I wish now I had collected more.

Your

FREYA

VENETIA BUDDICOM

24 St Leonard's Terrace.[1] 20 September 1936

Dearest Venetia,

Philby[2] has gone and taken Shabwa on his way from Najran. I find I do not grudge it him and I have just written to congratulate him: I feel much more as if we were all colleagues rather than rivals, and I think that is what one ought to feel (though not about little German worms!). Anyway Aden is all fuming because he came down with an armed escort and penetrated British territory without asking or even mentioning his intentions. I think this was tactless, but of course he *may* not have felt sure of bringing it off and then it is rather difficult to talk of one's plans beforehand. What is much more deplorable is that I rather fear he has done it *by car*: I hope for a refutation of this, but it sounds bad.

I read *High Wind in Jamaica*[3] some years ago and thought it a very subtle study. I believe one grows all the time in sensibility as one gets older (if one goes on growing at all) and starts as pure savage: and I liked the humorous ruthlessness of the book. But I am not sure that I would let him educate my children.

On October 16th I go for a weekend to Lady Leconfield and this frightens me and I hear it is to be a big party and I have not clothes (all too tight) and feel it is a fearful waste to buy any as I shall not need them afterwards. However this is not really one of the major worries of life, and not as disturbing as the state of Europe for instance. I feel that if I were at Geneva I should be one of the little nations who refuse to join in the hypocrisy about Abyssinia. I don't see *what* credit the League can hope for after this.

Your

FREYA

1 Anne Lawrence's house. She was staying in Asolo.
2 H. St John Philby, outstanding Arabian explorer of his time and adviser to King Ibn Saud; father of the spy, Kim Philby.
3 By Richard Hughes (1928).

Petworth. 17 October 1936

Darling B,

I must send you if only a scribble on this exalted notepaper. I am enjoying myself, and it is wonderful to be surrounded by so many beautiful things all in a perfect setting of appropriate splendour. The house has come down from the Conquest *never* being sold, but handed on from generation to generation, though changing name sometimes by the female line.

We seem to spend most of our time meeting for meals – an enormous table with Lady Leconfield very large and ornamental and rather like a picture of the Queen Anne period at the top. The rooms open out one from the other, all full of treasures and all with tables of china and large fires and high walls hung with priceless pictures. It is fun, for a short time: but what an effort to live so in splendour always! It is lovely to walk in the park and see the fallow deer enjoying simple things like cropping grass. The park is really lovely – such gentle lines as if the earth were breathing underneath, and bits of trees and water put in decorative places. The house is soft grey sandstone, austere and in beautiful proportion, with a stone roof and delicate little bits of decoration here and there.

I wonder why there is some feeling of fundamental discomfort – perhaps because one feels so padded round that all reality is far away. Lord L. in gaiters is real enough, but he looks on us all with rather a want of enthusiasm and rushes off as soon as he can to things I am sure more tangibly interesting, like manures or cattle foods. And yet everyone is individually charming.

Must stop and dress for dinner. Grey dress looks nice.

Dearest love,

FREYA

Duke's Hotel. 24 December 1936

Dear Harold,

This is a semi-business letter, though I will begin it with the best of Christmas wishes: may all your desires come true, and may I find you both in the Hadhramaut next year.

I am rather perturbed because every other archaeologist I hear of seems to think of wandering in the Hadhramaut next year – and this is really to ask that, if a dig is going, it may be reserved to me? I am writing to Sir Bernard [Reilly], and seeing the Colonial Office and Foreign Office here, but I thought I would write to you and put the matter more fully before you as you are to be, I hope, the person chiefly concerned.

Miss Caton Thompson wishes to join me and is looking round now for a grant and we thought of asking to dig either Meshed or Huraidha, as the Mansabs there are both personally friendly. It is of course possible that you will not wish *anyone* to dig; what I want to ask is that, *if* anyone is allowed . . . it may be us! Miss C Thompson is so well-qualified that one needn't even explain about her, but apart from that she is used to dealing with untrained natives on a dig, and I am as you know quite tactful (on the whole?!). I think we would do you credit and start your administration with the discovery of whatever there may be to discover in the way of archaeology. You will not want more than one expedition at a time I imagine, to see how the experiment works, and that is why I am writing now in good time, in case other people apply.

Your own
FREYA STARK

In February 1937 Freya left, by way of Asolo, for the Near East. She was ill again, this time with bad sinus, for which she was operated on. From Baghdad she travelled to the Shia Holy Cities of Nejf and Kerbela, and in May was in Baghdad again before returning to Europe, to join her mother at L'Arma for the summer. Jock Murray came to stay and together they spent a day in Monte Carlo where he anxiously watched her gamble thirty gold sovereigns she had unexpectedly found hidden away and was using to test a theory she had about doubling stakes. The theory proved to be unsound, and she never gambled at roulette again.

FLORA STARK

Kuwait. 3 March 1937

Dearest B,

This is a lovely place to be in: the weather delicious, hot at midday, but too cold to sit in the shade without a *very* warm coat. I got here with a little difficulty: slept in the train from Baghdad and woke up just in time for Basra. It used to take twenty-four hours last time: then people said 'Can't it be hurried up?' and with a stroke of the pen twelve hours were knocked off the timetable, and no visible difference in the comfort of the line!

Basra was rather uninspiring, but at the Post Office I found a polite effendi, young and fat with no chin and a rosebud mouth. I left them to deal with the motor company for Kuwait and went to try and get my hair curled. Mansur was the man, they told me. He was an old shambling Turk, very tall, with one black lock, oily and smooth across his bald head and a trembling hand with which he gingerly ran hot irons through my hair.

When I got back to the post, I was taken to rest at an awful hotel called the Alhambra: the effendi came later and showed me the new airport (Basra will soon be the greatest airport between Europe and the Far East) – gave me tea, and altogether depressed me so much by his kindness and quite hopeless inner self that I was delighted to let him see me along a dark deserty road to Zobair at 6.30. We got into its dark streets, heard of course that the car would not leave till tomorrow, and I was settled in with the postmaster of Zobair's family for the night and said goodbye to the effendi with relief.

The ladies of the family were all dressed in knitted cardigans, but otherwise un-European, and they had a Persian guest who was also on her way back to Kuwait and had just had eight days' pilgrimage at all the holy cities. She told us that at Kerbela a woman had been picking the pilgrims' pockets when the hand of 'Abbas stuck out from his tomb and struck her dead. There were ten ladies altogether, all very cheerful. They asked me which of the ladies I should like to have as a bedfellow, a trying question. Two of them shared the same husband, and they told me they were very good friends and that it all depends if it is a nice man and treats them fairly, night and night about. I was very tired, and having eaten eggs, bread, celery leaves and very scented sweet stuff made of fat, flour and sugar, I at last went to bed: it was a big four-poster affair with quilts and velvet covers but a very trying odour: the Persian pilgrim lay on a mattress on the floor, and one other guest: the lamp was left to burn itself out. Next morning I just had time to wander through the little arcaded market and then found the company's car ready to start. The 'company' was an old man in a yellow *kefiah* and a gown: I paid five rupees for my seat: the Persian lady beside me and three men behind: and the doors and mudguards all buried in bundles. We raced along, the wind icy, the desert faintly green and with many tents, and sheep and donkeys near them: we had an early lunch off a saucepan filled with *habisa*, a mixture of dates, bread and fat which they quite naturally asked me to share, and so I did: and finally drove up to Gerald's[1] gorgeous new palace and had to be lifted over the door and out by his rather surprised *farrashes*. He was very pleasant and gave no outward sign of pain at this method of arriving, though he mentioned it later. It seems that it isn't proper for me to stay with him but I rather hope he may get me a room out, and meanwhile I am with the Dicksons[2] while he has gone for four days to Bahrain. I

1 Captain Gerald de Gaury, now Resident in Kuwait.
2 Colonel H.R.P. Dickson was British Agent in Kuwait.

129

lunched with him, and this morning saw him off in Imperial Airways, a huge gigantic monster which stops twice a week outside the old medieval wall.

Your

FREYA

JOHN GREY MURRAY

Kuwait. 15 March 1937

My dear Jock,

This evening the whole British colony dined with the Sheikh. It was not too exciting for me, as I like my Arab society more undiluted and the Sheikh stopped being Arabic at the neck, where his black beard and white drapery ended and European grey flannels began. We walked from the drawing to the dining room across a short open space where two close ranks of slaves and servants stood with ewers and basins and towels alternately to wash our hands as we passed: and their black and brown faces, gowns and cartridge belts made the best of the show in the flickering light. It was an excellent dinner and fun to see the Sheikh's hand digging energetically in the roast lambs to give us succulent bits while the missionary and oil concessionaire ladies ate refinedly with their fingers. But other times when I have eaten so by myself in a Beduin party the peculiarity of it never struck me, and one realises how one can't combine the East and West.

You can't even *imagine* this sun and light, a sort of quivering gaiety: and the sunsets on the bay and its mauve edges and the shallow pools of the receding tide.

Do write. I am being so neglected.

Yours,

FREYA

FLORA STARK

c/o Mrs Sinderson, Baghdad.[1] *9 April 1937*

Dearest B,

I don't know what I shall have to pay to ransom fate for one month's perfect happiness in Kuwait. It was *quite* perfect – everything being right in the right surroundings, the lovely place and people, the comfort of the cool and empty house with nice servants running round in yellow embroidered gowns, and Gerald who was the pleasantest host in this

---

1 Dr, later Sir, Harry (Sinbad) Sinderson was Dean and Professor of Medicine at the Royal College of Medicine, Baghdad.

world, always thinking out new and amusing things for us to do, liking the same things, and with a pleasantly sympathetic mind ready to go from politics to literature or gossip, and so ready for conversation that I got no work done at all. I think he enjoyed it too, and sent a telegram after me to wish me *bon voyage*, and wrote to thank me for my visit – and altogether it leaves a pleasant memory of friendly comradeship; and I must say it *is* nice to sit and talk the same language and, if something funny comes along, to lift one's eyes and catch a corresponding twinkle.

It is strange how the things I have foreseen coming in these lands are now developing, so that I have an almost uncanny Cassandra-like feeling – and what no one would believe six years ago is now becoming commonplace. And perhaps I shall have some hand yet in the history of the future, though no one except myself and one or two unusually discriminating people will guess. Anyway it is good to be here and see the stream flowing.

Yesterday I went to a little female gathering of every sort – Iraq, Turk, Syrian, American and British at the house of a dear pretty Welshwoman who runs the girls' school. They meet once a week to discuss the universe and they asked me whether I feel myself more cut off from other races than from my own people – and I can truthfully say *no*: it is only a very small section of one's own people with whom one can talk the same language, and one may as well make up one's mind to being essentially alone.

On Monday we go to the Prime Minister's tea party: and then on Friday I leave and sit for two days amongst the ruins of Ukhaidr in the desert, an old Sassanian palace (or later) and then go for the week to Nejf to see life in the Holy City. Major Edmonds has been a dear and is arranging this, which is rather difficult as no one has done it before.

Dear love to you both,

FREYA

SIR JOHN MURRAY

North Gate, Baghdad. 6 May 1937

Dear Sir John,

I am going to try my strength by spending a week in the Holy City of Nejf and shall be there for the Coronation,[1] instead of at the British garden party – so I fear my last shred of reputation will go: the average British attitude towards the native here is quite incredible: one is amazed that we have any empire left at all between the Diehards and their

1 Coronation of King George VI.

131

atrocious manners on the one hand and the Little Englander pacifists on the other.

Yours ever sincerely,
FREYA STARK

VENETIA BUDDICOM

Nejf. 11 May 1937

Dearest Venetia,

It is rather nice to have got to the Holy City in spite of obstacles – first the Euphrates rose in flood: then my operation: lastly the tribes to the south began their usual summer rebellion. However the government acted promptly, intercepted a lorry-load of arms, took away the parliamentary immunity of three sheikhs and sent them to exile in Kurdistan: and I got away as quick as I could when the railway line was cut, for fear of being stopped by government – however, all seems quiet now. I got into a car with five Iraqis in the back and we ran into a dust storm, very unpleasant in the open – the lights throw no light at all and the soft dust comes pattering with every gust of wind, giving one an unpleasant feeling of being buried. The little driver was very good and crept along an invisible road telling us that his hand was on his heart while we said 'May Allah make it easy to you' in chorus. I got tea with missionaries in Hillah, and a bath. We ran out of the dust before that, as suddenly as we got into it, and stopped at a wayside tea-house, and the owner of it brought me a bowl of water to wash my face as I sat in the car. How can one help liking people who think of this on their own?

I got a car all to myself from Hillah and came along in the dusk. One has such a feeling of desolation and the power of time in this empty ancient land – the Tower of Babel on the right and the line of humps that once were the walls of Babylon. Ezekiel's tomb, under a crumbling minaret with a stork in his nest at the top – and Jews from Baghdad very blatant in their European clothes, sitting in hundreds along the banks of the canal to celebrate Ezekiel's feast. By the time we crossed the Euphrates at Kufa it was dark: it is such a pretty little town, all strung along the bank with sailing ships moored beside it and all the male inhabitants trying to get cool out of doors on benches – and the domes of its mosque lighted: and from there one goes into darkness and desert again – till the mosque of Nejf appears with the lights outlining it in the night. It is always a very moving place to come to – the end of so many pilgrimages.

Your
FREYA

Baghdad. 16 May 1937

Dearest B,

I am back in Baghdad, safe and sound with nothing but a cold in my head, the result of many varieties of dust. On Friday, with many handshakes, I left Nejf, sitting at ease in the two front places of a car in which various sayids with green headbands sat at the back: if one pays double fare one can get this advantage, and even so it is only 1/- for one and a half hours or more. It used to be three days to Nejf, and all flat desert with the Euphrates palms like a thin dark streak in the east and no life on the road except an occasional car bumping along a coffin with the mourners squashed behind it in the back. There is no peace for the dead: they are bumped to Kerbela and taken round the tombs in both shrines there: bumped along to Nejf, washed, and then with the lid off their coffin, taken round the shrine of Ali and finally buried. The only other excitements on the road were enormous pale yellow toad-like crinkly lizards with small black heads called *dhabb* who lifted their legs in a clumsy slow run and if they were on the road the driver amused himself by running over them. I said 'Don't kill them,' and he justified himself by saying that they creep unnoticed up behind the ewes and drink their milk.

Kerbela has no European in it that one knows of but a very neat European touch as you approach: an asphalt street with young euca-lyptus trees, all the work of my friend Salih Jaber: and when you come to the end of this highway you go suddenly into the real East, with overhanging houses and roofed bazaars, high, under ridged roofs of beams and corrugated iron full of holes, and fluttering doves; and a crowd less Arab and more varied than Nejf, many Indians, and women from Sind, like ghosts with their little embroidered gratings of eye-holes under the skull-cap, and voluminously gathered gowns. And here my host lived in an old house, two courtyards, and nice old brickwork solid enough to keep the heat out.

I took a car and went to Ukhaidr in the desert, about two hours' drive, and as we went along we saw gazelle bounding away and I saw three quite white against the desert, which I had often read of but never seen. They were far off and so white and flat that they looked as if woven in a Persian brocade, most lovely against the warm-coloured hill: and we saw nothing more except an old built-up column here and there with remains of blue tiles – made to show the way – till Ukhaidr appeared, incredible in the wilderness. It is an enormous size, square, with towers all along the walls and a walk round between two battlement walls to shoot from. One can still climb up three storeys and look from the battlements over the desert and the depression which they say was once the Sea of Nejf, and the ridge they call Jebel Tar (Gibraltar). There is nothing quite like this finding of ruins in the desert, something so august in its nakedness, and so dignified in man's courage and helplessness against the passing of Time. There were kites in the ruins and two little donkeys fanning each other's faces with their tails, and the cloak and sack and short sword of some peasant from the oasis.

We got back in five hours and saw the two minarets and Husein's dome floating on the horizon like a mirage before the palms appeared. One must know some early Arab history to appreciate a place like Kerbela: the place of a tragic battle where everything has a tradition behind it.

Dearest love,

FREYA

SIR KINAHAN CORNWALLIS[1]

Baghdad. 16 May 1937

Your question: *The feeling about the British* has become very much less acute in the past four years: in fact there seems to be hardly any anti-British feeling as such now, but a growing indifference and want of esteem for Europe in general (not to be wondered at!). I think that a really unmistakable smack in the face to Italy *anywhere* would have the instant effect of halving our troubles all over the East. The Germans are quite active here and thrive on such things as our delay in providing Iraq with guns. (This is causing real dissatisfaction and, as very little is required, perhaps your office could do something about it.) I have nothing tangible to go upon, but I should think it very probable that there is some sort of agreement by which Germany deals with the east and Italy with the west of the Arabian area: the Italians are doing nothing here at present and two agents they had are transferred to the west.

What I do feel very strongly is that the main point of interest has shifted since the days of the Baghdad railway and now lies in Arabia itself. South of Iraq lie both the natural air routes and the only oil fields that other powers may hope to get hold of. With the discovery of oil in a country like Arabia obviously doomed to exploitation, we are bound to have trouble if Germany and Italy can possibly stir it up for us: but it will be directed against us *everywhere* in the oil area – from Aden to Persia – and the defence against this coming attack – which is *sure* to come – ought

1 Sir Kinahan Cornwallis was Adviser to the Ministry of Interior in the Iraq Government; Ambassador in Baghdad 1941–5.

to be planned as a whole and not in separate bits dependent on half a dozen separate government offices. Here again, our ultimate position in Arabia will depend on our strength in Europe: but it seems to me that what is also necessary is (1) to unify our Arabian policy or at least to have some body of experts who are able to see the Arabian problems as a whole; and (2) to stop such vulnerable gaps as the Yemen etc. . . . before the local trouble can be started there which may involve the whole area. I think that if we eliminate any doubt as to who is paramount in Arabia we need not worry over the British position in Iraq. I have made no mention of the Palestine question, taking it as an axiom that no satisfactory position can be attained anywhere in the Near East till that is settled to the satisfaction of moderate Muslims.

FREYA STARK

FLORA STARK

Baghdad. 21 May 1937

Dearest B,

Sinbad [Dr Sinderson] took me for a bathe in the Club swimming pool this morning. It was very pleasant, painted a nice cool blue in the middle of a green lawn. I have a sort of deeply rooted inferiority complex in Baghdad and feel like a misanthrope in its social gatherings – and especially in a bathing dress now that I am so fat. A perfectly *awful* ordeal to go and get into the water while everyone sits round the edge and watches you.

I am dining out every night before I go and am asked about everywhere except at the Embassy which has never troubled about me at all. As Vyvyan [Holt] is living there I did think he might trouble to ask me to lunch or dinner. He is always dazzled by such shams.

Dear love, B,

FREYA

FLORA STARK

Damascus. 28 May 1937

Dearest B,

I am here in a lovely old Turkish house (eighteenth century) full of nice things and in an atmosphere where you needn't be apologetic all the time for being 'intellectual'. It is awful how inferior the wretched 'highbrow' feels in a place like Baghdad. There must be a strength in stupidity, or we would not, from the height of our Imperial splendour, look down with such absolute disdain on the activities of thought.

I left at four last morning, and dear old Sinbad came to see me off. The car turned out to be a magnificent Chrysler with two Iraqis behind. We left Baghdad in a pink dawn with the electric lights wasting themselves in it and went out into the desert – fifteen hours of it with only one hour's break at Rutba – oh how tired I was, in a sort of coma most of the way, neither awake nor asleep. Gazelle leaping about us, galloping across in front of the car, and then green patches and little red spots of poppies like bloodstains, and then all the way from east of Rutba to Damascus the camels of the Anezah – thousands of them, so that the desert seemed like one vast nursery for them to graze on.

I am here in the lap of comfort; I have been ruining myself buying a Nejdi dress made of hand woven silver and red brocade – simply irresistible. They are reviving the industry and the old patterns and making these lovely brocades for Molyneux, Worth, etc. . . . and this dress is the model worn by Miri Sha'lan's daughter (of the great Anezah tribe) at her wedding with Ibn Saud. I also saw there the fifth oldest carpet in the world: the colours are divine and it is in almost perfect condition – but they have just refused £6,000 for it.

Dear love,

FREYA

In the autumn, Freya planned to meet Gertrude Caton Thompson and Elinor Gardiner, to sail from Port Said to Aden, fly to Mukalla and to dig through the winter in Hureidha in the Hadhramaut. 'It was,' wrote Freya in *The Coast of Incense*, 'to be exploring no longer but archaeology.' Her health was not good; and this was not to be one of her happiest expeditions. It lasted four months. Early in March 1938, with considerable relief, she set off on her own for a 'last solitary exploration in South Arabia': a month's camel riding to the coast through the tribal borderlands of the west.

MRS LIONEL SMITH[1]

L'Arma. ? September 1937

My dear Mary,

I am very busy preparing for the winter excavations. Miss Caton Thompson is the archaeologist and her friend Miss Gardiner geologist – I am just nothing but expect as much fun out of it as any. I am going by slow boat and hope to stop some days at Jidda. Do you think Lionel would give me a note to his brother-in-law,[2] and do you think he would

1 Lionel Smith was now Rector of Edinburgh Academy.
2 Lionel Bullard, Minister to Saudi Arabia 1937–9. Then Minister and later Ambassador to Iran 1939–46.

put me up? I hear Philby hates me, only because I wrote a book. I can't remember if it was Solomon or Job who said 'Would that mine enemy wrote a book'?

Love to all,

FREYA

FLORA STARK

Overseas Club, London. 11 September 1937

Dearest B,

All the expedition stuff is more or less bought. We have bought two tents, chairs, a table, bedding – and an immense but rather dreary food list. The dietician looked Gertrude's list over and said it was sufficient for the 'very poor in a hot climate: for those who have nothing to do' or something to that effect: and she has added numbers of vitamins.

Your

FREYA

FLORA STARK

The Residency, Aden. 31 October 1937

Dearest B,

We woke up today to see the coast of Yemen, the Indian Ocean very blue, and were presently sailing into the bay of Aden. As I went into the saloon for passports, Mr Longrigg brought up a nice-looking, enthusiastic young man who had been reading *Baghdad Sketches* and welcomed me *most* cordially. His name is Perowne[1] and he is political here, and enthusiastic to dig and ready to give all help and encouragement – so pleasant, and he quoted Milton and Tennyson before we got off the boat into the Residency launch, where he took us regardless of the Oil party he was supposed to be attending to.

Mr Ingrams, who is here for some days, came to lunch. He has not got Shabwa under him and we shall have to tackle Colonel Lake[2] for that, but he was quite welcoming for his own district of which he is absolute king. It sounds *dreadfully* civilised: and you can address letters from now to P.O. Shibam – via Mukalla – Aden, and they will go from here by Anton Besse's plane: he has a weekly service and all the Hadhramis fly over for weekends. How glad I am to have seen the country still untouched, two years ago.

1 Stewart Perowne, from the Colonial Service.
2 Lt-Colonel M.C. Lake had raised and commanded the Aden Protectorate Levies. Political Secretary, Aden, 1934–40.

AB is away in Abyssinia and will not be back for a fortnight – rather a blow.

This afternoon I went to see Colonel Lake, but he was out – so looked in at the hospital on Captain Hamilton who has just shot himself in his own foot by mistake. He had been out, running a small tribal war, and had himself carried back to the assembled enemy whom he approached waving his leg and saying 'You needn't bother to shoot, I've done it myself for you' – and they gave him a marvellous reception and killed a sheep instantly. Mr Perowne has a lovely ruin also waiting for us in a place where they received him with a brass band of eight trumpets which marched before him, only pausing to drink by filling the trumpets at a stream, and then *blowing* to clear them when finished.

Tomorrow we must tackle the repacking and redistributing of our luggage – a ghastly job. But it seems deliciously cool here after the sticky heat of the Red Sea: one lay under a fan and perspired.

I find my own book[1] awaiting me and am longing now for reviews. I hope it will go well.

Dearest love,

FREYA

FLORA STARK

Aden. 4 November 1937

Darling B,

All our luggage, eighty-one packages, went off this morning at 1 a.m. on the *Amin*, and I put in my afternoon leisure fixing a cook and packing him off too. The oil party have snatched all the available cooks at high prices, but I found a gay young lad of twenty called Qasim, a Yemeni hillman, ready to get up at five and cook till midnight, though tea and stew are the whole range of his accomplishments. We fly down on Sunday by a plane sent to fetch the oil party, and it will be fun to see the coast from above.

I find I get through much more with far less exertion than my party. It is far more useful in this climate to sit quiet and make other people do things. A little chat about their own family affairs does more to get willing and efficient helpers than all the ordering about in the world: I think Elinor Gardiner still considers it a waste of time, being used only to Egyptians who can be browbeaten. The Arab has the charming attitude that anything he does is done as a kindness, so it is no good chivvying him about for it. It is a great mistake to look as if you can do everything

1 Enlarged edition of *Baghdad Sketches*.

yourself if you *want* people to put themselves out for you.
  Dearest love,

FREYA

Mukalla. 11 November 1937.

Dearest B,
  Today and yesterday have been very exciting because at first go off
Elinor went along a gravel ridge between us and Shihr and picked up a
palaeolithic flint. No one thought such a thing existed here and I was
beginning to feel a little dubious and Gertrude was afraid she would find
nothing but things about the Christian eras. Apparently you only find
palaeolithic flints in gravel: you can pick up the early tools – triangular
little notched instruments or sharp flat-pointed blades in flint, yellow,
black, or gold like amber. I found quite a lot myself and begin to learn
their look, and it is a fascinating game, though one will end by going
over Arabia with nose fixed to the ground so glued in the past as never
even to see the modern landscape.
  We have chartered a lorry for 200 rupees to take us and our food and all
our belongings to Tarim and Shibam and sleep on the road as often as
necessary. It is all very expensive and quite extraordinary how much
cheaper it is to be unassisted and alone: and we have to allow for lots of
blackmail to Beduin tribes later on. However that is quite a minor affair.
  You can't think of the loveliness of our drive along the sands towards
the sunset: the shallow wave-water pink and brilliant like a seashell and
rows of breaking waves like frills of lace beyond; the blue, tumultuous
ranges running out to their wild capes: the grasses and rushes of the shore
and some old boat with pointed prow or black quick-moving figure of a
Beduin like an incarnation of the Night: and on the wet sand, *millions* of
crabs running from us as quick as drops of water; and suddenly against
the breaking waves, four cranes or herons, three black and one white.

Your
FREYA

Seiyun. 22 November 1937

Darling B,
  I shall never be an archaeologist, I am far too fond of living things and
people. While Gertrude goes wandering with her eyes on the ground for
potsherds I am inclined to gossip with all the neighbourhood which

139

slowly gathers and drifts along with us offering bits of hopeful rubbish. We left Tarim yesterday morning. The old Sayid Abd ar-Rahman never came to see us, ostensibly because of Ramadhan but really because I alone was almost more than he could bear and three of us is above the maximum. But as I took a little bag to his wife, he sent along at the last moment a square blue box wrapped in a towel and inside it the most *awful* brush and comb with imitation gold flowers on an imitation silver ground you ever saw and with it two little boxes for razor blades and two depressing rings inside them.

It was awful starting off anyway and makes me feel like a Cook's agent because of the enormous amount of things Elinor and Gertrude need to have with them. They simply wouldn't go into one car, but a camel man happened providentially to stroll by so I pressed three suitcases and various bundles on him and he arrived here almost as soon as we, all for 3/-.

We lingered over ruins by the way – an old Islamic site called Senahiye, where the people led Elinor and me to a well built from the top down to the wadi bed – a hundred feet or more: it was interesting as we hadn't seen how these places on mounds got their water. I was led to the mosque, all in ruins but with an old wooden pulpit whitened by time with a date inscribed in beautiful lettering. This I found hard to read and the village teacher was sent for, a nice old man with an agate bead round his neck hung by a piece of string: if he rubbed his face with it, he said, it took away the toothache. He had a kind old face and we deciphered the pulpit together and made the date out at 673 which is thirteenth century: if this is true it will be a good inscription, as anything so medieval is rare from Hadhramaut. I offered to buy the pulpit, but there was a chorus of protest and the village said it was building a new mosque for it below.

We got to Seiyun in the afternoon, about four, and it was very pleasant to drive again through the dusty lanes and walls of gardens and find the feeling of peace that I remembered – the town gate open and neglected in the sun.

But instead of going to my nice white summer pavilion we are here in the grandeur of Sayid Abu Bekr's new cement palace and feel like a hotel at a watering resort out of season. You can't *think* what it is like. We dine in a columned atrium open to the sky and go to our bath along the edge of a princely swimming pool under a three-sided double colonnade of which the top columns stick up into the sky supporting each a small electric bulb. As one drives up through big iron gates under a mud gateway by a mud wall arranged in festoons, one comes to a second gate with a glass case hanging over it on which is written, on one side,

'Welcome' in Arabic and English, and on the other 'Godspeed': an electric light inside illuminates these messages for the arriving or departing guest. And one has fried eggs and liver for breakfast. The R.A.F. come here, and leave cigarette ash in their sheets. And there are taps, but not running water, in the bedrooms. It is all rather pathetic though nobody knows it so it doesn't matter. The only real shock I got was when I went to the wc and lifted the lid and disturbed about twenty huge beetles.

Sayid Abu Bekr came as soon as we arrived and was very pleasant. He is a fine man and has a manner of great gentleness and authority. It is he really who runs this part of the world. He asked what we meant to do and instantly vetoed Shabwa, which I push into the foreground as a sort of decoy, so that having refused that they may be less ready to refuse what we really want. When he left I went and had the most gorgeous bath just in time to come and sit in this incredible drawing room and receive five or six old friends all very cordial – and all saying how much better I look than before!

After dinner we went to visit the ladies in the town house, an old-fashioned one absolutely overpowering in its lovely harmonies after this. There was the musician from Qhurfa and many ladies. They come trailing in with bright chintz gowns that sweep over all the eatables as they progress slowly along, stooping and kissing their hands to one after the other of the assembly: they don't get straight between one and the other but just go along stooping all the way.

We sat for ages. The Qhurfa lady sang a long *qasida* while we nibbled melon seeds and smoked ourselves with incense and sniffed up the scent of coffee berries roasted: and eventually the Learned Sheikha Alawija came in and everyone rustled up to kiss her hand, and she came and sat talking almost as much as ever but not quite, looking very pretty with full red lips and very black eyebrows and her little hands, explaining such exciting things as the difference between a noun and a verb. Meanwhile poor Gertrude and Elinor were nearly dead and so was I, but we could not go till coffee came, and of course no one worries about late hours in Ramadhan. I have to go tonight but I rather think the rest of the expedition will rat.

Your
FREYA

JOHN GREY MURRAY

Shibam. 3 December 1937

My dear Jock,
Today is the feast day and Ramadhan is over. I can't tell you what

pictures I have been seeing (and I hope taking). Just as if a crowd painted by Memling had come to life. Sultan Ali arrived last night from Qatn and I sent to ask when I could call and he said 'at sunrise'. So I got up all in a pink light and crossed the wadi, the sand as cold as ice and a low mist along the ground; I went up into the old palace and found the Sultan most friendly and as nice as ever – with a heavy day before him. So I left and asked for a chair and established myself on the little platform that runs beside the city gate, with two drummers banging drums beside me – and there I waited and took pictures of the people as they came, little groups of mercenaries trooping in and running barefoot up the steps with their guns on their shoulder – until the procession came out, the Sultan in front and two banners behind, the soldiers in a fine chaotic thicket of gun barrels shooting here and there for fun: the drums marching ahead and a piper blowing hard – and all so gay with the whitewashed minaret and palace roofs glistening in the high sunlight and everyone out with a new cashmere on their shoulder or a new *futah* round their hips. These mercenaries are the bane of Mr Ingram's life and he wants to abolish them, but I must say they do give a nice swagger to the scene.

Dear Jock I am becoming such an Anti-Feminist, but you needn't say so. But I do much prefer dealing with men. We do nothing but fuss over our health and talk about tinned food, and the one day we had a little discomfort in the way of sitting in Ba Obaid's quite nice room with only about four people and ten million flies to bother – why they just *wilted* and then turned upon me for not keeping the inhabitants of the country away! (Elinor Gardiner was already sickening but Miss Caton Thompson is really *hopeless* as a traveller though a marvellous archaeologist – but so anxious not to take any of my suggestions that she won't even look at a perfectly good site if I have mentioned it.) Now *please* do be discreet and don't repeat this. I shall never risk an ordinary trek with them but keep them either in Huraidha or else go by air to Behan, and do my best to let them live here without being bothered by human beings. *What* a way to travel! I have come to the conclusion that there is a deep cleavage in human beings which the East and West represents – those who wish to *be* and those who wish to *do*: the experts, occidentals, and certainly archaeologists belong to the latter: but the proper traveller is the former and thinks it a waste to move from his own home if nothing happens *inside* him as a result. I mean something fundamental, like a chemical change when two substances come into contact. But to sit here and mix with none and just feel how far you are from Europe is a dreary business.

I would so like a long letter and to hear about your little house and all the nice artificial side of life. I think when I get back I shall settle down and become sophisticated. I am really getting rather old, all *creaky* in my bones and Arabia is very exacting.

Am I becoming very rich? I have seen *Time and Tide, Observer, Times* and *Country Life* – all very kind. I hope the book does well.

Ever so many good thoughts to you and love,

FREYA

FLORA STARK
Huraidha. 12 January 1938

Darling B,

Last night I made a list (for myself) of the seven cardinal virtues for a traveller:

1. To admit standards that are not one's own standards and discriminate the values that are not one's own values.

2. To know how to use stupid men and inadequate tools with equanimity.

3. To be able to dissociate oneself from one's bodily sensations.

4. To be able to take rest and nourishment as and when they come.

5. To love not only nature but human nature also.

6. To have an unpreoccupied, observant, and uncensorious mind – in other words to be unselfish.

7. To be as calmly good-tempered at the end of the day as at the beginning.

And I should like to see Gertrude trying to conform to *one* of them.

A wicked old man – old, old, with a hennaed beard and kohled eyes, sunken cheeks, a magenta turban – and his fifty-fifth wife came to call today. He is one of the chief people here and Qasim left him sitting on the dust of the kitchen floor while we were at breakfast. He came to ask us to lunch on Friday. He has travelled all over South Africa, India, Malay, etc., but is so old that nothing is left except a sort of ghostlike shell of antique gaiety.

Your
FREYA

JOHN GREY MURRAY
Huraidha. 27 January 1938

Jock dear,

We are quite marooned and it is ages ago since a few stray letters came up by devious ways – and your very dear Christmas telegram among them. Now however a small bomber has just appeared in our sky and I

143

am hurrying to write so that this may go to you.

I have been ill and I rather think a doctor is in the plane coming to look and give advice and go again. But whether or no, I am well on the mend and find it is just as easy to lead a quiet convalescent life here as anywhere else. Only for the last week have I had to stop the constant stream of conversation which constitutes Arab life and have been reading Jane Austen instead.

The dig meanwhile goes on: a cave-grave is being scooped out of the hill, and as Gertrude says there is enough work here for years it does not matter if I am not able to take them anywhere else. We think of getting back to Aden in the latter half of March.

Apart from this silly habit of always falling ill in Arabia, it has been very interesting to live and *grow into* a small unspoilt Arab town, and you can't think how much I feel a part of it and how devoted everyone has become. I am longing to write a book – but not pure Arab – the interplay of East and West which I have been watching. I will never be forgiven by Miss CT, but I think it will have to be done, and she *says* she likes 'Objective Truth'. She has never said one kind thing to me the whole of this winter nor to anyone else that I could hear, but the Geologist is a very different being – pure gold.

Anyway, dear Jock, I have come to one conclusion – that I am not going to be even the smallest of celebrities any longer: it is too bad for one's soul. I have seen what it does to women, and I am going to take warning, and sit in my garden and sew – and you can come and talk to me and tell me what the Young People are doing!

Yours,
FREYA

FLORA STARK

Huraidha. 9 February 1938

Darling B,

Today is the second day of the feast and we have been very busy with it one way and another. The great excitement of the whole town is that I have hennaed my hands! I wanted to see how it was done, and arranged to go to one of the neighbours, Sherifa Nur and her daughter Sheikha. The best beauty specialist in Huraidha was there with a pretty little pointed face and thin fingers sitting crosslegged on the carpets making a green paste of powdered henna leaves and water in a basin. When it was a little finer than a spinach puree she made me wash my hands with the powdered leaf they call *khotega*, to get the grease off: then I dipped my wet fingers in turmeric and rubbed it over my hands to make them bright

144

yellow, and then, being settled with cushions as supports all round me, I handed my hands over beginning with the right one 'for blessing'. The specialist dips her forefinger in the paste which hangs down in a thin drip with which she traces out rings and stars and trees and anything she fancies on your hand. It is no joke. I went at 1 p.m. and came out at five. Meanwhile the ladies came round, pressed glasses of tea in my free hand, looked at the process, and told the gossip. A feeling of leisure hung over the harem: one could not imagine anyone being in a hurry ever. When all was done, I was arranged on cushions full length and told I could sleep while one of the ladies did my feet and the rest had coffee in one corner. I lay with closed eyes, just feeling the little cold drops on my foot: henna is supposed to be very cooling, and they asked if I felt chilled by it. I dozed, and woke to find the work finished, a lovely sun with rays shining on each instep – 'taken', the lady said, 'from a printed book'. My hands had three little branches, and one up the middle finger, besides other small patterns and circles, and the first joint of the palm a solid block of henna: this elaborate affair is only for women who 'have a man', the others can have a simple band or so; but though I pleaded age and spinsterhood I was not to be let so lightly off.

Your
FREYA

FLORA STARK

Huraidha. 15 February 1938

Darling B,

Things are very gloomy. Gertrude is still ill with a small but irregular temperature: Elinor is in bed with a cold: Gertrude wants to dig out another cave, and it will mean either weeks of delay or a relapse: and I, though getting better, am rather afraid I shall not be strong enough for the trek to the sea I had planned.

Today however I did get out for a proper ride – and went in search of photographs to illustrate irrigation among the palm gardens of the big wadi. It was very pleasant to sit jogging in the sun, and go down the wadi bed with big open distance around, and men in fields hoeing with their pointed hoes before the *seil*, and the little yellow scented balls of blossom, soft as kittens, on the *samr* trees of the wadi bank against a blue sky. The people came out of two houses near the landing ground called 'Anaibat, and asked me in, and the women at once became friendly at sight of my hennaed hands which are always a great success. Altogether I came back tired but glad of the freshness of fresh air and solitude again.

Your
FREYA

145

Huraidha. 24 February 1938

Darling B,

We leave here in a week and take a fortnight to go south and *may* stop, but not likely as it is getting very hot – 106° in the sun at 8 a.m.

All are well again now, I hope it may last. I am enjoying the hot weather and begin to feel energetic again – and so slim that I have got back into my corsets of five years ago.

Your

FREYA

FLORA STARK

Huraidha. 4 March 1938

Dearest B,

My last letter from Huraidha. Everything is packed and three camels ready waiting, and as soon as the saddle-bags are settled on them I hope to start. The old Meshed Mansab is lending me his horse for the first stage. I hope to get down to the sea in a fortnight and to send you a telegram from Aden in three or four weeks. We were to meet at Bir Ali, but Gertrude changed her mind *last night at 8 p.m.* – and all is for the best. They both leave tomorrow by car.

Ever so much love dear B. I am quite fit and jolly.

11.20 a.m.

I have got half way to our resting place after a fearful hullabaloo to get off. At ten Elinor and I descended, leaving my poor little bare room looking very forlorn with only five boxes for Aden and two stools left in it, beside the boxes of skulls which support the dining table: as we got down my caravan appeared, a very proper-looking caravan of three camels with the paraffin lamps brightening up the luggage and the Mansab's orange quilt spread for me to sit on. The Mansab however had offered me the little brown horse, and I had just sent for it when the lorry and the motor for tomorrow appeared and distracted Huraidha altogether. Your letter was inside, and a mass of prints of Shibam sent by Jock, and Elinor and I looked at these in the middle of a thick crowd all wanting to see. The Mansab's son saw me off: Elinor was *very* nice, and offered to delay her journey to Palestine if I fell ill and needed her, which was *really* Christian, – and now I am off. We have driven by all the Himyaritic irrigation ruins of the plain, and are now almost opposite Wadi Rukhaime where we rode the other day – under a tree, waiting for the camels. A Beduin has come up who knows me from the other day.

He has just asked if Harold [Ingrams] belongs to my 'tribe'. Our camels have appeared over the sand against the background of scrub.

Afternoon

At 2.30 we turned the big corner of this wadi to the south, old bits of irrigation, but now all sand and stones. The camels had come up, and I rode along under my sunshade; it must be very good for the liver, but *very* tiring to begin with. Qasim is so overcome at parting with Salma that he just sits in tears, with blood all down his shirt from the burst boil, a quite revolting sight. People ought to be in love in private. I am not on a saddle but recline on baggage and the Mansab's orange quilt on top. The shoulders of the camel, lurching along below, are quite extraordinarily shapeless: he *is* ugly: his silly little ears and fluff of curls on his mane give him a look of elderly and dowdy coquetry. You would think in all these centuries he could have learnt to walk along behind his Bedu, but the wretched man always has to lead by a rope, and they change at frequent intervals, as it must be tiring to hold the rope so high. One has a feeling of not moving at all: the landscape remains exactly the same for ages, till one suddenly sees quite a lot of ground left behind.

Your
FREYA

FLORA STARK

5 March 1938

Darling B,

I was so sick with tiredness last night I could not write. I hope I shall get more fit for trekking in a day or two – it does take it out of one more than anything I know. It is the sociability after the long day which does one in.

Last evening was very pleasant. We got to our little town, called Zahir, in the dusk and saw it growing towards us, toothed ridge of houses against the sky and the cliffs in straight lines behind, one after the other like a stair. There is always a thrill at the end of the day in coming to your unknown resting place, all a mystery.

All the male inhabitants were gathered in a little group to watch our arrival, and took us to a very dark house on the hill top. We settled down, about forty of us, crosslegged round the walls for conversation. They are a rougher-looking lot than Huraidha, and also very different in type – lots of little English-looking straight noses and others with a sort of Etruscan curve. I was dead tired, but had to sit an hour, and then my bed was made and I went up to a tiny little clean room with a roof of its own to walk out on, and after the horrid shock of a huge green insect walking up me inside the net, and a short expression of mutual dislike before I got it outside, I went to sleep till a round mat was brought with rice and a kid for the Mansab (a nice long-faced peasant), Ali, Qasim and myself. I went down again after for another hour, and everyone got more and more cordial.

In the morning it was a fearful business to get off and meant being cross which is much worse for oneself than anyone else. It was 8.30 before we started, already exhausted with one and a half hours of medicines and talk.

It is extraordinary how far our influence has spread: all up this wadi people run up who have seen me in Huraidha and I hear my name called from windows as I pass. There is a great difference in manner between those who have heard of me and those who haven't.

This morning I have been three and a half hours on a camel and it is as much as I can bear. Now we have settled down under a big *'ilb* tree in the wadi bed and four Beduin have joined us, one smoking his hubble-bubble with a friendly bubble sound. I am only the second woman here from Europe (Doreen [Ingrams] came as far as 'Amd last year) and only three men I think. It all feels much more primitive than Huraidha.

Your

FREYA

FLORA STARK

Nu'air. 6 March 1938

Darling B,

I fear my trip is over almost before it has begun. We got here yesterday at 3.30 after three and a quarter hours' camel riding in the day, and again I felt so tired that I could have lain down and died. But there is no way out of it, one *has* to see people where one is the fourth European in a new country: the whole town was out to meet us. I was taken to the best house of the town and climbed up stair after stair lit only by shot-holes, to the top room which has four tiny windows and a door opening on to a high-walled roof of its own. There I was allowed peace and quiet for a wash and rest but in an hour's time Sayid Ali came to take me down to supper. He and Qasim and I had supper off one dish, and the other guests off another: it would be very difficult in any other country to manage the relations between master and servant on this basis, but it seems to work here. I sat on after the meal and talked to the ladies of Nu'air, about their maladies: then went down and found the whole of the male population sitting crosslegged in the half dark of the court outside in one big hollow square. Here Ali let himself go, stood up, folded his coat over his tummy and his hands over his coat and made me a speech of welcome, referring to me as the 'Beloved of the Government' (which would surprise them) and then asked me to address the meeting. I did this most inadequately, and got up only to find more masses of ladies upstairs and the sound of the coffee pounder going. At intervals the lady who pounds stops, casts up her eyes and invokes Allah in a short prayer to which all listen.

By the time I finally got up I felt so ill I thought I had better take my temperature and found it 100. I thought I would cure it as Dr Buchanan suggested with twenty grains of quinine. Well, it was disastrous. My heart simply fluttered about for the rest of the night, and the electric torch chose this time to conk out. I lay in great misery. Today I am quite flat and still and the heart is recovering – but it seems hopeless to go down into the most malarial part of Arabia if one's heart can't stand quinine. And I would not have arranged to go anyway if I had known that no one would appear to assist at the other end. So we have sent a runner to Seiyun and he should bring a car in three days to Zahir, a day's ride away – and that alas is the end of my journey on the Incense Road.

Yesterday at our lunch bivouac a woman called me aside and asked if I had medicine which would kill her husband. A Se'ari Beduin joined the party. All those I have seen are among the ugliest Beduin in this world, with huge mouths and long faces and eyes rather near together and curls so that they look like caricatures of Charles II.

FREYA

FLORA STARK

Shi'be. 8 March 1938

Darling B,

This adventure has begun and it is really an adventure with myself – because I decided I really would not be beaten by my silly old body. It may not get down to Bir Ali, but I am doing a *little* bit of new ground and getting up to the ruins of Redet ad Deyyin and then, if still ill, to Du'an – a two days' trek from there. It is four days from 'Amd instead of two, as they told me, and if I had known that I would not have risked it: but now I am at lunch under an *'ilb* tree, and everything seems more hopeful. I had a miserable night, going into semi-faints of weakness. It is one's *morale* that counts in Arabia: it is that which gives way under the constant strain of *people*: I realised it strongly by the immensely restful feeling it was to

149

get on my donkey and be off, with nothing but the exertion of riding.

This little bit of my ride has not been done by a European, it is all very feudal and pastoral. There *is* no way of getting on here except by sharing the life, and that is what makes this country so hard.

Your
FREYA

FLORA STARK

Husn Suwaidat. 10 March 1938

Darling B,

It was a very long day yesterday, and the fact that one can trust no one for distances is very trying. One three hours' ride took a good seven, and we left Zarub at 3.30 and got to this medieval fortress just as the sun set with shafts of yellow light behind clouds. Everyone was tired. Ahmed thought of nothing but his donkey who was really quite full of work but knew his master's lenient ways and would stay for solid minutes in contemplation of a boulder in his path. When he saw a donkey he fancied at Zarub, he nearly threw me off however, and reared with desperate cries: I did come off once, when he stumbled, and got more annoyed than ever with Ahmed who nearly smothered me in a firm and agitated embrace under the donkey's hoofs.

Head of Wadi Mothab. 11 March 1938

I am a good way on my way to Yeb'eth where we dip into Wadi Hajr and out again as fast as we can. We have left the highest plateau of the jol. We went on in peace towards the twilight and, coming to another shallow basin of jol strewn with early flints, saw in its stretch of cultivation a lovely little feudal company of four square towers with parapets and little top look-out and one big centre fort, and buildings low around – all in the last low sun with clouds behind – a *beautiful* sight: we pushed on, to a little agricultural turreted outpost with tiny huts round the towers, and the goats and peasants coming in. A hut was swept out for me where I slept in great comfort because of the total absence of windows, after dining with the company in the smoke of the chief room. There is the same lovely lively little chirping of birdlike creatures all night as we first heard on the jol, and the stars windswept and clear and the night very cold. I got up in the dark and found Qasim (now an *excellent servant*) making breakfast and finally got off at 6.40 before our camel-men had finished their dates.

6 p.m.

We are now in a high camp, 1,253 metres, back on Von Wissman's route and with a lovely horizon of hills across an immense dip of jol. We have been skirting the heads of big wadis that rush down both right and left to Hajr: they drop as if a trapdoor had fallen. Now the sun has gone, the gold streaks are dying as quick as candles snuffed, the green is sweeping over the sky, and an icy wind is blowing.

Your
FREYA

FLORA STARK

Azzan. 18 March 1938

Darling B,

I am having two quiet mornings' rest and found I needed it quite badly. It is comfortable having a room not to oneself (there are usually ten tribesmen or so in it) but to spread about in: it is in the palace of the Sultan's uncle, a square proper fortress and it is a lovely room, besides a bathroom of its own.

We left early yesterday morning. I promised bakhshish if we got here before tea, and the result was that the Beduin began to worry us at four! However we got up and off just, happily, as daylight was beginning and rode down from the watershed in a great curve, coming in a meeting of ravines and wadis stuck over with seven small towers, where the gardens of the settled people coincide with the track from Hauta. The people are not very settled, as the two little villages, near enough almost to touch each other, have only just stopped shooting and pouring paraffin on each other's trees: but now with Ingrams' peace they are beginning to sow and reap again. There is perennial water here, actually flowing, so that if there were real peace whole tracts of country would be cultivated, but the tribes are by no means under control.

A rumour circulates that if and when the English come the slaves will be liberated. The work here is all done by slaves and they are treated badly by the Beduin masters, and that is why the rumour has made us unpopular. At the first little village a whole bevy of them rushed out to kiss my hand with friendly demonstrations. It is an insult to pass by people of consequence so that one's progress in inhabited parts is very slow. I promised to come back however, and got slowly on to where the wadi narrows again between barren rock. Here on the left side a huge slab is written over with Himyaritic pictures and inscriptions, cut shallow in the rock. We have had nothing like it so far. There was a man spearing a lion in the mouth, two shooting bows and arrows, standing on a camel's neck, etc., and the writing is very exciting because I hope it may prove to be intermediate between Himyar and Arabic. I photographed, while a woman in the wadi below kept up a long scold against the foreigners who take pictures belonging to the country. Wherever one goes here a camera is looked on with suspicion and the men even are unwilling to be photographed. There is a party for and against you discussing like a Greek chorus, and your whole business is to keep the part *for* in the ascendant.

Yesterday I had a good rest and meant to write, but the Sultan's family and Ali all came to sit here and talk over their troubles. I got good proof of the difficulty with the Beduin in the afternoon when I went to see the famous ruins of Naqb al Hajr. Sayid Ali as usual was absent when wanted and nothing prepared. So I got on his camel and went off with a guard of a vague number of Beduin with rifles. We were very late and the sun low, so I hurried them on, and we began to trot, the Beduin giving unexpected whacks from behind and the camel's baby trotting on ahead in the outraged way they have when hurried. By the time we reached the ruins I was in a crowd of about 300 people. The ruins are on a long low ridge, quite bare and stony. There are two gates and on the inside of the south one, on the right wall as you go in, is the famous inscription which says that so and so began to build the fortress of Maifa'a 'with stone and wood and binding' (mortar) still cut quite plain. The 300 moved about with me in a solid mass, touching everything and talking of bakhshish. I copied the inscription, but having to keep up a running conversation all the time. They would have been charming if you had gone with nothing as a guest to their homes but the idea of money works like blood in a tiger. By dint of joking, smiling and scolding, the atmosphere remained friendly, and after one hour and twenty minutes we made off: I got on to my camel as quick as I could, handed my book, which was being snatched from me, to one of the bodyguards, and made off and I only hope the photos come out.

Everyone trooped off quite friendly without any bakhshish and the bodyguard, now increased by volunteers to about thirty, took me home at a trot in the sunset singing war songs in two batches on either side of the camel and shooting shots into the air.

Your
FREYA

FLORA STARK

Bal Haf. 25 March 1938

Darling B,

Do you know that my *average* camel riding for the last six days is nine **hours per day? I don't think I *could* go on without a rest now – yesterday**

152

was the most exhausting. It was to be so nice and easy, a sail in a *sambuk* to Husn el Ghurab and back in time to get on board the dhow before she sailed in the afternoon. We were to start at 5 a.m.

I woke at 5.30 and found all quiet: the *sambuk*, which fetches the only water Bal Haf has to drink, had not come back. Ali said it would be here in ten minutes, but the sight of a perfectly blank ocean shook even him: it was discovered that the wind was wrong anyway: the *sambuk* appeared in time, a small speck struggling slowly along the coast without a sail. I felt I could not cope with *two* things as capricious as the wind and the Arab temperament, so agreed to go four hours by camel instead. By eight o'clock and thanks to Nasir there were two camels and we were off: Nasir, Ali, five soldiers and the camel driver called Rupee. We went up and down the most depressing country – a slag bed of dead volcanoes, bubbling over with small craters and only beautiful where its blackness came near the jewel-green of the sea. Nasir walked and Ali and I rode till the steep untidy *aqabas* made us get off: by going along the coast I could do what detectives do – put myself in the place of the old writer of the *Periplus*[1] who saw what I was seeing and described it. He spoke of Cana as *between* two islands. I had already eliminated Bal Haf and another lovely little uninhabited anchorage called Kaidi because there is no water near: but imagine my joy when we turned a corner and saw Husn el Ghurab standing squat, a solitary crater, and the two islands one on each side of it out to sea. The droppings of innumerable birds have whitened them, and no one could help noticing them as a landmark coming as I did upon that wide view of bay and hills. I can only wonder there should be any doubt about the place. We went on till we came to the solitary crater where old walls in black lava stone still show. The flat land in a wide stretch on either hand sweeps beautifully up to a semicircle of dead volcanoes, twelve to twenty of them, all looking down with a feeling that they are alive and observant. Down their easy ridges the caravans can come by a dozen different ways. The water of Bir Ali is only a little way across the bay, which is green and white from the white sand that shines up through its clearness. To the east the land curves round to the black snout of Mijdaha, the only other possible place for Cana. And not a soul in sight in all that land except for the little treeless town (one palm tree only, visible beside it).

I went straight up and wandered over the crater and it was so big it took three-quarters of an hour to do so: with bits of wall, Himyar and later Arab, and four great water reservoirs: if it had been done in Arab

1 *Periplus Maris Erythnai*: a description by an unknown Greek of Alexandria in the first century AD of the coast of the Red Sea and Gulf of Aden.

times, I think some mention would have been made of it by historians: but it sunk to unimportance, probably because of the unsafety of the country behind. As we were coming down and thinking of sending to Bir Ali for a *sambuk*, the old 'uncle' came up with news of inscriptions and showed me two beauties on a rock wall: they must have been known and copied, but still I could not leave them while there was a doubt – so I said I needed one and a half hours more: the *sambuk* would take that time to come anyway and Ali went off for it with a camel and two men for water and food as well. The time passed peacefully: Nasir copied and I copied and the escort kept up a sort of Greek chorus on their own excellence in finding us the inscriptions and what about bakhshish? When I had finished it was four o'clock, and Ali still invisible crawling towards the town: when we came down the hill, tired and thirsty, a little stir was seen, and a crowd advancing. I wrote and took no interest: rejoiced in the solitary peace, the smell and gay sound of the sea, the old sea-wall of the port running down from its north-eastern precipice: until Nasir appeared with an inhabitant from Azzan and remarked in a pleased way that they wanted to come and shoot. I thought it was a reception of honour and said politely that we should be delighted but had no time today. The man from Azzan looked surprised and Nasir pleased: I could not have given a better answer, but what had been intended was that the inhabitants meant to come and shoot *us*. They wanted no strangers in their land they said. What really was the trouble was that Bal Haf and Bir Ali hate each other and I, in complete ignorance, was making an inroad into enemy country. Nasir, with his normal understatement, had said that there was a *little* feeling between them and the Bir Ali cousins. When I had understood, I said: 'Well, welcome and repose: when are you coming to shoot us?' The Ambassador explained he was a friend from Azzan and not a native of Bir Ali; that the more violent party had been dissuaded (we might have seen the tussle at the gates?), and that now they were not marching out but wanted us to go away. No *sambuk*, but they did let us have water. There was nothing for it but a camel ride back. We got ready; the dusk was coming on: Sayid Ali appeared, very twittery; I counted out his money on the sand, half expecting a haggle; but all the poor little man did was to burst into tears and kiss my hand and walk off sobbing: he and the two friendly Sayids walked back to the angry town, looking very small with the bay all round them. We collected together, our two camels, water skins, a few packets of sticky sweet stuff and some flour and a plank which one of the soldiers must have looted from the boat. Nasir, delighted with the whole affair, said to his men 'Dance a Zamil.' They went off ahead brandishing their rifles and shooting green flames out of them in sight of the town: Rupee and I were left alone with the camels till we got away into the lava foothills. 'They may cut us off at the pass,' Nasir remarked to his five men, who all opened their rifles and saw that all inside was ready and in working order. There seemed to be no path and the dark coming on in a cloudy sky among desolate little black ridges of lava; everyone scattered. I resisted the Western passion for giving advice, and waited, and just as the dark really came it turned out that a path did exist and we found it. The ghost of Cana, the squat crater, still loomed in a sinister sort of way behind us, a shadow in the low sky. We went on slow and steady and, as the dark fell complete, stepped into the totally black part of the lava: the path alone, I don't know why, showed pale and it was strange to follow its windings in a quite blind world, nothing else visible but the dim silhouettes of volcanoes. I had no proper camel saddle this time and ached everywhere, and we went on hour after hour. The Southern Cross moved across the sky: the clouds began to clear, but nothing brought any beauty to the blackness – and whenever we came out of one of the shallow dips we saw more shapes of volcanoes. I kept awake by balancing myself like an Arab, one leg up and one down to rest the pain, and as this meant one was in danger of falling from the camel's height on to stones, it did prevent the danger of falling asleep – a very real one your camelman guards against by shouting to you when you nod. However, poor Rupee was far too tired for that, or even to tell me to hold on for a bad place: but he would say 'oh-ho' to his camel and so I knew. As we got to the sea an old moon green and pale rose over the black ridge. We got in at 2 a.m. – an eighteen-hour day, thirteen and a half on a camel. I was just able to get off, creep upstairs to find that Qasim had packed my bed in the waiting dhow, put my quilt on the floor and sleep like a log.

5 p.m.

I am now lying in comfort on the deck of the dhow swinging easily in the sunset and feeling very near the water. The Arab coast, whose mysteries I now feel I know better, is just in sight, and the chief mate, a fat old stubble-bearded man from Dis, is standing near calling sunset prayer. Far away in the haze is the familiar and for the moment unattractive outline of more volcanoes.

It has been fun to do this all in the proper Arab way – to join a caravan to the coast, to be in for a threat of battle between the neighbouring ports and to start off in a sailing boat which traffics wherever its merchandise carries it.

Your
FREYA

155

ss Orontes, *in the Red Sea. 6 April 1938*

My dearest Juliette,

Will you please send me some good advice as soon as ever you can on the food and drink of lizards? I have a little one with a scaly tail: his name is Himyar and he is beginning to show signs of understanding when he hears it. He is a nice little thing with an intelligent eye, but so far appears to feed on air. I do think you and Julian ought to come to Asolo to see him. His Arab name is Dhabb and they eat him, and he seems quite harmless and can only defend himself by wrapping his tail round him and pretending to be a small thorn bush. He hates civilisation and its noises: the only thing that lured him from his box was Mr Chamberlain on the wireless, but whether that was admiration or fright I don't know.

Dearest Juliette, do come to us if you can.

Your affectionate
FREYA

Freya spent the summer of 1938 in Bavaria, taking a cure at Partenkirchen. She was at work on *A Winter in Arabia* and wrote tetchy letters to Jock Murray who felt that she was being unreasonably harsh on her companions. In the autumn, expecting the imminent outbreak of war, she travelled to London, fortified by a hat of feathers from Madame Suzy in Paris on the way. Despite Munich, despite her continuing ill health, 'the autumn and winter of this year were among the happiest I have known'. In London, her social life was intense. The spring of 1939 saw her in the Levant, visiting the Crusader castles and travelling home via Greece 'before the curtain fell'. She was anxious to finish her book and get to London to make herself available for whatever work war would bring her.

JOHN GREY MURRAY

Villa Freia. 25 May 1938

My dear Jock,

We got back two days ago and the unpacking *has* been an affair. Your mirrors are waiting for you – only one little bit chipped off. If this letter is incoherent it is because of Himyar who is so enamoured of the fire that he tries to commit suicide. He has only seen one twice in his life, but he makes a bee-line for it right across the room.

I very much fear I shall have to lecture to the Royal Asiatic Society. It is awful: I shall be exiled from England if it means lectures every time. The R.G.S. one is probably in November. I have quite decided on a small flat, so do tell me if you hear of one. What fun it will be.

And if you are in Richmond, I will get up early and go and *ride*.

Yours,

FREYA

JOHN GREY MURRAY

Villa Freia. 27 June 1938

My dear Jock,

Sir Sydney is busy choosing out photos for the picture book.[1] You have sent me no ideas about it and I wonder how soon you want the pictures. It *must* come out for a Christmas book or I shall be bankrupt in London! I am also at Chapter II of my own book. I tried my letters and true feelings about Miss Caton Thompson on Sir Sydney and see that I shall have to publish *in toto*: friendship went to the winds and he sat devouring every word and says it will sell like a whirlwind if I leave it all in. How one does enjoy the vices of one's friends!

He is such a dear and it is like meeting everybody one has ever heard of when he talks – and so many good stories.

Do come to Partenkirchen.

FREYA

FLORA STARK

46 Connaught Square. 29 October 1938

Darling B,

I do hope you are all right again and being careful now. My cure goes on, and is really a blessing in disguise – all except financially – as it prevents my doing too much. I am busy *softening* my MS: it has given Jock the shock of his life. He has doubts as to whether I am as nice as he thought!

I had a very exciting lunch at the Halifaxes, sitting on Lord H's left – very frightened but pleased, and we had a good talk though I did not dare ask him the things one longs to know. But we spoke about Palestine and I said I thought any settlement which pleased *general* Moslem opinion would be satisfactory, and the opinion outside the country is the most important. It is all very worrying. I was amused because Lady Halifax told me that the Ambassador to Germany, Mr Henderson, was dining that night and he and Lord H were going on to a film called *Carefree*!

Yesterday I lunched with two friends from the East – went to a private view of sculpture so crowded that not a bust could be seen; then to R.G.S., spending two hours over the negatives for slides. Then to Lady Colefax's sherry party. Rose Macaulay was there, very bitter; and Leigh

1 *Seen in the Hadhramaut* (1938), a book of photographs taken by FS with an introduction by her.

157

Ashton of the V. & A. and a charming man, husband of Rebecca West. I wore my Suzy hat which causes a cold glitter in the female eye, but a pleasant expression in that of man.

Dearest love,

FREYA

FLORA STARK

As from 12 Royal Avenue, SW3. 12 November 1938

Darling B,

It was nice to get your telegram. The evening was really great fun.[1] My dress quite lovely, but almost *too* bridal: yards and yards of tulle, and silver and gold shining through, and the diamond brooch in my hair! There were twenty-five people – Huxleys, Balfours, Lady Allenby, Jock, Sydney Cockerell, Mr Hinks[2] and Violet Leconfield whom I know, Dean of Westminster and his wife, Editor of *The Times* and wife, Admiral Little, three other Goodenoughs, Lady Stanley of Alderney (charming), Viscount Gort, and a few others I didn't know. I sat on the Admiral's right and the *Times* Editor on my right and I took the chance to talk of Palestine. I hope every little may help. He was an old friend of WP's.

After dinner Julian Huxley came and sat near me. Jock took me home – and the Admiral has written me such a dear letter of thanks. He is one of the best people in this world.

I can only just keep going, and feel like a bad swimmer in a choppy sea. I have now got the lecture[3] and speech both written but still to learn: and have been asked for four Arabic Harem talks in January (£10 each) and to speak to Chatham House which is a great honour.

On Wednesday I dined with a party of six with Elinor Glyn, and a Mrs Ghika from the Rumanian Legation. Elinor Glyn is seventy-four, without a wrinkle, red hair, green velvet and pearls, lovely eyes heavily kohled, and an emotional very delicate manner. And she told us all what we were in our former lives. It was rather trying, as she says she is inspired direct by God to say these things across the dinner table and the young men were all treated rather unkindly: but *I* –she fixed *me* and said: 'This is not a woman that I see – it is a man, a young man pure and enthusiastic: there is no falsehood here, no pretence: he speaks simply: he is caged in a woman's body and he hates it, but he is too great to rebel: he uses it gracefully, but remains aloof inside it: nothing but goodness and

1 A dinner given for FS by Admiral Sir William Goodenough.
2 A.R. Hinks, Secretary of the Royal Geographical Society, 1915–45.
3 For the RGS.

truth can come from him.' So now you know but it is a little overpowering.

I gave Jock dinner in my house and we had a pleasant evening talking. Mr Perowne came to sherry next day and told me all about the Opening of Parliament which he had seen – a wonderful sight it must be. It all fills me with such sadness now.

Dearest love to you both.

FREYA

FLORA STARK

12 Royal Avenue. 18 November 1938

Dearest B,

Do not bother about the money. I will see that you get £600 lent you and that should cover all needs. I am off to the Iveaghs today – a lovely sunny day too. I wish I felt more fit to cope with all these things. The lecture is learnt, but I have to repeat it once a day to get it fixed and that takes me an hour.

I hope for a letter soon. Cheer up and do be a little moderately careful. You say it is hard to learn. After I had been lying about on milk for two and a half years, I remember walking back up Wigmore Street after hearing I must spend another six months in bed. I do not think I shall ever forget that day and I walked home after that interview quite alone. And it is now fourteen years that I have *never done anything without the feeling of fatigue*: and I have only started on *one* of my expeditions without wondering if I was strong enough to face it. Every time I hoped to be free, and to begin to live a life worth living, I have been pulled back again – and this between the ages of thirty and forty-five when life should be sweet: and very few people have ever seen through the wretchedness of it or thought it other than natural to see me as a cheerful semi-invalid. So do not think that it is *too* hard to learn a little *ordinary moderation* at the age of seventy-six, dear B!

Your
FREYA

FLORA STARK

12 Royal Avenue. 6 January 1939

Darling B,

I have a sad little piece of news. My poor little Himyar is dead.[1] It was too much for him here and though I kept him warm, he just could not

1 After an eventful life: he had escaped in Delphi among the archaeological excavations, and caused a housemaid to faint at Petworth when Freya had hidden him in a drawer with a lettuce leaf.

bear the absence of sun. I don't think he suffered, but just got thinner and thinner and the day before yesterday I found him dead, and even now I can't think or speak of him without crying. It is absurd for so tiny a creature – but I think he and I were alike in lots of ways, both rather small and lonely in our hearts. It may be ridiculous to care so much, but after all there is less difference between us and a lizard than between us and God and we expect *Him* to feel an interest. I will wipe my eyes and go to less sorrowful things.

I spent most of yesterday at the B.B.C. – first doing the first talk to Arab women – very frightening. I only read the beginning myself and the rest and the remaining three will be done by the Egyptian interpreter. I had half an hour to practise and the man there told me that mine is the best Arabic they have had so far and far better than Ronald Storrs! I then spent the evening at Alexandra Palace in Highgate being televised – an even more alarming experience as you stand with a blaze of light turned on you from engines on all sides and answer questions. It was very amusing to see the studio full of people belonging there and six or seven come to perform – a Commander in the Navy, three schoolboys, an explorer from Greenland, a caricaturist, a Professor from Korea and a Zulu with a guitar! And one could see the picture on a screen at another end of the room and compare it with the original.

Three ladies coming to lunch – V. Sackville-West, Margery Fry and Rebecca West.

Dearest love dear B,

FREYA

GERALD DE GAURY

As from Villa Freia, Asolo. 19 February 1939

My dear Gerald,

It was nice to get a letter from you. I had heard all about your lovely journey and was just beginning to feel that you were abandoning your old friends for your new (and a little hurt), when it came. How good it must have been. I have already a great homesickness for desert air – but must wait for anything really good till the autumn when I am invited by two engaging young men to ride with them from Gaza to the Indian Ocean – the old frankincense road in fact. I think *two* is quite proper, don't you? not like *one*! Anyway it is rather tempting and the Colonial Office approves in principle. Sir J Shuckburgh,[1] whom I sat next to at

1 Deputy Under-Secretary, Colonial Office.

160

dinner, seemed a little vague as to what 'principle' means; I suggested it was something which can frequently be changed.

There is a wave of optimism here for which I see no particular reason except that we are beginning to feel ready for a fight if it comes. I still think it will, because I can't see what else the two dictators can do: anyone would rather fight than go bust all alone, and that is what it comes to, but most people now seem to hope we may just escape it.

I had a lovely time lecturing at Chatham House and said just *all* I thought about 'the future policy' of Arabia. The printed and, I fear, expurgated version will be sent to you, if they do print it. When I had done, Philby got up: he let me off most kindly but said I had been 'gilding the nettle', i.e. the British Government. Mr Perowne (from Aden) got up and contradicted and there was a lively passage.

The Arabs seem hopeful, and so do their friends. I have discovered a new champion for them in Peter Wood, Lord Halifax's second son, and hope he will write an article in the *Sunday Chronicle* – though perhaps not even he can get in on such a platform. Anyway he is out and out pro-Arab.

I leave all this until tomorrow and go to Asolo, till March 15 after which the British Consulate in Aleppo ought to find me till the end of April. I hope to be wandering among those hills and castles most of the time – recovering from this social whirl. Four months is just about as much as I can enjoy before the natural love of quieter things returns.

Shall I see you at all or anywhere?

Yours ever
FREYA

SIR SYDNEY COCKERELL

Train to Asolo. 22 February 1939

My very dear Sydney,

Your letter, so good and long, reached me on my last morning in London and now my London winter is over and, as for Cinderella, the clock has struck twelve. I have been thinking, to the rattle of this train, of all the good things the time has held. For the first time in my life I have had a swim in the Social World, and begun to find my feet among its reefs and pleasant places, and found that it is a good world too if one can bear in mind to live there *sans peur et sans reproche* – fear of other people or reproach from oneself. What do you say? I think if one remains truthful in oneself, the truth in others comes out, whether in society or desert: there is no particularly adapted locality for it apart from one's own heart.

My last weekend was with Jock to whom I talked about the folly of wasting *too* much time on work! Now I am here till the 15th when I go to Syria.

Your loving
FREYA

SIR SYDNEY COCKERELL

Hama. 14 April 1939

My very dearest Sydney,

I am just back and this is my first letter. I came tramping in with my poor old horse and mule and pack saddles and found quite a number of friends rushing out to greet me: Hama is supposed to be fanatic and unfriendly, but I have found nothing but welcomes and was taken out to an Arab supper in a stone house with carved fifteenth-century windows straightaway.

I can't begin to tell you the whole fortnight's history – except that I rode or walked from four to seven hours every day except one when it rained and we stayed in one of the Assassin fortresses whose single gate is still closed at night and whose old walls have been used to build the Moslem houses that now pack the citadel. It is really wild country for riding with valleys so deep-cut and lonely, and paths more like staircases of stones; the country is still, just as it must have been in crusading times, divided by deep hatreds accidentally located in villages which are all mixed up together so that it is impossible to get one guide suitable for all. When we reached the touristy part of Safita (such a *beautiful* fortified Templar church) I asked for a pagan to show us the way and one of the nicest (and best-looking) men I have ever known in the world came and stayed on with me for the remaining ten days. His name is Isa or Jesus, which is nice for a pagan, and he was the most perfect servant with that absolute devotion which one comes upon here and wonders how in the world one can deserve it. I feel he is far too good to waste and am going to see if something cannot be done to keep him, though an Arab servant will be more difficult even than Himyar to look after in Asolo. But it would do more than halve the discomforts of any future journey to have someone who could really look after one. It is very pleasant to be looked after, though almost as constricted as being married. If Isa considered anything he heard slightly improper, he would tell me that it was not suitable for me to hear, and there was an end of it! If a crowd came round me, he could hardly bear it: his eyes just became slate-coloured with anger, but he never lost his head or made a fuss.

It is a great thing to have had this time of quiet to gather oneself together. I read Villehardouin and Joinville as I rode and I think nothing could better prepare one for the ordeals of war than this return to a time when people thought so little of life and so much of honour. It was not mere words: the spirit that lives in those old chronicles is a genuine faith and I think no book would be so good a companion to a young man going out to war as one of them.

I am well my dearest Sydney, and happy – though I would like to have you near by to talk to. I have been lonely for some reason or other: but that is good for one now and then.

Jock has written me a long letter very involved and introspective. I can't help feeling one ought not to be feeling introspective when one just gets engaged, and I am not really happy about him: but I think I am built on rather simple lines myself and not much good with the windings of the ultra-civilised mind.

If war does not come yet, I shall be in Athens by May 7th.

Dearest love always,

FREYA

FLORA STARK

Aleppo. 9 May 1939

Dearest B,

I was very sad to come back here and find no letters from you after my fortnight's absence. I expect you are writing to Greece, and I shall find them when I get there on the 20th. A kind Frenchman of the Regie sent us, Mme Seyrig and me, to Sahyun where we got three horses and rode over the hills two days across a mountain bound with oak woods and the Orontes steep below. We had trouble with one of the men who was a thorough bad lot. His horse had seven bullet wounds (healed), caught while smuggling. He wanted to blackmail and was annoyed with us for trotting, and forced me off the horse. However, Isa made me get on to his and took the matter in hand very well, and we had the man cowed quite soon. It is extraordinary how, when one is angry, one never has the slightest trace of fear. Mme Seyrig behaved very well, but she had not the revolver she usually takes, which would have been really useful. Isa was first-rate, and so angry that he rode on in silence all the way to Jisr Shogr, where we spent the night, arriving just as darkness fell through lanes in damp and rustling gardens. When we got near, the man who had not openly misbehaved said they would leave us unless I promised to forgive. I was walking ahead, keeping my hands in my pockets, as the culprit was making constant grabs to kiss them: if he succeeded, I would automatically be obliged to forgive him.

163

Isa is to arrive on July 20th if all goes well. He is such a boon: he got us a hot bath every day, and washed our handkerchiefs and stockings: did *all* the bargaining and money affairs, saw to the fighting, and tells me when I have put on too much powder – you can't have anything more comprehensive than that!

Dear love to you,

FREYA

JOHN GREY MURRAY

Villa Freia. 28 July 1939

My dear Jock,

Your letter fills me with despair. How am I to make my point of view intelligible? Not God Almighty could I let loose with scissors in my book.[1] If ever you write a book yourself (and not a piece of journalism which might be *outside* you), you will understand all the horror of your suggestion, though Sydney Cockerell should come next after God Almighty if *anyone* were to do it.

Nor can I have GCT [Gertrude Caton Thompson] taken out. If you read my introduction, you will see that my object is not to write about Huraidha at all: it is to give a picture of *methods of meeting* between East and West. It is not a point of literature at all, but is something far nearer to my heart, and on which I have a thing I *wish* to say. Anything that goes counter to this primary object of my book, I will not entertain for one moment. On the other hand, I wish to put in no personal bitterness (which I have really ceased to feel anyway), so that any suggestion to *alter* passages I will do my best to follow, provided the *object* of the book is kept in view. At present, you are trying to make a different book of it, and that is a thing I do not for one instant intend to comply with; and you may take it as one of those points on which I would not compromise.

Sydney has not written yet; but, though I would always feel him far surer than I am in points of pure *literature*, I do not feel absolutely bound to take his advice in this point where non-literary considerations, valid only to people who know and love the East, also must have their weight. These you have brushed aside, regardless of my introduction where my whole purpose in writing is explained. Have I not made it clear? I tried to.

In 100 years' time, when GCT is forgotten, the picture of the type and its role in our history of empire will remain. I believe that the survival or death of our empire will depend on whether her methods or mine are

1 *A Winter in Arabia.*

164

followed. Do you think that feeling so I would write just another picture of Arab life alone?

I think, therefore, my poor Jock, that a *compromise* is clearly indicated. I will do what I can to soften if Sydney Cockerell will mark the offending passages; and, if that doesn't do, we can either suppress the book altogether or wait a year and then look at it again in more detachment. Your affectionate recalcitrant

FREYA

HERBERT YOUNG
20 Wilton Street, SW1. 2 September 1939

Dearest Herbert,

Last night London looked like a dead city – all the houses dark, a drizzle descending, and the streets very empty as everyone stayed as stationary as possible so as to make the evacuation easier. I bought: (1) a gas mask, (2) a little bag for all one's toilet things to take with me to the basement, (3) a winter suit, and (4) French face powder which I may never see again for the next five years. I shan't go down to anything lower than the sitting rooms where there are divans that one can go on sleeping on.

My ministry[1] constitutes itself on Monday. I have met one of my colleagues and know two others already. I appear to be the only woman. I feel very frightened and inadequate about it.

I am not writing to Mama till I get a letter and know that things come through. It is better for you to send on news you think will pass.

Dearest love. Do write often.

Your
FREYA

---

1 Ministry of Information, where FS was working as an Arab expert.

6

Information in Aden, persuasion in the Yemen, talk in Cairo.

Freya had barely settled in to the Ministry of Information when Stewart Perowne telegraphed to ask for her as his assistant in Aden, a British colony for just over a century, where he had been appointed Information Officer. She set out in early October, taking with her films for a projector small enough to be carried on a camel. She paused four days in Asolo, to collect a trunk of tropical clothes and say goodbye to her mother and to Herbert Young.

SIR SYDNEY COCKERELL

Sitting at Folkestone, waiting
for Customs. 8 October 1939

Dearest Sydney,

My first quiet interval in all these days. I left this morning, feeling more sorrowful than I can say. My host, and the Murrays, and Colonel Balfour to see me off in a grey drizzling morning, and a train bulging with promiscuous aliens. I hope it may not be too long before I see this land again and not too changed a land.

My last morning I spent having a very good talk with Mr MacDonald,[1] who seemed to me a really good sort of man. He was very reassuring, resolved to stand no Zionist nonsense, but to get our White Paper on Palestine observed. Also, I found him interested in my pet plan of a school for Arabia: the idea of a strong Arabia, as united as we can make her, he is as keen on as anyone. I feel I know now the direction we are going in and can work more intelligently. It is a comfort to me to think that I may have some influence now in settling a big question for the future. I said to Mr M that my own idea of propaganda in Arabia was to lay foundations for *after* the war. If we lose, our labour is wasted anyway; if we win (as I do not doubt!), we do not need *much* immediate work. But it will be useful to have all things so truly laid that we can build a good post-war world out there; and that is a happier work than

1 Rt Hon Malcolm MacDonald, Secretary of State for Colonies 1938–40.

merely the dealing with daily German lies. It is nice to be *building* in these days of destruction.

Love dearest Sydney. Look after your dear self and write.

Your
FREYA

FLORA STARK
Metropolitan Hotel, Cairo. 1 November 1939

Darling B,

Here at last and found your telegram – very welcome in default of a letter.

I seem to have lots of friends all congregated in Cairo, and they wrote to ask me to work here, but the letter never reached. Do you realise that it is almost *unique* at present to have been asked for by *three* Government departments? My nice gay little Colonel in Jerusalem, when he saw me in to the sherry party given for me, confided that he would give almost anything to have such a thing done for him and walk in as a Lion. And he does so much better things than I shall ever do. It is all just luck.

I am *so* tired, but it is rather pleasant to wear my Paris hat for the last time for years no doubt.

Dearest love,

FREYA

FLORA STARK
Aden. 19 November 1939

Darling B,

Stewart tells me that the daily bulletin has a *bite* in it since I came already! We don't even get Sunday off from it, but I hope to get time for a walk or ride by getting up early; and rest after lunch (noon) and then office again at four.

I have two rooms to plunge into, close behind the office: they contain two beds so enormous that Noah and all his family might have slept in them, two mirrors and cupboards, five night-tables and enough bird-cages for a zoo. But I suppose I shall find a means of squeezing in among all this bric-a-brac.

Your
FREYA

HAROLD BOWEN[1]

Aden. 20 November 1939

My dear Mr Bowen,

I found Stewart Perowne very much overworked with a tropical sort of cold, so he has been persuaded to take a day or two off. He is going about a little next week – Kamaran, Berbera, and such places, and that ought to act as a tonic. Meanwhile, I take over his daily bulletin which transforms Reuter into English prose – slightly tendentious. Daily we send you mournful moans, particularly for films, but also for literature, and very much so for photographs. *Anything* you send will and will continue to be welcome. What is not actual propaganda is always useful for the troops here, who need amusement badly. And where, oh where, is the Bell and Howell projector?

The very first evening after my arrival, Stewart took me to listen to his loudspeaker in the Maidan of Crater, the native town here. You would so much have enjoyed that charming sight: the square in starlight, a dim lamp here and there where traffic in coffee – and, I regret to say, the drug *kat* – was busily going on. The figures in white gowns, bright turbans, Parsee caps, tarbushes here and there, squatting in rows in the dust or strolling in quiet groups. The loudspeaker from a roof gave out first songs of Yemen, sad and slow and very pleasant – unlike the twanging of Egypt – and afterwards the news. Everyone listened, and when it was over, a spontaneous clapping broke out all over the square. You know how rare it is to get this sort of expression out of Arabs. There was something extraordinarily friendly in the sound and quite genuine, for there are no Europeans in that crowd. As we came away, Stewart had to tear himself from the embraces of his friends among the tribesmen – quite as disreputable in appearance as my usual native friends, I was glad to see.

I see that I am not keeping within the pale of official language, but cannot *feel* official when writing to you.

Please give my greetings and my boss's also to you all.

FREYA STARK

SIR KINAHAN CORNWALLIS[2]

Aden. 8 December 1939

My dear Sir Kinahan,

It was so nice to hear from you, the first news I had of the tornado that swept our department. I am sure that you are in your right place now,

1 Orientalist at the Ministry of Information in London.
2 Sir Kinahan Cornwallis was now at the Foreign Office.

and it is awfully nice to know you are there whispering the Right Thing to do to H.M.G. at the right moment.

My own ideas I give you here below, and you may take them for what they are worth. Aden and Hadhramaut are, as you say, satisfactory. Stewart Perowne has been extraordinarily good, and his loudspeakers keep public opinion just where we want it. He is now trying to get Arabic commentators at cinemas, specially newsreels. The Yemen we have hardly touched, and I think we may count it as an Italian preserve (to all intents and purposes). This is, in my view, *entirely* our own fault. The natural tendency would be for the Italians to be disliked there (and so they are in a subterranean way). Italy is more dangerous to the Yemen than we are, and her power would not be great enough to make her feared if we were anxious to prevent it. The fault is not here; our hands are tied and we have to sit still under every Italian infringement of gentlemen's and every other agreement. Now this seems to me quite idiotic.

We are far too prone to say: 'Italy doesn't matter.' We said it in 1935 when, by attending to her in time, we could at any rate have saved ourselves the troubles of the Abyssinian war. Even when that started very few realised its implications, but in three years' time, the threat which had been obvious years before had become a commonplace. The same thing is happening now. Nobody thinks much of her penetration in Yemen, but what is the point of allowing it *unnecessarily* when we could so easily put a stop to it? I do not suggest being provocative, but I do suggest a riposte to every Italian step, however veiled; the one way to impress on Italy the value of our friendship is to accentuate such powers as we have of being disagreeable if we wish. We are thoroughly bad at dealing with Italians, chiefly because we insist on treating the whole country as Fascist, whereas we have there (far more than in Germany) a small governing faction which will always be anti-British at heart, and the larger number which, if Fascism is overturned but not otherwise, would easily become genuinely friendly.

I hope to go up to the Yemen in seven or eight weeks' time if this is possible to manage. The idea is to sit there, visit harems, rectify rumours, and alter the atmosphere as much as one can from the standpoint of female insignificance, which has its compensations. Sir Bernard [Reilly] and Stewart Perowne have both agreed to this with their usual broad-mindedness.

I shall enjoy going immensely. Of course I may not be able to do anything at all. Everyone says that it is extraordinarily difficult.

Yours sincerely,
FREYA STARK

Aden. 12 December 1939

Darling B,

Two big boats are in today, but with nothing on board except two letters from Syria and Iraq that took a month to come.

Today I have been sitting all morning over a private view of newsreels with Luqman, our nice little clerk, who had to write out a commentary in Arabic. He got so worked up over the news, he could hardly write. 'That Hitler is cursed,' he turned to say at intervals. We get very good reels now, only they have not got beyond the sinking of *Athenia* as yet. The going down of the *Courageous* was very impressive, and the destroyers rushing like sleuths in search of the U–boat, and the great mountain-masses of water boiling up when the depth-charges were thrown.

This morning I got a ride for the first time. I am to have two rides a week, for ten rupees per month, and go out in starlight and see the sunrise over the great cliff heads that hang over the sea, and get back in time for breakfast and my office at nine. There is only one ride here, but no doubt one's thoughts can vary it.

Last night Stewart and Commander Coke and I dined with AB[1] who was charming and gave us delicious food and wines on his starlit terrace. There is a cachet about his evenings which is nowhere else, coming just out of his personality. Stewart then climbed up and sat talking on my terrace till 11.30.

One does feel in Aden how indispensable women are in this world after all. The men are all in bunches together and get rather tired of their own society, and we are not very clever – English women, I mean – at making centres of agreeable and easy intercourse. There is plenty of sport, but no home where I know that the poor things can drop in at any moment and be soothed by a restful feminine atmosphere. When I am older, I think I shall just take to sitting and making myself agreeable and fill a real need in this far too strenuous world.

Your own
FREYA

Dhala. 26 December 1939

Darling B,

We had one of the nicest Christmas days I have ever spent. In the

---

1 Anton Besse.

morning I gave each of the servants a stocking filled with all I could find to take to their masters: a bottle of beer, an orange, a cabbage, lumps of sugar, crackers, and some little presents I had with me. We started off (at nine) on a procession of five horses and a foal, and three donkeys running in and out with servants, soldiers, small boys, rugs – we wound up 3,000 feet nearly (we are already 6,000 here) to where the Amir has a mountain fort. I think we saw as great a view as anywhere in the world: mountains and mountains, studded on their lower peaks with little fortress towers, with here and there terraces and cultivated hollows, and ahead of us the great blue wall of Yemen. At this height there are villages; a Jewish one we passed, the Jews with their curly side-locks all grouped on rocks to see us, looking very biblical. We looked rather nondescript except the Count, who with a wide-brimmed hat might have just landed from Biarritz, and Colonel Lake and Stewart who were correct and handsome in *kefiahs*.

As we reached the centre of the plateau, which is a huge world of its own, we saw the whole male population drawn up with rifles behind their Amir – a sight in the clear sun. Colonel Lake dismounted and inspected them; the long column (about two hundred) wound ahead with drums and dancing, the Amir caracoled about on a young chestnut to show his horsemanship, we all wound up the steep way to a fort like an old painting on the very pinnacle of the hills. Hugh sort of cacti grow among the stones like candelabra. The landscape falls away, on a far peak is the tomb of Job. The little fort is built all of stone. At the gate the army halted in two long lines, and we dismounted and went in by the dark stairs and found our servants who had come on to cook our lunch. We stood on the roof and saw all the tents spread out below, and a sentry wrapped in this scarf sleeping on the battlement with his rifle sticking out over the edge, and I visited the harem, two ladies in silver and blue brocade with ropes of pearl and Indian veils.

In the afternoon we walked down by a cleft of a valley, and got home after two hours of this strenuous exercise in the light of evening.

We found that the servants at our rest house had decorated our table for Christmas, and we had a plum pudding with flames. We drank to all our beloved and I wondered what you were doing just then. Today, we are slack and pleasantly lazy. The old Amir uncle has come to see Colonel Lake and we have escaped round the corner of the house and are writing in the sun.

Dearest love, dear B,

Your
FREYA

JOHN GREY MURRAY

Aden. 31 December 1939

My dearest Jock,

I am indeed very happy here, and feel it is almost wrong at such a time. At least I have a Puritan feeling of the sort now and then, but crush it as unworthy of the Gifts of God. It is pleasant to be among people who are fond of one, with work that is interesting, and a most friendly office – from the Secretary, whose mind I am trying to lure from innumerable young men towards the fabrication of English news, to our translator, a dear little lad of twenty who is now translating 'Adolf the Wolf' from La Fontaine, to Stewart, who, as Boss, is a constant amusement and very rarely fractious if ever (and thinks me *quite* easy to get on with, I may say!). I rather enjoy being put in my natural female place for once and just watch all arrangements being made for me with a great sense of relaxation.

Isa[1] has at last arrived. I hope he will be all right; but he finds it very hot, and came with no clothes at all (except what he had on) and I have so little time to make him settle down that I have serious fears. And he is so good-looking that it is like going in an Ascot frock to a Mothers' Meeting. I *must* stop this or it will be 1940. May it bring us all happily through.

Love,
FREYA

At the beginning of February 1940, Freya set off in a lorry with a cook, a servant, three men and a projector on a six-day journey up the torrent beds of the northern frontier to Hodeida and from there to San'a, the capital of the Yemen. The plan was to show films – forbidden by religion – in a place where British propaganda did not exist, while the Germans were active and the Italians pro-German. Freya spent six weeks in San'a, living in rooms vacated for her by the Imam's Director of Artillery.

She was back in Aden when news arrived on June 10 that Italy had joined the war. Air raids came regularly. It was now that she started thinking about a project that was to occupy her, in one place or another, for the rest of the war: the setting up of a network of committees, or cells, which would meet and talk in a pro-Ally, pro-British spirit. The Brothers and Sisters of Freedom, as they were soon called, began in Cairo and then spread throughout Egypt and into Iraq. It was not, Freya would say, 'propaganda', for that suggested an uneasy twist of deceit. She preferred to think of it as 'persuasion'.

1 Freya's servant and guide in Syria, now come to join her.

172

San'a. 12 February 1940

Dear Stewart,

I am writing from bed, having gone under completely what with the colossal dinner given me yesterday by the hospitable Raghibs and the effort of the cinema after. I did it ever so much worse than you, and you can't half guess the agony it is to me to speak in public, and when I showed Nagy how to start the engine and the thing actually went I felt like one of those amateurs who succeed in calling up the Devil; but it all went without a hitch and I was able to see the effect on Prince Qasim who talked about the Ruler of the Waves for the rest of the evening; for the first time since coming up here I was told how necessary it is to strengthen our friendship with the Arabs. Before the show he asked me: 'Do not the Italians rule the Mediterranean?' I said 'You would hardly call yourself a ruler in a house when someone else has both the front and back door keys?' and I could see the really tremendous effect of the film afterwards. But whether I shall be able to show it more widely is very doubtful.

Your

FREYA

STEWART PEROWNE

San'a. 13 February 1940

My dear Stewart,

Curiosity is the one thing invincible in Nature. The Qadhi has just come to tell me that the royal family *must* see the cinema tomorrow night. You are implored to send more films soon. I am to go at 7.30 p.m. and, as far as I can see, spend the night there. *Do* wish me luck – if you knew how I wish it were you! But I am pleased, and hope you will give me a nice pat on the back, for walking on eggs has not been in it these days.

The Qadhi sat for a long talk about frontiers, all are very hopeful of a friendly solution. He said: 'The young men want to make themselves conspicuous and there are forty troubles at once. They do not know that it takes forty years of kind manners to make oneself beloved.'

The invaluable Nagy meanwhile has been teaching the Imam to make butter. I sent him out in the morning to chat in the *majliss*, and there they were pouring fresh milk into an Italian butter machine; nothing happened; try again; nothing; then Nagy stepped out and said the milk must be one day old and saved the situation. So that in a week we have made butter, have translated **King George's telegram, and shown the British**

Navy to the ladies of San'a. It makes one feel like a dictionary.

Your own
FREYA

STEWART PEROWNE

San'a. 15 February 1940

My dear Stewart,

I am just a shattered wretch again after last night, but it went off without a hitch except for one ghastly moment when the engine wouldn't start and I felt just as one does on the doorstep of the dentist. Nagy could only be allowed in the court below with the engine-cord coming up through a window, and I had to cope upstairs in dimness and tumult, wives, daughters, female servants, and Princes of the Blood all seething round me. The Imam himself I suppose I shall never see as women are quite beneath him, but his two wives were there (the elder, Fatima, so very nice) and four daughters-in-law, three sons (Qasim, Abdulla, Isma'il), and at *least* five daughters. The explosions were the greatest success; they wanted lots more and I promised more later on from Aden.

I don't really think it matters one bit not seeing the Imam himself so long as one gets to the harem: the two ladies live in two separate palaces, the Palace of Happiness (for the elder one) and of Thankfulness for the younger, with a garden between them so that they can see each other and live 'as sisters' and the Imam is very fair and stays one month with each. It seemed to me there was a lot to be said for this arrangement, but Fatima said it was worrying to see one's husband's heart go wobbling to and fro.

It is awfully hard work to combine social affability with the running of the cinema all by oneself, but I sat over tea afterwards, and chatted over this and that, and have been told to go when next there is an 'at home' among the ladies. I don't really *like* this job, because I hate having to be pleasant with a purpose. I mean going out deliberately to make oneself liked irrespective of whether one really wants to like the people. As soon as a real liking comes it is all right, but otherwise it makes one feel rather like a commercial traveller with the rival firm round the corner. However, I think it is a good work, both for them and us and I believe the sight of the Navy has really brought home the idea of British power. 'Meskin, al Yemen,'[1] was the Queen's comment. The children had great fun talking through the microphone.

---

1 'Meskin': 'poor thing'.

Today I am meeting all the foreign colony here.

Your

FREYA

STEWART PEROWNE

San'a. 21 February 1940

My dear Stewart,

Your letters are my great and only pleasure. I should hate it if you became conceited through me so hasten to add that very few other pleasures are available. Nagy says the Italian colony dislikes me; I can't think why. I do nothing but say all round how sorry I am for them all.

Last night we had a delightful evening in the house of the Governor here. We had the cinema (which is being asked for everywhere, but is only given after royal permission has been obtained). After that we turned Berlin on the radio – so as to hear if all the ships we had just been seeing had been sunk. They are sunk by the Germans regularly once a week I explained. I can't help noticing that Berlin is less credited this last fortnight.

I am sorry for your bankruptcy: it comes of not taking my advice which is nearly always excellent, but it is a horrid feeling and I don't suppose in an office one can meet it by just overdrawing as I do. Even the Treasury however should see reason, considering how small your estimates were.

I had one of Sidonia's [1] *most* crotchety letters, telling me it was hard to think of me with fondness! I think he just likes a temperamental atmosphere. The only thing will be for us to stage a quarrel when next we are together in his presence, and then he will love us both again – as long as I watch you rolling down the rocks with absolute composure.

I am getting such a chic coat for three dollars (to replace the £5 one that Isa lost!). I saw it on a camel man, and found out where they make them, and have invented a belt for it, and you will say it is Chanel when you see it. I notice that this is not strictly official news!

Your

FREYA

FLORA STARK

San'a. 23 February 1940

Darling B,

I have been wondering what the Jews here remind one of with their

1 Anton Besse (from the character in Disraeli's *Coningsby* and *Tancred*).

175

silky curls and soft eyes and lips, and gowns and barefoot walk: it is the conventional picture of Christ, which may therefore be historically quite accurate, but it is not one of the types one likes best. But they *are* intelligent: the only people ready to adventure into new realms here, and this great plateau, held by Religion, is very like a prison for them. I went to one of their weddings yesterday, and saw the bride of twelve like an idol, her hands blue with indigo, a gold brocade sort of hood-shawl over her usual hood, her breast plastered with gold necklaces. I photographed them all, but was annoyed by the rowdy untidiness, and none of the aristocratic Arab manner of welcome in it.

A very crotchety letter from Anton Besse talking of my 'success'. What a word. To care for it, because it is my success, is honestly not in me; I am glad that what we wish done should succeed, but I would really *prefer* someone else to be on the frontispiece. Success I think is apt to cut one off from many better things: it is barren if it is thought of as personal. I don't think I am ambitious; to be able to live without material anxiety, among a few beautiful things, to keep and enjoy my friends and possibly to find someone to share in it all (and not too dull to be unbearable nor too gay to care!). I think that is what I desire, and it is not what is called *success*. I think when this war is over, I shall have done what was in me to do, and can sit and give advice to the young. Stewart will carry on; he has so many faults that no one can help being fond of him and I hope may do well.

Your

FREYA

STEWART PEROWNE

San'a. 28 February 1940

My dear Stewart,

As if there were not difficulties enough to deal with, our poor little telegraph man yesterday fell and drowned himself in a well – the sort of thing one only expects to happen in *Ruthless Rhymes*. He was such a friendly mild creature (and I had *lavished* bakshish on him) and it always gives one an unpleasant shock when the un-safety of the world is brought home to one.

It is *awful* to live in this intriguing atmosphere, with everyone practically pro-German. I go as carefully as I can, but the very fact of being successful with propaganda rouses the other side: I no longer hear that Germany will win the war; the cry is 'Poor little Germany, so much weaker, why drive her to despair?'

Yesterday I had a call from an '*Alim* at 8.45; paid a harem visit; back for my mullah at 11; call from a Sayid and arrange for cinema; rest till 4; three veiled ladies to tea; call with them on new neighbours; cinema to the Sayid's harem after supper – typical day! It is amusing to see the difference of a Great Man in his own home; you find him sitting in happy deshabille in what looks like a late Victorian nightgown; he then goes wandering about, picks up a gown here, a scarf there, gold cap and turban, *janbiya* and belt, and goes out the venerable immaculate you see in the *majliss*: all done while entertaining the lady visitor!

This morning I have had the head of police, always a rather nerveracking visit – but it was only to quote poetry as far as I could see.

Your

FREYA

STEWART PEROWNE

San'a. 6 March 1940

My dear Stewart,

I have paid a farewell visit to the chief queen, who is one of the nicest women you can possibly imagine. She took me by the hand all over the garden, which is cornfields and fruit trees – fig, quince, pomegranate, plum, apricot and peach – with a cemented stream-bed running through and a little private mosque. The palace soars up from it, half brick half stone, and fine. Ladies of the other harem, whose doors also open to the garden, were praying by the *birket* (well), all robed in white. As for the Imam, I don't believe I shall see him at all; that honour will be reserved for you! Nor will I see the Qadhi al Amri. Some people *are* too exalted to talk to women.

Meanwhile I have made a social blunder by asking to call on Seif Islam Abdulla's wife. He is, I am told, the Minister of Education and I was told to write to him for permission to visit the cloth factory; after that you would not expect him to be *also* in prison! People said in an ambiguous way 'He lives in the Qasr', but I couldn't be expected to realise that this meant prison, especially as he was allowed out for the cinema! You see how *difficult* life is here. Another blunder I have made is to ask to subscribe to the local newspaper. There would be no difficulty, they said, in having it *free*, but to ask to subscribe looks very like spying and needs a special permission.

Your

FREYA

177

Aden. 1 April 1940

Darling B,

I don't know *how* many letters of yours I have found, but it is just an orgy, and *so* lovely and I am writing now in *haste* before being swallowed in the sort of Augean stable of papers that waits. Stewart being ill, and now off for a fortnight's convalescence, and no secretary except a kind rescuer in the mornings, does make the prospect gloomy. However, I just *will not* overwork: as it is far more important to keep well and anyway the Guinness is soon due! I got here yesterday after twelve extra hours on that fiendish ocean due to the worst storm remembered by the old Scot who has been on this route for thirty-seven years. I told him I was a Jonah. The sea was like a pond as far as Perim and we sat till sunset in that strange and landlocked harbour, built over with houses now silent and abandoned but not yet ruined – till the lighthouse shone out and we set out for a little detour to Jibouti – and then the *deluge* began: Noah must have seen no different and it went on all day.

Found Stewart much better, rather feeble and he ought to go off, sad as I am. Isa gone to the dogs, quarrelled with everyone, and in fact lamentable: he asked to go back to Syria which of course is quite impossible, but I said I could get him a labourer's job, which softened him and he is now a bit chastened. He may yet do, but I do not want him for *life*: one can't have temperamental servants in an already far too emotional world.

The clothes sound *thrilling* and what *masses* of them! I shall just wallow. But do you think *pink* for my age?! However, I long for its arrival. There is something extraordinarily vivifying in clothes. I have got *four* pairs of shoes from the man in Athens, so am going to do *very well*!

Everyone here is extremely cheerful about the war, though no one thinks it will be short. I must say it is a relief to get out of the atmosphere of the German and Italian broadcasts, both equally truthful. It is difficult not to be affected, however well one *knows* their unreliability.

Dancing with the Governor on Wednesday night; I feel I have deserved a bit of gaiety.

Your
FREYA

Aden. 28 April 1940

Dearest Jock,

Your letter, a proper one written from the country, was really a treat and I am writing to thank you though *dead sleepy*. I think it may not be solely work but the hot weather also which now increases day by day so that *La Nudité Complète* forbidden in Jibouti hotels would be simply delicious. You instead took me to birch woods in Gloucestershire! Apart from that I have heard (a) that you have the proofs: (b) that my two books in their new dress are out. I hope they will bring in a penny or two for the grim axe of income tax due to fall with an accumulated weight! When is the new book due?

We follow Norway with hope and a little anxiety not for its ultimate destiny but for what officials so strangely call the Immediate Future. Do you realise that I shall never be able to write uncorrupted English again? Stewart and I are dealing with his report, he making it up and I typing with protests now and then when he is misled by his official Past into the awful phrases that patter daily in our ears.

It is getting so hot that I now have left the swagger hotel (across an open square) and creep in the shade to the Marina – and like it so much better, with an open verandah, and a sea-blue brass-bound bar, and some nice soldiers and sailors to be pally with. An Irishman there this morning, who refers to our great man as Musso the Messer, told me that 'he believed in taking things lightly, especially those that have to do with God!'

Must send this with love,

FREYA

FLORA STARK

Aden. 1 May 1940

Darling B,

I am going to try and write a diary for you but whether it will ever reach you goodness knows. War is very near today and we, as you might expect, quite inadequately prepared down here. I went at seven to listen to one broadcast at Sheikh Othman – about 700 people squatting on the sand in starlight looking to where, among some trees, the palace stands like a village church with tower. I myself see things in rather a gloomy light and induced Stewart to put a piece of preparatory talk into the broadcast, to prepare for Italy to enter the war. The people listened in silence, then walked away clapping: the Sheikh who reads our bulletins showed me his small son Muhammad and assured me that he too was a democrat although only six. As I left, the great wide street was flickering with people and lights; and as one left the town, the wide sky opened with searchlights like swords across it. They cut like a huge span into the night with the lights of Aden across the bay below. An aeroplane was caught in a web: the tentative shafts held and refused to let him go!

Women may be evacuated. I called on Mrs Worth and found her packed. The Mediterranean is closed to merchant shipping – Colonel Worth says war is not declared but 'as near as dammit': one hopes it is we and not they who say go for a change, but the whole thing is gloomy. Stewart still thinks nothing will happen: I don't. Meanwhile the harbour has filled with ships – two cruisers are in. The five submarines have crept away. Soldiers are to wear uniform: officers to remain in reach of telephones; leave is cancelled. The air is soft, hot with cool ribands through it; the lights flicker on shore, in the boats in harbour, red on the wireless staffs; they glow from the hills where the belated caves are being bored to store the Aden oil.

Your

FREYA

SIR SYDNEY COCKERELL

Aden. 16 May 1940

My dearest Sydney,

You send lovely letters and I send only scraps, but I write at the end of the day; we are blacked out so the light is dim (as the closing of the windows would make the room intolerable); the fan just moves the hot air round and round; and the fact is that one is tired with emotion; *fatigue* is the result of it if prolonged for more than a day or two. I remember this when nursing even the dearest; one longs for a decision and an end. And so with this echo of war – I work for five hours in the morning and turn out the daily bulletin, and try to prepare for what will happen the day after. Stewart treats me as if I were his wife – he always expects me to be there, but never tells me the probable programme beforehand. I keep him in a state of mild but continuous exasperation: do you think that is a sign of love or hate? It seems quite pleasant anyway.

I have found a nice sheltered corner in the garden below to sit in during raids when the Somalis are said to be going to loot all the houses (but I don't believe it). Isa I regret to say is accused of getting drunk and insulting people's religion. It is sad, because he has at last learnt to iron my clothes and generally keep the two rooms that I live in – Stewart is so obviously pleased that I had to tell him that I could hardly regret the £26 spent on Isa's coming, since they procured him the exquisite pleasure of being right! One should always give pleasure if possible, and I find there is no such sure and easy way of doing it as being wrong

Much much love dear Sydney,

FREYA

JOHN GREY MURRAY

Aden. 18 May 1940

My dear Jock,

The news is grim.[1] Mama stays in Asolo; she has just wired. We must come down to such rock-like virtues as we may have gathered from our ancestors and ourselves.

God bless you dear Jock.

FREYA

JOHN GREY MURRAY

Aden. 26 May 1940

My dear Jock,

This letter still waits for a boat and I hoped to write more happily. Oh Jock, my dear – one can't help a feeling of sickness when the B.B.C. voice comes. There is only one thing to hold on to really, that unless one allows it oneself, no other human being can beat one. We shall hold on or *die*. In my heart I have already said goodbye to all things: even to Asolo, though a dull pain comes when I think of my poor old people in the garden there. I wish they had got away, because of the loneliness that lies before them. There is still a chance Italy may stay out, but a slender one *I* think: it hangs I suppose on that twenty-five mile gap in France. Poor Gamelin.[2] What that poor wretch must feel no human being can bear to think on. I suppose he has killed himself or perhaps he may be able to die fighting.

There is touching loyalty here. The King's speech was heard by many with tears. Every mosque and temple on Sunday was filled with prayer. It is one very happy thing to see that everyone (almost) *wishes* the British Empire to remain.

Meanwhile here we have a blessed lull in pamphlets and are seeing to sandbags instead. But I wonder if we have lost the vitality for rapid thought and decision? If so I put it down to three centuries of Puritan *inhibitions*.

I am better and sleep through the heat lying like a damp shroud, and the nightly drone of planes. The authorities are much relieved because

1 Germany had invaded Holland, Belgium and Luxembourg.
2 Général Gamelin was the supreme commander of the Anglo-French armies in France.

the various religions here are making no fuss about how they are to be *buried* in case of need! After an ominous interval, an Italian ship is again in harbour.

I wish myself in England and wish I were nursing wounded instead of dealing in publicity.

Today I hope Stewart returns from Cairo and I shall not have quite this feeling of loneliness which has been very heavy all these days. (Secretary also away ill.) How lovely your descriptions of Richmond spring. May it all be preserved for pleasant days to come!

I have read my two books again for the *first time* since they came out, and enjoyed the V. of A.[1] but to tell you the truth got a little *bored* with the S.G.![2] It is very sad to have to confess such a thing.

Your affectionate

FREYA

LAURENCE RUSHBROOK WILLIAMS[1]

Aden. 26 May 1940

My dear Rushbrook,

You left a great blank when you went away; I can't tell you what a pleasant interlude your visit made; and you left exactly that feeling of encouragement behind you which helps your scattered regiment to carry on.

I am now wishing that Stewart would behave like a dove rather than a raven and send some little sign of his whereabouts and possible return. Our new secretary just went to bed when you left and stays there; and what between the news and the Italians, we have been enjoying a new sort of problem daily since you left. Every different community has a different flap of its own. The Indians contemplate removal to India, and the result is that they cease to import goods just when stocks may be required. The Arabs are removing their harems to places like Lahej and Mukalla: they have the lowest opinion of the Italians and their power to annoy, but are terrified of their own countrymen; the British wives very sensibly refuse to let themselves be evacuated and when all else fails manage to miss the P & O. In the short time since you vanished from sight in the bomber the enlistment of a native Police Volunteer Reserve has been started to protect the people's houses from looting etc. in raids, and I hope it may be extended to Lahej in the next few days. I must say

1 *The Valleys of the Assassins* by FS.
2 *The Southern Gates of Arabia* by FS.
3 Freya Stark's Chief at the Ministry of Information. Author of books on India and Pakistan.

the authorities have been very noble to start such a new venture in the middle of dozens of harassing calls which shower down upon them.

The coming of all these new calls makes one realise that we are faced with a very important change in our propaganda situation; if the news continues to be bad, we can rely little on pictures or pamphlets; we will have to call on a reserve which we have hitherto scarcely tapped – the desire of average people to *give* rather than to *receive*.

A show of power is an excellent way to appeal to the Arab; but there is also I think a natural and almost universal generosity that makes people glad to be asked for sacrifice and service; and we have rarely appealed for such things outside our own race. Now we have a tough time ahead and it is not certain that the appeal of power will be at our command; we may have to rely on what we can do without the adjunct of success.

Does it not seem to you therefore that we must study deeply and swiftly all such methods as will rally to our side not the *interested* but the *disinterested* feelings of our districts? I have long wished to go more upon this principle – long before the war, I mean. It was for this reason that – when asked for a medicine against panic – we proposed the enlisting of the young Arab volunteers. It is probably quite true, as everyone tells me, that they will be no earthly good in a crisis; but I think the mere fact that they are giving something will inspire a loyalty which mere receiving will never do. Can you imagine anything more demoralising than to sit in a bombed town *being looked after* – with nothing to do yourself! This most trying of all situations is what we expect the average native to stand up under, merely because it is less trouble to do things competently. But I am sure that psychologically the other pays every time, and as our business is to keep our districts happy if we can, I am writing you this long rigmarole to ask if you agree and if you think we should develop this idea as far as possible.

Here I suggest that (a) we keep our local population busy *doing things for us*, so as to encourage the affection which is lavished only on the receiver of benefits in an unjust world, (b) that they should do them as far as possible in their way rather than ours so as to avoid any inferiority complexes. If we can rouse the feeling of service, we can count on loyalty in difficult times. It can only be done by wise personal contact (by people like Mrs Drower or Sindersons in Baghdad, Mrs Devonshire[1] in Cairo – hardly used by us so far). We have quite a few such to call on here and a touchingly docile public to deal with. In fact I think we are much more in

---

1 Long-established resident.

touch than in most places, owing to many years of friendly government in the past.

One is anxious about everything in the north these days, and listens to the news with rather a sick feeling. I shall be glad to hear that you are back – one can hardly say safely. May all yet go well in France.

Yours ever,
FREYA STARK

JOHN GREY MURRAY

Aden. 15 June 1940

My dearest Jock,

What days and nights we live in. We have been bombed three times in ten hours and I am ashamed to say that it is the only thing lately that I have *really* enjoyed. The Italians say we are in ashes, but that is rather exaggerated. As a matter of fact it was a revelation how over fifty bombs could do so little damage. One must admit that there is something in the theory of race, else why should the Indians all panic and rush off and the Arabs behave with perfect dignity? Dear Jock you will be in it all, far worse than we – and that is not pleasant. Nothing in Europe is, just now, except the spirit of our men and allies. One goes to the news with a sickish feeling – but someday the luck will turn, if one can call that luck which is the centre of the souls of men.

You will be glad to fight. There is a strange liberation when once you have looked into the eyes of Death and know that, beyond the natural human panic and recoil, there is nothing to fear. The earth becomes your garden and pleasure ground for ever when once you know that it is easy to leave. There are two families of mankind, those who know this and those who don't, and I am glad to think that you are among the freemen.

Harold is here and it is so pleasant to have him. He is a much less volatile friend than Stewart, who just leaves me in an air raid and forgets that I exist. I don't mind being alone, but the absent-mindedness is what pains one: Doreen is having a baby in Egypt and no one knows when she can get back. I myself think we shall not be so very long in clearing up this end.

Love to Diana and baby and the best of all luck to you. May we once more sit and drink vermouth at Feltre.

Your
FREYA

Aden. 3 July 1940

My dear Rushbrook,

The result of your telegram about Colonel Thornhill,[1] and of one from him in Cairo, is that Stewart is sending me for a thorough consultation – reaching Cairo on the 15th or thereabouts and returning here before the end of the month.

We have been busy here for the last fortnight cross-questioning prisoners from submarine and aeroplane[2] – and have come to some conclusions that have a bearing on propaganda. About a quarter of the men, if segregated from the others over a period of months, and carefully 'educated' by people thoroughly at home in their ways of thought and prejudice, would become reliably anti-Fascist and even more reliably anti-German. We thought of asking to keep them here and doing the job ourselves on a small scale – and then, when the months of war had done their disintegrating work in Eritrea, letting them loose there. But there are difficulties and it seems that the scheme might usefully be developed on a far larger scale – and that is the chief reason for going to Cairo to see what can be done. We have in Malta a reserve of people who could (if carefully chosen) do this propaganda work unobtrusively. It is a long-range policy – but isn't it time to be a little long-range in some of our policies? The war looks more and more as if it might develop into one of ideas, cutting across nations and even geography – and why should all the fifth column be on the other side?

We feel very *orphan* here: no mail since June 11th. Of course one wishes dreadfully to be in England just now. Every heartfelt wish to you all from this office.

FS

Cairo. 24 July 1940

My dearest Jock,

It is six weeks since I had any letters from anyone or anywhere, and may be just as long again before I get them for my plans are *fluid*. I may be staying here or going to Baghdad. I am in the flattering but distracting position of being wanted in three places at once. I was so happy in Aden, the thought of leaving makes me sad, but there is no doubt that there is far more to do here now and that *must* come first. Meanwhile no way to

---

1 Colonel C.M. Thornhill was responsible for anti-Fascist propaganda in Egypt.
2 One of Freya Stark's jobs was to translate for the Italians who had been captured and taken to Aden.

return to Aden is on the horizon: poor Doreen has been stuck for weeks and did not manage as I did to wangle herself on to a naval convoy by being 'officially nonexistent'. But I find so many friends here and am living a social life lapped in luxury and kindness – on Friday I broadcast. I dine tonight at Mena House; last night with Russell Pashas.[1]

I came up with a little scheme: I took infinite trouble and saw dozens of people from sergeants to generals – and have at last the incredible satisfaction of feeling that I have got it into good hands. One has to resign oneself to being a *Nuisance* if one wants anything done. I wonder if I could have been more of a Nuisance and if it would have pushed the balance over in favour of calling Italy's bluff last September? I still feel it the capital blunder. Now we go creaking on.

I have been out riding in the desert – over ruins of dead towns. Everything seems very *transitory* in Egypt.

How much I long for news. How do you like gunning? And what news of my poor little still-born child?[2] I wonder when I shall see it. And have you heard anything of Asolo? If you can hear anything and can cable me I shall always be most grateful. I think best address here till one knows for certain.

I am sending two things to *The Times*, to send to you if they don't want them. It may be too late to do anything with them and they must be censored, but that happens I believe automatically.

May nothing you dismay dear Jock.

Yours,
FREYA

GERALD DE GAURY

Cairo. 15 August 1940

My dear Gerald,

I am so excited – flying to Aden tomorrow in a Blenheim. I do hope I shall be allowed to pull the trigger *once* if we meet any Fascists.

Your letter was so nice to get and I do hope we may meet soon *somewhere*: I rather think I shall be based on Egypt and with a travelling commission for Baghdad: that is what has been asked for by the Embassy here and the army too, so they ought to do it, and I am going to Aden to pack up and await orders. It does seem more useful to come nearer the centre, and it looks as if plenty might soon be happening here. I have got a *lovely* flat with a terrace looking out over the Nile and all the barges

1 Sir Thomas Russell ('Russell Pasha'), Commissioner of the Cairo City Police.
2 *A Winter in Arabia.*

with their curved sails pass just below: one can sit and watch the gossip of the river. I think I shall have to learn how to drive a car. It is fun seeing so many people again but I have dined out twenty-five nights out of four weeks and am rather a wreck. Everyone one has known seems to be in Cairo and most of them doing Intelligence.

Yours ever,

FREYA

LAURENCE RUSHBROOK WILLIAMS

Aden. 27 August 1940

My dear Rushbrook,

Just before leaving Cairo I wrote you a long letter about plans for developing a sort of whispering campaign across the Middle East. I hope that in its slow course it may reach you: one is far too cut off to be able usefully to ask much advice *before* starting on anything in an emergency; one can only do as my godfather told me to do in writing – 'to keep one's eye on the subject in view' and, knowing that your end and ours is the same, hope that the means may be the ones you would approve of.

I am very deeply comforted that you approve of the scheme for lending me to Cairo for six months. By the time this reaches you, you will have heard from my letter more in detail. The idea of the whispering campaign began with Colonel Clayton[1] and has, as you know, been endorsed by practically everyone who knows what is happening in all the north Arab lands; but the details are left to me with the most generous confidence; and the enclosed paper which I wrote out for the Governor here, will give you an idea of the lines which seem most promising to work on.

Meanwhile with a week or two in hand Stewart and I thought we might begin the good work in Aden, so that a cell would already be in existence when I leave. We are going to have our second meeting on Monday next, when ten new members not in Government service will be proposed. The actual rules of this venture are of course still vague but there is provisional agreement on (a) entry by oath and absolute secrecy; (b) payment of entrance fee and subscription – for it would we think be a mistake not to let the people think of it as their own show as far as possible; (c) the election of a new member to be unanimous, and guaranteed by two existing members, but not on military service; (d) the obligation to assist any foreign member in every way; (e) weekly

1 Colonel Iltyd Clayton, Adviser on Arab Affairs to the Minister of State in the Middle East.

reunions when the material to be 'whispered' will be given out and short training lectures given to the recruits.

If the thing does develop, it might become very important, and I very much hope that then the *direction* might be taken out of my hands. I rather hate being at the head of things and only do so when I see my pet dreams about to die for want of support. I think myself that Stewart would be far better, and perhaps you will think of it if you decide to send someone else to Aden. It is not my business and I am merely 'conjecturing', and Stewart himself is at the moment completely involved in broadcasts. And of course it is possible that we may be too late with the whole idea. But we will do all we can. After all, if the Germans whispered Leopold from his army and France from her pledged word, we ought to be able to do something with people who are on our side already in their hearts.

I must thank you again, dear Rushbrook, for your invariable kindness and understanding. I am a very bad Government servant and don't yet know how to manage a file; it is balm to a rather chafed heart to have someone so generous as you as a chief.

Yours ever,
FREYA STARK

Early in September Freya was officially transferred to Cairo having found a flat in Zamalek on the edge of the Nile. Cairo was very gay. There were dinners and dances at the British Embassy, with roses and silver plates, lunches at the Turf Club, drinks at Shepheard's Hotel. Freya was also working extremely hard. There were 80,000 Italians in Egypt, most of them inclining towards fascism. The Brotherhood of Freedom began to take shape, first on her terrace over coffee, and then spreading around the city and to other towns.

SIR SYDNEY COCKERELL

ss *in Red Sea. 7 September 1940*

My dearest Sydney,

I am still wondering whether I was right or not. On the *pro* side were (1) the knowledge that I can do far more useful work; (2) the usefulness of a double salary just now; (3) the intuition that as soon as Aden gets dull and out of things, I should be left there and Stewart go away! On the *con* side: the regret of leaving Stewart and the feeling that he will never forgive me and this is made more so by the fact that he has started a new broadcasting scheme there which is rather much for him alone. I hope he may get away too and then all will be all right, for Aden now will I believe settle into a backwater while all our energies concentrate on Egypt. Anyway, it is decided and after a painfully stormy week Stewart and I had a happy harmonious and reconciled evening and I was whisked off unexpectedly at two hours' notice the next day. What does not go down of course is that a mere female *should* be able to go off and get £1,200 a year for the asking and both Stewart and Harold have been at ludicrous pains to miss no chance of telling me that merit, mere merit, has nothing to do with it: just pure accident. I am so fond of them both that it has been lacerating and more exhausting than weeks of hard labour. On top of this came the misery of hearing that Mama was moved from Asolo: but now news from America says she hopes to get back and they think they can get both her and Herbert to America – I hope this may be possible.

I am now in a tiny little merchantman with some Indian troops in a huge convoy full of military and stores and we have been bombed twice already and expect another any time, for we are just off the Italian coasts. Four raiders came over and the huge water spouts came leaping all around, our cruisers and destroyers flashed so that they seemed wrapped in a garment of sparkling gold. We have a little Lewis gun above the bridge in a nest of sandbags and it went off in great style, but the Italians kept too high.

You cannot think what an inspiring sight it is, this sea covered far and wide with the power of Britain floating along in clear and open sunlight.

Very dear love Sydney,

FREYA

STEWART PEROWNE

On the Nile steamer. 12 September 1940

My dear Stewart,

I found I had to wait five days for a ship in Port Sudan so it seemed better to come overland and I have just sent you a telegram because it seems such a long time already since I left. I don't really feel like Cleopatra (except in the matter of age and the fact that I have been witnessing a Naval Engagement) but the barge is very luxurious and you would look quite like Mark Antony in it if you wore your black and yellow dressing gown. It is so hot in these upper reaches and on the way up in the train that I am rather a wreck – wind water land and sky all seem made of brass – far hotter than anything I have felt except the Jordan valley in June.

18 September 1940

I am continuing this from Cairo – just in time to catch Colonel Lake on his way to Aden. He is coming to dine in my flat. I have just got into it and – oh Stewart – it is rather nice to have dinner with no one drunk about, and to sit at a table with embroidered linens and lovely fruit piled in bowls of amber glass. I have just bought peach-coloured towels for my bathroom and a bath mat to match as well as bath salts. There is a lovely spare room, canary-coloured furniture with a terrace on the river and the barges and their big sails just below. Do get into a Blenheim quickly and just come and look at it. I shall ask Mrs Cawthorn[1] if it would be proper for you to come and stay: *almost* anything is proper in war time one gathers. Everyone has said 'Why isn't Stewart here too when we *need* him?' or words to that effect, the parties still being divided as to whether Egypt or Iraq needs you most.

I think we shall just be in time to get the Aden model taken up instead of a quite *wrong* scheme of *paying* whispers: I don't believe one ever gets anything really dynamic by paying (do you think 'dynamic' a revolting word?).

Do write me a *nice* letter quickly – I mean one full of nice friendly kind things. If you do I may even admit that I *may* have been a wee bit tiresome: anyway it doesn't matter, as I am quite fond enough of you to forgive you for being right, if you ever happen to be so.

And do come soon, please, please. I will drive you in a car. I'm going to buy one. One has to live dangerously somehow in war time.

Yours affectionately,

FREYA

STEWART PEROWNE

Cairo. 19 September 1940

My dear Stewart,

I have had a letter from London about my mother – dated August 21st. They put her into a cell with five women criminals for three weeks – our poor old friend of eighty-six[2] with one prisoner in another cell – and were then sending them to a concentration camp but the doctor refused to sign what amounted to a death warrant, and they had five days at home before being allowed to go with their maid to Pesaro. This was before the telegram I got with better news in Aden. I have been telegraphing again and hope it may be possible to get them out to America. I think it is all this business that has made me feel so ill – one is so helpless. Nothing can hurt them, except in their poor darling old bodies. They are too good through and through to be harmed by these evil men – but one prays that one may not be driven to hate people capable of things like these. If you see him, will you tell that nice American consul? He was very good to me those two awful days in Aden when I first heard. Mama tried to get in

1 Wife of Colonel (later Major-General Sir Walter) Cawthorn, Head of the Middle East Intelligence Centre.
2 Herbert Young.

touch with the U.S.A. consul in Venice, but no communication with anyone was allowed. I will not write more about this.

I telegraphed yesterday to you about the Italians for broadcasting and also suggesting prisoners' messages if you can get any recorded in London. They are so very effective it seems.

FREYA

STEWART PEROWNE

Cairo. 24 September 1940

My dear Stewart,

I feel rather crushed by the size of the job here. In the morning I go to Colonel Thornhill to help interview Italians: the concentration camps at present are small Fascist republics where you sing *Giovinezza* instead of Grace before meals and never move without saluting the Idea of the Duce: it would seem a simple affair to put Fascists in one camp and antis in another, but it takes lots of doing. The poor little newspaper is now being harassed by both pro- and anti-Fascists – and suffering the fate of all Moderates, and we are trying to persuade Colonel Thornhill to let it be run by Italians even if they sometimes say things we don't quite like. It all means hours of talk with the most difficult people.

The Brothers of Freedom may soon I hope begin to materialise. I have got Lulie[1] there to look round the local Hadhrami colony to start a sister-circle to Aden.

Yesterday Mary Cawthorn and I went to look at cars – and I believe I am going to buy a baby Austin and have it painted green in memory of your little Beetle: at present it is chocolate colour and incredibly dowdy but they say it is good inside, a thing one is always hearing about the dowdy and I am always inclined to doubt.

I have had a visit from a charming old man called Darcy Wetherbee who sat talking about things like Crusaders in the Caucasus and the route from Burma to Siam (waving his hand to show just where you turn to the right) and he is going to try and find me a horse to ride: he kept hounds in Peking. When one talks to people of this sort it seems most natural that we should be ruling the world.

Gordon Waterfield[2] was with the French at the collapse and is hopeful for the future. He says they refrained from blowing up one of the Maine bridges because it was crammed with refugees. We on the other hand told a Belgian frontier village that all who remained in it after a certain hour would be shot, and we shot (the place crawling with spies): only

1 Lulie Abu'l Huda had joined FS's staff, and was later to open up the women's side in Palestine.
2 Reuters' Correspondent in Rome, expelled by Mussolini, and in Paris when the German offensive began.

hope that one does right. I go on doing this Italian stuff here with the thought of my mother constantly before me, and wonder in a rather miserable way. Gordon Waterfield's parents are also trapped and he has the same problem. They themselves would wish one to carry on.

Your photograph is much admired even by the Italian anti-Fascists in spite of its Dictatorial looks.

Yours affectionately,

FREYA

SIR SYDNEY COCKERELL

Cairo. 9 October 1940

My dearest Sydney,

A mail long overdue at last brought a glorious batch of letters from you, beginning with 26 June and ending 24 August – a proper *feast* and I feel remorseful at the thought that only one of mine went to you in the last three weeks. Here we are, if not ready, yet as ready as we can. The Army in good heart and pouring in in ever greater numbers; Cairo itself feeling definitely unheroic; and a small group of people, of whom I alas am one, trying at this eleventh hour to inspire harmless feelings into 80,000 *Fascisti*, most of them still at large. I don't know whether my work here is useful; but it is interesting and exhausting and means on some days a constant conversation of ten to twelve hours. My flat is lovely: the barges, the sunset, the ibis, all pass under or over my terrace, and I have bought two carpets and a silver coffee pot. Also a Baby Austin car I am learning to drive: it gives sudden bounds like the Ancient Mariner's boat, and very nearly sends me 'into a swound' too. I have had four driving lessons so far.

Dearest Sydney forgive this poor letter. It takes most dear love.

Your

FREYA

JOHN GREY MURRAY

Cairo. 5 December 1940

My dearest Jock,

It's rather ridiculous – your last letter to arrive is August 9th! I would like to have something more recent in these days of destruction. It was a very nice letter, and a comfort to me. All one's true affections mean very much just now. Ever since the uprooting at Asolo, I have felt most strangely lonely as if all my foundations had been shaken, I mean the visible foundations that depend on human habitations and relationships. And to tell you the truth it is a heavy task to have to do anti-Fascist work when one feels it may have such grim results over there. One just goes on and tries not to picture things. I would give I don't know what to know my two old people safely out. I believe Italy will be captured by Germany very shortly.

Here all goes steadily and risingly optimistic. I have been down with my third attack of 'flu these four days, not going out of the house, but rising from bed (a) to meet my young men's committee; (b) to meet my ladies' committee (far more exhausting); (c) to give my weekly evening party; (d) to give lunch to a mixed Anglo-Egyptian party; (e) to give lunch to the Air Marshal[1] and others – among them nice Colonel Bagnold who motors up sand dunes. All this makes influenza rather slow and I feel very old, worn and exhausted just temporarily (old possibly permanently, but one may resuscitate even from that).

I begin to fear that the war is going to elude Egypt after all and wish I had studied Greek instead of Arabic. Here we deal with nothing but the machinery while you are having all the explosions. I hope they leave you and Diana safe, dear Jock – may 1941 end well for us all.

Much much love to you,

Your
FREYA

SIR SYDNEY COCKERELL

Cairo. 6 December 1940

My darling Sydney,

I write this with only the vaguest hopes of its being a Christmas letter, but whenever it reaches you it will take some of those loving thoughts which go constantly towards you. Surely the air is fuller of love and anxiety than of bombs and splinters, if we could only see!

My work here is very interesting and I am almost *too* independent; I wish someone would step in and take the regulating of it which is far too big a job for me. I have obtained a very nice secretary who is also a friend, Pamela Hore-Ruthven. The Brotherhood of Democracy has grown to 200 members: the object is to make it 20,000 next year, but how am I to run a machine that size? It makes one in love with the idea of quiet obscurity in one's garden for the rest of one's life.

Such a variety of people come. Today it was two Yemenis, who have heard of my little society and want a branch extended to them. Then a Syrian came, and then the Air Marshal to lunch; my neighbours are people from Transjordan: the two girls drive their own cars and one has

1 Air Chief Marshal Sir Arthur Longmore, ADC-in-C RAF Middle East 1940–1.

an Oxford degree. Cairo is a sort of melting pot, with every race class and fashion in it and to pick the good and leave the bad is no joke. Many are very friendly: many too are saturated with propaganda: and few are courageous.

Dearest Sydney, all this gossip is merely the trimming to the one question I have at heart – if you are well and unharmed. I hope you are remaining in the country.

Very very dear love to you,

FREYA

STEWART PEROWNE

Hotel Cecil, Alexandria. 7 February 1941

My dear Stewart,

I keep on *beginning* letters to you and something interrupts. Yesterday I came here on a five days' evangelist tour and decided to try my little car on its first real journey and of course we ran into a *vicious* dust storm on the desert road, the sand just like small stilettos and if it weren't for the British army I should be there still, as the starter got clogged, and the pipe for water *burst* and the lovely paint seems to be losing its first-time careless glossiness.

I am coming more and more to the conclusion that my job needs a man as well as the womanly touch. Our Men's Committees go beautifully under our gentle hands, but a man would make all the difference in the Ladies' Committees. Apart from such levity, you know how little ice our sex cuts in the oriental mind. I think if we want really to make a big thing of it a more impressive standard bearer is required.

Do you know Stephen Longrigg? He is going off to govern Libya under Jumbo.[1] It is quite a business to keep track of all the stripes one's friends are adding to their sleeves. I am beginning to feel rather sadly that I shall soon know nothing but brigadiers: last year was bad enough already with all colonels.

Pamela and I have been lent a tent which we plan to put up somewhere beyond the Pyramids and go out to sleep there in summer. I do so hope that you may be joining this party. We think of having a small colony. Also of starting a donkey club. You wouldn't think from all this that I am a thoroughly over-worked woman, but I am and think longingly of a month's leave and to dash up, say, to Isfahan. There does not seem to be any prospect but wouldn't it be lovely?

---

1 General Sir Henry Maitland Wilson: GOC British Forces in Palestine and Transjordan 1941; C-in-C Allied Forces in Syria 1941; GOC 9th Army 1941; C-in-C Persia and Iraq 1942–3; C-in-C Middle East 1943.

Lots of love dear Stewart, do come soon.

Yours affectionately,
FREYA

STEWART PEROWNE

Cairo. 26 February 1941

My dearest Stewart,

Your letter, such a nice one, has just come and makes me wish I was with you. I feel that a little *Subordinatezza* is just what I should like. There seems no chance of it at any rate for the next few months simply because, as far as one can see, no Arabic-speaking English women *exist* and the idea of a return to Aden is just stamped on all round.

I go to Baghdad for six weeks in a fortnight's time leaving poor Pamela to deal with the committees of which we now have 524 members. What a *nightmare* and how I begin to hate democracy but don't, don't say this abroad. I don't really, but I feel the Committee is just too much with us. I long for a camel or even a donkey. There is a lovely feeling of spring about, all the fields full of young flax or corn or beans or flowers – a war or an office seems monstrous.

As for Momo Marriott,[1] I gave her your messages. She had just heard from her husband who is commanding the column round Barenta and said he 'had had a good day's shooting and got six grouse and a gazelle'. Nothing will ever make us comprehensible to the rest of the world.

News of Mama was good on January 20th and goes on being so *inshallah*.

Your affectionate
FREYA

SIR SYDNEY COCKERELL

Baghdad. 13 April 1941

My dearest Sydney,

I have neglected you, but not in my thoughts – but I have been, and am, very tired these days. We are in the midst of crisis: it looks a little less like breaking out militarily than it did a few days ago, but my only useful share in it all is endless Talking, and I am beginning to feel as Thomas Carlyle did about the Noble Silent men – I talk about ten hours a day, mostly Arabic and always politics, and that is why I have been too tired to write.

The crisis went off quietly enough, and I must say all the foresight and

---

1 Wife of Major-General Sir John Marriott, KCVO, CB, DSO.

good management were on the other side. We are now on the horns of a dilemma – either to use force in a very poor cause or not to use force and be rather small. I think that to push back a government on to a people who are not ready to lift a finger for it themselves is a *bad* cause. However we have a very good man here, and I think we shall get out of the mess.

I was in the middle of the only demonstration, being caught in it as I was driving up the main thoroughfare: about three thousand students with banners, and dancing, and patriotic yells. They engulfed the car and surged along on either side, giving it a kick or spit now and then: I kept smiling in an interested way and said 'Ya meskin'[1] when they spat which made their friends laugh at them – but I was quite glad to see the end of the procession and so was the driver who made things no better by murmuring 'Dogs sons of dogs' in a sort of recitative all through. There is no violent anti-British feeling – only a regretful fear that they may not have backed the winning horse in the war after all. Our news never gets to them and their thoughts are moulded by the Berlin radio.

A few old friends are left here and I am happy to find them just as they were.

Dear dear love,

FREYA

1 'You poor things'.

7

The siege of Baghdad, the Brotherhood of Freedom

In April 1941, four Iraqi colonels, known as the Golden Square and much under the influence of the Germans, staged a coup in Baghdad. Led by a politician called Rashid Ali Gailani, they took over the post office and the radio station but failed to arrest the British-supported regent, Emir Abdulillah, who had been spirited away from the city hidden under a rug on the back seat of a car belonging to the American minister, Mr Knabenshue.

Sir Kinahan Cornwallis had recently been appointed Ambassador. The embassy was besieged. Freya was one of the last to arrive in Baghdad, before its gates were closed on May 2. On May 30, Rashid Ali and the colonels fled to Persia. The siege was lifted. Freya wrote very few letters describing the event, but she did keep a detailed diary, of which the following are a few extracts.

2 May 1941 The Chancery is a bonfire, mountains of archives being burnt in the court, prodded by the staff with rakes; black cinders like crows winged with little flames fly into the sunlight.

Dormitory upstairs; uprooted women; horrid look of places meant for a few people and crowded.

Petrol tins of sand everywhere for bombs; cars parked on lawn; men sprawling asleep round the blue-tiled fountains in the hall to be cool; nurses. Lucknow feeling, very disagreeable. Pathetic looks of doglike trust of Indians; gloomy looks of Iraqis; imperturbable, hot, but not uncheerful looks of British.

3 May 1941 A mob came against us with war chant and drums – black silhouettes and their banners crowded against the sunset over the eyebrow arch of the Khota bridge.

I was given a mattress, pillow, and blanket, and laid it out with my Sulaimaniya rug on a terrace above the river and the police. The sunrise draws flaming swords behind the black of Baghdad's river houses and low domes. The sky turns green to blue; the clouds red to orange. The purple river – a hurry of small triangular ripples – rushes like the German armies to meet Eternity. I dress in the early sun.

Came down to breakfast at H.E.'s table: very nicely laid, no eggs. H.E. very calm: gives the certainty of deep feeling with no means of knowing

197

how he conveys it – by great honesty in his words I think. He has been through many a stormy sea before.

4 May 1941   I played bridge last night distracted by the news (false) that Rutba was taken. Extraordinary to see how a rumour spreads: four people had actually *heard* and all efforts to suppress were vain.

The most constant sound is the cooing of doves, like pacifists; as soon as the cracking of rifles stops they are at it again.

One of our dormitory ladies has a bad character, not supposed to be safe with property. A horrid feeling. She has quite a human smile. Difficult anyway to know a good woman by sight.

7 May 1941   Last night we had a concert, but we were not allowed to applaud, fearing that the sound of it across the river might be thought of as rejoicing over the air raid.

8 May 1941   Find my way through mazes of barbed wire and lorry barricades to the front gate to chat with police there. Quite quiet and apparently friendly world outside.

A horrible beauty there is about a fire in a town. The great convolutions of the smoke rolled northward above the quiet houses: still there in the early morning, when Baghdad above the water looks like some dingy but still beautiful version of the Grand Canal in Venice.

10 May 1941   The Lucknow feeling is settling down to one of ease and boredom.

Dined with H.E. last night: good to sit at a well set table and wear an evening gown. But the talk is rather shaky, as the guests are chosen in turn in order of merit and that has nothing to do with the art of conversation.

14 May 1941   It continues hot. The big doors are closed except in the evening and we have been told to wear topees (as if one could go out shopping) and to guard against heat strokes.

A spent bullet tied with a piece of string to a notice has been paraded before us all to impress on us the dangers of walking in the garden when people shoot. As the whole place has been snapping with machine guns and only *one* bullet was picked up, it seems to me that the argument works the other way, but that may be just my undisciplined mind.

16 May 1941   The policeman at the gate, staggered by the mass of cosmetics we sent for, said he couldn't think how the harem which is to be murdered in a few days could still be thinking of things like powder.

A woman asked if I didn't think it time for us to give up using our lipsticks but I mean to be killed, if it comes to that, with my face in proper order.

17 May 1941   A feeling of gloom I do not share, since one could not have a better field to meet an enemy than this of Egypt–Palestine–Iraq so far and difficult for him. We must wait, hoping that our importance on the Indian route may bring us relief – but not I imagine very speedy. The gloom I think comes from a silly habit of trying to hide the dark prospects instead of frankly asking the whole community to share. This treating of everyone as if they were small children would make a saint gloomy.

29 May 1941   Small arms they say have been heard from the direction of the iron bridge. There is something indescribable in the slow approach of this noise, so full of fate, so full of all the unknown, and so much a contrast to our stagnation here.

1 June 1941   All gates were open this morning; H.E. made a moving speech – was cheered – and all available cars went to meet the Regent. The crowd looked, I thought, very ugly – remarkable change from a month ago. We drive across the iron bridge – no visible damage anywhere except at the corner of Feisal Maidan. No friendly spirit visible.

I am the only woman in all this gathering (and worried at having no stockings and very short skirts) and reap perfect harvest of smiles. Long line of cars glittering in the sun; through the dust their back windows send sword-like flashes. We have done this with only two battalions – colossal bluff.

3 June 1941   All quiet this morning and the inmates of the Embassy are allowed to go out freely.

In the afternoon Bish[1] and I leave in a Lockheed. Reach Lydda just as daylight goes in a glowering sunset, and Jerusalem and the King David Hotel in the dark. What a dinner, with champagne, at 10.30 in the *Regence*! The people dancing look quite awful compared with our nice shabby crowd to which we have grown accustomed!

FLORA STARK

Cairo. 30 June 1941

Darling B,

It feels still very rash, like a tempting of Providence to write my daily diary to you – you should have left three days ago and the telegram was not clear whether to or from Lisbon; but anyway you should be on the way. I shall not feel safe till I get a telegram from U.S.A.

Of all my letters only one seems to have arrived, so you probably know very little of my surroundings here. I wish you could see them.

1 Adrian Bishop, a former employee of the Anglo-Iranian Oil Company and more recently an Anglican monk, was attached to the Embassy. He was killed in an accident in Teheran in September 1942.

199

My flat is so nice now, after its *iciness* in winter: a cool north breeze blows through it from the lesser Nile (the Blind Nile they call it), and the slow barges filled with straw, or cotton, or bricks, come sailing by, their masts taller than the landscape of houses and distant palms behind them. The first room in my flat is the dining room, with plain white painted chairs and tables and cupboards. I bought a Persian picture to look at during meals, all reds and gold, with a view that leads you away into a sort of Golden Samarkand distance. The drawing room is a double room opening out of this, and is also all white with brown curtains and lovely Kilims blues and dull pinks which look beautiful with red roses. Then there is a spare room, furniture all painted yellow, with a wardrobe used as my *cellar*, and then my bedroom, which is almost all windows, and furniture mauve, with curtains dark blue and magenta stripes and a violet bedcover. I have a Kurdish blanket given me in Baghdad, all crimson, purple, and green with gold threads, so that it looks very rich. I wish you could see it all. My little car is blue and is said to be one of the chief menaces to the general safety of Egypt.

Darling B, it is lovely gossiping to you – I ought to be at work.

Yesterday I lunched at Shepheard's and met Randolph Churchill whom I thought a quite insufferable young man with appalling manners. I was told afterwards that he is doing us more harm than any two Germans, just by being himself. He is extraordinarily like his father to look at except that his father is *solid* where he is *fat*. Perhaps he may yet emerge from all this chrysalis: but he is over thirty and should have done something by now.

1 July 1941

I began the morning going through the lists of my party on Friday. Every other Friday we have thirty to fifty people, half English half Egyptian – we find a speaker to talk about something non-war for twenty minutes, and nobody dresses, and any sort of people are welcome. I was told I could never mix social layers in this way, but it *has* succeeded, and my Fridays have been great fun: but it means a lot of work with telephoning and invitations and I am thankful now to have a secretary and not have to do it all myself. After all this I went and saw the Oriental Secretary and had a chat about things in Persia, which is the country he likes best. Then to lunch with Steven Runciman who is here from Sofia and then had a free afternoon and slept till six and am now ready for my Committee of Young Men which goes on from eight to ten. Then I go to neighbours to meet General de Gaulle.

There is a lull here at the moment but no one thinks of it as much more. The Alexandria raids have made people furious with the Germans. An enthusiastic young pro-British Egyptian said to me: 'I wish they would raid Cairo. Nothing we can say is such good propaganda!'

Your
FREYA

FLORA STARK

Cairo. 4 July 1941

Darling B,

I was impressed by General de Gaulle. He is rather like a Rodin to look at, cut out roughly and unfinished with beautiful and very carefully done bits here and there, such as his hands, and his eyes and brow, which are very sad. I had a committee so could not go to dinner but went to coffee and then he came and sat beside me and we talked about Syria and the Jebel Druse, and not about the war. One can't help feeling that one might get on quicker in Syria without the Free French, but that is heresy.

Wednesday is chiefly famous for my ladies' committee. They will come and tell me what ought to be done when every single thing they had to do themselves has been neglected. However one of them went away and said if there were 100 like me in Egypt no propaganda would be needed, and after all the root of propaganda is to make oneself liked. I had a lunch party with Peter, General Wavell's A.D.C.,[1] talking sadly about their departure for India. Everyone will miss them so much.

General Auchinleck, the new C-in-C, and his wife were very nice to me and invited me to India, and he seemed to me a very intelligent imaginative soldier. But General Wavell is more than that – a great man with a simplicity and gentleness about him that makes one love him.

I have been buying hats, one gayer than the other. One is like a cartwheel, pale blue, with the hours and dials of a clock on the top in pink braid. The other is red, with a *bouquet champêtre* on the top pinnacle of the crown. I went to meet a friend for a short walk in the zoo, and asked at the gate if an Englishman had just gone through. 'Yes' said the man: 'there are plenty of English in the garden. But would not an Arab do as well?' So I have had doubts about my hat ever since.

Your
FREYA

JOHN GREY MURRAY

Baghdad. 21 July 1941

My dearest Jock,

This isn't really written in Baghdad nor even in Cairo but midway in a little seaside Jewish colony where I am having three days' rest and if you

1 Peter Coats.

201

knew how tired I am you would think it wonderful of me to be writing at all. I felt I just could not go on without a stop: Baghdad siege, six weeks with both assistants ill, all arrangements for leaving Cairo (on three months' loan to Baghdad) and the Iraq summer climate before me. I felt I *had* to take three days and I have been enjoying every second of them, seeing *no* one, and hardly ever reading except *Paradise Lost* now and then, but lying under a parasol listening to the sea. It is a perfect place: clean pension with pretty girl, and garden to sit in, lovely food and fruit and cream in cornucopias figuratively speaking: a long yellow shore with leaping, biting foamy waves (very dangerous but I just sit on the edge) – and *nothing* to do except walk south towards Carmel or north towards Syria along a quite flat shore. If aeroplanes fly above, they go and raid Haifa where they have things much more worth while than us. And the Jews are quite a nice colony, mostly from Germany. Tomorrow I leave this haven and go on in my little car for Baghdad against everyone's advice. I picked up a charming Major to come from Cairo with me and he saved my life by snatching the wheel when I went to sleep, so I should be glad of someone to go on with.

Love always to you and Diana.

FREYA

JOHN GREY MURRAY

Mount Carmel. 1 September 1941

My dearest Jock,

How exciting the world is with all these comings and goings! I shall be proud to godmother little John. What fun! When the war is over I think I shall dedicate the remainder of my life to my godchildren – three girls and two boys at present. I shall either live in a village in England or in a white-washed villa in Greece – or of course both if you provide me with the income. In the English village I should like to keep the shop: that is the only way to have a finger in everybody's pie unless you are squire or parson – and it would be a much more amusing angle from the shop.

I have been amusing myself these idle mornings under the pines counting the names of as many books as I can remember reading and was surprised to find how difficult it was to reach 850: I then counted the people I could remember, and reached 1,200 easily. I think biographies could quite well put such a list in their appendices – one is very much made by the books one reads after all.

I now have General Weygand on Muhammad Ali, which has a secondary interest as it shows the depth of the General's anti-British feelings even before the war. In the account of the siege and fall of

Missolonghi he *never mentions Lord Byron*, in fact only gives one cursory reference in the whole account of the Greek war. You would think the whole history of the East Mediterranean was made by Napoleon. The most parochial nation in the world the French.

Heaps of love to little John and his Mama and sister.

Your affectionate

FREYA

SIR SYDNEY COCKERELL

Baghdad. 25 October 1941

My darling Sydney,

Your letter of September 3rd is the last I received and it came quite a long time ago; one does not get anxious, as there is no law or sequence here in mails, but I feel a gap. However, I have lovely letters from my little group in Cairo and they say at last the value of our efforts is being generally applauded: we have 1,800 brethren, all volunteer Egyptians in the cause of Democracy: we have the blessings of the Egyptian government (I got my prettiest assistant to interview the Minister); in fact we have everything but sufficient money to carry on. I got absolutely rabid, being provided neither with house car nor anything and made a protest direct to H.E., and now we are going ahead, have found a charming house and garden, are rapidly furnishing it in old rose and powder blue and a few carpets, and hope H.M.G. will approve. Every political officer gets more salary than I do, house, entertainment allowance – and it is *far* easier at the moment to get political officers than Arabistic women. Enough of this grievance; but when one sees how much time has to be wasted on making wretched little Treasury clerks at home alive to what may be necessary in Baghdad and not necessary in Tooting, it is very exasperating.

I am reading Storr's *Orientations* and think it's rather trivial: a trivial mind in all those great events.

My Pamela [Hore-Ruthven] is so lovely and charming – everyone falls in love with her – I feel now and then a little sort of *wistful* feeling, myself getting so elderly and never beautiful, but find how good it is to keep such loveliness about one, curing one of self and of that terrible walling up of one's own which sometimes comes to the middle-aged who wish to keep their illusions. Here is the end of the paper and no time for more except very dear love always.

Your loving

FREYA

Jerusalem. 13 November 1941

Darling B,

I ought to be in Cairo, but felt more than usually miserable on the aeroplane – very difficult to chat nicely with dear Pat as we drove up that lovely country and finally when I found an invitation to stay in Government House felt I must wait till after lunch; lunched at King David Hotel; felt worse and worse; drove up, grand car with crown fluttering in the breeze on the little flag: found nice Hermione,[1] a Cairo friend now private secretary here, who let me rest with tea in bed; discovered a temperature of 102, and am now convalescing from sandfly fever. It has all happened rather nicely, as I needed a rest anyway and Jerusalem is glorious air to convalesce in. The view from my room more lovely than words can say: the ancient city, with temples and walls, visible in a gap of the hills, with the valley of Jehoshafat running down to the Siloam pool in foreground.

Lady MacMichael[2] is most kind and refused to let me pack off to hospital as I suggested. The rest of the family I haven't seen but hope to go down a bit tomorrow.

I have just finished a book on Europe in 1940 by Clare Boothe[3] (*Spring Comes to Europe*), and thought the writer had a charming personality, and the very fact that all is put haphazard, in very racy language, makes that tragic picture of spring last year extraordinarily vivid. She says that only a new spirit of religion and faith can save the democracies. But my own conviction is that we are winning because we *have* that inner religious faith and the French gave up because they *hadn't* got it. Churchill certainly has that religious faith in his cause and so has practically every young fighting man. I think it is a pity we have made up a sort of game by which when I say 'pale mauve' the other fellow knows I mean 'bright purple' and answers 'shell pink' meaning 'scarlet': it takes years of a foreigner's life to know what we mean and then he rarely gets beyond the fact that it is something different from what we say. I was telling Pam the other day that I think truth much more important than modesty: they are not incompatible, but it doesn't seem to me to be *true* modesty to say you are a poor tennis player, when you know you are a good one: the only mistake is to think that your being a good one is a matter of any great importance.

Lady MacMichael is half French, and has a way of saying exactly what

1 Hermione Ranfurly, PA to General 'Jumbo' Wilson, later shared a house with FS.
2 Sir Harold MacMichael was High Commissioner for Palestine and Transjordan 1938–44.
3 Journalist wife of Henry Luce, proprietor of *Time-Life*.

she thinks which I like though I believe it has its drawbacks in an official setting. The other night at dinner I met a cheerful brigadier ready to take on a bet that war would be over next May – the most optimistic I have yet met. I don't think it myself, but stood for September.

Dear love,

FREYA

FLORA STARK

Cairo. 23 November 1941

Darling B,

Here now I am in the thick of it all and the Cairo life seems to be going on with its extraordinary atmosphere of contrasts and unreality. The battle is at its height out on the desert; we are smashing their tanks – and we took them by surprise, a feat almost unparalleled and very carefully thought out. We see a fantastic number of people passing by here from every corner of the world. Yesterday's party had Eve Curie, an interesting fiery creature with that curious rather fascinating rather repellent French hardness. I sat on Captain Lyttleton's right and had an amusing talk as to 'how to be rich'. He told me that he had been very rich and enjoyed it no end: I thought one could *enjoy* money if one began by eliminating philanthropy and then chose a hobby which would make you *feel* poor however much money you have.

On my other side was Victor Cazalet, who is A.D.C. to General Sikorsky[1] and a friend of Lionel Smith. He and I had a heated Jew-Arab argument all the way out: he told me he felt ready to die for Zionism though he has no Jewish blood in him. I liked him: full of contradictions and ardours. I thought afterwards that the Jews have now for the *second* time the chance of a *spiritual* kingdom, and for the second time are throwing it away because their understanding is only material: when their Messiah came, they did not recognise him, and now they could live in perfect peace in Jerusalem if they did not want the political control. I must meet Victor Cazalet again and have it out.

I lunched at the Wrights and sat next to Air Chief Marshal Tedder, a quite charming person full of dry wit with whom I agreed in deploring our inability to play anything but cricket. In the afternoon I saw Momo Marriott whose husband has the Guards' Brigade (just remembered not to give information of localities): and Joan Aly Khan came in and says she will work for me. I have plenty of women now but no man yet. Sir

---

1 General Sikorsky, the Poles' leader, later killed in an air crash, as was Victor Cazalet.

Walter Monckton[1] says he wants to help me all he can and that he has heard from everyone, including the Minister of State, that I have done good work: I hand on these bouquets because it will give you pleasure, and if you knew *how* many reputations have been lost this last year and how few survive in their jobs, you would be quite impressed.

Poor Joan has been having a lot of trouble with her Aly, who, having made himself most conspicuous with various ladies, went off in furious and unfounded jealousies over her. He told Momo that I was the only Englishwoman who could understand his sort of temperament, which – I said to her – I consider a very non-flattering distinction: the less one understands it, the better. Joanie, one of the best women in the world, looks very pale and thin.

I saw Amy Smart,[2] who knows the lady who is being sent to help me, and says she is governessy and quite unsuitable – an awful prospect.

This morning John Shearer (Director of Military Intelligence) came to breakfast and stayed just ten minutes before rushing back to his battle. It is by no means over, but goes well so far. *How* I wish I were out there.

Your own

FREYA

FLORA STARK

Cairo. 30 November 1941

Darling B,

The delay with this letter is due to the fact that I am trying to find some way of sending it with a reasonable chance of arrival. Perhaps they *do* arrive: I have just got yours from Lisbon; but the ordinary way seems very erratic and undependable.

I am very busy, but trying to keep fit (a) by always walking to the office, forty minutes and mostly very pleasant along the river; (b) by breakfasting in bed; (c) by going to bed early three times a week.

Yesterday I had Sir Walter Monckton and John Shearer to lunch and it was very interesting. Sir Walter told me, after, that John and the C-in-C are the two people whose contribution to the victory are most talked of just now. John told us about London and how inspiring it was to talk to the P.M., and how once when he asked him something about 'after the war', Winston just tramped about the room biting his cigar and saying: '*After* the war – I'm going to *win* the war, and other people can look to the *afterwards*.'

It seems that Eve Curie was flown to the front by Randolph with no authority. I said to John, I was hoping he would arrange for me next. He

---

1 Director of Publicity for the whole of the Middle East.
2 Wife of Walter Smart, Oriental Counsellor at the Cairo Embassy.

said: 'You *wouldn't* if you knew what the men at the front say about these visits.' For one thing he pointed out that all the sanitary arrangements are so public that everything just *stops* when a woman is in the camp.

I have now made an estimate for this year's expenses, which mount to £10,000, and I wonder if that will go. My little seed has sprouted so much that one can hardly keep pace with it.

Your
FREYA

FLORA STARK

Cairo. 25 January 1942

My darling,

I am back from Alexandria – a three days' visit filled with the Brotherhood of Freedom: there are over 200 committees, about 3,000 people, and I was incapable of dealing with more than a fraction: but it was rather touching, the most of them workmen, and all so full of enthusiasm. I had one crowded meeting of heads of committees, at least sixty packed into tiny rooms, and a selection of them got up and made speeches and poems: and the head of all the workmen ended a great harangue by coming to press my hand and say 'Tell them in England that the workmen of Egypt are with them.' I had to make a speech in Arabic. Oh B, I wonder if you can realise what it means to get up and go and talk to sixty strange workmen in Arabic who all look upon you as their spiritual leader, when you are just out of bed with 'flu? They are so touching: and they are so ready to throw themselves and all their troubles in one's lap.

In the evening the Naval Chief of Staff took me to a night club where we sat looking at revivals of 1890 costumes and turns till midnight. Alexandria feels far nearer the war than Cairo: nearly everyone wears the good thick battle dress and luggage is coming and going all the time. It was amusing at the station to watch the 'oppressed' Egyptians strolling by dressed to the nines, a porter carrying their little bags, while our licentious soldiery slogged along half-buried under rifles and packs.

I visited my ladies' committee which had 'done wonderfully till the raids discouraged it': I pointed out that raids are what it ought to thrive on! They were as a matter of fact very keen and I came away feeling that it is all ready for the next person to carry on. In sixteen months, beginning with myself and two young students, we have brought ourselves up to over 6,000 people, all Baghdad pledged to fight the fifth column, and none of them paid; all except Mr Fay[1] in his spare time, myself, and three

1 Ronald Fay was to hold the Egyptian Brothers together until the Nasserites closed them down in 1952.

attenders of committees, are Egyptian. And if we had a tolerable staff we
could treble our numbers in a month.

Your
FREYA

FLORA STARK

Gezira. 30 January 1942

Darling B,

I am just off to Baghdad and send you this last air mail from here.
When there I will make inquiries as to how best to reach you. It is horrid
leaving here while the desert battle is at its most acute, but there will no
doubt be masses of battles to choose from.

Momo yesterday gave me a lovely birthday party with a cake and two
little white sugar doves on it, and about fifty friends came and it was very
pleasant. I have made good friends here and everyone was so nice and I
felt they were sorry to lose me. The Duff Coopers came; they are passing
through; and I don't think I have ever seen anyone so lovely as she is; her
eyes are just like blue sky. When she looks at one it is quite literally
dazzling and it is a lovely kind of beauty too. I sat next him at lunch at the
Embassy and we talked literature as I felt he might prefer it to politics. I
said I hoped he would have time to write and he said 'Does that mean you
agree with the people who want me kicked out of a job?'

I have had a terribly tiring week but hope to leave everything as ready
as it can be for the three who take over but oh! how tiring people are:
yesterday I spent twelve and the day before fourteen hours *talking*. I am
going by train to Syria, lunching with General Wilson, and across the
desert by bus: shall be then settled for some time I take it.

Dearest love dear B.

FREYA

Freya was now transferred to Baghdad to set up her Brotherhood in Iraq,
officially under the auspices of the Embassy Publicity Department, but in fact
more or less autonomously. Her life settled into a routine it was to follow for the
next eighteen months. She moved into a bungalow in the suburb of Alwiyah set
among lawns and oleanders with three friends – Hermione Ranfurly, General
Wilson's Personal Assistant, Barbara Graham, one of her helpers, and Nigel
Clive, who was attached to the Embassy. 'My private life', she wrote in *Dust in
the Lion's Paw*, her fourth and last volume of autobiography, 'had become
singularly pleasant': rides in the early mornings, picnics on Sundays and a great
deal of the kind of social life she most enjoyed. Vyvyan Holt was still in Baghdad
as Oriental Secretary, and Stewart Perowne had been posted as Information
Officer to Iraq.

Pamela Hore-Ruthven had arrived to help her with the Brotherhood and later came Peggy Drower, a fluent Arabic speaker and the daughter of old Baghdad friends. The work was extremely difficult, not least because Iraq had been more actively pro-German than Egypt. Freya set them a punishing routine and herself travelled without cease, most often on Brotherhood business, but occasionally simply to get away.

FLORA STARK

Baghdad. 23 February 1942

Darling B,

I have just been made a full and proper attaché (only two of us in the Middle East) – and so I can rightly send my letters by *bag*. I go about seeing people all day long and feel tired. Vyvyan [Holt] says one might just as well whistle in a whirlwind, Bishop is just agin the government and anything that anyone is doing and Stewart is beginning to look pale again with far too many parties. Stewart, annoying as he is by never attending to anything that anyone says, has the rare charm of never crabbing other people's work: much will be forgiven him for that grace of nature. I had a lovely ride with Vyvyan today, with little clouds sailing in a clear northerly sky and wind, fresh after rain. Young luscious grass was out and my horse suddenly stooped to graze so that I came off, slowly and inelegantly, over its neck.

I have been visited by the Czecho-Hungarian-Rumanian Professor of Music and went to hear him play the 'Appassionata' to the troops. How lovely it was to hear something so beautiful and forget one's troubles! He played some Chopin after. I wondered what all the listeners were thinking, so far from their homes. They live in camps all among the dust storms and full out in the summer heat when it comes – and one has such a time driving one's little car in and out of their lorries.

I must stop darling B. I have been thinking of Herbert[1] today so much, how good and sweet, *naturally* sweet he was and how much happiness we owe him: all those years of a lovely home and all it meant – I hope he may realise how it lives in one's heart. Every dear wish to you and to all with you.

FREYA

---

1 Herbert Young had died in the autumn of 1941.

FLORA STARK

Baghdad. 15 March 1942

Darling B,

At the end of my ten hours' day I had Johnnie Hawtrey[1] to dine and hoped for a quiet early evening. Johnnie I hardly knew when first I came here and he was a smart young A.D.C. wearing fascinating stocks, and then I met him once last June and he invited me to Mosul: I thought to go next month, but he is now being sent off to the Far East and said last night was his last night and I was to go to the Ball: so I put on stockings and a white dress, and a little ribbon muff of red and white, and we danced for six hours on end in the Amana, which is a *huge* hall with plenty of space, a good band, and Johnnie a perfect dancer who said 'Paradise' at the end of every dance and told me I was adorable at intervals: in fact it was a perfect evening and I forgot all about propaganda and got back just before Nigel [Clive] who had been at the same dance with a far less glamorous party, and continued to tell me I was adorable, and I'm sure I let him do so far too much. Anyway it was a very pleasant evening.

Today the news is all bad again and one can't think of anything but our struggle in the East.

Your

FREYA

CHRISTOPHER SCAIFE[2]

Baghdad. 2 April 1942

My dear Christopher,

Of course no sooner was my letter posted than yours arrived – and I was so delighted as never was to get it. Dear Christopher, how much I *do* miss you all. You have your troubles and I have mine: possibly two positives would make a negative if we could put them together! I am a little weary of starting new things and new people, and leaving them as soon as they get going – and do hope to be allowed here to enjoy some fruits of the sowing if the Lord allows it to grow. As for difficulties, the Iraqis are bad, the British *far* worse and apparently think it quite normal that one should waste *half* one's valuable time converting one's own side; they have not yet realised the difference between a debating society and total war. It really is far worse than Cairo – the same criticism of whatever anyone in authority does from the Embassy downwards (by

1 Air Vice Marshall J.G. Hawtrey was Inspector of the Iraqi Air Force in 1940 and in 1942 was on the Air Staff in India. After distinguished service in Europe, returned to Iraq as Air Officer Commanding, Iraq.
2 Christopher Scaife, a good Arabist and recovering from a desert wound, had taken over from FS in Cairo.

people who do not do so very much in particular themselves), the same smug conviction that to have sat still in one place for twenty years and produced an unholy muddle at the end of it somehow entitles one's opinion to a consideration which mere probationers such as a Minister of State scarcely deserve; and far more bourgeois drabness of intolerant rectitude than ever Cairo saw – oh my, oh my –. In spite of all I think we are getting on. Ken Cornwallis is a big man, and most comforting; he says he will back us to the hilt, and went out of his way to say that his private intelligence speaks well of my efforts here. And I feel too that we have done some good spade work. In the next few months, if only we could get a victory *somewhere*, we should begin to show results.

With no assistant at all, I have been very handicapped, but now Miss Drower[1] has arrived, and she is very pleasant, tactful and with good Arabic; it is still too soon to say, as I have only had her a week, but I hope she is adding to these secondary virtues the two primary ones (for an assistant) of economising *my* time at the expense of her own and of preferring *my* policy to hers; you would think these virtues fairly obvious, but they are quite exceptional here, where everyone goes off at their own tangent.

Yours affectionately

FREYA

JOHN GREY MURRAY

Kirkuk. 30 April 1942

Dearest Jock,

I have been ten days in Kurdistan and won't say anything about it because I am having my diary typed to send it to you. It was lovely, though strenuous, and I felt rather like walking with those heavy balls they attach with chains to prisoners' legs – as I had two female companions, and I do think they have a disastrous effect on the *atmosphere* of a journey, and one was an assistant who had always to be reminded of everything so that one's labour was just a little more than it would have been without her (though otherwise nice). Also one had about nine hours a day to talk of politics only in Persian, and that in Kurdistan at present is like walking on eggs. Now I find your Christmas letter. *Dear* Jock, it is so lovely getting your little scraps.

Also found the Admiral's telegram saying I have the R.G.S. Medal.[2] This seems to me quite fabulous and can hardly believe. Delighted as one

1 Peggy Drower, daughter of Freya's friend Stefana, 'with a knowledge of Arabic and the country as good if not better than mine'.
2 The Founder's Medal awarded for journeys in Persia and South Arabia and for FS's books.

only is with what is quite undeserved. If the medal is wandering about I hope you will keep it for me.

The German offensive is later than we thought. Very kind of it to let me get my northern journey over. It is a year tomorrow since we went to our prison in Baghdad Embassy.

Love to you dearest Jock – and family. When will I see them?!

FREYA

FLORA STARK

Baghdad. 6 June 1942

Darling B,

I am having the usual difficult time in getting well here when the hot weather has once started: it is just that one hasn't got the 'kick' in one to resist anything at all. However, I am quite robust in myself, and am being *very* cautious, eschew all parties and limit my committees, and am hoping to be all right again in ten days or so, so as not to have to take my two months' leave till August. I have begun a gentle ride, going about 6.15 and back a little after seven and already any clothes one has on stick to one. If one had no work the summer would not be unpleasant in this nice cool house with fans in every room: a ride early, lie about and read till one bathes before lunch, sleep till five and then out in the cool: but when one has to fit in about eight to ten hours' work, it is not so good.

Later

My team of two ladies is now beginning to work nicely. We have now added a typist, a dingy little Jew called 'Summer Breeze'. We are in fearful straits for money as Stewart, supposed to give what we require up to my budget, suddenly went back on us and said couldn't give anything unless he approved every item. It is *I* and not Stewart who has to approve, but he is dreadfully jealous of my having a budget of my own and would I believe do anything to dish it (and has been talking most unfriendly to my boss, who however warned me long ago that 'Stewart is as jealous as the devil'). So we had a *scene*! and I had to telegraph to get the money put to my account so as to be able to draw without him, and then he apologised, but here we still are with nothing in the till.

Your
FREYA

212

Baghdad. 25 June 1942

Darling B,

We are just pulling ourselves together after the bombshell of Tubruk[1] – a horrid sickish feeling, only too familiar these three summers. I had a fight with most of my committee members and insisted on forecasting its loss a week before it happened, and this has had a remarkably steadying effect on the subsequent committees. Only one of all our ladies took the trouble to ring me up with friendly messages: one is very grateful for these gestures in these times. Otherwise there is a mixture of panic among friends and a silence which one knows is only in one's own presence among all the fifth column. Well, it is not a pleasant month for the propagandist. I do what I can and go out to about five different salons a day – and notice that our friends are the better for being talked to. 'Keep calm and carry on' is all one can do. If I had had five years instead of six months we might have had a more solid body in Iraq to rely on: as it is, I am always surprised at the number of people who believe in us rather than at their scarcity.

My week has been all full of committees and I have little energy left for anything else. The thermometer has touched 122° in the shade and the sheets are like ovens when you lie down on them. One has to be awfully careful about little things, servants tempers, etc . . . as everything is very explosive this weather.

I had a good afternoon on Sunday with Nigel: we started after lunch in a blaze of heat, and got down to the river, a sheet of ripples between crocodile snouts of mud and a thin line of palms lost between sky and water: and it was deliciously cool, and we lay afterwards in the shade out of sight and thought of all the world, with only two small boys in sight and a boat, and the baby melons growing in little potholes of the mud before the next flood comes.

The bag goes today so this must finish. I wonder how much longer I shall write to you from my nice little house. A sort of stability had built itself around it and I have more friends here than anywhere since the war began. One is oppressed with the wonder whether we are fighting hard enough to win. Our tommies are all right, and the sergeants too – but it seems to me that this war is putting a seal of incompetence on all our ruling classes! However, there is no doubt about our willingness to fight, and to fight to the end.

Dearest love,

FREYA

1 Tobruk was captured by the Germans on 20 June.

Baghdad. 26 July 1942

Darling B,

I have been so busy that I could never get down to a letter, but now I am all packed and leaving today for Jerusalem to hand over my budget and plan out the winter with Christopher. He was to have come here, but Egypt can't be left just now. The little brothers behaved *splendidly* and have more than justified their existence, going out into highways and byways and fighting the fifth column not only with eloquence but with fists (not too much pleasing the police!). There are 20,000 of them now – very different from our little gathering of four less than two years ago. I am very glad because everyone now says it was worthwhile, and the trial has strengthened rather than weakened them. Here we are now 325, with twenty committees, and I felt a pang at saying goodbye to them all yesterday; such inexperienced young things, with such a heavy task before them, to bring good government to a country like Iraq; and so grateful for any real interest one can take. If the news only keeps tolerable, we shall go ahead here I think. But I have *two months'* holiday from it all and am trying to go to Cyprus, where no one speaks Arabic, and all by myself – just to lie on the beach and then walk about in the hills and pine woods. I am really bone-tired and can't go on another winter doing strenuous work without a break. I went to say goodbye to Ken [Cornwallis] and he said such nice things to me and really made one feel that all one's little efforts were worthwhile. That is the secret of leadership I suppose.

The last fortnight has been largely filled by the awful business of balancing the budget. We have over £4,000 a year to account for and it drives me nearly mad: I feel that the items are like very shy wild animals which I have to trace in and out of their elusive columns. Eventually we appear to have a surplus of £60, which they say is fatal as the Treasury immediately think one has been given too much. I was amused in reading this document to see that they had considered reducing my salary 'on account of sex differentiation' but had thought better of it on Owen Tweedy's[1] recommendation. I would have *instantly* resigned if not!

Darling love to you all.

FREYA

1 'Nominally I belonged to the [Cairo] embassy, and first Reginald Davies and then Owen Tweedy under Sir Walter Monckton were my chiefs: they were all personal friends as well as the pleasantest people in the world to work for.'

Famagusta. 14 August 1942

Darling B,

Your letter of June 26 just followed me here – so lovely to get, and *delighted*! about the book.[1] Darling B, you are a wonder. If you go and write better than I do I shall be *jealous*!

It is not true that Kipling is a 'jingoist': his idea of Empire was one of austere discipline and *service* and it is our misfortune now that his was not the voice we listened to.

> 'Given to strong delusion, wholly believing a lie,
> Ye saw the land lay fenceless, and ye let the months go by
> Waiting some easy wonder: hoping some saving sign–
> Idle – openly idle – in the lee of the forespent Line.'

Thank God for our youngest. There is nothing wrong with anyone under twenty-seven that I can see. But the generation between thirty and forty – the lost generation Bish calls it – they are nearly all tainted somewhere. An engaging young corporal-painter here told me he had been a pacifist and then joined up when France fell. I said (rather brutally) that I hoped he was working double hard now 'as it's your war: you made it!'

I dined with the Commissioner here and his wife. They spent years in the South Seas and now eighteen years in Cyprus – the real inarticulate sort, with no show of word or look, but quite a lot down below and very pleasant if one is in need of kindness. She had been to see the daughter of a *cawass* who is ill and has no one, so she goes every morning to wash and tidy her: may such things be remembered when our Empire is no more! And yet they are not enough. Imagination and vision – we have been inhibiting them for a hundred years or more: how shall we make up for this loss?

With your letter came one which filled me with pride and pleasure – a note from General Wavell asking me to India: 'There will always be a room for you in our house.' It is very moving to get this from one whom one considers the greatest man of his time.

I liked your epigram that 'of all the things you wear, your expression is the most important'. This doesn't alter the fact that a new hat is one of the best ways to promote a contented expression.

In spite of being still in bed with only rice for three days, I begin to feel

---

1 *An Italian Diary* by Flora Stark, the account of her arrest and imprisonment in Treviso, after Italy declared war.

far better in myself. I believe one always collapses at the beginning of a holiday – the horse being taken out of the shafts.

Your own
FREYA

HAROLD BOWEN[1]

Prodromos. 19 September 1942

My dear Harold,

A telegram from Ken Cornwallis in Baghdad has come with the suggestion, transmitted from the M. of I., that I should go to the U.S.A. I telegraphed back that I would do whatever was most wanted, but that I felt very reluctant to leave my work for three months until I had time to arrange for it to carry on satisfactorily in my absence.

But I have been thinking about the matter, and I would like to put a suggestion to you whether you send me out now or later or at all.

It seems to me that if you do propaganda by *lectures* in the country where the Press is probably largely under Jewish influence, you may convert your actual audiences, but the account which is circulated to the majority of the reading public can be given any twist they like; they can in fact use your lectures to serve their own ends. Propaganda in districts where the other side is powerful should be as *intangible* as possible, so as to offer no target. It therefore seems to me that a tour of *private talks with influential people* would probably be more useful in results. One could send a series of people at intervals, and have small drawing room meetings – but with the Press strictly excluded.

I should feel much more capable of tackling this sort of thing than a lecture tour, and would gladly do so in a few months' time if required. In any case I merely give you the suggestion for what it is worth.

Yours ever,
FREYA STARK

JOHN GREY MURRAY

Nicosia. 23 September 1942

My dearest Jock,

I am on my way back to Famagusta and the sea for a week before trying to get away from this island with, (a) eight small bags, (b) a new fur coat of Cyprus goats, (c) a barrel of sherry, (d) twelve cases of wine, (e) a case of olive oil and possibly cheese.

I wish you could have seen the view of the island from the top of its own Olympus – a spread like a saucer as seen from the top of its own

---

1 Harold Bowen was with the Ministry of Information in London.

teacup (turned upside down to keep the dust out: Olympus is just that shape without the handle).

Do you know Lord Feversham?[1] He is the right sort of person and lives now mostly in tanks, and came to lunch and drove with me by the mountain road, so solitary, all pine trees, a few cedars, and practically no human beings at all, but a moufflon or two. And so down to Paphos, which I am sure Venus left rather quickly, as it is a dull place – and then back to Nicosia by the coast where there are white cliffs like Dover only looking as if it were sunlight and not moonlight inside them. The rocks where Venus really is said to have landed are there, in a foamy bay. We bathed there (not that the two events have any connection) and ate cold fried fish and partridge, figs and wine – and then visited the wine factory at Limassol where they gave us crème de menthe and cointreau local make and one after the other at 4 p.m. and tea to follow: in a mellow mood I got to Government House in time to dress for dinner.

Since then I have ridden, or is it driven in a tank. It *feels* more like riding. Jock I *wish* I could do tanks and not propaganda!

Love to you, lots and lots, from

FREYA

FLORA STARK

Cairo. 11 October 1942

My own darling,

I feel like the Prodigal returning. The Minister of State[2] has asked me to go and talk to him in his office today and his wife, who is *very* attractive, came to meet me, which makes me feel very grand and wonder rather why. I *hope* I may be meeting General Smuts, who is one of the people one would most like to meet in this world. Apart from everything else, it is a good thing to meet these people, who are building up the world of tomorrow, so that the ideas one has so laboriously garnered may bear some little fruit perhaps.

The desert battle is so near that people go out to it after breakfast and come back for a day off when they can! It is fantastic here just now – charity bazaars, diplomatic dinners, fashions in the shops, and the streets full of men who are within a few hours of their fighting lines.

Our brotherhood here is now 19,000 and has a most lovely house as H.Q., an eighteenth-century Turkish palace, and National Monument, which Christopher has got off the Government for £3 a month! We are

1 The Earl of Feversham, then in the Yorkshire Hussars.
2 R.G. (later Lord) Casey.

considered to be quite useful and are being now looked upon as one of the basic facts of propaganda – no small triumph after the scepticism of our beginning! We are getting Lulie to start in Palestine and are looking round for another woman here!

The R.A.F. have been doing marvels here. It was so impressive to land now on airports where a machine takes off every minute or so and to think of 1940 when they lay almost silent, and 1941 when I ran out to see our first five Hurricanes and felt tears rolling down my cheeks at sight of them!

There is a great feeling of confidence in our new generals (both Irish).[1] Their first pronouncement was 'No retreat; no prisoners; *no failure.*' Something went wrong for a young man here which was entirely *not* his own fault: the general told him that this was neither here nor there; he just *does not want* failures. I *do* so agree with this, the *only* point of view which wins a war.

Dear love from

FREYA

JOHN GREY MURRAY

Baghdad. 4 November 1942

My very dear Jock,

Your note 7th August came just as I was about to write to you with a very full heart, for news has come that Mama is dying. It was a week ago and I am hoping now that all may be over soon for her sake. It leaves me in a very lonely world. I will not say more, but I know that you will understand. She will leave more of a blank than most people and oh Jock I wish I could have seen her again.

I was luckily too busy even to think much – but wonder in between whiles what I am to do with my life after the war. It feels just now as if there were no one really to live for at all. I must not write things like this, but send you my dear love, and love to Diana and the family.

Your
FREYA

JOHN GREY MURRAY

Baghdad. 22 January 1943

My dearest Jock,

I am going to India for three weeks.[2] Doesn't it sound fantastic! One

1 Generals Alexander and Montgomery.
2 A message had been received from General Wavell: 'Freya Stark would be useful in India in connection with propaganda Italian P. of W. provided she can be spared and willing stay 3 months in India. Fairly strenuous work and considerable travelling. If willing can you arrange military passage by BOAC to Gwalior.'

gets into an aeroplane at Habbaniyah, sleeps in the grand hotel at Basra, next day one is in India. I am going to stay with the Wavells in Delhi. It still does not seem quite real and there were all sorts of hitches. First General Wavell asked for me for three months: H.E. here said yes, I accepted, Cairo put a china-shop-bull-foot down and said no. I wrote back (very annoyed) and suggested a fortnight compromise; no answer for ages (Cairo is like that, like the whirlpool of Niagara, things go round and round slowly but never get out). Then Providence, which is so apt to do the things you want in the most unpleasant way, gave me a combination of gastric 'flu and malaria (at least the doctors don't know which, so are dosing for both). That made me look so pathetic that *everyone* here says 'Do please go to India.' I decided to take a fortnight's leave and bother no more about Cairo. The dear Military here got all fixed for early February and the permission from Cairo has *just* come in time to save their own faces. So all is well except that I am not yet feeling quite my best.

I gave a very grand dinner party to Nuri Pasha[1] and Jumbo and A.D.C. and the A.O.C. (De Crespigny) and A.D.C. and the Director of Police and we were all so indiscreet saying things about the French that everyone enjoyed himself. I said to Nuri he must get *some* part of the Iraq army to do a bit of fighting as well as just coming into the war, but he said that must come gradually, and it is very difficult to fight anywhere in the Mid East and not annoy the French. He asked Jumbo whom he thought more despicable French or Italian: and Jumbo said he thought the Italians more despicable but the French more apt to let one down. Their speeches do really nauseate one rather; they might just *suggest* that they have something to make up for. I am quite convinced that they will hate us steadily for all our lifetimes anyway, and should therefore be sorry to see Italy too much weakened.

Oh Jock, when will we have time to talk over all these strange times. Bless you all.

FREYA

SIR SYDNEY COCKERELL

New Delhi. 14 February 1943

My dearest Sydney,

This is all enchanting. I landed at Gwalior three days ago, spent a night there and had time to stroll over the old Mogul fort that runs all along the cliff – and there was the absolute fairy tale palace (A.D. 1510 I think), a dream embodied in solid sandstone, ending against the blue sky with turrets, pinnacles, lattice windows all carved in stone, great pilasters and

1 The Iraqi statesman.

buttresses decorated with tiles canary-coloured and turquoise: and inside, courts, carved stone slabbed ceilings, narrow lattice passages for ladies, baths and prisons. One could live there delightfully today and look from one's window on the plain and city far below.

That is all my sightseeing as yet. I came here feeling very feeble (gastric 'flu and no food), but I have a room and verandah opening on to wide lawns, green trees, herbaceous borders full of flowers, parrots and peacocks in the trees, and the lawn mower drawn by an ox. One has India with country-house comfort.

I haven't seen Delhi yet – but have been driven in a phaeton by one of the A.D.C.'s round Viceregal Lodge and visited the garden and the stables: over all, with its splendour, there is a solid Victorian feeling – everything *good*, nothing of careless rapture; you couldn't see a stucco fancy set out amongst these trees, the very lamp posts are carved red sandstone in dignified designs. The gates have elephants on high pedestals which I am sure is wrong. The Secretariat is a very fine building. There is just something, I think it is this want of *enjoyment*, which leaves one dissatisfied.

I hope in two or three weeks to get back overland by Persia if I can manage it – I have a great hankering for the spaces of Asia with no committees and just a *chaikane* to rest in when night comes.

My dear dear love,

FREYA

SIR SYDNEY COCKERELL

Cecil Hotel, Simla. 6 March 1943

My dearest Sydney,

I have two letters of yours to answer, and there were quite a lot of questions, but before I do this I must tell you about this fantastic place. I have left Delhi, after three such happy weeks: my devotion to the Wavells much increased and the feeling that I was leaving real friends. It was pleasant too to talk about poetry rather than propaganda. Now I have spent £1,000 on a new car and all its appurtenances and am taking it all the way back across Baluchistan and Persia and hope to sell it for a large profit in Baghdad. If I don't, I don't care: I would any day rather *do* things than *have* things, and a journey like this is very alluring. An old friend in the R.A.F. is I hope meeting me in Quetta (with a revolver). My only anxiety is the *value* of a car now: in Persia and Iraq new tyres are worth £170 *each*! It makes it worth robbing.

Well now, I would write volumes about it all. The Mogul has been a revelation of real loveliness and the civilised art of living; the British is most fascinating: so much good, and something so wrong. In the building I have come to the conclusion it is the want of spontaneity; nothing is done for *fun*; no one just thought he would like a grotto, a fountain, or a lattice and put it there. While assisting at an investiture in the great marble throne room I kept on hearing in my head 'Nor in your marble *vault* shall sound my echoing song', – and perhaps that is what is wrong with all Official India. It seems to have preserved a Victorian rigidity, but without the Victorian passion behind it. And of course they take themselves seriously, which is always fatal. Even now, in most places, one feels our lack of training in formal courtesy. Here, for instance, none of the villagers ever say good day as they pass in a lonely footpath: I said so and they looked surprised, but coming back the same way, all greeted me delighted. The women here are *fantastic*: Kipling without a comma to add or alter, and quite frightful. But oh Sydney – the snowy hills! What a vision, quite unforgettable – the serenity of the Gods, peak after peak, a shining white barrier sea of steady waves hemming the north and east – even their names unknown. There is a map in the hall, it says 20,000 feet, 18,000 feet – belonging to the great Himalayan range. I told the Field Marshal I would not like my life over again, but I *did* feel when looking there this morning and remembering I am fifty years old that I should like to be young just to penetrate among them. (I have walked three hours today, which isn't bad for the first day at this height – but am all aches from my bruised back falling off a horse).

You ask whether I would have liked my life different. I think not. The years at Dronero I regret, but what came before and after was all good and I feel that I have acquired my philosophy such as it is and that that is what really matters. The object of life, if I were asked, I should say is to conquer fear: and 'perfect love casteth out fear.' One is only on the way, but at any rate it is something to know where the path leads that lies before you. I do regret now not being married: but not the marriages of those days I wrote to you about. The man with whom I would have been happy, and who cared, was killed by the Germans in Stuttgart in April 1939. And now – I feel lonely, but I know it does not very much matter. Also I have so much love for which to be grateful or humble. In that I am spoiled above most people; and at least, I do value it at its worth. It is nice to sit talking to you here in Simla, where I so little expected ever to find myself. One thing I have felt again very strongly today – that no *human* work ever moves me one fraction as deeply as does the sight of nature, but especially of mountains: only sometimes the Greeks, because in their holy places they have made themselves one with nature. The sight of these great giants has given me a sort of new breath of life today.

221

I have done such a foolish thing. I went to buy a pair of shoes in a little Chinese shop and there were two geese modelled in blue glaze, terribly fragile but so attractive, and I *bought* them – and have nowhere to pack them! They will begin the refurnishing of Asolo and I hope you will come to see them. Oh my dearest Sydney – you can't think how often I wish you were close at hand.

Your ever loving
FREYA

PAMELA HORE-RUTHVEN

Baluchistan. 15 March 1943

My darling Pam,

Baluchistan is a fine rugged country: the people up here are Pathans, very big and biblical with black beards and eyes like spaniels; they wear lots of loose cotton draperies very untidily, wash twice a year, lock their wives up when they go out (with every reason to do so it seems), and manage to live in a country which to the casual traveller seems to have hardly any houses or cultivation at all.

The Wavells gave me the loveliest three weeks. When one is lonely (and I have been lonely too since my mother's death) there is something very *healing* in people who are so genuine and whose affection you feel is just for yourself alone: one's acquaintances grow to matter less and one's friends far more as one gets older I find. I like the feeling too now of being quite by myself, well out of reach of all my superiors, with Asia all about me: I was picturing the world yesterday, the Himalayas stretching away glistening in the sun, the huge wedge of India and the Indus seeping down between its mud banks, and Arabia all brown and yellow, rocks and sand and a few palms, on the west – and my little grey car whizzing along like an insect, beautifully insignificant in all that immensity. Very few people I would like with me, but you certainly.

The blossom is all out up here, and makes a lacework neither white nor pink against the hills. The trees otherwise are still bare and there is snow in the high gullies – and I enjoy every *nip* of cold while thinking of the summer in Baghdad. India is extraordinarily un-war-minded: the women mostly still talk of summer in the hills as a matter of course and Lady Wavell is desperate for her canteens when the hot weather starts.

I will write from Persia and tell you about the journey, as I know you will like to hear. Do you mind keeping letters? I can't be bothered with a diary and I know some day I shall regret my laziness.

Your
FREYA

Baghdad. 16 April 1943

My dear Jock,

I found your very dear little note of November and one of 24 March asking me to write on Arab relations. I *couldn't* do that now: I am right inside them, with lots of Emotion but no Tranquillity – and it's quite impossible. If I could write a book it would be about a pre-war world in Italy, but I can't write anything till all this is over. I hope we may *talk* of all this: there is a plan to give me a week or so in London *en route* for America in August or September. I dare hardly promise it, even to myself!

Johnnie Hawtrey and I travelled 4,000 miles over one long stretch of gravel that represents the trans-Iranian road: it took us nineteen days. We did all this with numerous arguments as to who was to drive. Johnnie's opinion of my driving is terribly unflattering – but no quarrels, which shows how unlike he was to Gertrude (miaow) and it really was *most* restful: every sort of desert and never a bit of propaganda. Isfahan is just like a pale turquoise, sky, clouds, white-stemmed trees, faded painted houses with rickety dilapidated columns, and blue domes in the sky.

I am back now to numerous tangles as one always is, and have to tour the whole of my parish before it gets too hot.

Your

FREYA

CHRISTOPHER SCAIFE

Baghdad. 19 May 1943

My poor Christopher,

At the moment nearly all is visited, except the Holy Cities which you will have to go to anyway so I am going to try and avoid doing them myself as I am nearly dead with parish visiting. I have however now stroked down the bristles of every single political officer, called on nearly all the Mutasarriffs and their wives, most of the Police and lots of the Judges – and where the Brethren are gathered. I hope it may save you a lot of wear and tear.

I can't get away before July 10th or so, because Peggy must have her holiday before the heat of the summer. (I think I would be much fitter today if I had had any leave in the first two years of the war!) Peggy really does work *very* hard. She couldn't go before, because I had to fit in the visiting – and that was essential, for no one else could spot the troubles 'no bigger than a man's hand' and clear them up in time – and it would have been too bad to leave them all to blossom out for you. I think now all looks calm and bright for a good while ahead – *inshallah, inshallah*.

I *do* hope Palestine can go on. It is terribly sad not to bat when we are at the wicket. My tour has made me more sure than ever that this *is* the right road to take.

Ever so much love to you,

FREYA

NIGEL CLIVE

Algiers. 16 August 1943

Dearest Nigel,

I did so well to come here. Algiers throws quite a new light on Syria and the problem there: it reinforces my conviction of the absolute *necessity* of getting the French disinterested from Syria. Here they are just old-fashioned exploiters.

I got here quite safely but feeling almost as if *I* had been doing a parachute drill: left Continental 3.20 a.m. on the 12th and got here at 8 p.m. all on a hard little metal seat with everything sharp that one leant against: an Iron Age in fact. But it was thrilling to fly over that long desert route of the Eighth Army, and look down and see the criss-cross patterns of the tanks for miles and miles, and the pitted bomb-holes thick as moon-craters, and see the long coastline and the black road with little slits of dugouts, and Benghazi a white blur of ruins against the sea. Then a great expanse of chessboard squares so beautifully planted, with their little rectangle of house and court in the centre of each, where the colonies of Tripoli began. We looked down on the swamps of Ageila, oyster-coloured and puckered like the inside of a pearl shell; and then the huge salt swamps that close the Mareth line, like white veils drawn over the sands, and the ridges of Tunisia stepping up behind; they seemed like the spokes of a huge fan held in the hands of death, so vast and bare. And then suddenly the hills grew wooded and red roofs began, and we slipped down into provincial France. Luckily two kind officers, Army and Air Cooperation, took me along as the aerodrome is miles out of the town: I got to the chief hotel – no room except on military order and no food after 6 p.m.! However the kind Minister of State[1] took me up in a huge car and I am in the lap of luxury – going on some time after Saturday next. It is thrilling to see our aerodromes crammed with machines (over a hundred on one I counted) and the ships in harbour, and the diversity of troops.

My dearest love,

FREYA

1 Harold Caccia, serving with the Resident Minister, North Africa.

8

Putting the Arab case to the Americans, in India with the Wavells

---

The British Government's White Paper on Palestine, issued when war was clearly imminent in 1939, proposed the creation within ten years of an independent Palestine State, during which period both Arabs and Jews would be encouraged to take an increasing share in the administration of the country. Immigration certificates for an additional 25,000 Jewish refugees would be prepared immediately, and 10,000 admitted annually for the next five years. Thereafter further Jewish immigration would depend on the acquiescence of the Arabs. American Zionists were particularly incensed by what they regarded as a betrayal of Britain's obligations to the Jews, and in May 1942 they adopted a resolution by which the whole of Palestine should be reconstituted as a 'Jewish Commonwealth'.

Freya was now asked to give a series of talks on the Palestine question across America, a country widely and correctly regarded as being extremely ignorant of Middle Eastern affairs. She was not, perhaps, the most obvious of choices, for her one encounter with the New World in Canada had left her a little scathing of its culture, and she had never admired the Jews.

Crossing the Atlantic in October 1943 on the *Aquitania*, Freya developed acute appendicitis and was put ashore on a stretcher at Halifax, the troops lining the railings and watching. By November she was recovered and in New York.

JOHN GREY MURRAY

New York. 20 November 1943

Dearest Jock,

I am going mad in New York shops – fantastically expensive but *delirious*. Luckily I have no excuse to buy more costumes, but even little lacy blouses can almost bankrupt one and as for underthings with lace tops . . . oh my!

I can't get over the exciting beauty of New York – the pencil buildings so high and far that the blueness of the sky floats about them; the feeling that one's taxis, and shopping, all go on in the deep canyon-beds of natural erosions rather than in the excrescences of human builders.

I am being doctored now for anaemia, low blood pressure and all the results of operations, and hope to start the tour in January: that will not take me back to London till May.

225

Much love to you all.

FREYA

ELIZABETH MONROE[1]

New York. 20 November 1943

My dear Elizabeth,

My hostess, Mrs Otto Kahn,[2] and both her daughters, are very keen to help and are putting me in touch with the Anti-Zionist Jews here. I found that not one of them suspected the existence of the second clause of the Balfour Declaration:[3] – so I have given them each a copy of the text and they are going to spread it around. It seems to me very important that the moderate Jews should realise that we *have actually fulfilled* the Balfour Declaration and I notice that the second clause does make a strong impression on them. I met Mr Howard Dietz, who is a big man in the cinema industry, last night and quoted it to him, and also told him, more in sorrow than in anger, that Mr Weizmann[4] always leaves it out when he quotes. He said that Weizmann goes about saying there is really no difficulty for Arab and Jew to get on together. I said I thought this might be possible when immigration stops: the fact that there are already one Jew to two Arabs seemed to cause an impression.

Today I met Mrs Guy Rothschild at lunch – long discussion on Palestine and the Lebanon. She agreed that to upset all the Moslem interests of the British would not be compensated by the advantages of getting a million or so Jews into Palestine. She struck me as one of the Jews who would yield to the evidence of a firm attitude if H.M.G. could only decide to take it: I can't help feeling that a very great number of Jews would be in this category. Their social treatment here is appalling.

Yours affectionately,
FREYA

GERALD DE GAURY

New York. 24 November 1943

My dear Gerald,

This is the only town where one's looks are drawn all the time away from the ground up into the sky: the huge buildings are not too close together, so that they keep their individuality and are clustered rather

1 Director of the Middle East Division of the MOI.
2 Momo Marriott's mother, who had FS to stay.
3 'it being clearly understood that nothing shall be done which may prejudice the civil and religious rights of existing non-Jewish communities in Palestine . . .'
4 Dr Chaim Weizmann, President of the World Zionist Organisation and Jewish Agency for Palestine.

like the towers of S. Gimignano or Bologna – and from the canyon shadow of the streets you look up to their sunlight and the long vistas of the avenues, and would not be surprised to see clouds trailing about their summits.

I have gone mad over clothes and find that dollars melt just like water – everything is here, at a fantastic price, and so attractive. Of course it is marvellous seeing it all from the shelter of Momo and Mrs Otto Kahn, luxury, kindness, and pleasantness of conversation all mingled together. I think when I do begin to try to missionise, I will find it strenuous: the amount of nonsense talked is phenomenal. I discovered a proverb which says, 'The world would be a much quieter place if those who had nothing to say – said it.' I think of beginning any lecture I may give in this way.

The Lebanon as you can imagine has caused a spate of comment and the French are saying frightful things about us.[1] What silly things we do: like letting Mosley loose – no good to anyone and an absolute godsend to trouble makers. As if it mattered one bit if he did die in prison.

Affectionately,

FREYA

ELIZABETH MONROE

New York. 28 November 1943

My dear Elizabeth,

I had two messages from a Mrs Fitzgerald and a Mrs Forbes, both attractive, influential and enthusiastic, saying that they wanted to do *anything I could suggest* to help the Anglo-American cause of friendship. If I were in Iraq, these are just the sort of people I would rope in and work through. (I believe that in all propaganda one can do most by gathering and organising the already converted and leaving it to them to convert their own countrymen. This ought to be the Law and the Prophets of propaganda, but unfortunately isn't yet recognised.)

Yesterday I went to a party given for me by Miss Case (editor of *Vogue*) and had two long talks with Mrs McCormick and Clare Luce. Mrs McCormick (writes in *New York Times*) – Irish, middle-aged, twinkling and sparkling with life, fun, and sense – I thought one of the nicest women I have ever met: full of curiosity, sound comments, and a complete forgetting of herself in her subject. We talked of Arab

1 On 11 November the French authorities in the Lebanon arrested the President of the Republic, the Prime Minister and most of the Cabinet. As the result of an ultimatum by the British, whose troops had been in effective control of the country for the past two years, the arrested men were released on 22 November. The episode caused more bad blood between de Gaulle and the British Government than almost any other in the whole course of the war.

federation. I say, when asked, that I believe a unifying process is going on largely based on the fact that motors and aeroplanes have made deserts into a means of unifying instead of separating: and of course the past united history of the Arab world. She asked about anti-Zionist feeling outside Palestine, and I was able to tell what I had noticed in remote places like Yemen and Hadhramaut.

Clare was a very different affair and looked on me as an enemy at sight, with lovely eyes fixed firmly on the middle distance when forcibly brought up to sit beside me. She opened with no chit-chat, but said that what she believed in was Freedom: resolutely shut down on the Middle East and dragged me into India. She has, they tell me, about five secretaries who provide her with facts so that a war of statistics is to be avoided. I did however get her to agree that it would be a pity to open a door to the Japs at this moment: she fell back on a main line of resistance by saying that we refuse to say *when* the liberation of India is to be. I gave a little sketch of the 'freedom' of Iraq and the years of preparation to avoid its being a massacre of minorities. 'Let there be massacres,' said Clare. 'Why should the white races have a monopoly of murder?' She told me that a Moslem Indian had assured her he longed for freedom so as to be able to fight the Hindus. I suggested she should adopt 'Freedom for Fratricide' as a slogan. If she carries much weight now, I don't think she will in a few years: she is too much tinkle, really lovely though with a mouth hard and unhappy when you look at her – and she makes the mistake, eventually fatal to lovely women, of antagonising all the women.

FREYA

SIR SYDNEY COCKERELL

New York. 6 December 1943

Dearest Sydney,

A letter of yours has come to cheer me, and very opportune, for I am depressed and in bed with 'flu. I feel also that I am up against a most tough and uncongenial job, dealing with slanders, envy, detraction, and all malignancy as well as mere ignorance. If I had not got to tackle such a Hydra as Zionism I should enjoy America immensely and the *immense* personal kindness makes it very pleasant: but there is an undercurrent of Uncle Sam v. John Bull which not only upsets me as a British female, but as a thing so ungenerous and unsporting in itself, just now when we have so much on our hands. It is fashionable to say it is all our fault and our bad propaganda, but one should not need much propaganda to be generous to one's own allies when they are weary with four years' blitz and war:

and there is no valid reason for American papers to concentrate on things like Indian freedom and pass the freedoms of Ireland, South Africa, Iraq and Egypt under silence more or less complete. And at the bottom of all that is nothing but envy, the sort of feeling that has eventually ended in bloodshed ever since Abel and Cain had their row. I think the underlying cause is that this country does most of its thinking through business brains, and 'your loss my gain' is the basis: while we have some sort of public servant in every family, and that makes possible a more constructive philosophy. Yesterday a friend said to me 'You must be prepared to take second place after the war', unaware that, in a cooperative world, we would not *mind* second place. To establish such ideas here must be very wearying sometimes. It gives me a feeling of real misery to contemplate such an arid sort of universe and I really hate it: nor do I think that the ungenerous soul will ever be a leader either in men or nations – and I believe that if we remain steadfast and wise our poverty will still lead the world after the war in spite of the huge material masses here. However, everyone says that the real America is out of New York.

Your loving
FREYA

STEWART PEROWNE

New York. 15 December 1943

My dear Stewart,

It was so nice to hear from you: I know how difficult it is to write, but there is an 'orphaned' feeling west of the Atlantic which makes letters very welcome. This in spite of kindness beyond words, but it comes from the fact that the world just *does* look different from the opposite side. Or perhaps it is depressing when you have to meet so many people with opinions about things they know nothing about. They gather bright hard facts like magpies, and your logical mind is merely brushed aside if you point out that two contradictory facts can't be simultaneously true in the same place. I went yesterday to a ladies' luncheon – rows of faces with Grenadier mouths surrounded by grey locks on rectangular bases: it was like a collection of totem poles. I can't think why I have been sent here: I have no mass-appeal; I *hate* efficient women; I like truth and am bored by information; and sentimental inaccuracies make me sick. I am tired of being told how bad we are in India by people who can't keep their own negroes happy. When they ask me where the poor Jews are to go, I am beginning to ask if there isn't quite a lot of empty country in the States (there is). My hostess tells me that everyone gets this 'reaction' and I am hoping it may be better as soon as one gets away from the Intelligentsia which anyway is awful almost everywhere. How lovely it would be to go for a sail in Mayun! Those are the things in life that really matter – to sit still now and then and let Allah do the talking.

The news of Churchill's illness is a shock. It would be very sad if he could not see the victory.

Much love

FREYA

NIGEL CLIVE

Washington. 25 December 1943

Dearest Nigel,

This day must not go by without a word to you though I have no idea of where you are. I have reached Washington, have met the most entrancing Oxford don called Isaiah Berlin, a friend of Bish's, and the best talker I have met since his death.

I still feel so frail (hence pencil writing on my bed) the thought of semi-public speeches fills me with a feeling only comparable to drowning. Washington has none of the hard glittering New York splendour, but has a lovely quality, an eighteenth-century colonial air still traceable in and out of its classic avenues and hills and woods that nestle round it. And how lovely to breathe the cold winter sunlight and see between leafless trees the flat iced surfaces of streams.

May all go well for you this year my dear. Bless you.

FREYA

ELIZABETH MONROE

Washington. 2 January 1944

My dear Elizabeth,

I am now seeing so many people that I can't catch up and give a full account, but will try to keep up with the most useful ones. Among these, in the first row, *Mrs Longworth*,[1] a Queen of Republican Washington. I met her at dinner last week and we all went to tea on New Year's Eve. She is far away the most amusing, alert and individual woman I have met here, with a generous vitality and a devastating wit. She was delighted to hear of Archie Roosevelt's pro-Arab activities in Tunis and is fascinated by remote things like Grecian civilisation in Britain: anyone so imaginative can't be a Zionist if they know the facts, so Michael Wright and I plied her heavily with them and prepared her for a heavy and inaccurate crusade about to be launched: as the *Washington Post* and *New York Times*

1 Alice Longworth, daughter of Theodore Roosevelt.

230

had a full-page anti-White Paper display next day, we were just in time. I think she is an ally on the Arab side, and on the British too when it fits in with Republican ideas.

Mrs Truxton Beale, another social Queen, we lunched with and I sat next to Mr Beale, a man I should say disingenuous with everyone, including himself. He is not a friend to Britain and looked full of spikes when we came near Arabian oil, relieved when I told him I hated all big business and actually pleased when – in the less controversial field of buried Peruvian cities whose prosperous farmers were torn away by the Portuguese to work in mines – I suggested that there we had 'big business' at work again.

I had to do the same with *Mr Allen* of the State Department last night. He is just back from Palestine, very friendly, very anxious to help but he said he was wondering if it was any use to do anything at all in face of our P.M.'s Cairo statement that he was all on the side of the French and the Jews. Happily I was able to point out that this has not prevented fairly drastic action as regards the French and again assured him that our P.M. is far from being or wishing to be a dictator and the necessities of Britain will always come first. Time, which he knew would show more and more the essential nature of our Moslem relations, was all against the Zionist extremists if we could tide over the next six months or year till the Palestine side dwindled with the end of the war.

Mr Yale of the State Department also came to see me and charmed me altogether. It was Yale who in 1919 was breakfasting with Weizmann when he banged his fist on the table and said (of Palestine) that 'unless they give it to me I will break the British Empire'. I was pleased to have tracked down this elusive story at last. Mr Yale is an enthusiast, imaginatively liable to illusions, conscientiously disinterested, and with that pleasant capacity of being absorbed by his visions. He was captured by the East as a young man and has loved it ever since. He was under the impression that Mr Churchill might believe that he was pleasing the U.S.A. by assisting Weizmann, and was anxious to assure me that this was a mistake. His facts may be uncertain but that does not alter their influence if the Government departments of this country believe them.

Mr Walter Lippmann I have had little luck with: he seemed to me more interested in himself than in his ideas, I mean that he might think an idea was improved by being adopted by W. Lippmann – but I had no chance to get at the ideas themselves and shall hope to see him again on my return. I met the French journalist 'Pertinax' at his party and asked him how he liked America. 'A desert,' he said, 'they are lost, not in space but in time.' He blew them away off his fingertips into the outer darkness.

'They detest us all, but you British most, because they feel themselves inferior. Ce n'est pas une civilisation.' 'But the future,' I said. 'They may be growing into a civilisation. How long will it take?' 'I don't know – five hundred years perhaps. It is of no interest.' He shrugged his shoulders, lifted his chin and dismissed the whole continent.

Yours affectionately,
FREYA

JOHN GREY MURRAY

Washington. 6 January 1944

My dearest Jock,

I am now in the Chicago train, still surrounded by a mass of papers that is slowly rising up and burying me, so that it is very immoral to be writing to you at all, just for pleasure! But I have done so many minutes on Zionists I deserve a rest. The last days have been a whirl of Senators, journalists and influential ladies. It is a tough job to make the Arab popular, but it would be even tougher to popularise the British – I don't honestly think this is our fault; it is largely a puzzled jealousy because this country, running itself on a business morality, *can't* understand that we combine a different sort of outlook with success. I feel sure that we shall be far more powerful than anyone else after this war and that here it will be greatly resented. It is a pity: there is no reason in the world not to work together for the good of everyone including ourselves, but I don't believe America yet sees cooperation as better than competition and we shall probably go hand in hand with Russia while U.S.A. wonders how her slick methods fail when it comes to the outer world. It is fascinating to watch. I notice a drop in temperature whenever I mention the loyalty of the Canadians or the South Africans.

Washington is one of the pleasantest cities in the world – like a huge village losing itself in green avenues (now brown). We lived just above the creek, running brown and full of ice in a valley of brown trees with a zoo at one end and white wolves and grey foxes and bears. My only time off was a walk every fine day in the crisp shining air, with the lovely pale bleached colours of winter all about and the Shoreham Hotel just like that palace at Lhassa towering above. Also met two delightful people, Sir R. Campbell with a nice face like one carved in wood, and Isaiah Berlin who is an Oxford don but not at all like one. One goes into his office for information about people and he lets himself go in entrancing thumbnail sketches, in a low gentle voice that always seems to be tripping over itself.

I wonder what will happen before I see you again. The year has begun and so much is awaited.

FREYA

CHRISTOPHER SCAIFE

Chicago. 14 January 1944

My dear Christopher,

How I long for the Civilisation of the East again! This country seems to me quite terrifying because entirely godless. I am quite sure it will not lead the world in our lifetime: one can't do that on pure materialism.

I have given my two lectures and the people of the Oriental Institute here are as nice as can be: German, Jew, American, all melts away in the pleasant fellowship of a common hobby. The tower there is a copy of Magdalen, the halls grey stone with a feeling of cloisters. It is rather touching in this hard bright sun and amid the bouncing, barbarian, rich infidels of the Rejected of Europe that populate the town. In the snow I looked at a foreground of Greek colonnades and the skyscrapers behind them, fascinating to think what has brought it all together. But, my God, the *emptiness* of these faces! And I think I shall dislike the look of expensive furs for the rest of my life. The sad part is that they are all such good healthy animal 'raw-material'. But just think of raw material left to *civilise itself*!

The Zionists are gathering their ammunition. They are out for a fight to a finish and it is this year or never.

Affectionately,

FREYA

ELIZABETH MONROE

Chicago. 21 January 1944

My dear Elizabeth,

I don't know what to do about these newspaper notices: the plainer I tell it the more highly coloured it comes out. I am also beginning to get letters from Jews almost inarticulate with fury: I suppose that is a good sign, but it all makes me long for *private life* with a passionate longing.

It would be very regrettable (if we *did* change our policy on the White Paper) if the American newspapermen remembered all my eloquence and began to write about *coercion* of the Arabs. If there is any chance of this I hope you would send a wire to recall me as soon as you knew of it and stop my talking further!

A Miss Irwin, who works in the Chicago University Press, was there

233

and reported on it with the result that I was asked to lunch to meet Mr Brandt, the head. He asked if I would write a little book, popular and 'personal', about the 'Arab World' for them to publish – to give a picture of it as it is now and may be in future. They have of course very high standing and I accepted on the condition that I obtain the Ministry's consent. We will think how, when and where it can be done. It would take me two to three months I should say (looking upon it as propaganda rather than literature, which takes longer).

The outstanding (and most exhausting) events of Wednesday and today were meals with Zionists, shepherded by old Dr Olmstead. He got Rabbi Fox to lunch – one of the most influential Jews here and moderate; thoroughly Middle West, and very shrewd. We had a great argument, with the usual dead-wall at the end, but it does seem to have roused a certain disturbance in his mind and he afterwards asked Dr Olmstead to talk on the subject to a gathering of Jews – which is just what we want. The distressing thing is that I *like* the Jews I meet here and have to argue with, almost better than anyone else I see: there was a most disarming mixture of sharpness, kindness and humour about the Rabbi. But the man on my right called Kaplan, who had been Danish Consul at Tel Aviv, made me long for a pet pogrom of my own before we were through the soup. I said to him instead of goodbye that I regretted he was so shockingly anti-British and it seemed to cause him the greatest surprise and chagrin. I believe they are just delirious and don't know how objectionable they are. Rabbi Fox before we parted said that what he thought would happen is that Mr Roosevelt would 'whisper a word or two to Churchill and he'll be afraid to say no': unfortunately we reached our destination before I could refute this monstrosity.

The Consul gave a dinner for Mr Hodson (who did part of *Desert Victory*) and me: we couldn't talk much because, after our short and serious disquisitions, everyone else followed with comic songs (anyway it was refreshing to look on the Middle East as a Comic Turn). I do hope that after this war is over we will keep on separate people for Public Relations in all these places for it really is a job for which the 'departmental mind' seems unsuited. The gay part of the evening came when an enormous rubicund shipping director told us he was founding a Moravian church, and we all sang temperance hymns in broken American. It was a peculiar evening, very matey.

I have been coming to the conclusion that the root of the awful blankness in this country may be the fact that the *women are organised*: the one half of the human race that we still consider as believing in its duties rather than its rights, as being ready for self-sacrifice rather than self-advancement, as having leisure for other people in life and a mind sufficiently unpruned to be individual – here it is *canalised* into something hard, bright, competent, quite unendurable, much more intelligent than its average man, and I believe unhappy: or perhaps it just seems to me impossible that it can be happy. I only hope we won't think of 'organising' women in Europe!

Yours affectionately,

FREYA

PAMELA HORE-RUTHVEN

Los Angeles. 11 February 1944

My darling Pam,

Such a joy to get your letter in this arid land. I long for Poverty and Peace, not even so much the laying down of weapons, but the peace of people who see through the surface of the world and know the ties that bind them. I can't tell you what a feeling of discomfort it gives me to be out here, and it is not that I don't like most of the people I meet; but I feel their civilisation not only alien but dead and also have a horrid fear of it – that we may be infected and let ourselves be carried down this way of mechanical annihilation (because it is so comfortable just to turn a button for everything you want). And I also feel that it is all largely our fault: that if we had not deserted and sold our heritage of all the ages for a mess of false business ideas, this young energy might not have taken our example and made Business as Business its gospel. I am ever so glad to have come out here, for I shall never more feel the slightest doubt as to the relative worth of our values. I believe the Greeks said that the elements of great art are terror and wonder; anyway I don't think you can have any life worth living without that background, and your life's work to turn that terror and that wonder into the understanding of love. I seem to be degenerating into a sermon; but so would you if you were out here.

The work has gone pretty well I believe and Lord Halifax has already been asked if he pays me to be anti-Semitic. As a matter of fact, I take great trouble not to be so and continually tell people how much more ardently anti-Zionist I would be if I were a Jew. I think there is much more noise than substance to the Zionist voice out here and I found most of the journalists, for instance, very fair and anxious to hear the other side. I shall be glad however when it is all over and I can get back to something more constructive again; it is horrid to be 'anti' anything.

Very much love, darling Pam,

FREYA

Los Angeles. 19 February 1944

My dear Chief,

Your letter came across all the continents bringing more pleasure than I can say. It was very like a ride in the early Delhi morning (without the possibility of falling off!). It made me feel as the Arabs do when you tell them that it is a fine day. 'And you are the fineness of the day,' they say.

This is a monstrous country. They have an expensive cemetery where mechanical canaries sing through the funeral service. Everything in life or death is provided for you, as long as you are contented to have it exactly like everybody else. 'Equality is not enough' would be my title for a book on America (a thing I never mean to write for I am passionately longing to get away to any little town of Greece or Italy or England, however poor). Hollywood, however, has a gaiety – you feel it enjoys spending its money as well as making it and it is new enough to meet here and there people who still have a faint trace of the adventure that brought them West in their youth. There is a poem about this 'West' I think you would like. I am sending it as a Valentine.

Lord Halifax in Washington told me they used to get to Simla in time to give one grand banquet with the gold plates and bunches of red rhododendrons all down the table. I hope you will go, with or without the banquet, and see the rhododendrons against the Dalai Lama's snowy land. Some day I should like to ride gently up the banks of the Indus, beginning where the bridge of boats goes into Baluchistan and going on till it got too cold. It would be fine to get out again while you are all there – who knows?

I feel rather like a slightly discouraged David travelling across this land with one Goliath after another to meet and only a small packet of slingstones which the Mogul perpetually begs one not to use. But as a matter of fact I think the Zionist has much less popular backing than the sound and fury would make one suppose. On the other hand, every American seems to think he is born with a capacity to govern India: you would be surprised. I have met charming people, lots who would be charming if they hadn't got a complex about the British and everyone has pleasant and cheerful manners and I like most of the American voices. On the other hand I don't believe they have any God and their hats are frightful. On balance I prefer the Arabs.

One ought not to make sweeping statements about countries one doesn't know – but a people that *prides* itself on monotony deserves it.

Much, much love to you all,

FREYA

Washington. 1 April 1944

My dearest Sydney,

I am back from my tour, very glad to have reached the post without disaster: a sort of buzz is following, of all the little wasps' nests of Zionists, very annoyed that the existence of another side should be brought to anyone's attention: I was attacked in Congress and called a 'creature' of the British government (why should it be an insult to be called a creature?) – a sort of 'Molly McGuire'. Can you tell me about Molly McGuire, so that I may know what I am really like?

Your letter has just come with the news of Ld Wavell's anthology:[1] I am so glad it is out and hope one is on the way for me. I read the MS and liked the little prefaces and it is interesting to see the poems that people prefer: his is a very individual and clear-cut selection: all very sharply defined and gallant.

There is a fear I may not see the azaleas after all and not get to England till July. There is talk of a book on Arabs for Chicago: if I write it, I must get it plotted out and the first chapter or so approved while still here (to avoid endless delays) and that would take me into the summer.

On the other hand, I would have to resign my job, so that when I did come I would be free and get a good time before the book is out before taking another job – I am not deciding all this, but taking what comes and it should be settled in a week or two.

I am reading the Bible – the 'As Literature' edition. It is absorbing and I had never enjoyed it so much before in those horrid small-printed double columns – now it spreads in all its grandeur. I can't help feeling that the troubles of Israel, first with Leban in Iraq, then with the poor decent Hittites, show how the peculiar talent of the Jews for being unpopular with those among whom they settled was a very early one – all beginning with that detestable Jacob. The man who suggested how to organise them in the Wilderness was Moses' Arabian father-in-law!

Dear very dear love,

FREYA

Washington. 2 May 1944

My dearest Chief,

I have debts of letters to a number of the Wavell family, but your letter comes first for I have just read your anthology brought here by Chips

---

1 *Other Men's Flowers.*

Channon and it has been pure happiness. I think it will always remain on the shelves of discriminating people and be a friend. It rings as clear as crystal. It is a lovely book dear Archie: I can't tell you how like a little running stream it runs beside one's way.

Here am I with my lectures finished, no longer a 'public woman' thank God. It all ended three days ago in Boston when I radioed and the announcer, having finished me off with thanks, promised her audience 'A Circus of Performing Animals' for next day. That is how speakers in public should be treated! I thought myself ill with the strain and long hours of it all but here in a little guest house all by itself in orchard meadow, with ducks and robins going about their business and no one asking about Palestine, I realise that all I was suffering from was an indigestion of human creatures: how much and how often you must feel this, imprisoned in marble halls.

My propaganda has been quite surprisingly successful. Nothing could have upset my Ministry more, they do so hate saying anything which annoys their opponents. I believe they only sent me out because they thought it was useless! Now Rabbis here have been writing to Lord Halifax and a man with Zionist constituents has been saying things in Congress and Brendan Bracken has had to say in Parliament that nothing is farther from my acts than Arab propaganda: it is melancholy. I would rather be landing in Italy in some secluded creek: do you remember my suggesting this to you quite a long time ago? I am reading those days over in Alex Clifford's *Conquest of North Africa*; he is a good writer and says of you in those days what every one of us was thinking.

You will be pleased to hear, as you do take a civilised interest in *hats*, that there are Paris hats here now. Very few, incredibly expensive, they have been smuggled by the underground. They are recognised at once amid the horrors of New York, all gay and happy and hidden in mists of tulle. There is a gallant Gascon touch about them and the way of their coming.

People coming from India say how much you are doing. Oh I hope the world and time will bring us all once again into our orbit; one longs for *friends* after so many platforms.

My love to you and Lady Wavell.

Always,
FREYA

Boston. 22 May 1944

My dear Elizabeth,

I went to an incredible party yesterday, given by Elsa Maxwell for Clare Luce – 100 people to dinner in the 'Salle des Perroquets' of the Waldorf Astoria. We got lost among naked marble ladies and elevators till the noise guided us to the aviary of the perroquets and there was everybody – John Gunther, Dorothy Thompson, Anne O'Hare McCormick, the Republican speaker Mr Martin, Congressmen, journalists and the highbrows of New York – Clare looking beautiful in a sad and bitter way: Elsa Maxwell with her arms round everybody, genuinely rejoicing in having so many friends all dining with her. I went with the Marriotts (Brigadier John just out from England and seated with a quizzical expression beside Elsa). At my table were Colonel Bodley and Henry Luce. Colonel Bodley has written a book on his seven years among the Sahara Beduin and we were soon talking nomad shop which I found very interesting. I had not realised that these Sahara Arabs had kept their traditions and racial character so intact. Soon, however, when I realised who it was on my other side I tore myself from this pleasant Arab meandering and plunged into Anglo-American tangles with Henry Luce, a tormented soul with a wife who must worry him as the bow worries the fiddle-string, but likeable. We talked about China and the Arabs and I found him surprisingly sympathetic over the 'sentimental' nonsense about exotic peoples that we suffer from: he evidently does not share Clare's indiscriminate slogans. I spoke about the Mandates, and how they had been the means of avoiding the balkanisation of the Arab world, and – when he asked me – suggested that the role of the U.S.A. might be to help and enlarge this 'umbrella' with which hitherto we had safeguarded single-handed these budding nations. I think I did quite a lot of good with him, as he seemed very interested. We then talked about England and he expressed disapproval of Winston in no uncertain terms: I had been trying to explain that 'Commonwealth' has superseded 'Empire' but he refuses to look on the P.M. as anything but an old-fashioned Imperialist and made me feel once again that it is the name we give and not the thing itself that people out here mind: he was quite passionate about it. At the same time he seemed to have a great feeling for the English. I said I hoped and thought that we were once again becoming 'Elizabethan' and he leaped upon this as if it were almost too good to be true, and only doubted it because, he said, it was hard to reconcile with our present adoption of government interference of every sort. 'What we Americans dislike,' he said, 'is not your buccaneer who goes out into the world and carves pieces of it for his own profit, but we dislike the man at a desk who makes a slow safe dividend of 50% with no personal adventure.'

By this time speeches were beginning and went on, believe it or not, till nearly 2 a.m. and *all bad*: the crowning horror was that I was suddenly dragged in with a question on the Arabs in whom nobody was the least interested. I did it very shortly. It was most frightening and I wished I were in a uniform like John who got out of everything on that score. Clare ended the evening with a long and accomplished speech, beginning with her childhood and going right through her friends to the present moment. The smiles, the movements, the pauses, the daisy-like schoolgirl innocence, were all thought out beforehand and nothing was genuine – but the voice is lovely with a moving quality in it and she is lovely to look at, and laid the flattery on like butter (unrationed) and everyone was charmed, even I because it was a work of art. The only thing I thought unforgivable was her reference to her former husband: she said that Elsa Maxwell had interrupted their friendship for fifteen years while she was married to someone who was a *bore*. A ruthless woman!

The only real lightness was brought by a comedian (Eddie Cantor) who excused himself from a speech and instead dived into the hotel and re-emerged with a shy little blonde in a turquoise hat with whom he sang a song about having a baby which I must say, in that highbrow feminine atmosphere, I found extremely refreshing.

I am in the train for Boston and it is my *last* public week!

Affectionately,

FREYA

At the end of June, Freya ended her American tour. She took a flying boat to England from Baltimore, sharing its honeymoon suite with the only other female passenger on board. She had already completed the first chapter of *East is West* (published in America as *The Arabian Isle*), which had been suggested to her by Dr Brandt of the Oriental Institute in Chicago and was intended to give a readable, accurate picture of the Arabian background to the Palestine question. She spent the autumn and winter in England, writing, and waiting for the moment when she could return to Asolo.

MRS JOHN MARRIOT

London. 11 July 1944

My dearest Momo,

I waited to write to you till I had seen John, and now I have seen him, looking as well and cheerful as possible, in his flat with all your portraits all about him. London is so strange and exhilarating: lots of empty houses, lots of blank and glassless windows, and those insects come droning overhead[1] and very few people bother to look at them. My Ministry implores me to go away and write, but nothing is going to tear me away before I have had one little month of London at war. There is a strange fascination about the doodle bug. He walks like a lost planet over a town, rolling along in a flaming dress. When he is right overhead, one has that peculiar feeling about the middle of one's tummy which I suppose is fear. What people object to, I think, is the visibility of death, to see it coming with its clumsy dark silhouette clanking from the south and know that nothing will prevent its falling upon *someone*, and then to wait quite a number of seconds in silence when the machinery has stopped and the thing is slowing down and falling: then the explosion comes. But I can't help feeling all our years in this planet are quite *wasted* if something made merely of metals and material things is able really to unbalance us, and I think most people feel the same. Once one has faced the fact that at any moment one may be dead, the whole of life falls into a good and agreeable perspective, and I can see why the ages of great art and religion must also be ages of danger. I hope we may turn out a great age when we have time to settle down to anything at all. I dined with Chips, a marble table, candles and peaches, and Emerald Cunard[2] who fascinated me as a museum piece filled with a fictitious but glittering sort of life of its own quite unrelated to the world around it. I had an interesting man called Gladwyn Jebb[3] beside me, who has to reconstruct Europe, poor thing. Oh Momo, *how* good it is to feel nearer to it all again, to hear the day's battle spoken to us direct from the battlefields every evening (one can hear the excitement in the people's voices and the crackle of shells behind them). Dear London – so shabby and knocked about and wearing her rags so toughly.

Everyone says how well the Americans have been fighting: the real union must evidently be built on the battlefields and perhaps that is where the future is being made. Did you hear of the British officer who had to deal with the War Correspondents for D Day? U.S.A. had already about 400 and at the last moment sent someone to ask for fifty more. The British refused. The American protested 'After all,' he said, 'it is the most important event since the Crucifixion.' 'And that was quite adequately covered by four reporters' said the harassed Englishman.

1 The V1 – the German flying bombs.
2 The indefatigable hostess.
3 Gladwyn Jebb (now Lord Gladwyn) had been Head of the Reconstruction Department of the Foreign Office since 1942.

Chips says that the one thing that binds Tito and Prince Paul together is their common dislike of Randolph.[1]

Dear love to you all from

FREYA

STEWART PEROWNE

c/o Lady Waller,[2] Thornworthy, Chagford.
5 August 1944

My dear Stewart,

A letter of yours came yesterday – very welcome. It found me here on the eve of sitting down to the typewriter. I would give a lot to have a clear month before doing so – just to sit and enjoy a vegetable life. Instead of that I spent my month in London and I must say, though so tired as to be only half-human, I never enjoyed London more. Its lovely emptiness amid all its battered windows, and breached thoroughfares, the sudden beauty of unexpected buildings and the quietness of the faces and gallantry of odd little notices – 'Business as usual' or 'Now in such-and-such a street' over some hole in the wall. One sees people too in a pleasant way taking odd hours from work, and a party is rare and everyone likes it. I dined with Lady Cunard in her Dorchester rooms (Buhl, and brocaded curtains shutting out the Hyde Park bomb that afternoon), with Oliver Stanley[3] on one side and the Duke of Devonshire the other, and Londonderry opposite, and we talked about Major Mitford who had said at one of her parties, which happened to have two Catholic ladies, that he considered any Roman, even the Duke of Norfolk, as the alien in England. The Duke of Devonshire says staunchly he is quite right. O. Stanley lamented that 90% of the Colonial Office work is Palestine 'which doesn't really belong to us at all'. Lady Cunard fascinates me – a sort of Mme du Deffand all out of her century, with pencilled eyebrows and eyes made brilliant with belladonna shining like stars in her ancient face (still with a beautiful profile), very gallant and unreasonable.

I saw Patsy and Alan Lennox-Boyd and went to dine there. Commander Brabner attacked the First Sea Lord on the neglect of the Fleet Air Arm. The tough old man stuck out his underlip and defended himself with great downrightness and good humour against exasperated youth; and I couldn't help thinking what an excellent training politics must be for the *temper* – always being criticised: parsons and women and schoolmasters never get it and suffer in consequence.

1 Churchill.
2 Dorothy Varwell, later Lady Waller.
3 Then Secretary of State for the Colonies.

The Goodenoughs gave me a great lunch with Admiral Cunningham[1] and the Edens. What a dear the Admiral is. I said to him, 'It must have been the best moment of your life when you saw the Italian fleet sail in to Malta', and he just pulled himself up, shut his lips tight, gave a little nod and smiled. Anthony Eden[2] sat next to me and told me how difficult the Middle East is to anyone who has the Cabinet majority against him; agreed time is on our side. I like Anthony Eden, he has something very simple, like a nice boy, in his approach, but I should say that if he becomes the P.M. his success would depend more on the quality of his Cabinet than on his own? This is not disparaging – perhaps *better* than a man so strong as not to have good colleagues.

I was taken to the House of Commons in its new home and saw the P.M. answer questions. As he comes in, a livelier atmosphere seems to come with him like a pond when a stream of fresh water is let in. He stood with his huge hunched shoulders and head forward, and I noticed his hands moving as he stood with the Speaker's desk before him, with little delicate gestures almost like a Frenchman's, strangely unlike the solid massiveness of anything else about him. Of course you cannot get words like his without the delicate artist somewhere behind them.

I hate leaving in trains full of evacuees as if one were running away: still, very few people have been spending a month in London for pleasure just now, and I need a bit of quiet life rather badly. I am writing this on a boulder with little amber waterfalls of the south Teign all round me. It used to be our land,[3] and I read *Paradise Lost* here when I was fourteen – *long* ago!

Affectionately,

FREYA

FIELD-MARSHAL LORD WAVELL

Chagford. 15 October 1944

My dear Chief,

I am sending you a few paragraphs out of my book, in which you appear. I hope you will approve of them, but if not you must tell me and like the politician's principles 'they can always be altered'. The book is now about two-thirds done, and it is supposed to be a picture of the Young Effendi: it is rather hard on him to make him stand all by himself

---

1 Admiral Sir John Cunningham, Allied Naval C-in-C Mediterranean Theatre, 1943–6.
2 Then Secretary of State for Foreign Affairs.
3 Freya Stark had been visiting Ford Park, built by her father.

in the middle of the canvas, so there is a rich sort of Cinquecento background of the Middle East, with camel caravans walking through history and people fighting in tanks: rather like one of those Persian miniatures. I am calling it *East is West* as it is supposed to make Americans think of Arabs as effendis instead of sheikhs. The book has anyway given me pleasant hours remembering far more than I can put down about the days in Cairo and after. I wonder if you kept a diary and will write about it some day? You must write about yourself, that is what people want to hear about, now or later. All our Beveridges[1] are making the world so remote from its *people*, and it is a relief to go to men like St. Paul who saw it all in terms of individual souls. (I am quoting him against the Zionists: he seems to have been up against those of his day!)

Here on these high moors everything looks small and remote as if seen through the wrong end of a telescope. All the foreground is full of pleasant things like bracken-covered hillsides and granite boulders, with rowan trees over brown streams and starting south-west showers.

Ever with much affection to you all,

FREYA

A branch of the Women's Voluntary Service had been formed in India and in the autumn of 1944 Lady Wavell wrote to ask Freya if she would go out to Delhi to devise ways in which Indian women could become involved. *East is West* was written. She left, once again by flying boat, from Poole Harbour at the end of January 1945, to a world of pageantry and grandeur she particularly enjoyed. Wartime Delhi, like Cairo and Baghdad, was very lively.

LADY WAVELL

London. 26 November 1944

My dear Lady Wavell,

Your letter reached me a few days ago as I was leaving Devonshire for London and I am so very pleased and touched that you should want to have me out to work for you. I should love to do so because it is you and the Chief; no one I should like better to help in any way I can.

I have written to Rome to ask if there is a job for me – they haven't answered and Mr Harold Macmillan I rather think doesn't like women fussing about so that unless they write very affirmatively and very soon I should feel free on that score. I do however not want to tie myself definitely to any time after the liberation of Venice as I must then go to my village and do what I can there.

1 Sir William (later Lord) Beveridge MP, architect of the Welfare State.

Would you like me to go out to you temporarily and see what I can do to start the ladies, on the understanding that H.E. wafts me to Venice when the Germans are out? One could at any rate lay down the lines on which to work and if I got a good P.A. I could train her to carry on. (Both my assistants in Palestine and Baghdad are now doing very well on their own.)

It seems to me that in all these organisations in the *East* one should keep the bond a very simple and fundamental one so as to rope in the people of goodwill who are anxious to help but are not sufficiently western in their character to take kindly to being organised. I went on this principle in Egypt and Iraq and found it worked very well indeed. If you have a very shipshape organisation they tire very soon and anyway you draw on a very small number, but if you make something so elastic that it can fit into their own lives with just a *little* change of direction, then you draw on a very large number. I should love to try what I can do, if you would not mind my doing it in my rather unofficial way?

Yours ever affectionately,

FREYA

SIR SYDNEY COCKERELL

Poole. 28 January 1945

Dearest Sydney,

You will be surprised to hear from me still in England – but here have we been sitting while our seaplanes slowly freeze up more and more. Every morning they get us up at an unearthly hour in darkness to sit in a frozen bus that takes us to a dingy breakfast. Luckily I am enveloped in a small cloud of generals and brigadiers who, after bearing Democracy patiently for three days, have now turned and rent the Company and insisted on females and officers down to majors being taken in the good hotel: so this morning we got up only at eight and walked up a snowy hillside to breakfast with a tablecloth and are resigned to another day or perhaps two of waiting while ice is chipped off the engines. You never saw such an arctic sight: ice floes in sheets floating about the salt water of the harbour: the moon sinks into it in an Ancient Mariner way, dull and rusty in the dark blue morning: the sun without warmth shines like Pure Reason in a wintry sky. The B.O.A.C. are like a bewildered flock of sheepdogs trying to run the sheep without a shepherd: you realise what a lot is meant by a leader and what a poor world it will be if we try to get along without that quality.

Your little book of what happened in History has been a great solace to me – how excellently it is written – and makes it possible to disentangle what civilisation has done to us. The central problems seem to be two: the dealing with the increase of population, and the distribution of the *surplus* of wealth or goods. Perhaps the greatest invention of our age may yet be that of contraception which should allow one to adapt population to the means of existence. As for the surplus, it seems to produce the greatest results when in the hands of a small and expert class: but the very fact of being so creates a stagnation which prevents that enterprise from continuing: one is reluctantly brought to feel that eventually it is a matter of civilising *everyone* or not being civilised at all: the decay has always come from a *partial* civilisation. This is I suppose the modern theory, but what a long drab interval must be gone through before the general level comes to what we have been fortunate enough to enjoy in our own lives. The art of the future will be to be civilised with no more or little more than everyone else has: it surely can be done, since reading and thinking and the creation of beauty are not so very costly?

Your loving
FREYA

MRS JOHN MARRIOTT AND MRS OTTO KAHN
New Delhi. 7 February 1945
My dearest Mo and Mrs O.K.,

I am writing to you both for it will be perhaps some weeks before I get time for letters. Dear Lady Wavell has left on a tour of the south, so I have not seen them (only Pam and Felicity here), but she left me an ominous message that I was to be shown the Files. Having got through five and a half years of war with no files to speak of, I feel that perhaps the fate of a government official may be finding me out at last. That however is still all uncertain and the files are being held in check by Billy Henderson, the nicest of A.D.C.s who is by profession and nature a painter. He couldn't sympathise more with my views. I am in bed in the most lovely suite – luxurious that is, with a fire *and* an open window (which is real luxury) and three bowls of roses, and the down-trodden Masses of India in crimson uniforms full of gold braid coming in with breakfast, responding happily if one talks English but stupefied if I try my infant Urdu on them.

I can't understand how people are blasé about India. That immensity rolling out beneath one: across the flat Sind plains from Karachi, flying in the sunset, the earth a warm, mauve expanse with long low ranges, like parallel waves disappearing here and there, hardly breaking the surface from the height at which one flies. One can almost see the curve of the earth falling away into twilight, swathed with scarves of mists like the light floating draperies of those gods and goddesses of the painters: far above in the clear celestial atmosphere one can *see* what the earth looks like from outside it, and think what a remarkable thing it is that the human mind could actually imagine it all from its pinpoint existence down below.

I am now taking a day or two of easy and sumptuous convalescence (as one can't possibly deal with Indian ladies without a voice) and sitting in the garden. It is a Mogul garden: the trees are all alike, little cypresses shaped like bombs standing on end, and a long-leafed tree clipped about into the shape of a pudding on a stalk: they stand in rows in little squares of clipped grass separated by narrow tiled walks or straight water running between tiled borders. Eight fountains are splashing high into the sun. In some of the little squares, instead of grass, are coloured clumps of flowers. The broader walks have sand-coloured patterns in the tiles. And the Wavells have opened these gardens for a fortnight, so they are full of wandering families, which makes them cheerful, and no doubt very like what they were meant to be in the days of Akbar. It does look astonishingly like a Persian miniature, especially when the *chuprassis* with a pointed cap sticking up from their turban and scarlet coats come wandering by.

Dear love from

FREYA

SIR SYDNEY COCKERELL

New Delhi. 19 February 1945

Dearest Sydney,

Yesterday the whole party came back and we gathered in the hall to curtsey. H.E. asked after you, and we talked of *Hamlet* at dinner – also of *Henry V*, and H.E. told me he likes *King John* and prefers the bastard to *Henry V*: on the whole *King John* is, it seems to me, one of the most English of the plays: perhaps that is what H.E. likes. I find it very difficult to talk with six A.D.C.s sitting in almost complete silence round the table. They are as nice a lot of young men as one can meet and the A.D.C.s' room, where one is non-official and each young man has a dog of different breed, is a cheerful place where a telephone is always going and most people would say that very little gets done – I am more and more enjoying places where nothing much gets done!

Lady Wavell took me after tea and talked to me for two hours about the W.V.S. and I am getting more and more unhappy about my job. I think a *little* may be done if I am allowed to do it my own way, but I think that very doubtful. For one thing, they call the creature I am to look after a

247

'Special Committee for the W.V.S.': now *who* would lay their souls down before a thing with a name like that? 'Women's Voluntary Sisterhood of Service' is what I shall suggest (as Lady Wavell clings to the W.V.S. in it), and hope they may adopt it. I think there is already a rift in the committee.

There is a football match today with the Viceregal Indian Staff team playing – the opponents are to land on the ground by parachute (so very *hard*): I am hoping to go.

Love from
FREYA

GERALD DE GAURY

New Delhi. 3 March 1945

My dear Gerald,

I have just come back from a grand sight – the giving of five Victoria Crosses to Indian troops. It was a gentle pearl-grey morning and the drying grass outside the old Mogul fort was surrounded by a huge crowd, the red walls and the moat were behind, the mosque of Shah Jehan screened by trees still leafless in front; the detachments of the decorated soldiers were there in the middle. Their families sat on two long benches just behind the Viceroy; three were dead, so two widows and a mother were there to take the honour, wrapped in veils – the little Mahratta widow's face was uncovered so one could see how frightened she was standing out in this huge amphitheatre with the Gurkha band just behind her and the Baluchis and Punjabis, appearing most terrific warriors, on either side. The aides, looking as if it were terrific agony, walked at a slow step in front of H.E. as he inspected. It must be wonderful to step out to take your decoration with your fellows at attention behind you. Now the troops marched past – the Indian Navy; the British, looking tough in a very casual way as if they scarce knew it themselves; the Baluchis, every one like a scimitar out of the desert; the Rajputs, quite magnificent, very slim, and straight with thin little fierce moustaches; the Gurkhas, throwing out their chests with a quick little sure step of the hills. The Moguls spent half their time watching their armies march and one can see why. We were a very grand party with a charming Rajah in a tobacco-brown long coat, white jodhpurs, gold slippers, mauve and yellow muslin turban sweeping down in a long veil.

I have bought a tiny picture.

Love,
FREYA

New Delhi. 13 March 1945

Dearest Jock,

These days have been so full that I have not been writing to anyone. I am now in an aeroplane on the way to Southern India. All sorts of pomps and pageants went on at Delhi before I left. The Black Watch band played in the garden after lunch when sixty-five people were invited for an investiture: the bugles blow when their Ex.s come in, the echoes floating very beautifully about the niches and lattices of the great marble dome. The thrones have a velvet canopy draped almost to the ceiling and the English Arms embroidered: Her Ex. sat there in a lovely oyster-coloured satin and her white hair piled on top of her head, sighing imperceptibly now and then (but only those familiar with her would notice). H.E. in a grey frock coat: he looks so much what he is, good, and simple and direct. Nobody could fail to feel it. The people invited all came to lunch and were arranged in a long row in the state drawing room, which has painted ceiling and huge windows and is very fine. We, the 'house party', are always arranged on the opposite side, and just curtsey, with no handshake. Nobody was smartly dressed among all the sixty-five, so that it was only the great length of the beautiful polished table and the line of scarlet servants behind it that impressed one. In the evening I sat next one of the two Rajahs staying with us: Rajpipla an elderly and (to judge by appearance) dissipated prince who told me that the happiest day of his life was when his horse, Windsor Lad, won the Derby (I think). He has told this to everyone: it is his best bit of conversation. But the other Rajah, Cooch Behar, was very pleasant and brought up in England from the age of seven, so that he tells me English is easier than Hindustani to him. Cooch Behar has a kingdom in Bengal and is related to the families of Rajputana. I got him to tell me about his ancestors and their battles with the Moguls and how their family, though beaten, had never given its women to the Mogul harems. The Udaipur also never did this and that is why they are the leading state of Rajputana. It is fascinating to see all this mixed with an English education. I am sure it is a good thing, as the feeling of a tradition does make for a dignified and happy stability which is the chief lack of the Westernising Orient. Yesterday I went with Her Ex. and Pamela to the Assembly and saw the M.P.s assembled, a lot of them wearing the hideous white Congress forage caps. It was all a very depressing affair: the *faces* were so miserable, neither intelligent nor strong, nor honest. It is *impossible* that a government made of people who look like that can last: the first 'whiff of grapeshot' would blow it away. The proceedings were all in nineteenth-century English: the two

Englishmen who spoke were uninspiring: Sir Olaf Caroe is always angry so that one feels an animal must be biting him inside. And the Members spoke with Gladstonian phrases applied to a vacuum, in their reedy voices. The Indian government ministers were much better and indeed quite good. Quite a large public were sitting around the gallery listening: six or seven women (and two women members), but they were mostly young men, obviously political, and again a depressing lot of faces. The *chuprassis* standing ready to carry messages were a far more promising lot. I can't tell you what a difference there was between the appearance of these unreal postures and the good crowd of the 1st Punjabis whom the C-in-C entertained to dinner.

I went to lunch with him on Sunday and sat next Lord Louis Mountbatten – *so* good-looking and I should think very pleasant though I thought he was bored with me and lunch parties in general (he had just arrived from Chungking). He showed pleasure and animation when the C-in-C's two pet cranes came up to be fed (true British trait to prefer animals to conversation).

My job is making no perceptible progress though I have been meeting rather nice ladies, a group of Indian Communist social workers, very friendly and amiable, but every one of them says that they can't work in with our system 'all on paper'. Whether they would do anything on any other lines I don't know, but as there are going to be so few British after the war I am sure that the only sensible thing is to organise on *their* lines and not on ours, even if it means less efficiency. But as not even a *tiny* group of people has been found for me to work with, I don't see how under at least a year *anything* can be done, and it looks as if Asolo really might be free by June.

We are flying over Allahabad, a rich comfortable plain with trees and villages as thick as dotted muslin and the patchwork of the harvest turning yellow. A river is coiling about – Jumna or Ganges? It looks like the kingdoms of the Earth and their riches and would have pleased the eye of any old Mogul king. How those people in the Assembly think they can keep it by just talking is unbelievable: but it is also rather sad to see it falling from our rather nerveless hands. The Civil Service I speak to seem to me so defeatist: the one thing one would think obvious is that we can't *both* not govern and remain.

I am travelling in luxury with a bearer who goes below by train with my luggage: he in fact is 'the half that has the keys'. Even so I shall feel quite strange without the A.D.C.s around ready to arrange everything for one. One of them, Billy, has bought me a sari, white emerald and gold, on condition that he is allowed to design my dress. Everyone is nice in that palace: it is a lovely feeling of enormous rooms and constant curtseys.

Love dear Jock,

FREYA

Travancore. 29 March 1945

Dear Lady Wavell,

I have had two long talks with the Diwan, who is the most agreeable and intelligent person to talk to and himself laid down all the ideas we are trying to work out. Social and business relations, said he, are what we want to cultivate and they have been vitiated by politics almost past redemption. If you could re-establish a personal contact, he thought most of the problems would be solved; but he did not see any prospect of it and looks forward to a civil war here in *any* case. He did not seem to worry very much about it! Every Brahmin, nice or otherwise, I have met so far has given me an impression of intellectual arrogance even worse than the French and with less excuse. This however is by the way, and the Diwan could not have been more interesting and knew a lot about the old spice-trading routes which are much more alluring than the organisation of women. But when I came up against H.H. the Maharani, there was a much tougher proposition. She had just got your letter, and all your forecasts were justified: she is interested in no doings but her own and not at all out for any general good. She talked for nearly two hours and ended by saying she would like to know and help later on when we get things more fixed. But she was very unenthusiastic about putting me in touch with anyone else here and, as in Hyderabad, I think it is better not to press too much but go gently. They are terrified of interference.

Affectionately,
FREYA

Mysore. 8 April 1945

My dear Gerald,

I think that grandeur palls very quickly. I have now got a collection of the ways in which servants abase themselves before one. In Delhi it is quite moderate, they just stand straight as you go by (and are very slow in doing that on a hot afternoon), and only really perform by all raising their hands in white gloves above their heads when they stand each behind a chair and H.E. sits down to his lunch. But in Travancore as you arrive everyone holds his fingers in front of his mouth (the Maharajah does this in the presence of the gods and it is a rather gentle gesture). And here as one goes about the palace, they stand like statues with folded arms and head bowed above them. And as I drove up the hill to see the sunset, an old gatekeeper at the palace at the top actually knelt and put his forehead to the ground at sight of the government car. Of course if you are used to burn incense to a bull, you may just as well say your prayers to a governor, and real paganism seems to make one very uncertain as to where to draw the line. But even as a very tiny satellite whirling in the divine orbit I can see how boring it must be to be the centre of adoration. As a matter of fact women often find this out without being at all royal, when people fall in love with them and insist on agreeing with everything they say. There is a pleasant feeling of worship going on about the temples and the peculiarity of the objects they worship doesn't seem to matter very much: cobras and monkeys and mice all come in, and there is an endless supply of pictures and stories. I think one would get fond of the gentleness and 'earthiness' of the Hindu idea of the world, but I *can't* understand Western people shedding their own for something so far back in time in the human scale.

Mysore is all among trees, many with strange and scented flowers, and full of new white buildings, domes and arches, traceries and scallops – and as it is the most progressive of the Indian States and I have been seeing an overwhelming amount of philanthropic institutions, I think I may have a rather onesided impression of it. I would like to get it right by spending a few weeks in nothing but jungle.

I am getting more and more depressed with this modern effort of trying to give *everyone* a little bit of everything. Food and health and lodging as Beveridge as you like: but everything else, education, art, philosophy, should exist in its *best* state and let who wants it obtain it – not debase it down to anyone's level: explaining God, explaining music, making reading easy, flattening it all to the level of the second, third and hundredth rate. It *can't* be the way to get civilised.

Affectionately,

FREYA

GERALD DE GAURY

New Delhi. 11 April 1945

Dear Gerald,

Got back yesterday: nearly died as we met a storm and soared 17,000 feet up, much too near Heaven for comfort.

I am going to the swimming pool to meet Edith Evans at lunch.

It is a funny thing but I am getting more and more frightened as the freeing of Venice comes nearer. So afraid of what misery there may be. I hope I can get there. Am looking frantically for an assistant here who would take over: there don't seem to *be* any women who can do things not laid down for them on tram lines. *What* a world it will be: everyone in groups, leaning against each other like those bullock carts one sees, because I suppose it makes the yoke seem lighter.

Affectionately,
FREYA

LADY RANFURLY

New Delhi. 15 April 1945

Darling Hermione,

I am spurred by the news and am just begging you as soon as Asolo is free to do your bestest to get into touch with someone there and cable me news of my home as soon as it gets cleared. Hermione, I am *longing* to do all I can for Italy. One just can't let the whole of Latin civilisation go down the drain and it seems to be in real danger of doing so. I am not sure that the most useful thing to do would not be to sit in Italy and write for some English papers, so as to put her on a friendly map again? Anyway, I'm ready to do anything I'm asked.

Love,
FREYA

AUSTEN HARRISON[1]

Jaipur. 26 April 1945

My dear Austen,

You would just go mad with joy over this town. Imagine it enclosed in toy battlement walls, with toy gates and straight streets of houses with stairs running down to the pavement, and baroque arcades, all lacy but not too much, and little domes and pinnacles, elongated and curved like eyebrows, and lattice-windows *and all this washed rose pink with white designs splashed all over it*. It is just the Indian eighteenth century with no one interfering. The pre-eighteenth-century fortress is on a hill above and I am just in two minutes going up there *on an elephant* and will finish this when I get back.

. . . I have got back from the elephant. Did you know that they had pink ears? It was fun, going *so* slowly with a sort of circular motion, while the battlements of the immense fortress draw nearer. They must

---

1 Government architect in Palestine whom FS had first met in Cairo in 1940, responsible for Government House in Jerusalem and later for Nuffield College, Oxford.

have seen *thousands* of elephants in their day. A man with a red sash, and a round black shield with four brass bosses hanging on it, walked behind me. He hadn't shaved for a week or so. I suppose it was the minimum cortège an elephant can go out with.

Yours ever,

FREYA

GERALD DE GAURY

New Delhi. 6 May 1945

My dear Gerald,

I am just off to Simla by the night train tonight. My work is done, my successor found, nothing further can be done till their Ex.s return and till the Political Secretary rootles round and finds the necessary funds. I am told that two ladies knitting over their gossip were heard to say 'Miss Stark has come to India to *disorganise* the W.V.S.'

I have been a recluse this week since the day of my return; divided between the swimming pool and my large bedroom, sea-green, shuttered and air-conditioned, with Archie John[1] or an A.D.C. coming to drink sherry in the evenings. Pleasant and restful. I think I want to be one of those people who are always to be found at home, nice restful people whom everybody likes because they give a feeling of permanence to this rushing world.

Love from

FREYA

JOHN GREY MURRAY

Simla. 11 May 1945

Dearest Jock,

This high blue air is reviving me already, though I think the poor old creature needs a year of it. The ineffable feeling of getting up in the morning when you like, knowing you can do just what you like with your day!

It still seems incredible that the Western half of the nightmare is over. All sorts of clouds still lowering but the end of the actual destruction leaves a sort of blessed stillness. My God – may it be the last war in our time.

Simla is fantastic, a bees'-nest on the top of several hills joined by ridges – all trees and the shoddiest houses. No style either in building or people: the most sordid mixture of types, but a vague Victorian atmos-

---

1 Son of Field-Marshal Lord Wavell. Succeeded his father as Second Earl Wavell in 1950. Killed serving with the Black Watch in Kenya in 1953.

phere about it, and the best-looking people are the rickshaw coolies although they do sit about in rags. Felicity Wavell and I are in Squire's Hall, a small and charming house in the grounds of Viceregal Lodge, all balconies and windows, and the view sloping away and bordered by the great hills when they show. Simla lies like a *parure* of topazes high up under the stars at night. If one isn't a great walker, it is a prison: so high and every walk ending in a steep drop where the pines and the fields and villages go steeply down to the hidden clefts that drain to Sutlej: but if one could walk there would be endless days in the hills. What happens to you now? I suppose you stay on [in the army] till the Japs are finished? But I can't think it will be very long.

Love dear Jock.

FREYA

SIR SYDNEY COCKERELL

Simla. 22 May 1945

Dearest Sydney,

Yesterday all the Viceregal cortège came up here and I moved from the Officers' leave camp next door into a grand and comfortable suite that looks out over the falling terraces of garden to the Sutlej and the ranges beyond it. It is an oddly pleasant house: pinnacles, bow windows, rough surfaces of grey stone like a bad Scottish mansion, and inside a huge hall three storeys high, panelled in linenfolds surrounded by ornate banisters and carvings, and weapons hung in all the apparently inaccessible places. A shallow wide carpeted stair runs up; a wide open fireplace has a fire; there are silver sconces with electric lights like candles; there are portraits of Viceroys, C-in-Cs, Rajahs and Maharajahs; and photographs of a forgotten world – the Kaiser in spiked helmet sending 'good wishes for 1914'. One has a feeling that people have been happy here. The A.D.C.s' dogs have all got cold noses since their arrival. One sees how pale and lifeless everyone comes up, and they say I am quite different in this fortnight.

How heavenly to have a little leisure. I have read *Othello, Macbeth, Timon of Athens, Pericles* and now *Antony and Cleopatra: Pericles* seems to me a pot-boiler for what was later to be *A Winter's Tale* and *Cymbeline*. But *Timon* is a strange outburst and comes strangely after *Lear* and before *Cleopatra*. Perhaps that too was the rough material, the acute vision of the bitterness of life which when he had time to *digest* he moulded into the meaning of the great tragedies – the last two pages, when Alcibiades and the Senators talk, seem to give a clue. Both *Macbeth* and *Othello* give an overwhelming feeling of the *danger* of life, the power of evil ready to

255

swamp every moment of weakness in people who so easily might have escaped, who were not inevitably bad. Timon sinks and fails at the sudden sight of it: but in the last pages it seems to me that Shakespeare's own sane and moderate estimate is sketched and that in that rebellion and agony and the moderate conclusion can be seen the *ingredients* of which the greater tragedies are compounded – I may be talking nonsense.

Dear love,

FREYA

JOHN GREY MURRAY

New Delhi. 7 June 1945

My dearest Jock,

You can't think *how* disappointing – I was in bed for the great arrival and now that these historic days are here am like a mouse in the wainscot; members of the family come and give me crumbs of the gossip as it goes on.[1] Poor H.E. having got all and more than he asked for (eleven hours before leaving England after all those weeks waiting) now finds his Council all prickles. I can't help feeling that this was well to be foreseen as the Council are the eggs which have to be broken when the new omelette is made and having seen how things like the M. of I. and such receive the news that their dissolution may be advisable have no illusions as to how people in office react. These are rather doddery old people for the most, so that they are not all likely to go on from strength to strength.

I suppose it will all be settled in a matter of days. Dear H.E. came up to see me after dinner last night. He looks aged since he left, but I expect it is just fatigue – he had a council meeting the *night* he arrived and ever since! He was his usual completely equable gentle self, dismissed all these weeks' struggle as all in a day's work and we talked about his visit to Ibn Saud in Riyadh. He flew in from Jedda just for a night and it was a great meeting: I wish I had been there – H.E. tried to sit on my bedroom floor cross-legged in his evening clothes to show me how it was, and I wondered what his Council would say if they could see him after the time they had been giving him. He got Ibn Saud to tell him the story of his conquest of his capital which must have pleased the old king very much – I was so pleased and touched at being visited while all this is on.

Tomorrow I hope to get up a bit. It is a sort of fever, 'flu, cough – and very annoying. It is 112° outside and dusty and the fact is I have had as many hot summers as I can take for the time.

Love,

FREYA

1 This was the eve of the Simla Conference on the future of India.

New Delhi. 11 June 1945

My dear Gerald,

I was charmed with your story of the young man smiling after the prison in Poland. There is, with all the troubles seething here and there, a pleasant feeling now that a great many people are happy.

I hope to be so soon. Before leaving Simla, John Wharton brought a soothsayer – the handsomest old Punjabi Muslim you ever saw, with perfect features, very clear and straight. He told me that in about two months' time the best seven years of my life are to begin, with a journey overseas. He also said that I had a 'tiger face' which means that no one ever dares to be impertinent in one's presence. Also he said there is a *very rare* line in my hand which preserves me from telling lies, flatteries, or feeling envy. Nice people, I thought, who still feel it comforting to be assured of such virtues: nobody in the West would think it worth while to mention such non-utilitarian things.

H.E. has written to Field-Marshal Alexander to ask if I may disembark in Italy. I still hope to hear I may and perhaps get away by the end of the month from this cage. It is *incredibly* uncomfortable to live in splendour: one feels like a railway station – every time I have been away (four times) every single paper or piece of clothing has been taken out of my cupboards and drawers and put higgledy piggledy somewhere else. I thought only female housekeepers managed to run households with this sort of inhuman discomfort and am cured for life of the desire for royal lodgings. No sooner are you accustomed to your servants than they go, sometimes to hospital, but usually just for a general post which is the timetable of the house. The garden is so arranged that it never provides coolness at any easy walking distance. And instead of the cooing doves which soothe the Middle Eastern summer, we have a variety of birds whose throats seem made of brass and every sound that comes out as if we were twisting them. It is not nearly as hot as Baghdad, and merely less tolerable because of the uncivilised way of life we lead.

There is a quiet time at the moment, but the thunder of a tide approaching and I suppose any moment it may be on us. I am glad to be here for this historic moment. Everyone seems pained at the fact that every secret instantly oozes out of the secret sessions of the Executive Council. I should be much more surprised if it didn't and do wonder how we keep our optimism in the face of years of oriental experience.

Love from
FREYA

New Delhi. 18 June 1945

Darling Pam,

This just a scribble in haste to tell you that I *hope* to get leave to go to Italy in a week or two. I can get no news of my home except that I think I would have heard if it had been burned down altogether.

Meanwhile however we all go up to Simla. Poor H.E. already head over ears in the temperamental fireworks of these peacock-vain politicians. The saintliness of Gandhi seems to me more bogus with every word he utters – all directed to the Viceroy and addressed to the public. However H.E. goes steadily on and no one could be better, since he gives that rocklike feeling of sincerity and integrity which people who are used to nothing but façades do recognise and value.

I suppose you are deep in elections and cries and calls. I am relieved that I have no vote. I believe that I would vote Labour or perhaps Liberal: it seems to me there is want of a good Gladstonian Liberal party now. On the other hand, Labour, so long as it sticks to Conscription, would not do much harm now and might be far worse later. And I believe anything that comes in now will be pretty unpopular in six or seven years.

Dearest love,

FREYA

SIR SYDNEY COCKERELL

Simla. 24 June 1945

My dearest Sydney,

I know you will like to be written to on this historic day, just as we are all waiting for Maulana Azad, Head of Congress, to call on H.E. this morning, and the Mahatma has crowds ready to greet his arrival in the little electric train from Kalka, down the hill.

Billy Henderson, the painter A.D.C., whom you may have met, a charming person who wanders like a lost anchorite among the official affairs, took me in his little Austin Ten at 2 a.m. from Delhi, with our luggage in the back and his woolly Tibetan dog on the top of it. Even the stars seemed hot with dust, and that huge airless pile suffocating in its own heat, stagnant in the night. We drank some iced soup and then were away through the dingy streets, between the motionless drooping trees, out past the ridge and the pre-Mutiny houses, out along the Great Trunk Road, all quiet with the trains of bullock-carts walking gently through the darkness, their eyes shining as they came into the shaft of our car. Little wandering breezes began to meet us as we got into the real country, however flat and dry. We passed Kanel, about eighty miles out, where the old indigo planters had their houses, now still lived in by local Zamindars: one could see their pleasant eighteenth-century lines and little pagodas and etched arches in the light of a sinking moon. At 7 a.m. we had passed through Umballa and reached the little hills where the streams spill out in flat sheets of water to the plain – and there, just before Kalka, the Maharajah of Patiala has a walled Mogul garden with gates and towers, and old wide trees round it with bricked platforms all interwoven by their roots, where people can sit. We spent a delightful hour having breakfast here, with doves and the cross-tailed iridescent bird they call the king-crow hopping about on the ground. We got away and went curling up, and halfway to Simla discovered an *old shoe* tied on by a fellow A.D.C. for our elopement! We passed the police just turning out along the road for the Viceregal party following grandly in the heat of the day. We were the *avant-couriers* (and rather disreputable ones) when we reached Viceregal Lodge.

H.E. and his Secretaries are very busy and there have been all sorts of alarms and hesitations: and do they want our cars or will they have their own or come in rickshaws (not many people are *allowed* cars in Simla). Gandhi was offered one of the Viceregal small houses and has taken it for some of his party while he stays with friends near by. Today is all interviews, one this morning with the Congress head (who speaks little English) and Gandhi and Jinnah this afternoon.

This was interrupted yesterday by the arrival of the Head of Congress in the morning and the rest of the day seemed to be spent (for me) in stalking these eminent ones with my camera – Maulana arrived, a very tottery old man, with an extra and unexpected Pandit (Pant of all names) to interpret for him. Azad is the show-Muslim of Congress and joined it apparently long before it was a weapon to beat the Government with. I photographed him driving away in his rickshaw and in the afternoon awaited the arrival of Mr Gandhi, who came ten minutes *before* his time, almost giving a heart attack to the A.D.C.s. Luckily they were there and their numerous dogs shut away in their bedrooms. The Viceregal rickshaws had been sent in full rig, blue and red – red woollen stockings with no feet, red sashes, red peaks to the turbans – and the crown in brass and a monogram on their chests. In their little crowd the old Mahatma sat very small benign cheerful and, as it seemed to me, *tough* – obviously cordial and pleased to meet all the good-looking young Englishmen in uniform gathered on the red-carpeted steps of the porch. I haven't spoken to him, but he had an atmosphere of great charm which one felt at once. After more than two hours partly with H.E. and partly with Her Ex. (so annoying I might have been there if I had known) he re-emerged and decided to walk, his thin spindly little naked legs and glasses making him look like some insect with white drapery fluttering about the middle like wings. The rumour has come that the press tormented him as he got out: it is now confirmed that the crowd pressed up to him and he lost his temper and took one of their cameras and threw it into the air. (The Indian police never will make a stand against any European or American pressman.) The result is that he felt so tired today and slept till 9 a.m. and has not attended the Conference opening, which everyone regrets. What he said to H.E. of course we do not know, but he talked to Her Ex. about air travel, the Legends of Rama, the Dean of Canterbury, Eton, the Bishop of Chichester and the *Hindustan Times*!

After him came Mr Jinnah looking as sleek, sinuous and neat as a lovely grey serpent. One can't help thinking of one as one looks at him, but not in an unpleasant way. Merely because he is so sinuous and graceful with a feeling that every ounce of him is *energy* and no waste.

I went up and had a few words as they were all gathered on the lawn this morning before Their Ex.s came out and the Conference began. It is a pleasant grassy flat bit with the intaglio of the grey stone house piled up in decorated tiers behind it and the Union Jack floating on the tower. There is a big shady tree built up on a gentle grassy round platform and the lawn spreading to a wide English flower border; there are other terraces descending along the ridge in tiers, and then the woods, and then the mist with hilly shoulders. Jinnah asked me where I came from and said 'Devonshire cream' in a heartfelt way when I told him. He has an attractive face because it is just *sparkling* with intelligence, small features, eyes rather near, but strung to a tension like a bowstring about to shoot. Sitting all by himself (he talks no English) was Maulana Azad the Head of Congress and I was taken to him and found he spoke easy Persian and Arabic and had a father from Mecca – so we were very happy. And then Their Ex.s came and went round talking to everyone down the line and nothing could have been pleasanter. The press were there in a varied international group and H.E. spoke a few words to them and there were lots of photographs – and they all went down to the Conference. Now they are out again and sitting in groups on the lawn and those who like can have a carefully selected vegetarian lunch in the ballroom while we females have been moved to the Council Chamber.

With dear love,

FREYA

9

Home at Villa Freia, marriage and the Caribbean, social life in Barbados and London

On 20 July 1945 Freya landed in Rome. She reached Asolo a week later, making the last stage of the journey in an army lorry. The house was intact and Emma and Checchi, the maid and gardener, and Caroly Piaser, her mother's assistant in the *tessoria*, were there to meet her. She had been away almost six years. Flora and Herbert Young were both dead, as were her two nephews, one lost in Russia, the other killed in the fighting in Piedmont. Only a niece, Cici, was left.

SIR SYDNEY COCKERELL

Rome. 23 July 1945

My dearest Sydney,
   How strange it is to be here, and Simla, and India, and all the East has rolled away to the other side of the world. I flew in one long day from Karachi to Cairo, spent three days there and saw the few friends remaining in a comparatively empty, quiet and dusty town, far more expensive than I remembered it; left at 2 a.m. from Almasia aerodrome which I remembered in all the bustle of war – breakfast just before sunrise in Tobruk – and about eleven was seeing the coasts of Sicily and landing on the Continent of Europe. It comes with a terrific impact: every day brings some deep feeling, either of familiarity or change. Naples sat among all its fields, tended and ploughed and planted as in peace – but then one reached the town, what a desolation: the airfield surrounded with tumbled ruins, and the town not really ruined so much as defaced; the plasters and stuccoes are peeling or blasted and the poverty of building appears; but not nearly so bad as London. It is the misery of the people which is so awful – the *gay* Neapolitans walking their streets silent, with dull eyes, with clothes incredibly drab; houses half-empty, and the children listless about the pavements.
   I came back to my hotel weeping and felt miserable at the thought of finding this everywhere: but here it is very different and Rome is what she must have often been – a cloud over her of immense prices and poverty and lack of transport, but a living city and oh *how* beautiful.

People lodge in their *palazzos* with the lovely things that look better for being shabby and worn – and they stroll about the gardens, and are gay.

I leave for Venice tomorrow. My hopes of a quiet life are I fear to be shattered, for someone is coming this morning to try and make me work for the M. of I. But I have said I will only do something that can fit in with at least half my time at home – I am the first person to get back to Italy like this on my own (and everyone rather surprised): they say it will be six or eight months before permits are given. There is no transport except military in the north and the problem of food is not too easy. Fuel also. The whole life of Italy hinges on coal, and there will be many sorts of misery and trouble if she gets none.

But the *vaporetti* have just started again in Venice and the road-bridge is intact though the railway doesn't yet run. Ordinary travel is beginning in lorries with wooden seats they call Pullmans. By great luck, Boni and Teresa Roascio, my sister's nephew and niece, have just come down to Rome and were able to give me lots of news and good news of my own little niece Cici, so happily married. The Germans annihilated a number of villages I used to know, as reprisals: the mountain valleys behind them were held by partisans, and it would be most desirable if such of these partisans as don't belong to the district were got to their homes as soon as may be – as they are liable to go on being partisans indefinitely. All sorts of problems are looming ahead and one still feels very near here to the naked facts, hunger, poverty, isolation, that the politicians in India for instance seem to be so remote from.

The young military man, Colonel Piggott, has been and wants me to be Public Relations Officer for all North Italy with a car to go about in – oh, my dream of quiet! I don't think one *can* refuse, and perhaps it will not be needed very long. Anyway I have accepted only if not a full-time job, so that I may spend part of my time in Asolo and go on tour from there – and it would not start till September (and perhaps the M. of I. in London may not agree).

I leave for Venice tomorrow with three bottles of olive oil and twenty-four lemons from here – a little coffee, tea and sugar from Cairo and two cashmere shawls and a pair of furry slippers from India to face whatever there may be.

Dearest love,

FREYA

Asolo. 13 August 1945

Dearest Jock,

I have been here over a fortnight and never a moment to write – it feels like some very remote, landlocked bay, right out of everything. A puny little rag from Venice can occasionally be bought for thirty times its prewar price, but it says nothing and we don't even know if peace has come or not. It has here, anyway, though with a shadow of famine in its train. Have I written to you since I came? It was so strange. In a lorry from Padua, over a makeshift army bridge, by a German tank head-down in a canal, along the familiar tree-shaded roads and the peasants in their soft felt hats and decent Sunday black gathering in groups while the church bells tolled. And then (the road not so good as before) up the hill and all just as it was – the little fountain, the group of children, the front-door bell with its same unbalanced tinkle, and Emma opening the door and Checchi behind her. All is there in the house, except the people who made it: I still almost expect to see them as I walk about the garden – I am still struggling to get everything right again.

18 August 1945

Was interrupted and never got back, and am now in a hurry as someone is leaving for England and calling at any moment. The house is slowly beginning to look like itself again, though every chair has to be re-covered: the Fascists must *sit* much more roughly than we do – they have rubbed bare places with their arms. This poor little town was made G.H.Q. for Republican Italy and the General stayed in my house. The grass path is worn bare by the *carabinieri* sentries walking up and down and eleven unexploded shells were lying there beside it: the laurels were cut down to take away cover from snipers, and the General (a little self-important man fond of the cinema) would go out with two guards before and two behind holding their tommy-guns not casually over a shoulder but level and ready in their hand. *How* the people here all hated them! The German S.S. only came at the end and were going to make Asolo into a last centre of resistance; but things moved too quickly, luckily. There was no bomb damage, though everyone lived in fear, and Pippo, a low-flying bomber of ours, patrolled the roads and dropped a bomb on any light that showed. Pippo is a sort of Frightener, like the name of Boney. Up in the Grappa the partisans lived and also a lot of innocent men with flocks, who were rounded up and their houses burnt. About forty-eight young men were hanged and left on the trees of the avenue of Bassano: a little withered garland of leaves now hangs on each of those trees.

Everything however looked so peaceful and luxuriant, the year leaning towards autumn with a rich profusion, and we were counting our grapes and tomatoes – when a frightful storm came rushing at us: a sort of waterspout which turned to hailstones as big as pigeons' eggs (and I mean this with no exaggeration) and in five minutes *everything* had gone. You never saw anything like it; the bark was torn off the branches; every fruit, apple, grape, tomato, was on the ground; and all the winter's maize vanished. There is an awfulness about anything so sudden and complete. Then the rain came, and soaked through everybody's roof into the houses: we put buckets here and there and watched it pouring down through cupboards and ceilings. Then the wind rose; the garden was illuminated like a hissing, tossing, roaring sea and there was no interval in the lightning flashes: it was light enough to read in my room. Dozens of trees were blown down in the plain and a monument was carried off its pedestal and smashed (the only good thing done by the storm). Next day I drove into Treviso and it was like a stricken winter land – no trees, even the grass ploughed by the storm. And the spectre of hunger just a bit nearer! I am collecting what I can, but everything except silk stockings is hard to get – soap, cigarettes, sugar, to say nothing of the bedrock of flour, butter, rice etc. Luckily the *tessoria* is still holding itself just above water: Mama ceded it to her secretary,[1] who changed its name, so it is not legally mine till I buy it back, but she is a dear and does all the hard jobs for me, and her family keep a food shop, so I shall not starve. How I wish you could come out, even if it meant finding food for you! I think I must try and keep a diary for you. It is rather fascinating to be here, with the country just beginning to feel its life after the awful nightmare.

I am all right for money. I am selling some old cameras, glasses, etc., and the pianola: and that and what I have will see me through to Xmas: then I have asked Knopf to send so shall need nothing from England. If I need any here, I shall borrow from the local bank.

I don't suppose I shall hear news of the books for ages.[2] I did ask for six copies here of both, didn't I? Dear Jock, do come out as soon as you can.

Your loving

FREYA

1 Caroly Piaser.
2 *An Italian Diary*, by Flora, and *East is West*.

MICHAEL STEWART[1]

Asolo. 16 October 1945

Dear Mr Stewart,

Thank you for your letter – I hope you have received mine by now explaining the only difficulty in my way: if my £100 a month is an 'allowance' I can accept, but if it is called a 'salary', it involves English (as well as Italian) taxes on my other income to such an extent that the result would be a deficit and not a salary.

I would be very grateful for a letter telling me what you would like me to do exactly. Major Alexander is most helpful and we have plotted out a rough idea for your approval, trying to cover as wide a field as we can and to help each other without overlapping – while he does the straight 'British' information, I would travel about and try to get independent centres for books and paper-reading to start in the smaller as well as the larger towns. In this way one may hope to get both the people who want to read us because we are British and those who want to read what we have but do not like to come to the British Government for it (like the Communist Vice-Sindaco of Venice whom I met yesterday). I suggest that while we supply the papers etc., the local Italians supply everything else and run the thing on their own lines, with occasional visits and perhaps a small apparently private donation now and then – so they feel it is their own effort. The difficulty is going to be housing, as there is very little room left in the towns here. The other difficulty is going to be to keep it non-political and generally inclusive. Anyway I think it might succeed, with any luck.

Yours sincerely,
FREYA STARK

GERALD DE GAURY

Asolo. 18 October 1945

My dear Gerald,

Nearly a month for your letter to reach me. My quiet days are over and M. of I. has thrown their lasso over me for 6 months: after that, wild horses will not make me take another job: I have surely done enough, and why should one not be allowed to lead the good life in one's old age and enjoy pictures and music and the books one likes, and journeys at leisure, and the views and flowers of one's own garden? It seems almost immoral to have all this in a year like this one, so I am doing this job out of a feeling of austerity, but it is jolly well the last! You can't think how pleasant

---

1 Then in the British Embassy in Rome.

Asolo is now. Nigel (who has come for a fortnight's leave from Athens and sends his love) and I walked over the hills to Maser[1] yesterday, and the slopes are turning pale gold with a brilliant blue sky. I took him for his first sight of Venice. Fancy seeing Venice for the first time! We spent two days there, not grandly in a whirl as you do, but pottering about in a gondola in the evening under the little arched bridges, in and out of the Middle Age and the Renaissance, watching the marble lion or sphinx masks over doorways, spending a whole morning among the Tintorettos and the Ducal palace: the mornings for Culture – Adrian Bishop said – and the afternoons for Recovery and Pleasure. Archie Colquhoun and his gang joined us to talk Communism at Florians. They got their Communists to meet me at lunch, one a most charming person anyway: one in three is quite a good percentage! Venice has become gayer and more normal: the shops are *filled* with pre-war things at vast prices: Nigel presented me with a piece of soap for 380 lire. I think if people are selling, it means they expect this inflation to deflate fairly soon. The shops are open too till 7 p.m. now and there is a natural look due to the fact that fewer Allies are about.

I now get all the papers and realise how they spoil one's pleasure in life. Those Belsen faces! Mr Molotov! Our poor diplomats trying to say it doesn't matter! What a world! I believe poor little Molotov is quite genuine and honest and can't see that it matters whether one tells the truth about a conference or not: and what have we all been doing and saying all these years to make him think any differently. We have allowed the use of words to become debased and are now paying for it by seeing nothing but counterfeit coins!

Love to you from
FREYA

FIELD-MARSHAL LORD WAVELL

Asolo. 9 November 1945

My dear Chief,

It was very good to get your letter. Even the crown on its envelope did not make it travel fast and it was over six weeks on its way, but I had been wondering about you all and feeling the whole half of the world, and such a deserty half, that lies between, and then it came and brought everything quite close.

Now that the enemy has gone, the people have pulled their copper buckets out of hiding and go to fetch water at the well as they did after the

1 Palladian villa near Asolo, owned by Contessa Marina Luling Volpi.

Vandals and the Goths and the Huns and the Celts had come and gone in their turn. The roads are filled with ruts and holes and the country people come along and shovel in a little earth and stones to keep them going. We have bandits roaming at night in bands and holding up lonely houses and the people who live outside the towns are setting alarm bells up that can be heard and may bring help. Our small Polish garrison, like medieval mercenaries, patrol Asolo at night. A deputation of citizens came to ask me what they were to do when the Poles, rather drunk, open doors and shout 'We want women' in bad Italian. I felt this was not my sort of job to cope with and suggested a good lock to the doors as the best answer. I enjoy living so far away and am reading histories of the Dark Ages and feel them almost contemporary.

I wonder what will happen after your elections? It seems to me that the only thing people are feeling more and more strongly is that you are the only person who can tackle that huge job. Did you find in London that last June had cleared the air and made the problem appear plainly to Whitehall? The Palestine question seems at last to be showing its genuine shape to the people who write about it in England. What a *horrid* world it is just now.

Please write again dear Chief: it gives me one of the best of pleasures.

Much love to you always,

FREYA

P.S. One of my Dark Ages historians says that Queen Brunehilde was paraded in North France in the eighth century on a *camel!*

MICHAEL STEWART

Asolo. 4 December 1945

Dear Michael,

I am initiating the new typewriter, so all sorts of things may (are) happening. That, and the car, and all are here: it is very exciting. Apart from the Venice circle, at which we all worked and which is to be inaugurated on Saturday and which Major Alexander will have told you about, I hope to have planted four more little shrubs, at Conegliano, Bolzano, Bressanone and Trento. The Civil Liaison lent a jeep; it was very bracing, crackling over the ice at ninety klms. to the hour in a wind that made one's face feel like falling off.

Bressanone seemed quite important, as it is the ecclesiastical centre for a wide district, and the church is the least political medium in that troubled area. Father Malden, an English Catholic missionary, having travelled all over the world is ending his life in a cheerful quiet way in the house of his Order at Brixen. His native talent for administration shows instantly; he lost no time at all, fixed on thirteen members interested in English and a room in the Elephant Hotel for our papers and took me off to see Miss Weth who has been a governess in the best sort of Scottish families all her life, and now, with stiff corsets, black brocade and pearls, leads a benevolent and refined old age knowing everyone in Bressanone. Father Malden says he will see to the rest.

At Bolzano, I happened to discover that there is a *Università Popolare* and got some acquaintance there to bring along the School Director and his wife to an evening at the dreariest place of amusement you can imagine. I sat him next to me, while everyone languished all round, and talked him over; he thinks he can get us a room attached to the *Università* and will make an all-party committee and write and let me know. He came away quite mellow and enthusiastic; poor man, his wife so plain and knows all about Kant and Schopenhauer.

I drove out to Merano where I only knew of a Graf from Styria who turned out to be one of those aristocrats you think of only in operetta and far more dead from the point of view of ideas than I ever hope to be in this world or the next. He had an Alsatian wolfhound and a lot of antlers all about and periodicals bound in dark leather firmly settled on their shelves. The Russians have looted all his castles. Merano, he told me, is full of commercial people who never read.

In Trento we visited the Partito d'Azione and found a young partisan with Renaissance hair who said he would love to do anything so long as I assured him that Britain will not insist on the Italians having a king. I told him that if only he had been reading some of the British papers he would realise how unfounded were his fears. The only thing we stipulate is a non-party committee, so that as many readers as possible can improve their minds.

Is this a sufficient sort of Report? I hope the next one will look neater. Do you think my money could be sent to me in Turin by December 31st? I am getting rather low.

Yours ever,
FREYA

JOHN GREY MURRAY

L'Arma, Ventimiglia. 6 January 1946

My dear Jock,

It is a relief to get even to the ruins of L'Arma.[1] The roof is going to be put on next week and the rest of the damage is more superficial. I am

---

1 Cottage bought by Robert Stark for Flora and Freya in 1918.

scraping £250 out of my salary (*lucky* I have a salary just now) and Cici and Franco can spend it as they like and must do anything left over themselves. It ought to do everything that is necessary to make it habitable. The furniture is mostly there, though in a horrid state of chaos and neglect: all the backs of the books have been eaten by mice. But it ought to be ready for camping in by May and Cici will go down there for the summer and have a heavenly time setting a house of her own in order at last.

She has had a very hard time poor child. What I feel about my brother-in-law is unprintable. He left my mother without a penny in an enemy country knowing she had nothing but what he owed her and took the opportunity of not paying; he let my cousin, who had worked for him and been devoted to the children for years, ask in vain for money from her concentration camp, where she finally committed suicide; and he practically turned Cici out of his house. I have done with him thank God, now that the children are out of his hands. As for his face, all his vices are printed on it, so that one does get punished in this world after all.

I have got three reading centres started up and down the coast and only spent the holidays at L'Arma when no one was in offices, and tomorrow we go back to Turin and I shall have a fortnight of miserable cold going round the little towns of Piedmont, but hope to squeeze in the weekend on skis. I would like my work if I did not feel perpetually cold and very tired: but who doesn't this winter? One thinks with real longing of the first spring days and the last, I hope, of the war winters.

You can't think how happy I am at the thought of having got rid of a possession. That L'Arma will go on, being a means of happiness, and that I have not got to keep it on, gives me a feeling of such pleasure that I realise how necessary it is not to have one bit more of the goods of this world than one can constantly enjoy. When I have got rid of Canada, and am left with just Asolo all nice and centralised, I shall feel beautifully unencumbered.

Dearest Jock, are you quite a civilian with the New Year, and happy to be one? *When* are you coming out?

Love to you all,

FREYA

JOHN GREY MURRAY

Turin. 20 January 1946

My dearest Jock,

I think I have done well by the M. of I. and started something for them in nineteen towns already: the people I meet are all eager to receive, cooperate and go ahead: the question of finding rooms free and for nothing and with lights and windows (one doesn't hope for heating) in these bombed towns is the greatest difficulty, but even that is overcome: and I like meeting such nice genuine people. I like the lunches in provincial hotels, market-town centres filled with substantial middle-aged men clumsily dressed but with a very discriminating eye for the wine, the cutlet and the gorgonzola. You get everything in these places (except real coffee): loaves of white crisp bread, grated parmesan, every sort of meat: you pay immensely, feel happily benevolent and return sadly in the evening to the Military Transit Hotel where the Victors eat their dismal meal of margarine and camouflaged bully beef, suited to the poverty of their incomes. It *is* a strange world.

I thought I would take the weekend off and go with Cici and Franco up the valley towards Modane to one of the skiing places. We went to a little hotel at Sauze d'Oulx with a glorious view of peaks shining in sun: the air tasting of snow; a lovely world I had almost forgotten.

I would have been on my way to Milan today but we have had a terrific snowfall and everything everywhere is blocked.

Love from
FREYA

SIR SYDNEY COCKERELL

Asolo. 14 March 1946

Dearest Sydney,

I have suddenly been offered the Freedom of Asolo. I believe it has never been given to anyone before, and everyone is telling me how glad they are, so that I am much touched by it all. It also makes me feel what a very real thing the small city is in Italian life: I have been reading so much history lately, and this seems a continuation of it all.

It really was a great event, even though it poured with rain. A huge bouquet of carnations with two small Union Jacks inserted and tied with a huge Italian bow arrived in the downpour, with friends from Venice. They all came in and then went to the Municipio while I was told to wait like Cinderella till my hour came. Then Cici and Caroly and I walked out (with neighbours waving from all the windows that overlook my gate), and found a crowd of the populace of Asolo gathered about the Munici-pio, and two municipal guards all shaved (which they rarely are) and saluting smartly. There is a beautiful hall, and it was crowded with everyone here I know or my mother or Herbert Young ever knew before me. The people invited were down below and the 'public' were in a gallery above, overlooking: and the prefects of Venice and Treviso, and the Sindaco of Treviso were there: and Major Harrison representing the Allied Commission, and John Miller[1] and the 'boys' of Casa Genova 13th Corps Liaison, from Venice, and the Venice Sindaco too. And presently I was seated on a red velvet chair, flanked by the prefects and Monsignore; and our Sindaco, who is very young and nice and had thought of this, and very shy as he had never made a speech, went to the middle of the opposite row of chairs with the Municipal table in between, and stood there flanked by his *Quinta*, who are all the blacksmiths, upholsterers, house painters, masons, etc. – people we have long known. In the hush, someone upstairs got so excited that he dropped an immense umbrella which came like an incendiary bomb floating down and narrowly missed the Municipal heads: and I mistook my way and was for sitting in the Sindaco's chair.

But we all got sorted and the Sindaco read his speech and it was so touching and friendly, and remembered my mother, and sounded so sincere, that by the time I held my scroll of Citizenship in one hand and my bouquet in the other and had to speak also, I found my voice wavering and had difficulty in starting; but then by saying just what I felt and thanking them for all they had done during the hard days – and mentioning the *tessoria* girls, and the lawyer, and Caroly, and Emma and so on, and telling them how the house was first bought in 1887 by Herbert when he and my father were students together – I found the audience all with me. I can't tell you how simple and moving it all was. Cici was in the audience, and people were crying. I think it was a sort of return, a symbol of peace and the old friendships restored. We then went again in a downpour over the cobbles to the castle, where a wonderful spread of food and cocktails was waiting and we talked for an hour, and everyone mixed, and the workmen who are on the *Quinta* told me how pleased they were. Letters have been coming in; and the Communist head of the library in Venice has telegraphed, and so has the English language professor in Padua. I think everyone feels pleased that Asolo thought of this symbol after my mother's treatment by the Fascists.

I had twenty-four of the Venice people to lunch – a sort of picnic all over the house which went on till after tea time. Now I am leaving for Mantua and must hastily end this with much more to say.

Dearest love,

FREYA

---

1 Author of *Friends and Romans*.

BERNARD BERENSON[1]

Rome. *1 April 1946*

My very dear BB (if I may?),

There is no longer the lovely leisure of I Tatti, and in any case it would be impossible for me to tell you all the goodness and pleasure of my visit to you. I am *so* grateful for it. It was like a return to all that one has lived in and dreamed of, and a consolation to find it blossoming under your hand. Thank you, and Nicky, for the warmth and loveliness of your welcome, again and again.

I arrived in Rome very late, with so much to beguile me on the way. The car behaved in the most obliging manner, breaking down *in* Siena and Viterbo, so that – although, like Mr Churchill, I am '*très bon camarade*' with my conscience – there was no need to strain it, and I lunched in Siena in the *piazza* after seeing the Duccio, and waited till the palace was open to see that incomparable Madonna. What a glory! As for the *piazza*, it took my breath, just as the first sight of the Himalayas, or of the tower-towns of Southern Arabia: it seemed that *it could not be possible*.

It was already getting late, but we deviated to Pienza and how delighted I am that you told me. The position is so beautiful, and that Gothic-Renaissance church and its gold pictures. I wondered as I came away if Aeneas Silvius had named the little streets: Via dell'Amore, Via del Bacio, Via Buia, Vicola Cieco. The sequence amused me.[2]

So much affection to you,

FREYA

JOHN GREY MURRAY

Asolo. 11 June 1946

My dear Jock,

Already I wake up in the morning without that horrid feeling that Life is Real, Life is Earnest. I know it isn't and that nothing will be very different if I lie in bed and read *The Testament of Beauty*. There is a lotus atmosphere in my garden, and as nobody gets up for breakfast it is always afternoon.

Asolo has voted for the Monarchy, but I have put out two flags for the Republic today. A nice man in Venice who makes beautiful glass is saddened by the fact that the only thing the new masters of the world, the Americans ask for, is 'cheap, cheap'. It is the only word he has learned, he says. Here the poor still think it worth while to give a little extra for

---

1 The art historian and critic. FS had been staying with him at I Tatti, near Florence. 'Nicky' was Nicky Mariano, Berenson's secretary and friend.
2 'Love Street, Street of the Kiss, Dark Street, Blind Alley.'

Beauty. I have made a New Year's resolution to save no more money and spend whatever surplus the Gods may send on beautiful things. It seems to me as good an object as any philanthropy.

Do come soon, dear Jock, and sit and talk in my garden.

Love from
FREYA

SIR SYDNEY COCKERELL

Asolo. 14 September 1946

Dearest Sydney,

I am just back from Venice and find a good letter from you waiting. I hope for more news too, for Jock rang up and is on his way here tomorrow: it gives one a beautiful feeling of reunion with the world when a friend really arrives – not just a pleasant person unknown before who happens to be in Venice, but someone who has really come on purpose across the waste of Europe to see one.

I follow India only in bits when a paper comes, and feel so sorry for H.E. He told me in his last letter that he often sees Nehru and likes him, and this *must* be having an effect: no one could withstand the *truthfulness* of H.E.'s whole person. But Nehru seemed to me a sincere but a weak man, and not one to hold the reins of such a plunging team as India. Jinnah I believe H.E. took a dislike to (and he went in smoking a cigar, too, which I do think the A.D.C. should have saved him from). It seems to me that Jinnah's whole policy is bound to be to *prevent* our efforts from succeeding: it is obviously against every plan of his that we should succeed, and I don't see why one blames people for not being ready to compromise when their whole line of policy goes in another direction? I am sure we ought and must hand India over: I don't believe they will let Russia in: it is not that they want anyone more than us, and perhaps we may build up a far better relation quite soon. But all this only when the present deadlock is overcome. Anyway I can't help feeling that one good is done – a close personal relation is built up with H.E. which must have altered their ideas of British statesmen a great deal.

I am being called and this must catch the mail.

With dearest love,

FREYA

STEWART PEROWNE

Asolo. 6 October 1946

Dearest Stewart,

How very rich to have two letters of yours to say thank you for – I am always so glad to get them and you have left so many friends here that all are delighted with news. Marina has a small infant child still peacefully unconscious of the fact that it has to carry the name of Diamante Deodata right through life and I was to be godmother, but it seems the rules of Rome forbid. I saw them in Milan, when I took Jock to get his train.

What a relief to have Nüremberg over.[1] One would have thought it a relief even for the culprits, though it must be fearful to face death with no such very good prospects beyond. What can go in those minds these last days? Do you remember Montrose, sleeping his peaceful sleep before his execution? Raleigh's letter to his wife? It seems strange how very little people are worried about how they are going to meet that time, which is so sure to come.

With love from

FREYA

SIR SYDNEY COCKERELL

Asolo. 29 October 1946

Dearest Sydney,

I thought this might be my last letter before leaving, but now I have postponed my sleeper in Milan to November 28th because Nigel Clive has sent a sad wail begging me to let him have a short leave here, and he can't come till the 12th. So I shall spend I suppose a week in Paris (getting a white chiffon gown and a *hat*) and be in London by December 7th at latest. It seems almost incredible that I last saw it with V1 and V2 bumping down at intervals.

Bernard Berenson came here on Monday, in wonderful good form, and quite exhausted by his tour of friends and picture galleries. The Duff Coopers also came to lunch and have asked me to stay in Paris. She is no longer so lovely that one cannot bear to take one's eyes away: in fact, many people of her age are better to look at because there is more interest in their faces – a sad penalty for the perfection of youth! Marina tells me she came to her (Marina's) coming-out party and as Marina was distributing garlands for the cotillon she stood so ravished before this lovely vision that she put one garland after another round her bare shoulders and made her seem a sort of Venus in a foam of flowers.

Dear love dearest Sydney,

FREYA

East is West was now out. Freya needed a new book. Pausing in Paris for an enjoyable look at the clothes, she reached London in the late autumn of 1946 to

1 The war crimes trials.

discuss with Jock Murray the possibility of a collection of essays, an 'Every-woman philosophy' to be called *Perseus in the Wind*, on themes 'beyond our grasp, yet visible to all, dear to our hearts . . . a comfort for the frail light they shed'. She was also planning to start work on what were to become the four volumes of her autobiography. Her life was on the verge of taking an entirely new direction: that of marriage.

GERALD DE GAURY

British Embassy, Paris. 1 December 1946

My dear Gerald,

It is fun being in the big world again. Everything has a glow and zest: pictures, plays and clothes. I have been to Schiaparelli and Molyneux, with rows of hard-faced women with narrow eyes looking at the newest detail as the mannequin walks around holding her label in her hand. Diana and Duff are the most kind and imaginative hosts: one just sees them now and then, is asked to stay in for the gay things and allowed out for the dull ones. Taken to plays – yesterday *King Lear*, which had a tremendous ovation. I was greatly moved by it: it was beautifully cast and staged and Laurence Olivier a great actor in the part. After it (*long* after, it was one o'clock before they arrived) they all came to supper and I sat next to Laurence Olivier and found him a charming person, very easy to talk to. He told me he had wished to grow rubber in India, and his parson father persuaded him to go on to the stage. I asked him when he was going to give us Antony, and was pleased to find him agreeing that this is one of the supreme acting plays. But he said Antony can't be acted by a young man and it will be in about ten years. Like all arts, he said that it is the technical part which is the hard labour, and when the instrument is ready, the inspiration comes. I am sure this is so in writing: he thought the sign of the real artist is the willingness to undergo all the pain and trouble. We talked about *Richard III*, and he told me he had incorporated in that great first speech a whole chunk taken from *Henry VI*, and that not one of the critics had spotted it!

I am staying here for a week. A beautiful Schiaparelli chiffon is being concocted, and a hat like a small pillarbox with a veil – it is just heaven to be able to think of a Paris hat again, though most difficult to procure the necessary francs. Diana introduced me to someone as 'an explorer who is interested only in clothes'. It is quite a *disinterested* passion: I really prefer seeing them beautifully worn by her than having them myself. The very latest thing is to have a wide full skirt and garters of fox worn *under* it below the knee.

Much love to you,

FREYA

Paris. 9 February 1947

My dear Gerald,

It was very nice to hear from you, just in the last two days when life in London was far too much of a rush to do anything in the way of answering. Now I am here, with Juliette Huxley who is Queen of Unesco.

Do you know the latest romance? Biddy Carlisle[1] and Walter Monckton.[2] They are looking rejuvenated and radiant and are hoping to be divorced and married this year. For some extraordinary reason, they thought I might disapprove of it (as if I ever worried about people's private affairs!) until Pam saw them and I was asked to dine.

London is altogether a hopeless place for seeing one's friends and I think another time I will go straight to Oxford, which still preserves a pleasant atmosphere of civilisation, where you can find your friends at home and pleased to see you if you happen to pass by. Isaiah Berlin[3] was in bed with a chill in New College, lying, as he described it, 'like a prostitute – people come knocking at my door all day'. I lunched with the David Cecils,[4] and found Lionel Smith, who showed me the cross that still shows the place on the pavement where Cranmer was burned. It was snowing and, in London, most people's pipes had burst. What other country would let them do this every year and not put them *inside* the houses? There was general gloom over Palestine, India, coal, and everything else.

Here it is a little less cold, but on the other hand, there is even less fuel. Only the Embassy is lavishly warmed. I went to the Salon Vert last night and found Diana surrounded by Generals, and Mr Masaryk[5] looking like a pleasant and intelligent frog. General Morgan, just on his way to take Jumbo's [Wilson] place in Washington, told me he had left blocks of ice in the Venice Lagoon.

I had one very pleasant evening before leaving, with Harold Nicolson[6] at John Murray's. We got him to talk about all sorts of people – among others Edmund Gosse, who was once visited by an old lady who had inherited the MSS diary of Byron's doctor and wanted to know what to do with it. Gosse himself told Harold that he 'advised her to burn it', which she probably did.

1 Eldest daughter of the tenth Lord Ruthven; married to the Earl of Carlisle.
2 Sir Walter (later Viscount) Monckton, lawyer and politician.
3 Now back in Oxford as philosopher and academic.
4 Lord and Lady David Cecil, old friends of FS. Lord David became Goldsmith Professor of English Literature at Oxford the following year.
5 Jan Masaryk, Czech Foreign Minister.
6 Author and (1935–45) Member of Parliament. Married to Vita Sackville-West.

He also told a nice story about Churchill, who, when complimented on his obituary speech on Chamberlain, said he hoped the Divine Providence would spare his ever having to make one for Baldwin. In spite of this, when Baldwin was out of everything, he invited him to lunch and, instead of taking his usual afternoon nap, took him all over the secret rooms where the invasion of France was being mapped and planned, knowing too much how he must feel, being kept away from all the news.

Yours affectionately,

FREYA

SIR SYDNEY COCKERELL

Asolo. Easter Day 1947

Dearest Sydney,

This is a very hurried note, as everything here is happening all at once: Osbert Lancaster,[1] Lulie, and the Wavell honeymoon pair are in the house; there are all the social calls and Easter greetings; this morning eleven children from the *tessoria* (including the two youngest work girls) came to hunt for Easter eggs in the garden; and the bathroom is *still* being worked upon. We leave on our tour on Tuesday, so you see it is rather hectic and no writing will get done till I return, anyway. I enclose one more chapter and an improved ending to Chapter Four. I am most anxious to hear whether you think it is going to be a book worth writing.

We have now had two fine days since mid-February and it seemed like a resurrection to sit out and have tea in the garden. There is very little there but grass. The few poor shoots and buds were crushed by hail so that the elements are really spitefully directed this year. I hope Tuscany and Umbria will be warm, but I am starting out in my tweeds all the same.

Osbert has brought a most enthralling book: the account of Hitler's last days gathered from all the evidence by a young don called Roper.[2] It is extremely well done and, of course, Hitler has succeeded in his *Götterdämmerung*. The story is so dramatic that it will never fade out of history. The awful *stupidity* of the Nazis is what shocks one most. I took the book up reluctantly, but am now unable to put it down.

Always your affectionate

FREYA

---

1 Osbert Lancaster, writer and cartoonist.
2 Hugh Trevor-Roper, *The Last Days of Hitler* (1947).

Rome. 26 April 1947

My dearest Jock,

We reached Rome two days ago, happy and in perfect harmony, but Osbert has seen eighty-five churches since his arrival and I fifty-two, with all my reading centres added. Osbert is very tough, but I have been in bed with a temperature. I am up today and told Osbert that I could have a car from 4.30 to 7. 'Oh yes,' says he, 'there are two churches I am most anxious to see.' Insatiable!

I am delighted today to get your letter with Harold Nicolson's criticism and so pleased with it. I had hoped to give the effect of a tapestry, rather rich and not too sharply defined and it is a great joy when one's attempt is taken as it is made. And I must say that your first words, and especially SC's, were *very* discouraging. Sydney has a kink against anything mystical or religious: it rouses a quite unintellectual animosity in him. So we will have to agree to differ, while considering his remarks on technical points. As a matter of fact, I would have been even more depressed, but I had showed it to BB, who embraced me and said that we 'live in the same universe' and that it is the best I have done. Lulie and Cici, who are both sensitive and not particularly literary, said the same. So it is evidently one of those things that people either like or don't like.

I hope to get some more done when I get home. I thought of calling it 'Perseus in the Wind'. It is a title I thought of years ago when I saw the constellation at the head of all the Persian passes; and, as it refers to the stars that lit my path, it seems suitable, and I could get in a paragraph in the text to explain it.

Oh Jock, I *wish* you had come. *What* haven't we seen? Zig-zagging between Trecento and Renaissance like mad. Lulie lost something in every resting place; Osbert makes a habit of walking away with his hotel key, but is very expert in returning it; I only forgot my passport. We spent the last night on the shores of Lake Bolsena where the Corpus Domini was invented; otherwise it is only known for its eels.

Thanks for all,

FREYA

SIR SYDNEY COCKERELL

Asolo. 19 June 1947

My darling Sydney,

You (and everyone else) are being so neglected, but it is the fault of this book. I struggle to get a little time, and even so, it is very rare to have a clear morning. I am only in Chapter Eight, but hope to be at L'Arma in a fortnight and to work there every morning. Meanwhile, visitors come and go. A quiet little female party of Pam [Hore-Ruthven], Juliette Huxley and myself is being broken into by Steven Runciman tomorrow. It will be so nice to see him again, after last lunching with him in Jerusalem in 1942! Today a young buccaneering Irishman called Leigh Fermor[1] is coming to lunch with Joan Rayner who was Osbert Lancaster's secretary in Athens. But Pam and her two adorable boys are leaving. It has been a great joy to have seven weeks of nearness of such a real and dear friend.

The *tessoria* gives a good deal of work, but it has at last paid off its debt and we can buy our new lot of raw material out of our own resources. As for the garden, a *pink* lily has blossomed! I go and look at it with adoration at intervals through the day. If you see any very exciting and beautiful combination of flowers at Kew, I shall be so glad to hear. It takes very long to try out colour schemes in gardens, as one has a year's interval with each effort. I now have a lovely mass of great Regal lilies under the ilex trees, and orange day lilies just beyond. The sun shines through them against the far background of the plain and they fill one's mind with peace.

I am buying a tiny motor bicycle left over by the commandos. It can pack into a suitcase, and will be very useful for getting about.

Dear love, dear Sydney,

FREYA

NIGEL CLIVE

Asolo. 14 September 1947

My dearest Nigel,

Such a peculiar thing has happened: I have promised to marry Stewart. I have not written to anyone to tell them yet; but I must say so at once to you, for you are very dear to me, nor do I feel that this or anything else will affect it. I hope you will feel this too, and make me happy by saying so. If you had been old, or I young, we might have lived our lives together; or perhaps we might not have cared for each other or not realised it. As it is, we hold hands across a river of time. Nigel darling, please remain my dearest of friends.

It is one of the happy things that Stewart likes the people I like. We have a common world to set out in. He is being sent to Antigua. I believe he just couldn't bear to go alone and had to have a wife among his tropical kit. Anyway, I am by way of going out in a few months, and

---

1 The writer Patrick Leigh Fermor.

going now to London to see it all through in a deplorable hurry. So it all seems very unreal at the moment. I think, too, it will mean no Greece in January, and I don't mind in the least if you are not to be there. But you *must* come here when next I am back, probably in the summer.

Don't mention anything till you see it officially announced.

Dear love,

FREYA

SIR SYDNEY COCKERELL

Asolo. 24 October 1947

My darling Sydney,

Such neglect, but you can imagine what a mountain the poor little mouse, my pen, has been eating its way through. Apart from the ordinary business of a honeymoon, and the extras of masons and carpenters, hammering all the wrong places of the house, a garden party on the last of the warmish days, for Asolo and the *provincia* to meet Stewart, and so on. Now his day for leaving is upon us: we go to Venice tomorrow and he starts next day; and I shall follow in January, I hope, and see you perhaps on my way through. I shall be buried in my book for the next two months, in the hopes of getting it done by Xmas.

How happy I am, dear Sydney, that you met Stewart and liked him. The process of getting married was so alarming, and it seems to me so monstrous to undertake such solemn things without in the least know-ing whether either of you is going to be able to carry them out, that if it had been at all possible, in that last fortnight, I would have done like an unwilling horse at a jump and taken the nearest gap in the nearest hedge. Many feel like this, I imagine.

Now, however, I am going to miss someone who requires such constant attention, and I am glad I accepted the adventure. It is so hard for human creatures to get near to each other. A relationship that makes this easier is happiness. Even a misanthropist would say that marriage gives one the advantage of having someone to get away from occasion-ally and increases one's capacity to suffer? Please don't show anyone this letter, or it might be misunderstood. Now we are building up a whole number of things together: books we read, evenings by the fire, the arrangement of the new rooms, and I hope each is making a little bond. And, in spite of being such a middle-aged couple, we do feel very happily alive.

Today is the first day of cloud and cold. The country is so beautiful, just turning to copper and gold.

My dearest love always,

FREYA

Villa di Maser, 13 November 1947

Darling,

I walked down here, only to find that Marina had mistaken the day and is in Venice; and has just telephoned that she will not be back until ten tonight. I have been sitting very happily reading Napoleon's letters to Marie Louise. He always says exactly the same thing six days running. But they are very touching all the same; and, it seems to me, there is very little to be said for ML, even remembering she was a Royal Austrian. The only point I would like you to imitate is Napoleon's way of dealing with his wife's journeys. Here is one specimen:

'Amica mia. I desire to see you. You will leave on the 22nd and sleep at Chalons: the 23rd at Metz, and the 24th at Mayence where I will join you. You will travel with 4 carriages for the 1st service, 4 for the 2nd, and 4 for the 3rd. You will take the duchess, two ladies [I would dispense with all those], one prefect of the palace, 2 chamberlains, 2 pages, a doctor, and two red and two black ladies [their clothes, not their faces it seems], and your dinner service. Take a coach for yourself. Prepare it all. Adieu, my darling. Yours entirely, Nap.'

Your
FREYA

I Tatti, Settignano. 8 December 1947

Darling,

I have been driven out by the ancient chauffeur to see a villa that has been bought by Lionel Fielden.[1] The villa is very fine: rather a fortress, with only two heavily barred windows on the ground floor, and a garden hung in space on high old walls; and then the land drops and sweeps away, and the hills fold one behind the other, all smoke-coloured with cypress and olive, and houses at intervals. An incredibly sophisticated landscape, refined through so many centuries. BB's garden has a wonderful triple hedge, immense, of cypress, and then ilex, and then cypress again cut broad and flat on either side of a central cascade of steps, and grass. I admired the sunlight which seems to *die* onto the darkness, and he said, 'Yes, they are the nearest vegetable things to metal.' He always has these happy phrases. A woman with dyed hair and lots of bracelets came into tea, and he said to me, 'Ever since I have known her,

---

1 Lionel Fielden had come to Italy in 1945 as Director of Public Relations, Allied Control Commission.

she has been this *article de commerce*. What I call a woman of clank and fashion.'

I am working like a slave at the book; I have all except the epilogue done, and am half way through the revising. It is extraordinary what a help it is to be in a sympathetic atmosphere for writing. BB makes me talk about it, and reads it, and it does help a lot. But I *am* longing to see the last page sent away, and so relieved to think that tomorrow morning, instead of finding adjectives, I am going to buy a hat.

The name of the Greek theatre between Halicarnassus and Alexandretta is Aspendos. Do let us go!

Your
FREYA

STEWART PEROWNE

I Tatti, Settignano. 13 December 1947

Darling,

The Marchesa Fossi, who is half English and very pleasant, brought me a tiny silver Madonna and child, two inches high, as a present yesterday. I do hope she will see to it that we lose no more of our wedding presents. I will bring her out and keep her in great honour and comfort on my dressing table. Otherwise, I am sure I shall drop my wedding ring one of these days, as I have just lost Patsy's[1] little ring. It is so *sad*, and BB says think of Polycrates who couldn't lose a ring when he tried, as if that were any comfort.

Victor Mallet, the new Ambassador in Rome, came and lunched today. He is an agreeable man, but I sat on BB's other side and listened to him all through lunch saying the wrong things. BB very dangerous and urbane. How desperate it is when public servants come to think that just making a noise with their mouths is pleasing to other people! He evidently thought that it made BB happy to have the wrong names stuck onto his unique pictures. 'A Baldorinetti, I feel sure. Ah, no? How *could* I have thought it?' And all he had to do was to ask and be interested in hearing *who* it really was, or else talk of something that he knew.

14 December 1947

We have had a fine day: Florence like a statue with a veil, in her mists in the hollow, and every gentle line and colour of grey and green and rose in the hills that rise about her. Hoping to send off all except the Epilogue to be typed for the third time, tomorrow, before I leave for Asolo. So I do nothing but eat, talk, sleep, write, and take two little walks with BB,

1 Lady Patricia Lennox-Boyd.

who makes the whole of the last century live again in his memories. He was telling me about Oscar Wilde. They were great friends, until Lord Alfred was so objectionable that BB couldn't bear him, and told Oscar not to make them meet again. Oscar was passing through Florence and visited BB, and there was this (so he says) dreadful man. And when Oscar came to apologise, BB told him that he was courting destruction. Oscar said to him, 'I am like God in every way and must have constant praise.' He brought him the first copy of *Dorian Gray*, and BB read it and told him he thought it appalling; and Oscar was almost in tears, and said he knew it himself that it was bad, but they offered him £100 to write it, and he needed the money so badly. And the whole continent of Europe has been reading it ever since, apparently unaware of how bogus it is.

BB dreamed that at last he wrote something which delighted him; and, in his dream, said to himself, 'Now this is prose like Freya's' (such a kind thought in a dream), and woke and not a *word* remained. I have often written long poems in my sleep, and would like so much to remember; but one only sees a sort of form disappearing into shadows when one wakes.

Your
FREYA

STEWART PEROWNE

Asolo. 4 January 1948

Darling,

You sound awfully cluttered up with domestic problems, and so many more will be bearing down upon you when you are a Married Man with a Household (though I will save you from dealing with the servants); I hope you won't repent and wish yourself a bachelor. It's much easier to think only for oneself, but rather arid; you can always look upon a wife as very good for you (I believe Socrates did). I am finding it rather sad to leave Asolo (Emma in tears at any moment and Caroly, also); and I long to be so far on the way that you are growing a little more real on my horizon!

The bathroom is finished and is such a gem that it is worth being in debt for years. It is not opulence, but it is so beautiful. When I first came back here, I made a five-year plan, and it is now three years done all in one go. So it is not bad, and such a comfort to have all that mess and trouble behind one. And you can go in and shut the door and turn on that beautiful light and forget that the world of Utility exists. I feel as if I had purged away a little of all the ugliness of all those years of war.

I have packed five big straw hats and four parasols (the hats are bigger than the parasols), two fans, and some mittens. All this because you have given no really intelligent information of what is worn; so it will be all the worse for you if parasols are 'not the custom'. I am feeling so unflatteringly sad at leaving. I wish you were here.

Your

FREYA

MR AND MRS JOHN GREY MURRAY

SS Ariquain. 3 February 1948

My dearest Jock and Diana,

This is the first day I feel alive again. The hurricane (it was an official hurricane) is over, the sun shines, the portholes are open at last, and a soft, tropical breeze is flapping this paper on deck, and my bread and butter letter would like to say thank you for so much more than bread and butter (and I am not referring even to claret and stout). One makes oneself such various homes in this world. When I left Asolo, I was feeling homesick for that, and I imagine (hope) there will be a growing 'homeness' out here; but I know that I shall always think of you two as one sort of best sort of a home, where one can be oneself and find oneself together.

Malory was on my rack ready to be opened for the birthday, but alas! this poor little boat is very light, having no cargo, and she creaked and rolled. One clung to a perpendicular bunk like a fly on the wall. The waves looked like the stony desert hills, huge and full of barren ridges and shining like mica in pale grey gleams of sun. It felt almost *indecent* to be there, like intruding on a family scene with the winds and waves howling at each other, or jostling like huge herds of grey elephants, and tilting us up and down their great slopes. I felt much too ill to enjoy it; and the stewardess is a good old type and, without even pausing to think, contradicts anything any passenger may say. In the calmness of the Bristol Channel, she went about as glum and disagreeable as a funeral, grudging one even a hot water bottle (and furious if one got it for oneself). Then suddenly she appeared, beaming with cheerfulness and kindness, to tell us that 'The Captain says it's a hurricane' and enjoyed every minute of it, with her tray cloths all sopped down with water to keep the things from slipping, and everyone ill in every cabin. She liked me better after she heard I had had appendicitis on the Atlantic, where she went to and fro in the war, 'getting the bacon and eggs home: it had to be done.' Now she is quite a friend and would love me if another hurricane came to bring us together.

We had a day's lull in the lee of the Azores. I *would* like to stop off there for a week. Nothing can be stranger than to come upon them there in the middle of nothing, with huge cliffs; and, on the top of them, flat lonely pastures, well tended and walled with hedges, but no houses, until you look toward the softer slope of the islands where sparse little white groups are scattered and there must be small hidden coves. Terrific white towers of spray were breaking against their dark red walls, and there was a big distance of sea between the islands and, of course (I was told), a strong disapproval of one for the other. We went right in towards the mouth of the chief harbour (Fayal) and saw a little clean white town, prosperous and quiet.

No more now, except love to all five.

Your
FREYA

JOHN GREY MURRAY

Bridgetown. 25 February 1948

My dearest Jock,

I have been here a fortnight and haven't written. Really not lack of time, but a sort of caged feeling; and I felt if I wrote it would be just a wail. I found Stewart turned into the perfect Civil Servant, completely occupied by files and minutes and the *things that are done*; people with cards (three of them) in shoals every afternoon; and days filled with groceries and servants. Don't repeat this, Jock, but I did look down into an abyss and am still very wobbly. However, the household now goes smoothly with a minimum of my time; and the callers are beginning to develop individual faces; and, no doubt, there are casements here and there opening on the foam. I do think there is an element of *darkness* in the Government Service; it makes people think themselves important, a *frightful* thing to do. I will rather sit among the Negroes in their touching little Methodist wooden chapels (called Pilgrim Holiness) than take an official view of my only life in this earth.

I have pulled out the autobiography and will look it over next week.

Dearest love, dear, dear Jock.

Your
FREYA

FIELD-MARSHAL LORD WAVELL

Bridgetown. Easter Day, 1948

Dearest Chief,

Your lovely letter came a week or so after mine had started, and now I have just heard from Sydney that you are back from South Africa. It is

Easter Day so that one *must* be allowed to do what one likes, and I am doing some Russian. If I had more time and this were a less sleepy climate, I might do you credit and speak quite a bit when next you see me; but it is a lotus-eating island and always afternoon. And an hour's work makes one go right off to sleep. Even the cars here are not allowed to go over thirty miles on the loneliest roads. The country is charming and gets wild in a small way at the north end; and one looks down steeply to the rough coast where the long rows of breakers come in. One can wade out there quite happily with water scarcely to the knee, and a backwash comes suddenly – a terrific rush of ten feet deep or more – and carries one out to sea.

There is an Anglican sort of smugness about the island which would make me hate it to live in. I was told the story of a German governess who went off her head and decided to worship the Sun God. So she took off all her clothes and swam into the sunset and was seen miles out to sea. A boat put out to rescue, and came up with her, saw she had no bathing dress, and turned back to shore to fetch one. When the poor thing could be rescued with propriety, she was very nearly drowned.

I am going to be back in Asolo some time in June, I hope. One ought to be delighted to be here out of all the turmoil, but I feel as if I were imprisoned in a dewdrop and long to be a part of the living world again.

Love always,

FREYA

JOHN GREY MURRAY

Bridgetown. 19 April 1948

Dearest Jock,

The marriage business is not going at all nicely. I had a miserable time, and now the decision is made and I feel better, like after an operation. Perhaps a summer away may do good. I don't want to quarrel and I won't, but I will just go. And this would be such a dear little island with anyone who was a little bit in love with one. What a letter! Dear Jock, bless you.

FREYA

STEWART PEROWNE

Asolo. 1 July 1948

Darling Stewart,

So strange and so lovely to be here again. Great waves of Peace come lapping up against one. The roses and lilies are nearly done, but there is a sort of lush wastefulness in the garden. The house is coming to life as I go

286

into one room after another, all polished by Emma and Maria to the nines. And suddenly I feel beautifully happy and optimistic again. I *know* Barbados is not right for us; it seems to make all the wrong things important. The East is big enough for one to keep one's own scale of values; and, anyway, our values *are* to be found there.

All here are asking after you and so much hoping for your coming soon. A pure *New Yorker* character, Peggy Guggenheim, is in Venice, with a face as amusing as if it were a caricature of herself, and a collection of *modernissimo* pictures which she travels about with and hunts for houses for (and took BB to see, with the results you can imagine). Venice is ravishing, but sad: there is no work anywhere.

Bless you,

FREYA

STEWART PEROWNE

Asolo. 11 July 1948

Dearest Stewart,

I have suddenly realised *why* I dislike a complete autobiography. It came to me while reading Dickens. It is because nearly always the end of one's life makes an inartistic anti-climax, a tailing off which leaves the reader depressed after all the promise and fire and achievement of youth. Whereas, if you take it in bits, you can start low down so to speak and always make your climax somehow, like *Samson Agonistes*, or *All Passion Spent*. In fact, every age ought to be an artistic achievement of its own kind; and therefore it's a mistake to put old age, which needs a subdued and gentler sort of lighting, into the same work as the fierce illumination which adds to the excitement of the earlier chapters.

Your
FREYA

STEWART PEROWNE

Asolo. 22 September 1948

Darling Stewart,

So difficult to get paper and pen and five minutes' quiet; and now we are back in Asolo with the addition of the two young Eustons, the most charming young happy couple.[1] All came crumpled into the Youngs' van, Hugh at the back extinguished under the Venini lampshade (for I may as well confess that that is your Xmas present; I thought we might be enjoying it meanwhile).

1 Hugh and Fortune (Earl and Countess of) Euston. He had been an ADC to Lord Wavell when FS stayed with the Viceroy in New Delhi.

287

It will be rather nice to have this rush over, and be quiet. There must be something wrong with the sort of social affairs that leave one depressed at the end; or perhaps it is only I who feel that flatness, and prefer a quieter life? Anyway, I find that I go to bed happy after a quiet evening with real friends and good talk, and go to bed with a feeling of *futility* after all the whirl and stir. I feel the same with books. Your Graham Greene novel has just come and is already making me unhappy; whereas nothing but a lovely serenity follows on *Paradise Lost*. I will tell you what I think of it when I get a little further. With most of these writers I think there is a lack of final balance which the classics never omit; I mean that the misery and squalor are obviously real things that exist, but they are not the final sum of things. The great writer never forgets to put his work into the proper perspective even if he is only concerned with some squalid aspect. I believe that is what we have forgotten in our lives, too often, and therefore in our art. One should never specialise so much as to forget that the bad patch is only a *detail*. The beauty of life is that the good and the happy exist, and even if it is we ourselves who miss them, it doesn't *really* matter, does it? If one could feel this strongly enough I believe one would attain happiness, and certainly serenity?

Dear love,

FREYA

FIELD-MARSHAL LORD WAVELL

Asolo. 6 October 1948

Dearest Chief,

A beautiful letter from you; and the days and weeks have been passing and I haven't written, partly because it's so *difficult* to make up one's mind as to what gifts from a fairy godmother one would prefer – health for the body, I think, though I would choose beauty if I were *braver*; it is such a sharp-edged thing that cuts oneself so deep, so I shall keep plain and contented with health. Then poetry, or perhaps painting: it doesn't matter what it is so long as it opens 'the casement on the foam'. Poetry does it more than anything else to my mind. And for the soul, I think I should choose a feeling like that of the Greeks or even the early Christians, of a sort of divinity all around and inside one. Perhaps that and the poetry are rather alike, so that if *one* of the three has to be given up, I should do without the middle one and jog along contentedly with Good Health and the Grace of God? Now what made you think of these questions? I will be very curious to hear whether you approve of my philosophy when *Perseus* reaches you; he is due out in four weeks.

Momo and her general are coming to lunch today.[1] He is taking a fortnight's leave, so I hope the European crisis is not quite so acute. I am simplifying life by not reading about it; at intervals of a month I look, and it is always either Stalin or Molotov refusing visitors, and what is the good of looking at every swing of the pendulum when you are not consulted about the striking of the hour? So I have been reading Shakespeare's comedies and trying to decide whether Beatrice or Rosalind is my favourite.

Love to you both,

FREYA

SIR SYDNEY COCKERELL

Asolo. 24 October 1948

Darling Sydney,

All my plans are accelerated by a month by Stewart who has written to beg me to be out by December 1st in Guadeloupe, where he has a conference, and suggests a little holiday among the islands. So I am going. There is no point in disappointing him for only a month. I wish he had been able to come instead; but he can't. Anyway, I am crossing that weary ocean again (but by air this time) and am a little fearful of Barbados.

Dearest love,

FREYA

PAMELA HORE-RUTHVEN

Gaudeloupe. 12 December 1948

Darling Pam,

We are here at the end of a fortnight's Conference; and, my dear, it is so much more like Evelyn Waugh than like real life that one feels all the time as if one were removed from the world and inside a Work of Art. This poor little island lives on dreamily in the year 1850 or thereabout; the Napoleonic Age still its criterion, and the evening parties (with bows, chignons, and flowers in the hair) looking like so many scenes painted by Renoir. There is a circular, good road made by the home Government to go almost round the island; and a volcano with mountains and forests in the middle where one has to walk. The forest eats up every small path unless it is cut out fresh every four months or so and the banana plantations are cut out of forest as if it were a solid slab, and the solidity

1 Major-General (later Sir) John Marriott was at this time GOC London District.

is left all around to keep off the wind that tears the broad banana leaves to tatters.

One hundred and forty West Indian delegates were poured onto this remote provincial peace. The aerodrome to receive them is only half built; so is the model village to house them; and even the stock of wines and perfumes (which is all this island offers from France) is now coming to an end. The islanders have been so hospitable, and turned out of their own houses. Delegates are parked about in villas, bogged with the rain; and the 'Administration', which promised to give them fresh sheets every few days, has not even been able to deal with the laundry problem. The strike of chauffeurs threatened to leave the Conference quite para-lysed, scattered about in remote banana groves. And after about five days a U.S.A. medical circular asked us all to abstain from water, ice, salads, fish, fruit, and Coca-Cola. The Coca-Cola agent came down from another island in a fury, and it must have been very good for the Gaudeloupe sale of wines, but it gave us all a tinge of gloom. Stewart went down with fever, and I spent a strenuous day plodding down our banana grove in search of a doctor and food.

This is a much nicer island than Barbados. It isn't so municipal; it is just what one reads about, romantic sunsets, solitary bays, remoteness. The people are so charming and greet you with no inferiority complex as you come to their little wooden shanties in the hills. They speak a formal, forgotten sort of French, and are pleased and proud of their traditions and not the rootless sort of creatures that sadden one in Barbados.

A happy Xmas, dearest Pam,

FREYA

GERALD DE GAURY

Barbados. 8 March 1949

My dear Gerald,

Such a nice letter from you, – all about the things I like to hear about, the views and the spring days, pigeons and swallows and the women gathering their firewood by the stream: it makes me very nostalgic.

Stewart is governing this island, pro tem, and it means a fearful lot of general amiability; I *like* people, but I like them much better when I can look on in obscurity and not be looked at myself. I always thought this a normal reaction, but here is Molly Higgins from Jamaica staying with us, lecturing, visiting baby welfare, rallying girl guides, calling everyone darling, smiling beautifully, and completely at home in the limelight. How enviable! Yet I still think the world is nicer when looked at than when looking.

290

I am so anxious to talk about Euphrates with you. I hope to finish my autobiography next year and be free then for new adventures.

Love from

FREYA

JOHN GREY MURRAY

Bridgetown. 19 March 1949

My dearest Jock,

The last of the book has gone to you. I hope you will like it now.

I am coming over earlier, so you should see me in London on, say, April 26th. Is that going to be inconvenient for Diana and you? And, dear Jock, will you get my appointment with Miss Kelsey at Hartnell's[1] made earlier, as early as possible? A little black corduroy is in the air! In return for all this, I will send you a picture in today's *Advocate* of myself planting a tree, looking almost worse than in any picture ever before and that is saying a lot, as you know.

Love,

FREYA

STEWART PEROWNE

Train from Cliveden.[2] *15 May 1949*

Darling,

I think I must have reached my highlight in weekends: lunch at Hatfield, Friday night at Magdalen with Tom[3] and the David Cecils, and nice Italian d'Entrèves, Saturday night at Cliveden, and now on the way to spend the day at Sissinghurst.[4] It does gather the cream of England, though it would be nicer to do it more slowly. Nancy[5] insisted on this one night, and I said, weakly thinking it impossible, that I could only do it if fetched from Oxford. She mobilised the whole Rhodes Scholar department (the only ones who have petrol) and two charming young men and a wife came along and drove me across the fat peaceful land, oozing with serenity and peace, till one feels that nothing in this world can break it, neither invasion nor conquest. Albert Hourani[6] came to see me and said he would be interested to see what happened if England were occupied by the Germans. Tom and I agreed that something would happen, but it would be to the Germans. The comfortable land would

---

1 Dress designer.
2 Home of Lord and Lady Astor.
3 T.S.R. Boase, President of Magdalen College, Oxford.
4 Home of Harold and Vita Nicolson.
5 Lady Astor.
6 Writer and academic: Head of St Antony's Middle East Centre.

slowly swallow and digest them and stamp them with its character as it has done before. The gardens of Magdalen were all a foam of hawthorn and chestnut, the old walls deep in wistaria, forget-me-nots and tulips and narcissus in the long grass. And the young men and girls punting along through the sunset. I am avoiding Cambridge out of a *delicatezza* and I hope you approve, for I thought you might like to be the one to show me round there.

Cliveden was so beautiful, the azaleas yellow in the woods and the red masses of rhododendron just beginning in that sort of valley as you go up the main drive. I crept out early this morning while all were asleep and am now rattling mistily through Kent.

Dear love,

FREYA

STEWART PEROWNE
Train to Bradford-on-Avon, Wiltshire. 16 May 1949
Darling,

Sissinghurst yesterday was beautiful, a sort of labyrinth garden, all mellow walls and rare flowers, kept rather sparingly and cut down and carefully chosen. Vita showed me how to get roses low down by pegging creeping branches along the ground. I shall learn so much for Asolo before I leave. The visit was rather spoilt by Rose Macaulay[1] being there. She is rather old, virginal, and embittered, until she smiles, very sweetly. She has strange goat's eyes and pale suffering lips, and I was quite surprised to see how self-centred authors can be for she kept the whole party discussing her review for about twenty minutes till Harold came and asked me if I was an egotist. I said I didn't feel anything particularly mine once it was out and done with. I was more interested in living than writing, and he agreed. Vita roamed about with her slow big stride in plum-coloured trousers and a corduroy jacket and coral earrings; she has lovely young lips, full and generous, and slow eyes, understanding and unhurried; and she wanders off on domestic errands which she forgets as she goes by some rosebush in the garden, and then Harold comes along and copes, almost quite amateurishly but with more concentration. The son, Nigel, was there and has the charm of both. Vita told me they had always been very happy on a basis of complete liberty both for themselves and their children, and there is now a charming mellowness in themselves and everything about them. The Weald of

1 Novelist and travel writer.

Kent stretched away in a dream of blossom; it lay like a mist over all the hills.

Love,

FREYA

STEWART PEROWNE

Ditchley,[1] Oxfordshire. 5 June 1949

Darling,

I suppose this is one of the loveliest houses in England. Such a façade of old grey-yellow stone, with the old panes of glass shining with *mauve* lights as they catch the sun. Such a courage of simplicity about it, relying on space and value for its beauty. I have sent you a card, from us all.

Ronnie Tree's two boys are here, very gay with the world at their feet, all going to parties and dances. And Michael Wright told me how Evelyn Waugh had been describing Peter Quennell 'looking as if he had just ordered himself from Asprey's.' 'He is in bed,' he said, 'trying to grow a club foot like Lord Byron.' He *is* witty, but how horrid, and everyone listens and despises him for amusing them.

There is a lake in the dip in front of the terrace, and a little temple, and many trees, and a great peace. Yet how glad I am not to have the burden of owning so much. It seems to me quite perfect to be poor enough always to want something and not to need too much time for looking after what you have, with just enough to make it possible to come and enjoy the life of your friends. I think one can improve on the gospels by being 'of the world and not in it' instead of the other way about.

Dearest love,

FREYA

STEWART PEROWNE

Paris. 18 June 1949

Darling,

The Parisian has studied the Art of Living to a hair's breadth, but you have to go further, to the Mediterranean, for the Joy of Living. Perhaps it is the sun. What a *feminine* town Paris is: women move in it as if they knew it for their own, and what a good business they make of it. All the serious things, the style, clothes, food, social life, small commerce, art; all seem to be run by their capable selves or else in such a way to please them. While in London one feels that the woman is incidental, and all the

---

1 Ditchley Park, Enstone, then home of Ronnie and Marietta Tree.

city life throbs to things happening in China and Peru.

Love and many happy returns,

FREYA

STEWART PEROWNE

Chantilly. 20 June 1949

Darling,

I sat between Cecil Beaton and Duff at dinner. I can't think why people are so very nice to me; when everyone who comes is either young, brilliant, or beautiful, and I feel like the ugly duckling. But they *are* nice, and Duff asked me to stay on over lunch today. One gets to like him more and more. He is spontaneous and human and ready to give and take. He has first editions of Scott, Jane Austen, Dizzy and Peacock, and much more, and loves them. He was describing Diana as a schoolgirl weeping and throwing flowers on Meredith's grave (she was called after Diana of the Crossways); 'drowned in emotion, as she is so often', he added in an undertone, which made everyone laugh. Cecil is agreeable to talk to. What a *medieval* face he has: with a velvet cap on one side he would make a Dürer or Clouet, with those sad eyes and frustrated mouth, and small artistic impotent hands. He told me that photography is not what satisfied him and the setting for *The School for Scandal* gave him far greater pleasure. He wants to come to Asolo.

I don't know how the Duffs can go on with such a stream every day. Diana says it is becoming too much for her. It would keep me from ever wanting a house so near Paris.

Your own
FREYA

STEWART PEROWNE

Train to Verona. 22 June 1949

Darling,

Everything looks a little shabbier than when I left it seven months ago. The ruined edges of the towns, and dusty fields, and ragged paper monies; but now the hard Lombard plain is past and the gentle Venetian background is taking me to its heart; it is like someone not beautiful or grand, but very dear and known in every wrinkle. I am filled with a sort of sadness, for it is silly that you are not here; not physically, with the C.O. as it is, but in your heart, so that it might be the sacrament between us and not drunk off like table wine. I wonder if it will ever be so, or if you meant it to be so? I think often of St. Margaret's and all the mystery we undertook there, and would still like to keep my pledge if I could. I will have faith and wait for your heart to find its way. Perhaps it is silly of me to write like this, but I have been thinking of you and must say what I feel when it comes.

It is very strange that, with all the belovedness of this countryside, I never feel quite that twist of the heart that is given by the English fields. And I have lived here so much more. What is it, do you think? Is it being fundamentally Protestant? I love this always as if it were outside me, while any English hedgerow gives a sort of passionate feeling of being a part of me.

Your loving
FREYA

STEWART PEROWNE

Asolo. 27 June 1949

Darling,

The nightingales have returned to the garden; they shout in it all night. I have been reading Claudel, rather like Blake and the Bible, and he describes a lark singing in the sky as 'ce furieux peloton de plumes'.

Yesterday Jock and his sister Evelyn arrived, all sending you messages. So good to see them, and specially because Jock is so worn out, I think he needs this sort of a resting place. I wish it weren't quite such a hectic week with BB. Jock brought out twenty-three little rock plants, and *watered them every six hours*. Now which of my friends other than him would do that? I doubt if even you would! The result is that they are the only plants ever to arrive fresh and ought to grow beautifully. I have been counting the casualties among lilies and, alas, fifteen out of forty-eight have vanished, but some may still be thinking things over underground.

Yesterday we practised the Vespa. Jock is very expert and he has a Corgi; but this, he says, is almost a motor car (with three gears) and beautiful for him, but not for me. I am far too accustomed to these attempts, and listen to all the imploring of friends without turning a hair, and yesterday succeeded in making second gear without being lost in neutral (as is too easy).

Your loving
FREYA

STEWART PEROWNE

Asolo. 26 August 1949

Darling,

Two lovely letters, August 11th and 14th. I was so glad to get them, thinking that if we had not been fortunate in both of us being alike, able to put ourselves into our letters, if we had been tied up and inarticulate, these months of separation might really cause a total separation? As it is, they do the opposite, for we do talk of the things we really need to say. What a blessing!

Yesterday I took the day off at Maser and went on Vespa. How terrified I am of the little beast. When you put her into second or bottom gear, she goes up hill *shrieking*, as if she were a Maenad. I was pleased with myself, though it is still a matter of pure chance which gadget I turn on. At Maser, in front of an admiring staff, I forgot to turn the engine off, so she started going towards the largest statue, luckily not too fast to be caught and stopped.

I have just been reading in More's book how philanthropy flourishes in non-religious ages, because it is fundamentally an enlargement of the self; while in real religion, there is no need for it and it comes unnoticed as a consequence of deeper things. I was delighted, as you know how I loathe philanthropy!

Your
FREYA

STEWART PEROWNE

Asolo. 1 September 1949

Darling,

What a nice day yesterday, Diana arriving looking like a vision. She is getting to have a sort of unearthly beauty as she gets older, and a great white straw hat absolutely plain and one of those simple little cotton dresses only produced round about the Place Vendôme. Duff, smiling, and the son, John Julius, one of the nicest young naval things, writing poetry in his spare time, all of it the quintessence of England. And no *Tatler* atmosphere. Lunch under the wistaria (making the wasps drunk with vermouth imprisoned in those little glasses), and siesta, Duff with Benvenuto Cellini on the lawn. 'He loves a book more than he does *any* of us,' says Diana; and then after tea she drove us all to Possagno and we looked at Canova in that sea-green atmosphere and the enchanting landscapes one sees through the columns of the Temple, just like Veronese. I thought how pleasant it is to see what amounts to a Greek portico *in use*. We ran out of petrol on way home, and JJ had to pour some in from a tin, and poor Duff went through tortures while Diana backed at a smart pace all down the zigzags of the Asolo hills jerking at the reluctant engine till at last it went. How you would have sympathised!

I feel you will need a rather more restful leave this time, breathing the air of Europe. I have been having insomnia, too, and am quite sure it is only fatigue. I get it when my life is unbalanced, too much mental, and too little just ticking over, and cure it either by walking, embroidery, or weeding. I wonder which of these you would adopt? Weeding would please Checchi most. I have nearly done him the whole of the grass path up to Bacchus, and the great advantage of it as an occupation is that, having reached the end, you begin again at the beginning.

Your
FREYA

STEWART PEROWNE

Asolo. 8 October 1949

Darling,

Your telegram with remembrance, thank you, so warming to the heart. They must have crossed each other on that beastly ocean and I hope made it a little less unpleasant for all passengers as they passed. If you had been here today, it would have been one of the pleasantest days. I realised that this is just the sort of day I like: a fine morning, all alone, walk with Checchi round the garden, post arrives, and then three hours spent over the writing of English (the article is done and goes by surface). A little meditation after lunch under the wistaria, looking at the Japanese anemones now like a white and pink halo round the pool, and then a heavenly walk all by myself for one and a half hours in and out of the slopes of the Rocca that drop quite steeply on the north. It was a day sweet and heavy like honey, a white sky, and all the country sounds, voices and laughter, animals, the crackling noise of carts in the plain below. I sat for a little while enjoying it all, and found another stony little climbing path home. Caroly came in for tea: I wrote to Jock and Peggy Drower (who has a girl); and then Rory Cameron came over to find refuge from what he calls 'the hard glitter of Italian hospitality' and sat for one and one half hours talking about India and Moguls and Hickey, very agreeably. And then a bath and a little chat to you, and soon dinner. If you were here, don't you think that is the sort of day to have? I hope for it so much, just beauty around one, pleasant relations, a little work, a little exercise, decent food, and letters to one's friends?

It is awful however to open my first paper for weeks and see that Russia has the Atom Bomb, but perhaps just as well to *know*? And it does seem to have exploded at the wrong moment.

Dear love,
FREYA

Asolo. 12 October 1949

My dearest Jock,

Here is the contract, but I am not really happy about it – only I will never fall out with you over finance D.V. – and, with that in mind, would you set my mind at rest over the following?

Is 17½% the summit of what an author attains to as a first royalty? Is it, for instance, what Osbert Sitwell gets?

Because: I have now written ten books, and every one a success: so that I am so to say at my apex. I don't see why you should ever give me a higher royalty than now, and soon you will be saying that I am like that Bishop who was read in his lifetime and forgotten when dead, – and therefore there may at any moment be a decline? If 17½% is the ceiling, so to speak, – that is an end, and I am quite content: but if other authors attain to more, then I think that this is the moment (after ten successes and four stationary royalties) that I ought to reach the level of *the best*, of which I consider myself to be (modesty apart). Now will you please give me a clear answer to this?

Your

FREYA

Asolo. 26 December 1949

Dearest Jock,

What a lovely stocking or valise of books. I am so looking forward to the (inevitable) end of this Christmas sunshine, so as to sit by the fire and read.

Stewart descended from a blue sky, all the Alps without a cloud behind him. May it be an omen! I met him halfway between Milan and Domodossola, as that is where they land in winter to be out of the fog, and we drove back through the Lombard mists and reached clear weather again in Asolo. It has been heavenly for Xmas, crisp and blue, white with frost in the morning and roses opening by midday and all the Christmas roses and winter jasmine coming out as fast as they can. We pulled ourselves together for Midnight Mass at Maser; I told Stewart that it would surely not begin till Marina telephoned that they were ready to start, and sure enough, nothing happened till long after midnight as they had forgotten to send to fetch the Friar, and then he came without enough Communion wafers to go round. But only the plebs suffered, a meek little crowd right on the outer circumference of the little cold round church, in which we sat on two privileged benches just in front of the altar. After that we had a far too sumptuous meal at 1 a.m. (shrimps, turkey and plum pudding, champagne) and Stewart, between Marina and her sister, never got in one word: and then Xmas tree, and back at 3 a.m., and now here we are, cosy and idle, with no social engagements till tomorrow when we give a party of our own.

Much love darling Jock,

FREYA

JOHN GREY MURRAY

Rome. 11 February 1950

Dearest Jock,

Such a lark, we have Vespa'd down to Rome from Perugia. Of course it has been icy ever since we left Asolo in a snowstorm to come south (that awful Mediterranean cold that cuts through you like a knife): the Vespa had to be fitted into the car to get her to Padova. Then she had to be emptied of petrol and put on to the train. Then in Florence, rain, snow on the hills, huge cloudy skies, everyone said I was killing Stewart – so on to the train again, to Perugia. By this time we began to look on the Vespa with aversion as a holiday pet. We warmed to her after a fine day at Assisi, but then more rain came down and Stewart was all for waiting and doing the whole train business over again to Rome. But the little page boy of the hotel, who had become passionately interested in us and the Vespa, said the wind was in the right quarter (the North Pole it felt like), so there was no more dallying. We spent the afternoon going to Todi and slept in a primitive little set of rooms over the pawnshop – very cold, but Stewart was cheered by discovering a Roman forum and I would suffer a lot for a sight of the deserted *piazza* by night, those gaunt thirteenth-century palaces and churches staring at each other, with the wind swaying the electric lights, and puddles glittering below them, and the Song of History made audible as it were in the solitude and severity of it all.

Next day, yesterday, we came all the way to Rome – about eighty miles I suppose – along the beautiful ridges that slope down to Terni and then by a small despised forgotten non-tarmac road that reaches up and down over small ranges to the Tiber in the south. The sun came out, and a valley opened where every spur had either a small fortress-hamlet with walls and castle towers built into its houses, or some fortress-farm: it was just Romantic, and we might have been travellers any time in history between 1500 A.D. and the invention of railways – the Vespa is quite a good substitute for a horse and does for the same sort of country. We got here for tea and risked our lives across Rome where no one thinks of traffic rules but only gives a look to see whether the opposing vehicle is larger or smaller; of course the Vespa is fair game for anyone to run at!

Found a telegram from the Wrights which confirms Cyrenaica[1] to anyone except Stewart, who is shocked at my hearing in this unofficial way *before* the official news. But anyway there it is, and such good news, though it may curtail England by a good deal.

Love,
FREYA

PAMELA HORE-RUTHVEN

Benghazi. 1 April 1950

Darling Pam,

It seems very natural to be back among Arabs, though alas! that democratic fluency has gone and we both find that the necessary word is most often missing. But the air and the light and the cheerful guttural noises, and the suddenness of life, and the dust storms, are all here, and I hope you will come out soon.

Oh Pam, I think of you so much here, and of Pat.[2] We broke down and were towed to Tobruk in the moonlight and the whole desert seemed alive with the young, the gay, those who will never be old. It was strangely happy for the gigantic corridor of death, so many hundreds of desert-miles long. We drove by Ain Ghazala, a glittering solitude of ridges and sweep of sea breaking in long white foam on its empty beach. Never is there a stretch without some wreck of tank or lorry or armoured car, wheels gone, and chains lying loose on the sand, or sometimes only bonnet and shaft remaining, or empty gun pointing like a useless question to the sky. I think you would like to see all this, you must come soon. One understands so many new things, the hours of thought and loneliness for instance that must have comforted all these boys, the immense peace so august that I believe it made death more easy to meet. As we drove along and the afternoon melted all the low ridges, and the mirage built towers and white walls out of the scrub and dunes, and as the evening fell and a man or two showed walking towards the small tents pitched near a bit of grazing, and even the derelict metal took on a sullen sort of graciousness in the soft light, I suddenly had one of those happy times that come like a visitation, a feeling of enveloping *mercy* into which all this turmoil melted, so that one knew it cannot matter in the end. I am sure many must have felt this, and welcomed the end when it

1 Stewart Perowne had been made British Principal Adviser, Cyrenaica, a post he held for only a year before it was abolished.
2 Pam's husband, killed in 1942.

came. I believe I should do so if it came tomorrow, not from any dullness of life, but because the big adventure is beyond, and it would be nice to get rid of a lot of things, the constant irritation one causes to one's dear ones, for instance, by merely being oneself (and one can't not be oneself or try to change things that are quite good and nice. . . Oh well!).

Stewart has written what I think is a very good report on his first journey. Everything is to do, and I have a fear that we may have a lot of heartbreak, for what is this nation to be carried along *with*? We can't compete with the Italians, who poured all the money in they should have spent at home. I shall be much surprised if we don't hear how much better it all was under Italy in a very few years. Anyway, it is a fascinating work and I believe Stewart will be very happy over it, and is getting on finely with his Ministers. They are a nice people here, with pure Greek features as often as not.

Love dear Pam,

FREYA

JOHN GREY MURRAY

Benghazi. 26 April 1950

Dearest Jock,

The first sheet of Volume II[1] is written! I have got a desk at last, made by taking off the front of a hideous Fascist sideboard, and a room with that and a chair and nothing else inside it, not much but a *little* out of the noise and dirt of all who say they are building but appear to be demolishing this house: and so I hope now to go on. It is a frustrating feeling not to be able to get to one's proper work – I had an idea that my proper work was to love and be loved, but it isn't: it is just to *write books*, so what is the good of not doing so? And anyway *you* will be pleased.

I am reading Byron with much enjoyment – but why all those asterisks? Quite maddening! The conversation with George IV for instance? Where one *doesn't* know what is left out, it is irritating, and where one *does* know it makes it just a little more masked than it would have been otherwise.

Today I Vespa'd into Benghazi, but not yet across the bridge of boats which makes our approach rather like Venice. I am going to be very rigid, cutting out parties here so as to write. I *hope* to do two chapters a month: that would make eight when you meet me at Zante or Asolo in September or October. Tell me soon which it is to be.

Love,

FREYA

1 *Beyond Euphrates*, 1928–1933. Volume 1, *Traveller's Prelude*, was published that year.

Cairo. 28 June 1950

Darling Pam,

Your lovely letter made me very happy, good news of you and my Skimper,[1] and Hermione [Ranfurly], all giving a warm feeling when it comes. Darling Pam, don't let *anything* interfere with Asolo in October. As for Cyrenaica, we should be there with open arms from November to March, and April again in Asolo.

We had a three days' ride along the coast, by little bays visited only by the Beduin and perhaps a pirate or a Commando since the days when the Minoan traders beached their boats on the white sands. Such a pure sea, made more of light than water. My dear, I shall never be able to let Stewart come exploring. He made a great scene and said I was to take no interest in anything, *everything* was organised and arranged. In spite of this I did put both feet down and make him telephone to ask about food and find out, to his surprise, that we were expected to bring it. Otherwise we would just have lived on a cucumber or two and the sight of flocks feeding far away. Nobody looked at a map with any eye for distances. However it really was all so beautiful, and the aches and pains go and the beauty remains. Coming into Tolmeita in the sunset can never be forgotten, with the cold waves lapping the submerged quays where the Greek promenade, by tombs and quarries, must have heard a lot of gossip in its time. Even there there was no firewood, no lantern, no water, and the beds not unpacked, and food only because mercifully I had refused to disinterest myself from that basic necessity and saw that a sheep with fat tail was dangling from the basket that contained my underwear (as saddlebags had also been omitted). What rankles of course is that, with three geographic medals, one should be even associated with such a shaming exhibition, and never even consulted. But we will sort it out and when you come travel by quiet stages and see that there is leisure to enjoy those hidden places and lovely wild villages. It is such a pleasure to come upon the people in their low tents, visible only by their smoky fires in the scrub, and barking dogs, and so happy in their freedom, and a good feeling to be in a land where no one need feel cramped for space. There are, I believe, about 200,000 to 250,000 inhabitants, and I suppose the Italians could have crowded in two million at the expense of the Beduin lives. It is not a very easy problem to answer, and a great luxury to keep a land empty in this age. But it is good to enjoy it while it is there.

Tell me soon when to expect you. Dear love, dearest Pam,

FREYA

1 Lady Ruthven's younger son Malise (and FS's godson).

Benghazi. 29 November 1950

Dearest Jock,

Such a long time without news of you: was it that week in Paris – too strenuous? – or have you come back unable to write without a *coupe de champagne* every two hours? I meanwhile have the most ridiculous piece of news to give you: I am to be made an Hon. Doctor of Laws by Glasgow University. Did you ever hear anything more exhilarating? So many laws I have broken. It is just what happens to those young men in the *Arabian Nights* and delightful to find in real life – and will take place in June next year. You become it without a lecture, but only a hat and gown to buy which of course is pure pleasure.

As well as this excitement is the enclosed proposal to make a film of Luristan. I have written to say that I should love to see my books filmed but that *you* decide all these matters.

I am sending Robert Byron's *Byzantium*. What a first rate book: I think the analysis of the Greeks in his first chapter is masterly. What a pity he died, and stopped writing anyway in the welter of war.

Love dear Jock,

FREYA

BERNARD BERENSON

Benghazi. 6 December 1950

Darling BB,

So many days gone by without writing. I came and found a nice cook, full of goodwill but no cookery: and a sort of minor Byron of a parlour-boy, with twirling mustachios and a gay way with life – but not domestic. Since then a second parlour-boy has come and gone, brown ebony from the Fezzan who told me he got drunk 'only on holiday' and said his luck was bad. 'Well,' said I reasonably, 'you might make it better by working a little?' 'Perhaps,' he said, and added, 'but perhaps I am lazy.' We now have a nice earnest young Berber, and I am teaching him from the beginning and hope to be settled in time. It is frustrating to have to devote so much time and energy to mere *living*, the mechanical parts of it I mean. I have done seven pages of Volume III in all this month, and that is all. I hope that you have got the *Prelude* by now?

Our King[1] is not yet really made, but everyone behaves as if he were and the buses have new flags with a red stripe not nearly as smart as the former black and white but I dare not say so as Stewart helped to invent it. We went last night to leave a letter at his palace out in the country, and

1 The Emir Idriss el Senussi was to be King of Libya.

303

there was an inscription of congratulation over the door in electric lights. I hope it may end happily for him: he is gentle and benevolent, and yesterday in the afternoon, as I was coming home from my walk, I met his outrider, and grand red car behind, and police jeep behind that – and he and his Emira were having a quiet little country drive together side by side. It is rather unusual and pleasant to see that in a Muslim land.

Darling BB I hope for lovely days with you in March. Keep well and get no colds through the winter. Here a cold blast is coming in from the desert south, but narcissus and crocus and cyclamen are out among the rocks. Stewart sends love – so do I, always, every day, to dear Nicky too – and Christmas thoughts.

Your
FREYA

STEWART PEROWNE

Asolo. 19 March 1951

My darling,

Things are so sad and superficial between us that I have long been feeling that they cannot go on as they were and have only waited to write or speak because I could not bear you to think that any trivial cause, or want of affection, made me do it; and also because I hoped that you yourself might feel this thing so near your heart as to make you speak before I left.

I don't know whose the fault, anyway it doesn't matter. If it were just that the thing has failed, it would be simple. We are both independent, and we could separate and go back to where we were. I do care for you, but I have tried to take myself out of this account and to think of the whole thing without any bias as far as I can; one of these days I believe you will discover that you do care.

Let it be friendship meanwhile, and not just acquaintance. Half a dozen people around us tell me their hearts more intimately than you do. Better just to come and go as friends and that I will always be. There is nothing but true affection in my heart.

I have kept this for a day before sending, feeling perhaps that I might not send it at all, but there *must* be a truth between us, and it is the truth. Let it not make any difference to what we are to each other, such dear friends, and with true and safe affection, let it only take away what there was of pretence. I long for you to come here and you know it is your true home.

Love,
FREYA

CHARLES RANKIN[1]

My dearest Charles,

I had begun to think it about time for one of those rare letters, and I was so glad to see it arriving. I've been here a month, and I begin to think I never want to leave Asolo again.

At the moment I feel that a garden is far preferable to any husband, and I don't even feel like Eve, looking round for someone to share an apple with. Tulips are out and roses beginning, and I am designing my patent writing desk and never looking at a paper. On June 13th I shall be in London for five days and hope for a glimpse of you; but I hope too to be a little less hurried later and to have half July and all August in England – though mostly out of London. I go to Scotland to wear a red gown and become LL.D. – such a good *easy* way of doing it: you will have to tell me what it really means. I only wish I could try the gown on beforehand: I feel sure that tucks will have to be taken in at the last minute.

Everyone here asks after you.

Love,
FREYA

STEWART PEROWNE

Asolo. 10 May 1951

Darling,

We are all gloomy with the continuing rain, and the house covered with dust from masons. But the porch takes shape, and a lovely design of beaten ironwork for the door has just been spread out on the floor by Reginato.

I have been thinking hard over your precious leave, and feel that you would want it as soon as possible; so unless I hear soon to the contrary, I shall consider the first available day, September 16, as the happy day of your arrival! If, however, you prefer to go to Stamboul, I will try to join you there; but think that a home is a precious thing and needs a lot of building and care like every human affection, and that, in the world as it is, you may not have the chance of enjoying it for long. So make your choice and let me know.

My fourth chapter is done and only one left, and I now come on all your early letters. What a long time ago it is, London in 1938 and '39. It all comes back as one reads and really, if one keeps letters, one mustn't be

---

1 Charles Rankin had been an ADC to Lord Wavell when FS stayed in New Delhi in 1945.

afraid of one's past. I have kept yours here, but all the rest go to Jock and I rather think I may never read them again.

I have just been told that I am being given the Sykes Memorial Medal of the Central Asian Society on June 13. It is very flattering. I wish you could be there for some of these occasions. Do you realise this is my fifth award? I wish I could *wear* them!

Love, dear Stewart,

FREYA

Early in June 1951 Freya left for what was to be one of her grandest and most enjoyable social seasons, first in Paris and then England. She received an honorary degree from Glasgow University and paid a series of visits to the country houses of her friends, after which she returned briefly to Italy before meeting Stewart in Paris for one last attempt at marriage. They were there three months. By February 1952 she was back in Italy; and on a long, solitary walk in the mountains she decided her future.

STEWART PEROWNE

Paris. 9 June 1951

Darling,

I am quite an *habituée* of my little hotel and was greeted like a friend, rushed off an hour after arrival to try the velvet gown, which is magnificent, and have bought white gloves after all, not kid, but *antelope*, like whipped cream so soft and lovely – and washable so that one can wear them for day, too. But I thought that if there is an evening reception with the King and Queen, I shall have to have long gloves. Six guineas, your present. Thank you ever so much; it was nice of you to want me to wear something from you.

Paris is more and more expensive, but so gay. I was taken to see Christian Dior's dress show, and this afternoon we went and looked at Toulouse Lautrec's show. He is not great, not in the range of Manet or Renoir, but with a very human quality, wistful and sad over the sad world he looks at. It seems to me that the difference is that the nineteenth-century artist is still on the side of the Good when he is painting the underworld. The Graham Greenes and Mauriacs have really crossed over, however much they disguise it from others and themselves.

11 June 1951

It was the French Derby and there was a huge lunch-party at Chantilly, two tables of fourteen, Duff at one and Diana at the other, all in ravishing clothes. The most extraordinary thing was that four people at my table had been to my own house in Asolo and I didn't recognise one of them! Shaming, but there it is.

Tomorrow to London and will write from there. Hope to find a letter. It is rather nice of me to be thinking of you in Paris, isn't it!

Love,
FREYA

STEWART PEROWNE

Glasgow. 19 June 1951

Darling,

Just off. So glad of your telegram. I have a telegram, too, from Asolo Municipality. Rather touching! Very nervous and wish it was you and not me being robed. I would enjoy it so much more. The Clerk of Senate yesterday told me that the doctorate gives me the right to decide on points of both canon and civil law. I said they seemed very rash, that I was just thinking of writing a handbook on smuggling.

It is such a comfort to be with the Kers;[1] they think of taxis and *everything*.

21 June 1951

The cap is on. All went well. There are still lunch, dinner, and two celebrations today and I am nearly dead.

22 June 1951

It is just 11 a.m. I have slept like a god and got up with the wonderful feeling that the day is my own (and not feeling a bit like a doctor inside), have sent off five telegrams of thanks including one more heartfelt than the rest to you, and have had three letters from you in the mail. So good of them to come so rightly timed. And now I shall tell you all about it.

I got up on the 19th in a train about half a mile long and found the station dotted about with sweet girl undergraduates all in red gowns and dear Charles Ker. We called in and took an enormous sheaf of tickets and introductions from the Senate House and tried on the gown and cap and asked about the wearing of decorations and all that, and next day gathered in the great hall of the university to watch the delegates of two hundred other universities and Learned Bodies hand in their addresses. I seemed to be the only person not wearing anything academic! The delegates were all one more strange, coloured, and gorgeous than the last, the French going in for gold and ermine, the Lutherans for ruffs, the Rhine for great medieval robes with velvet collars. It was fascinating to

---

1 Charles Ker, brother of WP.

see how medieval the *faces* became with these robes. There were three women delegates, an English one in blue and silver, a French and a Belgian. Will Spens[1] represented Cambridge in black and blue (but only came next day). The Scottish Academy wore a maroon-coloured velvet cape with gold tassels on the sleeve and (as he had a gold beard) looked like Sir Walter Raleigh. The old Chancellor with white bushy eyebrows and a cape of black and gold sat in his chair and the delegates came one by one, handed in their scroll, and bowed before him. Some little orientals brought their greetings in the Office Folder and I thought suddenly of the policemen on the Western Desert road. There were Indian universities, Madras, Malaya, in red silk. I suppose there is nothing left so colourful as the academic world today.

Well, after this ceremony I came upon my fellow doctor, Dorothy Russell, who turned out to be very friendly and easy and the professor here with whom she is staying added me to his lunch party. From there we went on to the solemn procession and service in Glasgow Cathedral and that was beautiful. The sun shone, and the gowns glittered and wound in a semicircle with the dark Gothic walls behind them and the only slight anticlimax was the Moderator of the Church of Scotland who appeared to be sleeping all through his fellow clergyman's address (but he *may* have been thinking with his eyes shut?).

The Kers live half an hour by car outside Glasgow (and refuse to let me pay for any of the daily taxis I have been using) so I just had time to get back and dress in my white Paris frock (and diamonds) and get to the dinner where I had a Canadian doctor also getting his degree on one side and one of the Glasgow professors on the other, a charming lawyer obviously immensely relieved to find me Normal and not Academic. In fact about a dozen people have come up these days and told me how pleased they were to find me 'feminine'.

Next day I joined the sixty-seven other graduates all robing with far more concentration and fussiness than men are credited with, and we were formed into a long double procession by the harassed Clerk of the Senate, Divinity first and Laws after. The doctor ahead of me was a nice old boy, adviser to the College of Surgeons, and the one behind was the most charming ex-professor of medieval history in Oxford, radiating gentleness and goodness and humour. He was smaller than I am, and the next man was Sir John Reith of the B.B.C. who is six foot four. I was so glad not to be next him, the man who put his hood on had almost to *jump* up to reach. Churchill, it seems, always calls him 'Wuthering Heights'

1 Master of Corpus Christi College, Cambridge.

and he made me think of the hero of *Barchester Towers*. He looks so bitterly righteous and incapable of being happy. He was one of the speakers and made a very heartfelt sentimental speech but so egotistical down below that it jarred (I wonder why sentimentality and egotism go together so?). But this was all later. We are still going in slow procession onto the platform past a mirror into which every single man turns to look as he passes, with slow music, and a packed hall and galleries in front. We sit in tiers and then the Chancellor's procession comes in and he sits on his throne. And then one after the other goes down, kneels, is touched on the head by a huge purple velvet sort of mushroom cap very worn at the edges, gets up, shakes hands, and has the hood fitted on from behind and retires. I had tied my hair tightly and neatly in black tulle and carried it through, I was told, with composure, and got a great clapping. But the audience was so nice and wise and gave the greatest ovations to the foreigners and especially the coloured ones. I wish the Barbadians could have seen!

After this long morning we had a great lunch and then there was another reception in the afternoon which I skipped from sheer exhaustion. I went out again in the evening in the black gown with the red and purple LL.D. over it and a little black veil on my head just covering my eyes, which I thought rather dashing, and the black enamel and ruby pendant which looked very fine, with my little white cross of St. John beside it. The whole of the City Corporation with the Lord Provost at its head was there to receive us and we shook hands and bowed and went on into the huge ballroom. Everything here was done very solid and good about 1880; solidity is the word. This was a very pleasant evening. All sorts of people came up and I really ought to be very rich, because everyone seems to have read my books. A nice professor from Denmark who is an orientalist came along and told me how he had lost his wife after twenty-five years and how lonely it was. And suddenly everything seemed so much less important than that one human fact. I looked about at all the faces and so many are pinched and made mean by worrying about their honours, promotions, degrees; when one saw them in rows it was just like those pictures we have by de Monvel of the Inquisition trying Joan of Arc, the world writing hard things on the features.

There was another great University reception, the Scots Guards (rather dim in contrast to the Robes of Learning) playing on the grass of the quad till a shower drove them in. Then back in time to bath and dress and return for the dinner given by the Senate. The wives were being entertained separately, but we academic ladies were with the men, four of us, including the Vice-Chancellor of London University who made a speech really *shaming*, arch, argumentative, and inaudible, in a squeaky voice. I had said to my Glasgow professor (who was again my neighbour) that every woman who deals in education should have a past. So now, when it really was too appalling and I said to him, 'I could make a better speech than that,' he said, 'Well, of course, you have a past.' 'Several,' said I! There must be something terribly wrong with female education when it is taken for granted that an academic woman is to be avoided.

Some day when I can afford it I think I must get a cap and gown. You can't imagine how noble it looks with jewellery and decolleté – far better than ordinary evening dress!

Love,

FREYA

STEWART PEROWNE

London. 26 July 1951

Darling,

Back to find two letters of yours, rather sad;[1] I do wish I were with you, and yet I don't suppose it would help. Haven't we known what governments are from the very first? I believe in the long run it may all be for the best if we take it wisely. What about beginning all over again and spending three years on a degree in archaeology? We can afford it. I asked Steven [Runciman] what he thought, and he is for it; he says it would give just the 'mental discipline' you need.

I am rolling along to Henley to lunch with Peter Fleming and Celia and go on to Cliveden. So dear of Nancy, she has got Pam, and asked me what men friends I want and I have asked for Christopher Sykes and Fitzroy Maclean. One's friends are wonderfully good. I sometimes wonder at what age this kindness stops, it would be too much to expect it to go on for ever.

Cliveden. 28 July 1951

This is the room with the view you love, a still summer day, a little haze lying on the river, the trees as if cast in metal so warm and still. The most peaceful view in England.

Nancy not peaceful! I think she is desperately unhappy inside. She has gone for the public things and now begins to find them dust and ashes I suppose, and here is Pam on the edge of a penniless marriage with the only person she has ever felt like loving since Pat died. Everyone is at me to dissuade her, but I can't find it in my heart to do so. All I suggest is to

1 The post of British Adviser in Benghazi had suddenly been eliminated, leaving Stewart without a job.

live in sin for a couple of years before deciding, which is advice that none of these old ladies would approve. Christopher is in Paris but Fitzroy is here and very pleasant, and also Professor Rowse the Elizabethan, an arid little combative man.

Nancy says she wants to become a saint so that everyone may feel her influence when she comes into a room. I told her I have only known two people who gave this impression of making a room different, one was Gandhi and the other the Mufti and neither were saints!

Waldorf looking better, wheeling himself in a chair around his woods. How beautiful they are. The long garden a dream, all colours shut in by the box and cypress.

Love dear,

FREYA

STEWART PEROWNE

Houghton Hall.[1] 5 August 1951

Darling,

Queen Mary came at 4.20 and left at 7.15. She was very erect in grey glacé kid shoes, the kind of 1910 with little waisted heels; and a Liberty silk of pink flowers on pale blue under a pale blue coat with little cape, and pale blue marabou; a high tulle collar of the sort held up with whalebone; a pearl necklace, diamond brooch and earrings of a little diamond and huge pearl; a very pink make-up, and blond-grey hair nicely waved; and a pale blue toque with a bunch of pink and yellow primulas and a white narcissus among them; and a grey silk parasol with a Fabergé handle of crystal and diamonds. She came along very anxious not to get her feet wet, with Lady Wyndham (whom I had met years ago at Petworth) very dowdy behind her with untidy hair. Perhaps a Lady-in-Waiting ought to be a little dowdy? Sybil made me sit on one side while she sat on the other and she said, 'I know all about you. I've read your books.' She has a wonderfully short, decisive way of speaking, but kind, with a readiness to be interested in anything that comes. Everyone offered her little bits of the conversation that might please her. I was very shy, as you can imagine, but I did talk a little and showed her my ring which amused her, and told her Lord Wavell's answer to Churchill from Somaliland at which she looked at me with a *flash* of the eyes. It must have been terrific when she was young. I think it is this spontaneousness and kindness together which charms everyone. She remarked on Lady Wavell's shutting of her eyes and imitated her.

1 Belonging to the Marquess of Cholmondeley.

At 7.15 we all curtseyed and kissed her hand, and she drove off and slowed down for a little knot of people in the park who waved their handkerchiefs and cheered. As she went she wrote her name and the date in the visitor's book and wrote 'aged 84' after it. Wonderful woman. She gives me the feeling that she *enjoys* every bit of her job, and likes her people, and to know about them, and to give them pleasure. She makes up her mind instantly on anything that comes before her and if she thinks it nonsense, says so in that crisp little voice that no one would contradict.

Love,

FREYA

LADY CHOLMONDELEY

Asolo. 14 October 1951

Dearest Sybil,

Stewart has been offered a job in Paris on November 1st.[1] So he leaves for a few days in London to see about it, and I go to lecture in Milan and Genoa, and all being well we meet in Paris and look for a small, quiet, inexpensive hotel on the Rive Gauche. It is fun to think of, as neither of us has ever *lived* in Paris (except when I was born there). It seems to me that it may be more probable to see you there than in Asolo? I hope so.

Much much love, dear Sybil, to you both,

FREYA

JOHN GREY MURRAY

Paris. 15 November 1951

Dearest Jock,

A lovely letter, and I am glad to hear how the Publisher's mystery works, and delighted to have at last crossed that whirlpool of the 17½% out into the gilded lagoon of 20%! It looks as if the bathroom may be paid for after all.

My drawing comes along nicely and charcoal nudes decorate the walls of the Bristol bedroom. I go every day to Julian's Atelier, quite near where I was born, tie my head in a handkerchief and wear a burberry and look as like the Left Bank as I can, find an easel, shove it in amongst the young shock-headed girls and boys, and sit down to take whatever view I like of the model. Twice a week the Professeur comes around and with a stroke here and there revolutionises the efforts. Otherwise Mlle Joubert, with a blue overall and lots of chins and kind old sensible eyes, waddles around and gives a hint as to how you foreshorten, or shade, or

---

1 Liaison with Arabs and United Nations.

take away. It is wonderful how the time passes; and it is like adding a new *sense*: I begin to feel the delight of a pure line, the beauty of the bone at wrist or ankle, a whole new world of delicate pleasure. Perhaps dear Jock I shall never write any more and only make pictures? Anyway I believe I may be able to illustrate.

I do nothing about the United Nations except sit at lunch with a delegate or two now and then and take the Iraqi wives to dress shows. Stewart is at it all day. I would take a hand if wanted, but I'm not really and do you know, I am glad to be left out of it: it is a temporary affair, and too much like what the three witches in *Macbeth* were cooking. After fifty one wants to emerge into the more substantial world. Diana and Duff now live in it: she tells me she goes to bed at six, Duff comes and reads and they dine in her room, with time for walks, gardens, friends: the only way for ageing. Paris is crowded: the dresses *dreams* – Dessé's had a grey evening gown scarfed with black chiffon and held in a sort of Milky Way of diamond stars. How I hope I may go somewhere in the next world where clothes are worn (and with a nice figure to wear 'em).

All concrete plans are still hazy, though I did go and buy a book on the Roman frontiers of the Euphrates.

Love,
FREYA

JOHN GREY MURRAY

Monte Mattanna. 22 March 1952

Dearest Jock,

Isn't it extraordinary how the things one has thought about come along, years and years afterwards, but as if a gentle, unconscious pull were taking one towards them? When I was about fourteen, I used to look up at these fine marble mountains from Carrara and think how I should like to see them close by, and here I have come, walking two days from the Lucca valley, and am going to sleep here and walk a day or two along the ridges before dropping to Massa on the southern slope. I thought, as I put one slow step before the other up the worn stones of the mule-track, so smooth and round, what a pattern our footsteps would make: a sort of graph of our life, in and out, round and round, with a straight bit here and there, our own private drawing of our life, which everyone makes for himself. Perhaps the imaginary footsteps ought to count as well as the real ones?

I came yesterday by train and bus till the road stopped and then left my sack to be brought up by 'the mules' in the evening and walked for two hours beyond the reach of wheels, keeping along the edge of a valley filled with young chestnut growth where the Germans had cut the old trees of the gullies to get a clear view downward from this Gothic line. All is growing up again and the trees cover the round wounded trunks with new shoots and look happy. What a difference when the wound is made from outside and *accepted*: a rush of life comes over it. It is the want of acceptance, the want of vitality, that makes all ill and dead. I comforted myself with this feeling about the chestnuts, because it has been such an effort to get going again in solitude, the aching legs and cold evenings, and energy necessary to pull oneself up by the roots and deal with new people every day; and now the rhythm is coming again, and the hills are not so steep and long, and a beautiful passivity comes with the body at peace in the sun or by somebody's fire. The life of the little places trickles in and one feels *convalescent*, a nice lizard-like feeling on any warm stone. And the people are so nice in this remoteness as soon as one is away from mechanical things. The knapsack is left at a casual dark little shop and comes safely to the next village in the dusk, and my guide this morning is given 300 lire for his morning, a little boy who asked for 500 being sent about his business by my landlady. 'We have to keep the young ones down a bit,' she said to me with a flattening gesture of the soup ladle, 'or they take advantage of strangers and give the village a bad name.' We dined all together with the village schoolmistress and I slept in a bed warmed with the *scaldino*.

Aulla. 25 March 1952

Arrived yesterday, such a day, and the only one without a view, alas. Just as we got to the place where all the western hills should open out, the mist came boiling up and has continued ever since. So it was just discipline, one foot before the other; one's thighs feel as if they would die going up, and one's knees feel as if they would break going down, and the thin places with nothing but steepness below give an air-raid sensation in the tummy. Why does one do it, at my age? But it is wonderful to have it done, and be safe down in the valley with the earth-surface solid and flat enough to feel safe. I luckily had a good young guide, for the path, such as it was – a little worm of worn stones scarce visible, had been sliced away for marble and there was a nasty smoothish slab. How surprised I was to find myself negotiating it, and so was the guide.

Massa was full of ghosts. I sat at the café where my father used to give us ices forty-five years ago, oh my! And there were all the little orange trees and the red palace with twenty windows with Roman Emperors above them taking all one side of the square, and the other two sides bombed.

314

And I came here and carried my knapsack to the castle in the dusk and have been sleeping and writing all day.

Love,

FREYA

LADY ASTOR

Asolo. 5 April 1952

My dearest Nancy,

Your letter is very dear and I would love to talk to you, but I am not going to go back to matrimony with Stewart for a long time, if ever. He doesn't want *me*, he wants a home and a lot of odds and ends, and I would like to give him as much of that as I can, true friendship, a place to dump his things and come back to, a feeling of safety. But marriage is more than that. We must go back, and having made a false start, retrieve it by not undertaking more than we can. Friendship is as far as the thermometer will rise, and there it must rest for the present. And Stewart can come here and be most dearly welcome like any friend, but I think as things are, it would be a good idea to wait a bit.

I think of you in your loneliness so different from mine, for there something has gone that *existed* and that is very hard to bear.

Dear love,

FREYA

CHARLES RANKIN

Asolo. 7 May 1952

Dearest Charles,

Asolo is heavenly now. Tulips over, roses beginning. Everyone getting very old, but gay – Malipiero and Cavalieri houses so full of animal smells that one almost faints going in. La Mura giving trouble as usual with Brian Howard[1] as a tenant, drunk or worse, and turned out of Harry's Bar[2] for jabbing at his boy-friend with a fork. Luckily I have avoided meeting him, but he has at last put the lid on the Lawrences as tenants and the Rucellai are looking for someone 'respectable' who will take it on a long yearly lease: they want to give only the front and will do it up for them. *Do* find me a pleasant neighbour!

Let me have a nice gossipy letter with news of yourself, Lulie and other friends. I wish it were to say you are coming in June. I shall be here till July 10th. Then Dolomites, Zante, Athens, Anatolia . . . the whole world.

Love,

FREYA

1 Star at Eton and Oxford in the 1920s.
2 In Venice.

315

10

Turkey, in the footsteps of Alexander, Lake Van

It was during the years of her marriage to Stewart Perowne that Freya began reading more deeply in classical history. She had never much cared for the Romans, whom she found brutal and dull, but she was increasingly admiring of the Greeks and the excellence and beauty of the civilisation they had brought to Asia Minor. In 1952, she turned her attentions to Turkey. It was to lead to a natural sequence of books and a fixed pattern to her life: a journey, a London season, a calm period of time in Asolo in which to write.

JOHN GREY MURRAY

ss *Iskenderun. 4 September 1952*

Dearest Jock,

The adventure is on. I am still in Piraeus harbour, but the anchor is making noises, the radio has been put on to drown them, the few Greek words I have are useless already, and a request for money-changing with my Turkish vocabulary in hand has produced results.

We are now creeping out past the prize Greek ocean liner and I will soon go out to see Sunium on the left. This is a spacious, clean, and attractive Turkish boat, *much* nicer than any Italian, French, Greek, or English I have been on, and I was seen on board and a wonderful cabin fixed for me.

I must also tell you that I think I am buying an object longed for for years – a white Lekythos vase, about eighteen inches high with two little graffiti figures. One man in Athens has a few and I think will give it for £50. And if I can get permission to take it out, I shall eat olives for six months, but buy it! These are the most beautiful of all the vases, I think, with a sort of Matisse or Picasso modernity, and were only made in Attica, and only during a fifty-year fashion in the fifth to fourth centuries B.C.

Smyrna. 6 September 1952

I kept this after all to add my arrival: a wonderfully comfortable cabin on deck let me watch the sunrise over the Bay of Smyrna, an hour-and-a-half-long bay with low, pleasantly outlined hills all running here and there with various shapes, a green bright sea smooth as satin in front and

316

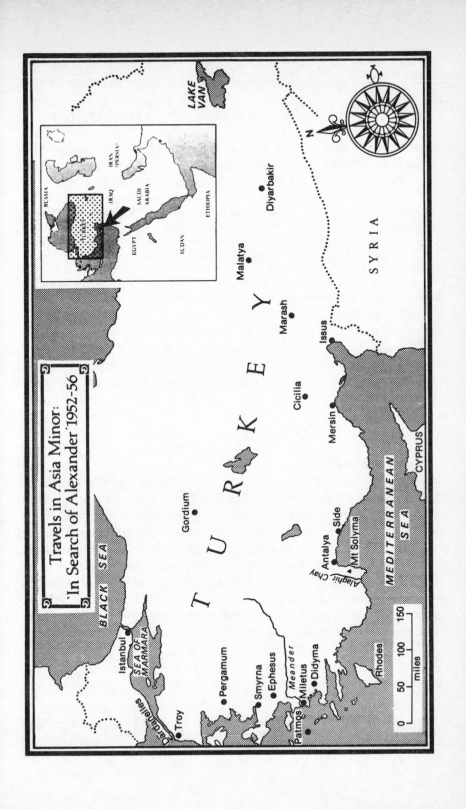

Travels in Asia Minor:
In Search of Alexander '1952-56

BLACK SEA

LAKE VAN

SYRIA

Diyarbakir

Malatya

Marash

Issus

Cicilia

Mersin

CYPRUS

MEDITERRANEAN SEA

Gordium

Side

Antalya

Mt Solyma

Alaghir Chay

Istanbul

SEA OF MARMARA

Pergamum

Smyrna

Ephesus

Meander

Miletus

Didyma

Patmos

Rhodes

Troy

Dardanelles

T U R K E Y

0   50   100   150
miles

RUSSIA

IRAN (PERSIA)

IRAQ

TURKEY

SAUDI ARABIA

EGYPT

SUDAN

ETHIOPIA

N

an orange dawn behind them, all with a strangely 'classic' feeling, and a solitary dolphin leaping black out of the water to make it even more so. What a world it is!

The consul, Eddie Wilkinson, who is a great-great-grandson of the first Whittall, has found me an Anglo-French-Levantine *pension*, and knows all about what to see and how – Ephesus, Miletus, Pergamum, and *hundreds* of little ruins unknown. But I am weekending with the David Balfours[1] opposite Chios first, and then spending a week here quietly with Turkish lessons, then ten days with Seton Lloyd[2] in Ankara, and back here when it may be a little cooler and also the International Fair will be over, for September in every year it fills Smyrna with visitors and mechanical objects.

There is still an oldish bit of town climbing uphill with small blue and yellow houses and cast-iron supports for oriental bay-windows, and minarets like candles and Victorian snuffers. But all the flat land was once harbour, then swamp, then built on, then burnt in 1922, and is now modern with red tiled roofs and a Kultur Park in the middle with the fair inside it and a parachute tower where you pay to fly down. It was fantastic to watch them last night, the two umbrellas opening out and descending, illuminated against the dark sky. I long to try, but don't want to break a leg before my sightseeing.

Love,
FREYA

BERNARD BERENSON

Smyrna. 14 September 1952

Darling BB,

I have a Hellenistic sort of *pension* and am keeping to Smyrna for a little to get some Turkish lessons: I seem incapable of learning the vagaries of its pronunciation and can now say a few things but understand nothing of the answers. I ought to settle here and study, but the land is too alluring, and now – after a visit to Ankara for a week – I shall slowly go south and look at Priene and Miletus and down to Halicarnassus. Here I am going about the places of the little towns mentioned by Herodotus; and it is an enchanting thing to do. Did you not feel that you were in the very heart of the Greek secret here – a something made naturally by the landscape and climate, the mixture of land and sea, so that it all feels spontaneous and different from all the Greek anywhere else?

---

1 David Balfour, once a Greek Orthodox priest, was now Consul General in Smyrna.
2 Seton Lloyd, a friend from Baghdad days, was Director of the British Institute of Archaeology in Ankara 1949–61.

What a lot to tell you when next I reach I Tatti – next January I hope, darling BB.

Your loving
FREYA

JOHN GREY MURRAY

Smyrna. 23 September 1952

Dearest Jock,

I am just back from Ankara, seven strenuous days of reading, staying in the British Institute and hardly moving from the library. I read right through the Bronze Age from first to last, with Phrygian and Lydian art thrown in. I hope it has begun to give me a fine background against which to travel, but it would need a year or two rather than days. There is nothing like living in an atmosphere of specialists to feel on how very thin ice we amateurs are skating! Seton has had a marvellous season, not only the missing tablet of the Creation epic, but a mosaic of moon-worshippers, a whole family, of about fourth or fifth century A.D. The fascinating thing is that they are wearing practically modern Arab dress with full trousers. It is, I imagine, a unique document, found at Harran in a cave.

Mr Nigel Gosling writes that my article assumes a certain knowledge of Greek history in the *Observer* readers. What have we come to that this can no longer be assumed? I think this is nonsense anyway, one doesn't need to know all the facts to enjoy an atmosphere of remoteness. But what a shipwreck of the European-Graeco-Roman world when a reference to Clytemnestra is not even to be understood by the *educated*!

David Balfour has just been in to say would I be ready by Thursday to go in his little boat down by Patmos and Rhodes and Kos, to Halicarnassus and south of it. So I said yes, and all is settled except the passport, and we hope that may be done tomorrow. A Russian friend of his and a cook may be coming. I sincerely hope the latter anyway. What strange things happen all the time. If only I am not seasick it will be entrancing to get at places like Xanthus and Cnidos from the sea. Should be three weeks away, so you have just time to write and let me find a long letter on my return.

Love, dear Jock,

FREYA

Cheshme. 28 September 1952

Dearest Jock,

We are back in Cheshme because of the south wind. It started veering round yesterday. We got off in a gay swell, delicious to sit on the deck in the sun, and took two friends and a stray doctor to Chios, meaning to leave after dinner. It seemed a dead calm. We were shown Chios town, its library, its museum where there was an original letter from Alexander the Great to the city, carved on a solid marble slab. (How lucky I don't have to do that with yours!) And there were also three young English archaeologists working away with glue among deserts of potsherds, beginning with the fourth millennium. It is rather awful, there is a sort of flutter when my name is mentioned; it makes me feel as if I were already dead.

What I like doing in a town is to look at its fortifications and then sit at a café. We managed this as the daylight ended and drank the mastic which comes from there and is the only drink of that kind I like. It tastes of aromatic hillsides in the sun. It was fun to be suddenly in a Greek crowd: the difference with these people is *curiosity*. They are all fascinated by every human concern that comes their way, their eyes restless, their lips mobile, their children all with so much vitality. The towns there are just as poor but they do it with gaiety and of course are happy *talking*. All the same, I would rather have the Turk as a background. I thought of this as I lay trying to sleep, with a quayside lamp shining onto my bunk and the green and red harbour lights going on and off alternately.

DB has gone home to take his wife to Smyrna and I have the *Elfin* to myself till tomorrow with Mehmet and Husain. It is so cosy, the light just bad enough to send one early to bed and a safe feeling of being in harbour, but not the dull quayside which makes one feel a mere annex to the land. We ride at anchor with the steep town coming down to us on three sides. I took a walk in the afternoon, in time as well as space, for we moored our dinghy to a Greek capital stuck into the quay, and walked past the Genoese Crusading castle, by a Roman or Byzantine ruined storehouse, through the Turkish town with charming domed fountains Seljuk or early Ottoman, and by the latest ruins of the Greeks. I reconstruct the story like this: a late Hellenistic or Roman port going on through Byzantium which gives a trading permit to the Genoese, who build their castle and use the old khan and the little market town, till the Seljuks or Ottomans (more likely) took it all over and built a Muslim castle-entrance and then continued with minarets and overhanging windows along the small flagged streets, until these last awful massacres which ruined all alike. The Muslim graveyard is as horrible as anything Greek, all the turbaned graves agitated and askew.

At six o'clock the sun went down. I rowed out and sat under the *Elfin* awning, watching a caique with its hanging lantern lit and a star above, and felt that an evening like this is worth almost any price that Fate can ask. What can one want more than to feel right *inside* the world, so much so that time seems to stop? It only lasts a short while, but it is like that glimpse in the fairy tale.

Love,
FREYA

JOHN GREY MURRAY

Off Pamphylia. 21 October 1952

Dearest Jock,

From Telmessos, if you look at the map, you will see us sailing round the southernmost points of Lycia, DB fishing (which I think waste of time), and I looking at Byzantine remains (which he thinks the same). As a matter of fact, I like the meditative part of fishing and he is becoming quite keen on sites. Who wouldn't, on tiny islands in a sea the colour of this one?

What a good way to learn history by going to *see* places. I feel far more intimate now with St. Paul, having wondered what he felt as he saw his view dwindle away, such a wild romantic horizon of hills on hills. The sands have silted up round the Lycian tombs, leaving only their lids unhidden, and have made great dunes to choke the river harbour so that now one lands in a bend of the sea and has to walk forty minutes to the city site. Camels unload onto a platform of cement at the water's edge, like a picture by David Roberts or Lear, with a huge mountain background behind them.

Finike. 22 October 1952

I shall be five days in Smyrna getting sorted out again, and then fifteen days or so on my own in the Maeander Valley, Ephesus, Miletus, etc., back to Smyrna to see what I still can of Herodotus' Ionia, and to Cyprus by the first boat in December. I feel now I must have a week without new things to absorb. I do feel, however, that I now know how a Greek city came to be born and how it became what it was. There is a sort of touch of *Greekness* that one can recognise, a type of little headland with isthmus behind it where you instinctively look for the acropolis.

Love,
FREYA

LADY CHOLMONDELEY

Kyrenia, Cyprus.[1] *5 December 1952*

My dearest Sybil,

It is months since I meant to write, but I only emerged from Turkey two days ago and the time there was too strenuous for anything but a line to Sydney now and then squeezed out of very heavy days: fifty-five Ancient Greek sites or cities in less than three months! It sounds American but wasn't, for every one of them was earned with hard up and down or battling a way through thorns. I am back now with the feeling of the casement opening on the foam: a world so ancient, new, miraculous – such incredible beauty and loneliness. In all these fifty-five ruins I found only *once* a fellow tourist (at Pergamum); otherwise there they wait, sometimes only one fine-cut Greek stone to show where the business of all we are today was going on; sometimes a whole street with marble steps, a sarcophagus with togaed figure slipping into the sea-edge, a harbour town well over 2,000 years old, with the sponge-fisher's caique sheltering for the night. We slipped along in a little boat with long stretches and never a house in sight, and at night all the perfumes gathered by the sun wafted out to sea so that one could tell in the darkness what grew on land. I do hope to tell you all about it.

Am now slowly on the way to Asolo – by way of BB, leaving here at the end of the month and getting home by Jan 20th – then to sit quietly and work till May. Is it possible to get a sight of the Coronation and where will it pass by? As it is the last and only (I hope) I shall ever have a chance of seeing, I am very tempted to go over and stay on for a month or two. Must get over to see you all before the summer goes: there is this frightening increase in the pace at which life goes by as one gets older. What a good world, dear Sybil, in spite of all; so full of such different things. No wonder the Lord doesn't want it *all* good but likes the pattern unexpected.

Love and good wishes to you both.

FREYA

JOHN GREY MURRAY

Kyrenia. 6 December 1952

Dearest Jock,

Austen is a charming person; and really this autumn has been very happy, spent with men (which I like), in real friendliness and nothing further. How restful and agreeable, and one of the pleasures of age to

1 FS was staying in Cyprus with the architect Austen Harrison.

enjoy friendship undisturbed by oneself or others. Here sitting over a fire in a beautiful long whitewashed room with three white archways on carved pillars down its centre, Austen reading Betty Miller's *Robert Browning* and commenting at intervals, there is an intimacy and cosiness I have been without these last five years – and I realise how I missed it. One doesn't need anything very passionate, but just the gentleness of life, the eye that looks pleased when you enter, the feeling that there is no barrier.

Love, dear Jock,

FREYA

BERNARD BERENSON

London. 27 July 1953

Darling BB,

I have neglected you, in appearance not in fact – for I think of you so often, and talk of you now and then with a number of your innumerable friends.

I have had a very strenuous eight weeks, ending on Friday by having my ribbon pinned on by the Queen. She stood in the great ballroom with the scarlet throne behind her and the Beefeaters holding their pikes upright at the back of her dais, all scarlet and gold – in a little dark dress like a butterfly, soft brown, smoothing out the ribbons before she put them round the necks, with a sort of quick and zestful determination and grace, most alluring to watch. There were only four women C.B.E.s so we were put in first after the knightings and Ks, and she talked a little to the Matron of Guy's Hospital who came before me, and to a very young girl who was being decorated for *skating* (such a pleasant motive for decoration); and when she came to me she just said 'Dear dear dear dear' as she hooked it on, like the sort of hum of a Gregorian choir in Eastern churches where they have no organ – but in a gay way which made me smile, and she smiled. And so I walked out with my little box in my hand feeling like an infinitesimal cog in the great machine – whirling into what unknown? What a time it is, BB: on the tiptoe to what? I feel it is one of the biggest corners in history we are turning, and am quite sure that no statesman has much of an idea of what it is turning to.

Dear dear love, darling BB, to you and Nicky.

Your
FREYA

SIR SYDNEY COCKERELL

Asolo. 5 October 1953

Darling Sydney,

I long now to forget my book and immerse myself in Turkish, and in the Roman part of that vast history which is the most typical of Cilicia and Pamphylia where I hope to spend my spring. I hope so much to be able to give a little of all these riches to my readers. Otherwise it is almost *too* much for one human being to have all these ecstasies to herself alone!

It is wet day after day, and I have lit the central heating and am very cosy, so glad that this autumn I can afford it for once even without a lodger. But I still have no tenant for when I leave in December, and am rather anxious to find one. Then I hope to look at Greek temples in Sicily for a fortnight and go off to Cyprus in January.

Dear Sydney, I think of you these darkening days and hope you are nicely tucked in for the winter out of the way of colds. BB came here and we gave him lunch and sat in the garden (luckily our one fine day) and he was very sprightly and took me over the Lotto exhibition in Venice, like a royal ceremony with deferential bowing all round us. He told me that he couldn't understand how people don't *know* who the painter of a picture was, by sight, just as one recognises a face. What a gift!

Love, dearest Sydney,

FREYA

MRS DEREK COOPER[1]

Asolo. 19 December 1953

Darling Pam,

This is going to be a scrap of a Christmas letter, but I hope to do better in Cyprus, if leisure ever comes anywhere again. Never more, I hope, shall I try to finish off one book and prepare a journey simultaneously! Jock has just been for six days and '*Ionia: a quest*' ('q' not 'g') is off my hands, after sitting up till 1 a.m. looking out mistakes, headings, maps, pictures, etc. Whether it is good or bad etc. I can't tell, but it took a lot of hard work to do.

Jock was so overworked and strained, and with a sort of fixity as if he were being happy on principle but not inside – and that is a state when all intimacy goes, because one is always being warned off the things that come naturally. How few people seem to realise that friendship really does mean talking about the things that one is *feeling* and with no guard,

---

1 Pamela Hore-Ruthven had married Derek Cooper in 1952.

so that one can for that little interval banish fear from one's life.
   Bless you all, dear Pam,

Your
FREYA

Kyrenia. 18 March 1954

Dearest Jock,
   So glad of your letter; and here you will find the answers, most of which I seem unable to give – but I *have* got a plural for acropolis! I hope to leave in six days' time and have been spending two happy days copying out the sieges of Miletus and Halicarnassus, and the Battle of Issus out of Arrian into my notebook – very laborious, but at least I now feel I can *see* the battle almost: Alexander with *white wings* on his helmet, crossing the stream.
   I like living in this little pub, all on the outer edge of other people's lives. If I were a novelist, what a lot of material there would be: my Turkish teacher and his matrimonial drama; the young Armenian with a Graeco-Roman head who came to my bedside to ask whether he is to marry the twelve-year-older-than-himself army wife with whom he is having a love affair, or not? She is a nice woman although she is at her third husband, but I advised very firmly *not*, pointing out that if this had not been already settled in his heart he would not have asked the advice!
   Harry Luke[1] is here and we go for gentle little elderly walks, telling ourselves how much more solid a generation we 1914-ers were. Marie Millington-Drake is here too, writing a book for you – a very pleasant person, young, rich, good-looking, and not happy. But Lawrence Durrell, who is a charming person with a lovely child of two years and no money at all, is near exhausted by overwork and no money but has all the *capacity* for happiness ready to bubble up if given a chance. Perhaps it is something in the quality of being an artist after all?
   Forgive this poor letter, dear Jock: head still very weak and buzzy. But I hope to send you nice news soon. My next book begins to shape.

Love,
FREYA

Aleppo. 31 March 1954

Darling Jock,
   It was like a turning back of time to land under Lebanon and see Beirut

---

1 Sir Harry Luke, traveller and diplomat, Governor of Malta and of Fiji.

grown with skyscrapers to twice its size and the pines on the hillsides full grown again since the wreck of the First World War, and suburban villas up all the slopes. Christopher Scaife took me up in a jeep that has come to look quite Oriental and we lunched off artichokes and local truffles in his house that looks down over a Druse village and slopes of pines to the olive stretches and Beirut below. There is a strange quality of peace which I remember on these Lebanon slopes, even though one looks out on numberless red roofs of little ugly houses – uglier and uglier, and cement taking the place of the fine limestone, and the three arched windows and decent roof giving place to a horrid convention that no two sides of a house must ever be alike. But there is something in the actual bones of the Lebanon that makes it good to look at, especially when one is a little high up and can see the tremendous clefts of the valleys and the bold sweep of ridges descending. Christopher's house was built by Victorian religious eccentrics in the last century and it is full of beautiful arches and stone walls and austerely furnished with books, and the pines have grown huge around it and the olive terraces covered with little flowers and cyclamen in the crannies of the walls. Such flowers I have seen: yellow asphodel, and a black iris, and here little yellow-green iris, vermilion tulips, shrubs among wild rocks, and the green low round hills of the Hama valley splashed with swathes and pools of crimson, the anemone of Adonis.

It is unexpected to find it still as beautiful as I remember – for it is fifteen years since I was in Aleppo. I came up in the diesel train of a single coach, rattling along from Beirut in early mists, by a lakelike sea, by orange gardens whose scent came in waves through the window – fishermen in boats and people digging sand, with the coast going in and out in small bays and Phoenician tombs cut square in the rocks above. Little cement squares collect salt on the edge of the sea. Then we came out on to a wide green coast plain, where there was once a city called Marathus, which welcomed Alexander.

The next book is vaguely shaping: various things I want to write about. I think for one thing that I have found the spring of this Eastern enchantment – it is the *acceptance of insecurity*. The West is a constant fight against it and we try not only to thwart but also to hide the real insecurity in which we live. The East accepts it, and so one feels an essential truthfulness in life as soon as one comes here. Another point I have been thinking over in the Greek city state – and that is that it, and the Italian Renaissance republics, and the English commercial eighteenth century – all the most *civilised* ages of the world – were based on the prosperity of the middle classes (and commerce). I think that is a thread to be followed.

One thing about Ionia I must put while I remember: there must be a mention on the jacket that the later Seljuk and Ottoman ages in Turkey are to follow – this for the sake of the Turks and of my future permits to travel. Ernest Altounian[1] agrees that this is absolutely essential. You can't think how touchy this nationalism is becoming: a man here who was photographing an unprogressive donkey with panniers had his camera confiscated!

As for Egypt, I give Neguib two months before they bump him off.[2] It is sad; he is a decent man I think – perhaps he missed his chance and should have got in first with one or two murders while he could.

Love to the godchild and the others and Diana; and much to you, dear Jock.

FREYA

JOHN GREY MURRAY

Alexandretta. 1 April 1954

Dearest Jock,

What a wonderful arrival! *Pouring*, buckets of rain all day – the landscape invisible, the luggage sodden; but then here I am in a new clean comfortable hotel, and my Turkish carries me incorrectly but swimming, and four charming letters unexpectedly waiting for me, sent on from the non-existent consulate of Adana – and one of them is your nice chatty one of March 23. I am on top of the world, and only hope the Turkish cooking will let me continue there. The consul too is very kind and offers a car and a junior official to take me to Issus tomorrow: (two of my letters have little crowns on the envelopes and that has a wonderful effect on consuls). Oh how good for one it is to be loose in the world now and then: nothing matters – I can come or go, I have no date to tie me, I can melt into my landscape.

2 April 1954

Issus is all there if one could only see it. We drove along by the coast way Alexander took marching back over his tracks at nightfall and seizing the Syrian gate in the middle of the night. It slopes down there in a regular, steep, but not precipitous, slope from about 5,000 feet to the sea and is one of the great places to hold. A bit of ancient masonry stands against the sea, and a castle above patched by all sorts of rough garrisons, and now has a rather pathetic Turkish notice saying 'Danger: don't come

---

1 FS had first stayed with Dr Ernest Altounian (who had been a friend of Lawrence's) and his wife in 1939.
2 There had been an attempt to oust President Neguib of Egypt in February 1954. Colonel Nasser became Prime Minister in April, Neguib remaining President until he was dismissed in November 1954.

near: dynamite.' We did however get in round a wall regardless and saw a toothless old heap of walls and a little hut with cement roof where presumably the dynamite is kept – and there, below the immense sweep of bay, the narrow dark green strip with cracks of gorges spitting out their torrents, the etched line – clean as a cameo – of Cilicia and the hills that fringe the plain: a factory, a railway, the new wide American road building, and the sharp horizon of the sea, dark but with the Aegean darkness where one *feels* the invisible light. It is the most exciting of all horizons, as if the whole intensity of life were there hidden; it makes one feel as if a siren sang.

Alexander descended from this slope at dawn and led his troops along the coast in column till the plain spread out and then he opened out his phalanx and went across what is now olive groves, corn and orange gardens, but was then probably all cistus and asphodel and patches of rushes by the sea. The mountains grow gentler and down one of their passes the armies of Darius had descended. And we reached the bridge on the river which is said to be the right one, and it was rushing down with curls of yellow foam, all the poplars and plane trees out on its banks with tiny leaves and shining white stems, and the river bed itself a light grey, with gravelly banks steep here and there but not high, and loose – so that the horse could manage and the stakes of the Persians on the bank could be pushed about. And no doubt they were. One could *see* the battle: the foothills where the Persian left tried to get round and was driven up by a preliminary action into the heights; the cavalry fight towards the sea where now, among the flats, a low green mound goes by the name of Issus; and the wide grey bed where Alexander and his white-plumed helmet pushed in with his guard about him (across a very small stream, as it was November). How glad I am to have seen it. What a fine way to learn history. If I can come back here on the way home I shall try one of the hill passes and see if Darius' flight can be made visible. We asked about ways across the mountains and it seems there is one where muleteers pass across in ten hours or twelve.

4 April 1954

This letter must get off – I meant to send it from Adana yesterday but was exhausted. We rolled on in sunshine beyond Issus. The way out at the back looks steep; I do want to try it to see *where* Darius went if possible. We came to green hills, corn and grass, sloping to open passes towards the Euphrates highlands. The Amanian gates are there, and beyond them on a mound, with a diagonal wall going up with towers, a fairy-tale castle – 'Toprak Kale'; and another splendid 'Castle of

328

Serpents' on a knife-edge of black rock with sheep and a river before it – what a land!

I shall rest for two days and look at Soli which is near, and then go to Silifke and Antalya till the end of the month and then back here (Toros Oteli, Mersin); then to Ankara for a day by air and Smyrna, and see what David Balfour proposes for May.

Do you like these rigmaroles or do they waste your time? I like to feel I am talking to you, much more than writing a diary all to myself!

Love,

FREYA

JOHN GREY MURRAY

Antalya. 19 April 1954

Dearest Jock,

I have got myself scattered, from not knowing the communications, and shall not feel happy till reunited with luggage, money and mail. Am hoping to concentrate all here, and pick it up in a month's time before going back (by sea) to meet Derek[1] in Adana.

Meanwhile I have been seeing great things: Aspendos and Side, Silyon and Perge. Side the most endearing, so beautiful a Graeco-Roman city by the sea, spread with its walls along the sand; and theatre rising out, like Beethoven's Seventh Symphony, its great arcade repeating itself in tremendous arches of stone. The houses of the village are in among the ruins, tucking their gardens into old foundations or pedestals of colonnades. The harbour is silted, and only a tiny break of foam shows where the entrance was; the sands have poured in east and west; and the city itself is all among bushes, with bits of its mosaic floor or marble panels showing. The scale of riches, the amount of carved marble, is inconceivable. What a coast it must have been – but always in *islands* of civilisation, for there is little left in the country and I believe the feeling was always like Bedu *v.* Effendi today.

Silyon we approached from the back by a track that ran through villages and corn. It can't have changed much since Alexander left it on his left without attacking its Persian garrison, watched by the sentries as he marched between them and the sea. It has older things than the others, and long stretches of Hellenistic wall. As soon as one reaches that period, the ruins are *alive*, more alive than anything around or even inside one I feel! They are the only ruins of which every separate piece is beautiful –

1 Derek Hill, the painter.

every stone as it was taken up out of the workman's hand and fitted with no mortar nor anything but its own perfect fitting into its place in the wall. There is a modern *functional* feeling too about that period: the doors and windows straight, the economy, the clean lines.

I am coming to the conclusion that Turkey is not a country for travelling in alone – not for any reason except that of boredom. I realise what makes the Arab travel so constantly stimulating is for one thing the bit of danger, which doesn't exist here; and secondly the liveliness of the people who are always good company and full of unexpected fun. Perhaps it is my poor language: scenery isn't enough, one longs for someone to talk to. But of course this is my hardest time, with not enough language for anything interesting anyway. Yet so far no one has made a single remark of that abstract and unexpected sort which the Arab is always providing.

Love dear Jock,

FREYA

VICTOR CUNARD[1]

British Embassy, Ankara. 3 May 1954

My dear Victor,

I was lured by Alexander's campaign, which leads into the middle of Turkey by a route straight up from Antalya. So I got my baggage – and such of my post as had made the running – sent by boat, and followed Alexander in a taxi, over *most* exciting and beautiful country and really not too bad roads.

I explained the Battle of Sagalassos to the taxi driver, on the ground. One can really reconstruct it all and see the phalanx moving up the hill with all those young Macedonians who could move up these steep slopes in heavy armour without puffing, though they did say that most of the defenders got away among the rocks because the hoplites were unable to follow. Their city is now all shuffled by earthquakes into heaps of stones, cornices, and bits of carving and figures of goddesses jumbled about on the hillside, but the theatre with the door of the stage still standing among its ruins, and a beautiful marble figure in the market place of the village below.

In a week I hope to be off again, but in the little boat and with David Balfour doing all the hard work of *organising*, so that I can just sit on deck and look out through my field glasses for ruins. We are going down the coast looking at all I missed when last here.

1 A friend from the wartime Political Intelligence Department of the Foreign Office.

But one needs *years* for this country. Everything that has ever mattered in history seems to be represented.

Love,
FREYA

SIR SYDNEY COCKERELL

Smyrna. 5 May 1954

Darling Sydney,

Here in Smyrna I have had one of the most moving moments of my life looking at the bronze found in the sea near Halicarnassus, the head and bust of Demeter. The draperies are encrusted with roughness of the sea, but by some miracle the face has escaped and there it is, living with that Greek radiance that has never been again. It is a *wonderful* face: it brings a sudden catch of tears. It looks long, but is not really for the cheekbones are wide, the nose slightly curved, the upper lip short and just a little different on one side from the other as if the breath of life and thought were going through it. One feels as if this were the one reason for which the whole world has been made. I wish you could see it, it is one of the few very great bronzes of the world.

Love, darling Sydney,

FREYA

JOHN GREY MURRAY

ss *Kadesh, Antalya to Mersin. 2 June 1954*

Dearest Jock,

The little *Elfin* has fallen back into its enchanted memory. We came along with another passenger, a very charming woman called Hilda Cochrane.[1] I liked her so much, but it made me realise what is wrong with yachting parties – the mere *existence* of every other person takes away the reality of the landscape; it becomes more of a background with every addition. But it was lovely all the same, and at last warm enough to bathe, though I was rather anxious sharing a sunset bathe with a shark. David told me it was there, in a calm way, looking down on us from the deck, so I thought it was a joke (rather poor) till Hilda and the cook confirmed it: the shark was on the other side and smaller than me, so I continued with the belief that no one would bite something *bigger* than oneself, but I didn't swim very far.

We had lovely still days (and no difficulty with the Chelidonian cape), and made a little detour to look at the three islands – waterless rocky

---

1 Wife of Air Chief Marshal Hon Sir Ralph Cochrane.

peaks where seven eagles were playing in the sun. We passed a rocky little island which belongs to the swallows, and bathed in a bay with pine woods and oleanders and a slide of straight rock that was Mount Phoenix high up on its sunlit sides. And then saw Olympus again and Phaselis, and dined at the chrome mine with the young Turkish couple I had met in Antalya a month ago. When we had left Phaselis I decided I must see the country through which Alexander sent his army to Pamphylia. So *Elfin* went along the coast and DB took these films of the place where Alexander himself waded – still negotiable only in good weather, but a road is being bulldozed just above. I, with agonies of doubts and hesitations, set off on a pony with a guide and took two days to get round the back of whatever Mount Climax was. There it all was: the fierce gorge, sheer up on either side with a wild loveliness of trees, every sort – plane, pine, cedar, wild almond, olive, fig, pomegranate, high arbutus and myrtle, laurel, and others I didn't know – and a green river and white boulders below. The rocky steps were worn smooth, perhaps never changed since the Thracians cut them.

We went on riding up from one level basin to another, till we came to the high pasture lands on the Lycian-Pamphylian watershed – and it was very exciting because I could at last *see* what the reason was for Alexander's campaign: all tied up with the mastery of this vital coast road. But we had come into fearful storm: mist and thunder and rain: it smelt and looked like Scotland, made more so by the fact that they have *gates* in this country, made roughly of boughs but the same shape as ours. We rode through them sodden to the skin, with ghosts of misty pines around us and I felt back on Dartmoor. By the evening we climbed down liquefying hillsides to a village and lodged in the carpenter's house. I felt as if the country had enveloped me: one accepted and was a part of it, with no bother to criticise or ameliorate. It was very restful in a strange way, though I feel I am getting too old for the strain of the seesaw of emotions this sort of travelling means: things either going well and then it's heaven, or badly and then the effort to put them right is so great. But it is only the physical resistance that gives way, the happiness of travel where things happen to one is as great as ever. The next day was sparkling, all the mountains showed clear as we rode down in a wide high fertile valley with crops thrown here and there on all its ledges and slopes that led to ridges, the far ones streaked with snow. We did nine hours the first and ten the second day, and dear Jock I am not as young as all that, I was pretty tired.

I feel I have enough material for six books inside if I could only sort it out. Most excited about the four or five chapters on Alexander. I sometimes feel that the time is non-existent, that everything is *now*: such a strange feeling, climbing up that gorge with the rocks, the landscape, the difficulties, all there the same.

Love,
FREYA

Most often, Freya travelled on her own. Loneliness, and the desire of others to join her, occasionally caused her to change her routine and in the summer of 1954 she set off to Marash and Malatya and on to Lake Van in the company of Derek Hill, who had been introduced to her by Bernard Berenson. The idea was that Derek Hill would look at Armenian churches, while Freya pursued Alexander. In the hall of I Tatti, in Florence, they had laid out a divided tent that they intended to share, with much laughter. In the event, it was not the easiest of expeditions.

Not long after her return to Asolo, the first of the books on Asia Minor, *Ionia: A Quest*, came out, while she started work on the second, *The Lycian Shore*. The travels continued.

JOHN GREY MURRAY

Mersin. 8 June 1954

My dearest Jock,

Derek arrived last night and we start tomorrow – I full of misgivings, especially as he has told me he is going to keep a diary and would like to publish it. This seems extremely cheap to me and brings this journey into the sort of category I loathe; so I hope he may think better of it. Anyway, as I have to do all the talking, I am going to shunt all the business of food on to his shoulders and shall jolly well make him too tired to write. Nothing could be more out-of-tune-putting than to have someone at hand collecting one's stray remarks for a social travelogue. Having so expressed my feelings I may say that this little cloud is no bigger than one's finger at the moment and as Derek promises to show me all beforehand, I will be able to delete all references to myself! He also tells me that Patrick[1] hopes his book will be out before mine? *I* hope this is groundless, as mine was finished long before.

I have been lying hot and idle in this squalidly rich little town except for yesterday, and then after many efforts I got a Land Rover to come at 4 a.m. and we had a day, such a one, finding the priest-city of Olba in the hills. It is a summer resort behind Silifke and people go and live in little shanties through the hot months, from Adana, Silifke and Tarsus – and probably did so in the days of its greatness, for there is a great upland, not mountain but yet uplifted almost out of sight of the sea, and all pinewood

1 Kinross.

333

or limestone pockets deepening into defiles, covered with scrub and interspersed with pines: not beautiful like the gorges and valleys of Lycia but with a delight about it – thin high pine-scented air. We had thirty-five kilometres after Silifke of a shocking road, part of it still with the ancient paving slabs, and then came by a funeral tower on a hill, and there was a sight: the temple, with eleven columns each side – four with capitals still and the rest truncated. What an excitement it is to see columns in a landscape. And how these sites vary: some have little intimacy, and others, with nothing – some strange little detail – make you feel it as a place you know. There was nothing heroic here: a comfortable city on a hill; a lovely early Roman gate; a dilapidated theatre; the temple with its surrounding wall like an Oxford quad, shadowed by almond trees, a row of delicate Corinthian capitals against the sky in the market place; and then the steep road down to the sacred city in a little plain in sight; and the northern road to Karaman, down a tortuous valley filled with tombs. From it, the traveller approaching saw the gate and the columns and felt the joy of nearing a City on a Hill. As we drove away, in the narrow part of the defile with caves and limestone overhangs, a little boy appeared in the solitude – perhaps a shepherd: but there is something poignant always about the sudden sight of a human being in these places. I have been wondering whether that is not the origin of the Greek feeling in tragedy, the frequent sight of the human creature so *alone* with huge forces of nature all round him – the feeling one could understand on the downs or the moors, but not at Margate?

I saw a porpoise turning over and over in the bay, which was a strange electric unnatural blue and all the low capes with their white edges of hard stone lying in it as if chiselled in that Aegean clearness.

Dear love dear Jock,

FREYA

JOHN GREY MURRAY

Malatya. 16 June 1954

Dearest Jock,

I have been thinking about it, quite a lot; and come to the conclusion that the tourist is content to *see* places, the traveller wants to *be*. It is not difficulty of character that prevents them from being happy together, but the fact that neither is comfortable in the other's world. You may have guessed that I find Derek a tourist at heart and feel like strangling him at frequent intervals – but hope to stick it out to Van and then turn off to the Tigris while he concentrates on churches in the north. He arrived a week later than the date, so I have to choose between the two directions anyway.

We are now about half way to Van and already out of the Greek–Roman into the steppes of Asia world. A wonderful drive yesterday, from Marash (where Nestorius was born) by round hills with cultivated fields, till the snow appeared on long bony ridges, with all the lovely colours of the Asiatic rock. How can the sun and air work the miracle, to give that gaiety and lightness of colour? There is a feeling of size that grows and grows as you climb up here: and all is surprising, for at Marash you feel already that Central Asia is round the corner: the people have Turcoman features, the town is mostly flat one-storeyed houses on two hills; the streets are stone-flagged and go up and down with dark corners under trails of vine; and the shops are shut at night with wooden shutters, and look as they must have done in Roman days. Then one climbs and climbs: through a pass where the first Euphrates tributary to be met with from Tarsus pushes as if through the debris of Chaos, such wildness and variety of rock; and then the plateau, and nomadic solitude and wide expanse, until with the moon risen we drove in to Malatya, with new factories and shops everywhere, electric standards, a square with monument and an aerodrome. It was President Inonu's home town, so has had a favoured dose of progress.

17 June 1954

We went on by old Malatya to see the sun set over Euphrates. It is quite near, only about twenty kilometres, and we crossed a tributary by a long narrow bridge on the Sivas road and turned east through a village of neat mud houses done charmingly with Byzantine and Crusader window patterns, each house with its winter heap of dung fuel piled beside it. A wonderful nostalgia seized me: I just wanted to settle down on a roof in the cool of the evening and rest my shoulders against cushions and chat about politics and crops and watch the supper cooking on a fire. There was the *cleanness* all about – with village dust now and the trampling of goats and cows returning, but emptiness all around. And then we came to Euphrates: what a river, a royal amplitude all about it, winding down with streams that meet and part, deep and swift with ringlets of current in the middle, but overlapping round flat islands into quiet places.

I must tell you an interesting psychological reaction. It happened a few nights ago: I felt a little scratch on my thigh, threw back sheet and nightdress, and an enormous insect (about 2½ inches) shot away to a corner of the room. I felt I couldn't help screaming but, instinctively, before doing so put on my dressing gown and boudoir cap: and of course by then I didn't have to scream any longer. Now what on earth goes on inside one to make one behave like that? Was it the German governess?

Love dear Jock,

FREYA

ss Barletta, in the Adriatic. 23 August 1954

My dearest Jock,

How kind everyone was to me in Greece: it is, like London, a place where I always seem to be happy. I hope it may continue in both. An old lady of eighty-one is here all alone, leaving Athens to go back to her country – Lausanne – after fifty years: she has just said to me sadly 'On ne peut pas être et avoir été.' May one be enabled to 'être' always, in some way or another.

Asolo. 29 August 1954

Wonderful to be here again. The house full of Millers, two charming little girls:[1] I love to have all that going on and no responsibility – I really *must* find a nice family of lodgers soon.

Love,

FREYA

P.S. I had two fashionable Venetian days – lunch at the Lido, two cocktail parties, Duchess of Windsor (dreadful face, heavenly clothes), a dream-luxury-yacht black and gold and Van Goghs in the saloon and rubber non-slip stairs and air-conditioned, belonging to a Greek called Niarchos (sounds like a Triton), which made all the other millionaire yachts look vulgar; Momo among tuberoses in the Grand Hotel, Diana, at the Bestegi: all wonderful for two days. Chips,[2] Peter Coats, John Marriott buying turquoise blue trousers; and Dali's pictures which greatly impressed me.

I enclose a note of thanks to Stewart for his book which I found here. He hasn't answered my kind little note. The Arabs, when their salutations are not answered, say: 'The politeness is to God!'

Asolo. 27 September 1954

Dearest Jock,

The book[3] came on Saturday and your letter this minute just as I was going to write. I think it looks *beautiful* – the jacket very alluring; and the pictures inside look to my fond eyes very fine. I hope it will be a success – but anyway it is done. I can't go into agonies over my work like Alice Meynell: it always seems to me that it is the living that matters, and the

1 John Miller and his family.
2 Chips Channon.
3 *Ionia: A Quest.*

writing comes out of it if it can. But this is a Benjamin of a book: I do hope it will be liked, and anyway you have liked it. I will try it on John Sparrow who comes tonight for three days.

No more dear Jock, but thanks for all the loving care and attention to my Child,

FREYA

LADY CHOLMONDELEY

Asolo. 21 October 1954

Dearest Sybil,

Three weeks since your letter was written: where do they go, and the months and the years? Since it came I have done nothing but look at photographs, write little signs on their backs, and fit them into sheets of white paper; and I have sworn *never* to be away so long again, as it makes me come home with seventy-two Leica rolls to deal with. But they will make fine pictures, and some day when Turkey is all Welfare and suburbs, it will be fun to look at the Chelidonian islands with eagles flying in their sky, and at the track behind Mount Climax just as Alexander's army saw it.

I have just received *Lord M*[1] and am looking forward to it as a change from the Peloponnesian War. The only other reading I have 'for amusement' is *The Wilder Shores of Love*.[2] How charming Lady Ellenborough is and how dreary Isabel Eberhardt. Doughty, when asked why he never pretended to be a Muslim when in danger, answered that 'one must remain a Christian and a gentleman', and I think the female traveller should remain a lady and not be quite as squalid as the Eberhardt?

Ionia is off my hands and blessed by the nicest reviews (all except the *New Statesman* and that is praise of a sort). I am pleased, because I worked so hard and joyfully and loved it all so much. How does that come through? It seems to be something more than words.

Very much love dear Sybil,

FREYA

JOHN GREY MURRAY

Asolo. 12 November 1954

Dearest Jock,

I am writing this in a last little burst of liberty, as chapter 1 of *The Lycian Shore* is awaiting to be started. That is a better title don't you

1 Lord David Cecil's biography of Melbourne's later life.
2 By Lesley Blanche.

337

think?[1] It has a touch of Milton without being the same, and that is what one would like to live up to – and I can explain as I go along that Carian, Pamphylian and Cilician shores are to be added. I am deep in my six volumes of Diodorous Siculus – still sadly hampered by want of the eighth volume of the Loeb, which is unobtainable. It is a tribute to Alexander that nearly everything that touches him is out of print!

My winter plans are all settling and all nice. The Geoffrey Youngs,[2] to whom I am lending the house, are landing on December 7th so I shall have them for ten days before I leave for Cici on the 18th – stopping to see the David Balfours in Geneva on the way and perhaps get them to join for Xmas (as they will still be homeless, though I have got them two good servants). I then leave about January 10th for twelve days in Ischia trying to cure rheumatism (in my hands too) and go to Sicily for February. And I have Barclay Sanders,[3] a charming young girl, to come with me and then to come back here and do my typing and be an adopted daughter for a month. This all makes me very happy – and in fact I am wondering how long the golden weather, inside and out, can last. But perhaps a bit of credit was in the bank on both counts?

Love,
FREYA

MRS DAVID PAWSON[4]

Asolo. 21 April 1955

Dearest Pam,

How good it always is to get a letter from Athens, and yours particularly. I wish I were going, but am not; and on the other hand shall be here all through June and long to see you and of course no question of hotels. I am alas not getting Eastward at all this year but go for three months in winter to England, hoping to make up next year for all this virtue and spend a Levantine spring. I am trying to write my book, and it refuses to come easily. The trouble is that I love pottering among obscure abstract historical oddments, and constantly have to put the tiller right over in a more readable direction. It is also a very difficult period to fix, just before Alexander, and so full of fascinating problems that I find I can't reach Alexander at all and he will have to have another volume all to himself. But it is all blissful reading for me and I feel more comfortable in the Graeco-Roman world and never want to leave it.

1 'Markets by the Sea' had been the first choice of title.
2 Geoffrey Winthrop Young, poet and Alpine climber.
3 Grand-daughter of Herbert Olivier, a painter friend of the Starks, who bought a property at La Mortola in 1921 and, wanting to make a 'small Versailles', built hanging gardens in the terraces.
4 An Athens friend, who occasionally travelled with FS.

It is colder than winter here – below zero at night and all the tulips wilting. Venice too full of Germans, their revolting little Volkswagens are everywhere. I had the Rodd family[1] for Easter and Rosie tells me that the Flying Saucers and their inhabitants are going to set our worlds to rights. I had John Sparrow, the Warden of All Souls, here at the same time and it was so amusing to see the helplessness of the reasonable trained mind in the face of feminine logic!

I think of you all so often. Whatever happens we have seen Olympus at its best: never to be forgotten.

Love to both,

FREYA

AUSTEN HARRISON

c/o 50 Albemarle Street, London W1.[2]
27 November 1955

My dear Austen,

There are so many things I would like to talk to you about, and here comes your letter about Alexander to add one more. I am indeed contemplating a book. I thought of taking it down Asia Minor as far as Issus in Alexander's footsteps. It would not be a life exactly, but it would cover that first marvellous epic of youth and I think it might be made nearly as good to read as it would be to write it. That campaign down Asia Minor, so far as I know, has not had a book to itself and so little is known, it leaves wide room for the imagination.

I am going north now to give five lectures. Never again will I do such a thing! I could almost have learned to draw in the time it has taken (apart from the agony of speaking them) and, after sixty, one's rule should be never to waste time over things one doesn't want.

I have to go through a hard job verifying all the references in my book. Professor Andrewes,[3] who kindly vets the classical part, says they are 'unnerving'. As a matter of fact, I love spending days in a library and not trying to create; not for *very* long, but for a certain time it is a delightful way of running through one's days.

All best wishes to you for Christmas. I hope it may be a better year for Cyprus, but it looks gloomy.

Ever affectionately,

FREYA

1 Taffy Rodd, younger son of 1st Baron Rennen of Rodd, British Ambassador to Rome, 1908–19.
2 The address of the publishing house of John Murray.
3 Anthony Andrewes, Wykeham Professor of Ancient History in Oxford 1953–77.

MALISE RUTHVEN

Asolo. 3 March 1956

My dearest Skimper,

I hear you are to be confirmed and I am ever so sorry not to be there. I shall think of you and put up a special little prayer that your life may go – smooth or rough as the case may be – towards its beautiful estuary of peace and happiness, with all the richness that can be gathered on the way, the only harvest that really matters, and that one carries about inside one. I feel sure that unhappiness is *wrong*. I mean that it has the nature of sin; a result of something out of tune in oneself: and therefore I wish you the happiness that can't be seriously shaken. Dear Skimper, I do hope to see you out here again. A visit has been promised for the autumn and perhaps you can make it on your way to Eton? It was lovely to see you.

    Lots of love from your affectionate godmother

FREYA

JOHN GREY MURRAY

Aleppo. 25 April 1956

Dearest Jock,

    How this East has eaten into one. It is twenty-nine years since first I came to Aleppo and the enchantment still holds, though one has to wander away into holes and corners. These idiotic Syrians – Egyptians and Turks too for that matter – seem to have got their blessed nationalism so mixed that they are ashamed of everything that isn't foreign, and though they reluctantly let one photograph an antique gate, no human being moving beneath it is supposed to be included. I have taken some pot shots in a hurry, sadly, as one could get lovely pictures if given time. Even so it led to a vivid argument with a pale young *effendi* full of 'angst' who made me a long speech about the wicked British colonial empire – a crowd all clustering round. 'Thanks be to God,' said I, 'that words are cheap', at which everyone laughed and the young *effendi* vanished – but it was done with my picture; and the same happened more or less in every place that was crowded as the city gates all are. I am never thought to be English, but when I said that I *was*, 'You love the Jews!' said another *effendi*, and smiled most amicably when I said I didn't indeed. What a *disaster* the newspaper is in these lands! I drove in a little gharry all round the four gates, but the walls and towers between them can scarcely be traced, buried in new streets. Between them and the citadel, the covered city of bazaars still exists and carries on its life filled with bars of light and shadows and not too apologetic for its existence. But the balance has

340

been tilted and the modern side has won, and there is a doomed look about everything that appears. It is sad, as this was still the old Graeco–Roman world lived more or less as it always had been. As I strolled about the bazaar I bought two little towels for my camping and chose them out of sentiment – with two winged cupids and roses, and 'Towel of Happiness' all woven in Arabic in the cotton sponge: any archaeologists would date them about the first and second century of our era.

I am now going off for five days to lodge in a village called Dana with a man who has a horse and car available, one or the other, to explore those little dead Byzantine towns.

On the Antioch road. 26 April 1956

A day of paradise seeing five of the little towns – the last three quite deserted, their colour the rock-colour which built them, their churches, shops, streets, baptisteries, two- or three-storeyed houses all with bits standing amid a chaos of their huge chiselled blocks. One can still feel the solidity of the life, with summers in rich homes when Antioch grew too hot, and the enchantment of these hills when the grey walls showed through grey slopes of olives. Now there is a strange ghostliness – strange because of its solidity: the ghosts of hills reduced to their lace-skeletons of rock and the ghost-towns scattered on them. Far below, the plain or wide valley that stretches towards Antioch lay, emerald corn and red plough, and quite flat because the earth of the hills has flowed down like water and settled; no trees to notice, only a few yellow daubs of modern hovels in some of the ruins, or tents among the stones and flowers; and one temple on the hilltop built with quite a different freedom from the hillside churches with their houses around them.

Love,
FREYA

SIR SYDNEY COCKERELL

Aleppo. 4 May 1956

Darling Sydney,

I can't think that it is really I who have been riding over the hills of Antioch these last four days. Everything, the sky and rock and grass, is pale, as if at any moment they might become a little whiter and disappear.

We set out at five, before sunrise, and started either by lorry on the only road, or off it on a donkey. I saw about twenty of these lost cities. They must have been summer resorts for the people of Antioch, when the hills were not denuded, and covered with vines and olives. My companion's grandfather still remembered the olive roots left on the slopes, and a few old straggling trees survive along the heights, but most have gone. But the presses for grapes and oil survive. The bits of churches are there, and villas, all cut in the limestone which was creamy and has weathered to the dove-grey of the hills.

All the comfort and luxury and civilisation seem still to hover there, though lost in Antioch itself. But it has grown so faint that it only comes back to those who give it time, and do not hurry on the road in cars, but ride slowly from ruin to ruin, letting the country and all the meaning sink in slowly.

Love always,

FREYA

JOHN GREY MURRAY

Antalya. 9 May 1956

My dearest Jock,

I am treating myself to the luxury of a permanent room to come and go from, so as to leave things unpacked and all clean. Anwar manages to make beds, sweep and bring hot water always with a cigarette in his mouth, and is I hope helping in the perennial struggle to get to places *not* on the tourist lists. I spent the afternoon at Perge yesterday and bought a tiny coin of a gazelle and Artemis' crescent moon as I climbed the acropolis – low and wide and empty but for shrubs and stone. On the way up stone sarcophagi are carved in rows, shoulder to shoulder, all heavy, some with Greek inscriptions, but all the same shape. The gate led into a semicircle of tall rounded niches with a marble bench and column pedestals arranged below. Lovely draped figures that seem to me fairly early (Hellenistic or early Roman?) have been dug out here; they are ranged round the 'Teachers' School' at Murtana nearby, and the gate itself has had the white marble, *shining* marble, of its great triple way unearthed. How grand it must have been! A stream of water in stone lips made the water rise and sink again so as to glitter in the sun. (That at any rate is what the old custodian said, and I like to believe him.) The theatre beyond is crumbling into ruin. From the acropolis the ways up show towards the northern passes, which Alexander must have studied; for he started from Perge towards the hills.

I hope to get up tomorrow. They say alas! that a jeep can do it. I was hoping for a horse. But Phaselis as yet has no road and Alexander's way round Climax is still in the sea.

I am feeling old, my dear Jock. That is to say that I am just as ready to do things, but would like someone young to take on the unbelievable wear and tear of 'getting a move on'. I met an archaeological party in Aleppo and they had already been delayed for *ten days* getting their things through the customs. My struggle is simple in comparison, but it feels like Sisyphus and every time one gets near the top the stone is liable to roll back. But here I am on my terrace and the view so lovely that it makes up for anything.

Love,
FREYA

MRS T DEUCHAR[1]

Antalya. 15 May 1956

Dearest Dulcie,

Just as I went down with the first of those beastly little tummy troubles that spoil one's Eastern adventures, Alan's book arrived,[2] a real godsend for such occasions. I am deep in it now, though it is almost too poignant for my generation. One of the little midshipmen of *Queen Elizabeth* was my friend, and another wrote me after he left in the last boat from Suvla Bay. And now to read of the *bungling*, one can hardly bear it. I think Alan has done it superbly, with both emotion and restraint. So glad. Will write to him.

I am finding Alexander difficult. The great wall he attacked here is turned the *wrong way round*. I went yesterday and looked at it from every side and there it is, an utter impossibility, already noticed, as a matter of fact, by two young naval officers a hundred years ago.

Otherwise, the world is heavenly apart from my own inside. I don't think any bit of coast anywhere can be more grandly romantic than what I see from this terrace, the mountains blue with snow at the top dipping into a sea that looks as if air and not water had made it. As soon as I get up again I hope for a week or so of riding in one of the few places left 'where a jeep cannot enter, lest herself fast she lay'. They are making a road where Alexander waded round the cape, but it is not yet made.

Love, dear Dulcie,

FREYA

---

1 Tommy and Dulcie Deuchar were new friends with a house in Surrey, where FS was to spend many weekends.
2 *Gallipoli* by Alan Moorehead.

Antalya. 18 May 1956

My dearest Jock,

I must say you are neglecting me rather – and here have I been four days.

2 June 1956

I leave this to show you how sadly I left, and now come back after a fortnight and find two lovely long letters. Thanks for telling me about *Lycia*.[1] I hoped it would sell more than *Ionia*, and perhaps it may. But don't you think the reviews, apart from Harold [Nicolson], the excellent *Times*, and the *very* nice *T.L.S.* item, rather depressing? They seem to miss the point altogether and go on asking why I don't write about modern things, or people, or all the things the book is *not* about.

I started off feeling like death, having caught a horrid feverish cold. The first week was spent all over the Chelidonia peninsula and all on horseback, and at the end I rode to where the huge wall of the plateau cuts it off and the Pisidians looked down on the Greeks from 5,000 feet of rock and more. There is a pass out into the valley of Finike, and I slept in a farmer's house near a little ancient town called Idebessos, very rarely visited. It took eight hours to ride up to and lies on a ledge against the giant wall. It looks as if one could drop a pebble onto it from the plateau above. There these old Pisidians vulgarised the Greek pattern, and yet built an elegant little theatre and ran their water supply in stone runnels and built expensive tombs; and looked in earlier days on their enemies in the valley that runs to the open bay, where the sea and its traffic showed.

The theory was that Alexander came this way into Chelidonia, and I grew more and more unhappy about it as I rode out next day. You can't imagine a fiercer gorge. First a little ribbon of orange path that is washed away every winter when the rain rolls down the stones, going round the head waters of the valley for an hour or two till it opened up to high fields and we let the horses rest for an hour on the last plot of good grass they were to see. Then it began to go down, and went on doing so for two and a half hours, a river of stones and pines half a mile wide or so: not a sign of habitation except one bad patched remnant of an ancient wall. The nomads were coming up in little parties with poor little packs on donkeys; and here and there on the blinding white river of stones, the plane trees showed there was water below. It was far too steep to ride, and of course my horse's bit had come to pieces and now its shoe was so

1 *The Lycian Shore* was published in April.

old that it slid, and anyway it was too bad underfoot for riding – so we walked and walked and I felt surer and surer that Alexander took an easier way round! Far down the western side, Ahmed and his jeep were waiting and wafted us to Finike in comfort; and next day I left the horses and the peninsula. I have now crossed four passes there and visited eight ancient cities, and I believe I have that part of the march pretty clear. But the part from Xanthus to Finike is still obscure, though I have now crisscrossed it for eight days.

We were making for the east side of the barrier that closes in the Xanthus valley: two high snowy mountains pouring waterfalls down naked gullies, where people come from the coast for summer coolness. Somewhere Alexander made his way through this wall: the southern way, that skirts the slopes and long ledges of Ak Dagh *may* have been his more likely route in winter. We looked at it across the valley, but our road took us on, not into Xanthus, but straight through the cedar forests of the south – which Antony gave to Cleopatra for her ships. I had never seen a cedar forest. It makes every other tree look dowdy. Here, for miles, over passes and shoulders, there was nothing but cypress and cedar, and here and there pine. The old way must have gone deeper in the black defiles, but we kept high on the forest shoulders and at last descended into the great trough that has sunk like an amphitheatre in these hills and carries the whole water-system out through the Demre-Myra gorge. The middle west–east way came through here from one little fortified town to another and one could (and can) reach the southern coast track through or above the river gorge. There are therefore three west–east routes Alexander could equally well take: I have followed the northern all but a small piece, and now decided to follow the southern and see only this dip into the middle one. It is I believe the most probable, but also the most easily imagined.

My next three days alone would make the whole journey worth making – from one little vanished city to the next. They stood with their stone walls and towers, surrounded by their tombs, with some pillared temple or portico to make them beautiful, all a few hours one from another over a land like a medieval painting of spiky ridges and points of stone with pockets of corn between. On one side the sea, often out of sight but always felt, and on the other the long trough of Cassaba and its northern rim and the snowy summits of Ak Dagh (Massicytus) or Alaja Dagh appearing. With terrific steepness, the tracks plunge down to the little harbours I knew; but the main route runs, shockingly surfaced but windingly level, along a broad backbone that makes a landscape of its own. One could never understand this travel unless one suffered its discomforts – the welcome of shade, the joy of water, the sudden scent of some shrub in the *maquis*; and when the young men walked along and the little towns were intact on their hills, with broader fields about them, the contrast and the beauty must have been infinitely greater.

We got down to Myra. There is no other way anyway with the cleft of the gorge to cross. And there I found St. Nicholas being repaired and an enchanting basilica being brought to life, like Pygmalion's statue, dug out of the earth that buried it. Ahmed and the jeep went back, and I got another horse for the last pass – Myra to Finike. What a pass too – 5,000 feet slap up and as many down, as steep as a horse can do, with loose stones on one side and sloping slabs of limestone on the other. It was five and a half hours' good going not counting a halt at the top where, perched on the promontory, a little unknown town was feeding the goats in its stone courts.

What a letter, my dear Jock – just dipping into the mixture and taking out a few items, and so much more to say. And your letter opened up *vistas* of speculation. Certainly, as you ask me, I think that I have *nearly always* the thought of death in my mind: not morbidly, surely, for it does not make me sad; but I have been too near it ever to forget it, and it seems to me to be the significance of life: I would hate to shut it out. But then I am a lonely creature and the people who really loved me are nearly all dead – so that it will be like finding *home*. If one's love were here it might be different. Perhaps if Stewart had cared for me it might have made the world harder to leave. But as it is, I love it because I feel it like one of those landscapes from the train, seen while one is going somewhere else? Words however are different: they should dip down into something that has immortality and this constant effort makes the joy – of any art I suppose? And of love too? And that is why neither art nor love are worth much if at least a crumb of the Best is not in them.

Dear Jock bless you,

FREYA

JOHN GREY MURRAY

Antalya. 11 June 1956

Dearest Jock,

I finished Antalya with a sea expedition to the headland round which Alexander waded. It has been tantalising me as it is in sight, but a river makes it impossible to reach by car from here, and anyway the new road stops half-heartedly in the middle of the huge red cliff. I thought that probably the places where Alexander and his men waded were the flat beaches *between* cliffs, but now, having examined, I think he *did* wade round as it avoids an enormous inland up-and-down detour. I went with the owners of this hotel, who have a little motor boat; and the young daughter and I got into our bathing suits and went round the cliff, not out of depth except just at the tip where some huge boulders have rolled down and made the sea-way deeper. The cliff goes sheer up, slabs of red and yellow out of a pale green sea that has smoothed the boulders underwater to a satiny smoothness.

Close to the north end is a slit in the face, and a small cave, small as caves go, but big enough for coolness and shade. Till I saw it, I could not think why they meant to picnic on this scorching bit of rock and sand. But the cave was damp and cool, filled with a noise of drops falling onto the gravel from a sort of double canopy that stretched across the river wall, covered with rounded curves of moss and pockets of water and dripping all over with a quiet glitter, never a stream but only drops, onto the rounded pebbles and the pink and yellow boulders at the back. It was a sort of cave out of the *Faerie Queen*, or the earlier mythology. We made our fire of pine sticks and had tea there – and cheese, olive, tomatoes, cucumber – and then slept in clean solitude. I don't know if I was half awake or asleep, but I *saw* a young Macedonian, with a helmet and his armour very bright, come round the rocky wall and the rest behind him – not with that half-light one usually has in dreams, but with all the Aegean brightness, as if they had gathered it in: I can't tell you how vivid it was.

Love,
FREYA

JOHN GREY MURRAY

Ankara. 4 July 1956

Dearest Jock,

I have been reading Milton here, in bed in the mornings. Making allowance for the greater fierceness of that time, *Samson Agonistes* is a wonderful vindication of the dignity of man and his relation to the awe of God and fate. How one manages without faith I can't think. But then I don't think I can understand pride either, because it excludes love, and what a dusty world that makes. It excludes not only human love, but that openness of heart which lets the love of God come in. How can one prefer one's miserable singularity to that? I think as one gets older the barriers go on falling and the love of God, the feeling of *oneness* with everything, the certainty that neither death nor sorrow can really matter, nothing can matter but one's own shutting of oneself away from this deep unity – this feeling grows and grows. At least I hope it does.

A curious thing happened to me when I was very young – I think sixteen or seventeen, but can't quite remember. Anyway I was deeply immersed in these problems, and one night a wonderful *Answer* came to me – so absolute and satisfactory a conviction that for several days after I went about in indescribable happiness, feeling that I need never trouble any more, that I was safe for ever. Now I remember this feeling of security and delight quite perfectly, but I can't – though I have tried and tried – remember the grounds that gave it. But I take them on trust.

A very social life here. Arrival of General Templer the CIGS – with such an intelligent face, and apparently a terrific temper. Band on the aerodrome, and a polo match yesterday – the first for Turkey: I thought quite creditable especially as the *horses* hadn't yet learned to be interested.

Lots of love, dear Jock – and please take my words to heart. I will copy out a bit of *Samson* to comfort you about the human race!

Your
FREYA

SIR SYDNEY COCKERELL

L'Arma. 27 August 1956

Darling Sydney,

I have only just reached Italy again, by a roundabout way, sailing from Piraeus round Cape Malea in the moonlight, an hour not to be forgotten. The light on the water was pink, like pink pearls, and the foam softer than any I have ever seen, so that Aphrodite could be expected at any moment and no doubt it was only the noise of our engines that kept her away.

Now here I am for another week and then look forward with joy to autumn, winter, spring in Asolo, and to get down to my book. I had a little Turkish money left over and spent it on a gold stater Alexander in Stambul bazaar. It was mounted in a ring and has a little head inside, and gives me pleasure to look at, and I shall wear it to bring me luck with difficult passages.

I am reading the life of your Abbess.[1] A proof copy has been wandering and found me here, and I don't know whether the book is out? Are you pleased with it? I found the early part, frankly, dull, and the musical part I don't understand. But the human portion, that is the last five chapters, in which you figure, are deeply interesting. Now why was I never taken to meet her? It would have been an unforgettable experience. I don't believe there is any glimmer in me of a nun-like vocation! But unlike you, I can understand it. It is not that I don't feel and believe in

---

1 *In a Great Tradition: Tribute to Dame Laurentia McLachlan, Abbess of Stanbrook.* Published by John Murray in September 1956.

the mystic life, but I do love the world and feel that there is a time for all things and that, while we have mortality, we may as well enjoy it. At the same time I am never unaware of its relative *smallness* in the general picture. The world seems to me like one of those walled gardens full of happy things where one can sit and look through the little windows of the wall to the expanses of Reality. And why hurry so much to get out into those spaces? Sufficient to know them there and that we shall be taken there in good time. So it seems to me that I am about halfway between you and your Abbess?

Love, dear Sydney,

FREYA

JOHN GREY MURRAY

Asolo. 13 February 1957

Dearest Jock,

I am late in thanking you for all remembering that too swiftly recurring date – thanks to John for his thought of his godmother – for the telegram and letter all so welcome. Someone must have talked of birthdays here for I was invited to tea at Maser and there was a cake, one candle, two balloons, and a pen! And I have had Rose Macaulay's book[1] sent as a present – I thought it fun but not enough to bear a second reading: is that the test of a book?

Alexander is plodding along and two thirds are done – that is to say thrown down in a formless way – and I hope to have got this first draft ready by April when the Cecils come and the summer pageant starts. I know how almost impossible it is to sit at a desk once the garden wakes up. Crocus are out now, new ones every day; winter jasmine, the Christmas roses nearly over. Every morning we wake to brilliant sun and sharp snow-lines of hills, and see the mist like a sea below; and now (by ten) the mist has risen and all the fineness is being wasted on the upper air or possibly Cortina.

Diana Cooper has just spent two days – beautiful and dear but alas, for the first time, she looks no longer quite *eternally* young. I wonder if she will mind? I fear she may – it is such a tremendous supremacy to lose.

Love,

FREYA

1 *The Towers of Trebizond* (1956).

11

The Romans in Asia, travels with godchildren

After Alexander, it seemed to Freya natural to move on to explore the Roman frontiers in Asia. If her energy, at sixty-four, seemed almost undiminished, the way she viewed her writing was changing. In the 1930s, she had regarded her role as that of traveller writing about herself and what she saw, and introducing history as and where it became relevant; now she was conjuring up the past, recreating history out of the landscape.

LADY WRIGHT[1]

Asolo. 9 July 1957

My dearest Esther,

I am making enchanting plans and they will, I hope, take me to Baghdad in the autumn. I do hope you will be there (latish October?). I look forward to it so much.

The main journey, however, is farther north and I am rather stuck for permits as it seems there is difficulty in getting across from and to Turkey or to and from Iraq. Can Michael find time in the interstices of the Baghdad Pact to drop a useful word? And, if no official channels exist in that particular district, perhaps a letter from one of my friends whose word carries weight might do the trick? The Turks are all out to help, but can only do so within their own borders.

I shall be settled for a few weeks in and around Mardin, visiting all those old Roman battle grounds. Then I thought of spending a week or ten days around Mosul, going to Hatra, etc., and then to *relax* in Baghdad. And while I am about it I promise Michael not to go dotty either about Kurds, Assyrians, or anything else explosive, but to confine myself to the wars of Nushirvan and Sapor.

I have just finished my book on Alexander's route in Asia Minor, and am now trying to find a likeable Roman to succeed him, but how difficult that is. What a beastly fascist people they were!

I long to hear Eastern news and to see you all again. I hope you like

---

1 Sir Michael Wright was then Ambassador in Iraq.

Baghdad? I love it unreasonably, like the mother of a beetle, but it really is much better than that.

Love to you both, dear Esther,

FREYA

HARRY LUKE

Asolo. 27 July 1957

My dearest Harry,

My royal lunch was as pleasant as anything could be that is so awe-inspiring: it is rather alarming to be the only woman present except the Queen! She went down the line and then came and talked to me: they had just been to Glyndebourne, and she said it was rather distressing to have no carpet in the box, so that every sound, even a programme falling, echoed loudly. I asked her whether the story was true about John Christie dropping his glass eye as he showed her in, and she made a little gesture of impatience and said: '*no*: those are the papers!' But, she said, 'he did ask me in the middle of dinner whether his eye was in straight: rather a disconcerting question to have to answer suddenly, isn't it?' I told her about Archie Wavell and his glass eye, which he lent to his A.D.C. who could not get one during the war, when he was anxious to look well in the eyes of the pretty Wavell daughter. Then we went in, and I was set between Prince Philip and Martin Charteris[1] (whom I knew), with Benjamin Britten beyond within reach to talk to. I can't tell you how easy and interesting Prince Philip was to talk to. We began on modern art. He told me that he was being shown a room full of designers' drawing patterns for dress materials, and saw one rather like a heap of spillikins, and looking out of the window noticed that it was taken direct from the straight lines of the scaffolding round Big Ben: all those modern cubes and square lines come, he concluded, from the brains of city folk who see straight streets and houses. I told him about the student at the atelier in Paris who asked me if I really *saw* the fat woman we were drawing 'all in curves', and brought me his own version – all cubes. 'And do you really *see* her like that?' said I. 'Yes', said he. 'How sad for you.' I asked about Gordonstoun where the individual is encouraged, and he told me how he had wished to learn carpentry, and to build a pigsty, and had been sent out to learn to do so. He has an extremely narrow, quick and nervous face, not handsome, but as it were almost too alive to remain inside oneself, so to say. While the Queen, walking slowly and very

---

1 Later Provost of Eton. Created Life Peer 1978.

composed but a little timid among her guests, seemed to keep all her vitality under control, so that only an observant person would feel it. She ate very little – for her beautiful little figure no doubt – and after lunch led us to the next room, with columns, looking out onto the lawns, and with a marvellous service of Meissen china in the corner niches: and then she walked from one to the other with a little pool of silence falling around her – how hard to be royal and to have always to begin the conversation!

London was a terrific rush. Only one meal at home and so many odd things to do as well, but great fun.

Love and au revoir from
FREYA

BERNARD BERENSON

Ankara. 4 September 1957

Darling BB,

How often have I thought of you, riding up the Lycian passes – looking at the beautiful tomb of Caryanda, a horseman spearing his prostrate enemy, a lovely B.C. fifth century thing of which I hope to show you a picture. And little forgotten cities, with barbarous names – Bubon, Balbura, Arana, some with theatre or agora, most only with tombs remaining.

I met Michael Stewart in Smyrna and he drove me down and we reached the village where the Muhtar promised horses last year, and for four days rode up and down the passes, and on the fifth rode to where the Xanthus river comes in strong green waters from its gorge: the cliffs rear up about three or four thousand feet, and the water looks happy to be free and tastes like life.

We had two long days' driving to get back and I hoped after a day or two to get on to Diyarbakir and the Roman Limes, but the Syrian situation is interfering and I have had to change and will go to Brusa instead – and then on to see Iraq for October. I shall have a longer time there and hope to see Hatra again and visit Sinjar – and not get back to Asolo till November. But then hope to find you well and tell you all about it.

Dear love to you and Nicky. Michael talks of you with the devotion and admiration we all feel.

Your
FREYA

Brusa. 25 September 1957

Dearest Jock,

I got down from the Ulu Dagh last night – I must say the dullest mountain I have ever been up. One walks along a ('jeepable') road for an hour, and then begins to climb up a steep zigzag to get on top of the semi-crater which is the rather dull shape of these limestone ranges; and I would probably have renounced it if an old old man had not been tottering ahead with two mules. I asked him to take me for ten lira, and began to feel more pleased with the world with the nice jogging animals beneath me. We went on, very fatly and slowly, and got to the top in an hour. It was spread out like a rather rough flattish tablecloth of stones with all the world below: ranges and ranges, towards Smyrna or Troy – but the Aegean magic is missing: they are just unimaginative, empty hills. Never never again shall I see a coast as lovely as Lycia; it is just the difference between all other birds and the nightingale.

The plan for the next book is slowly and dimly appearing and threatens to be quite different from what I intended. I believe that whole Roman Limen is going to appear to me as one colossal mistake – a cutting of the world's great life line of intercourse and trade. It may be that we are still suffering from that basic error, and that the (historically) good and bad empires or supremacies may be known by their keeping those Asiatic doors open or closed. A vast subject, and too little life left for it – but I would like to be able to look at the scenery next year.

Love dear Jock,

FREYA

Trebizond. 22 July 1958

Dearest Victor,

It is sad to write with the world crumbling and all our friends being killed. I knew Nuri and the Regent and Faisal for years and years, all the happiest years of my life.[1] The whole thing feels at an end and here is what we feared, the ditch we have so constantly made for during the last years seems reached at last. As I go about here, I feel very strongly how Asia is building herself against the West. She still needs and uses it, but will try to stand alone when she can. There will, I suppose, be more bloodshed. The middle people in Iraq will follow the King and go under,

---

1 On 14 July 1958, King Faisal II, the Iraqi Prime Minister Nuri Said and the ex-Regent Abdul Ilah were among those assassinated in a military coup led by Brigadier Abdel-Karim Kassem.

there will be army leaders and many more murders. If we could *recognise* the cause of our failure, something might be retained. There is no one in the Cabinet I imagine who can contemplate these murders as a part of ordinary life, but any one of the men trained in the Middle East could do so, and would scotch or prevent in time.

Now I must give you my news. Plans, all vague except that Persia is almost certainly inadvisable (no way out), and my ride through the Hakkiari also. I go to Sivas tomorrow and get there in three days: I will make a centre there for the battlefields of Lucullus and Pompey, and come and go.

This is a sort of dim transparent city at the end of our world, quiet and prosperous on huge green hillsides scattered with little farms, with a new harbour, and vast silo, and commerce in hazel nuts and tobacco and asphalt on the transit road to Persia. But the mists are round it, hiding its capes both east and west, and its sands are black though bright, and its churches scarce to be recognised, mosques ruined or changed, or storehouses for timber. The Greeks put Medea near by, and magic, and midnight in dragon-sown fields and one feels that all these might hide in the misty coasts that are scarce ever seen.

Your affectionate
FREYA

JOHN GREY MURRAY

Giresun. 28 July 1958

Dearest Jock,

If you remember your Xenophon you will know that this is the place where the fat boys were produced by a diet of chestnuts and the local morals shocked the Greeks. I have come to the conclusion that hazel nuts is what he meant, for the whole of these wooded slopes are covered with hazel trees, growing beautiful and well cared for like fountains and their fruit exported to Germany.

The Trebizond archaeologists brought me here in their jeep and left yesterday morning and I walked up to the acropolis which Lucullus took by siege. The town now spreads over both slopes of the peninsula below, and is full of nice houses with signs of wreckage when their (probably) Greek owners were pushed out.

The bay is far more beautiful than Trebizond; the ranges behind open deep valleys, the rivers come down under high trees, one can see six headlands looking east and here my west window looks over the new harbour building. All yesterday afternoon a caique was unloading amphorae, some polished with glaze others plain terracotta, made at

Uniae just down the coast. There is something so strange about this sea: not like the Aegean, far away but still our *home*, but as if here one were already half in the other world. The black sands which yet glitter silver, the sea so thin and pale which yet one feels black underneath, and which has no horizon, or so pale that nothing ends there: it is all subdued like the daylight in the landscape of a dream. And all with English smells and plants, autumn-wood brambles and bracken, hazel and alder, grass and dew: an English sort of Elysium or Limbo all wrapped in vagueness and mists.

Tonight I hope to reach Samsun by bus and get to Sivas tomorrow and there find news. And according to what it is will make my plans. I have not much heart for travel with all that has happened – but I will probably never be here again so will see what I can. Perhaps it is time too to go out into a sunset and wave goodbye: all those years, when in spite of failures we went on building, seem over. Other sorts of building no doubt will come, but my own generation's work seems closed and I begin to feel that I belong more to that other side. Perhaps this Medea sea has this effect: one feels half there already.

Love

FREYA

JOHN GREY MURRAY

Ankara. 15 August 1958

Dearest Jock,

I hope for an aeroplane to Van tomorrow or next day and then to get into those mountains and emerge back here about 7th September.

I am reading through the *Divine Comedy*, and the last time I read that all through from end to end was up the Alamut valley in 1931! It seems to me that this is civilisation – to be constantly in touch with *excellence* in some form, so that it becomes the yardstick for one's life. This happened through Bible, cathedrals or any great architecture, poetry or art: when a town was small, its fine buildings had a *daily* influence; the Greek plays were familiar to *all* their citizens; it was a constant yardstick provided by the *best* that humanity could do. If one thinks now of the numbers of people who pass days and months without even the sight of great *natural* beauty, one can't think of them as civilised human beings.

Love,

FREYA

JOHN GREY MURRAY

Athens. 22 September 1958

Dear Jock,

I came back and found your note – very pleased and excited to think of *Alexander*[1] out and waiting in Asolo when I get there.

I had only a day here and then we went off for the weekend to Santorini – a fierce fantastic place, exciting because one can see what the world looked like (and how disagreeable) when it was new. In the middle of a crater that climbs out of water too deep to anchor there are two islands, one that came up in the sixteenth and the other in the eighteenth century and a little welding operation in 1925 stuck them together where the lava has not yet gone quite cold. One can boil an egg in a crevice. All this is black cindery ugliness, but a few shrubs and poor grasses have started and I suppose in a few more centuries fine vineyards will flourish. In the late afternoon we were landed on Paros in very different landscape of gentle pointed hills descending to rounded lands and flat snouts – all limestone, pale brown and mostly treeless; and a whitewashed town with long sea-promenade and classic remnants built into its church and ruined castle. This morning we got back and tomorrow I go to Paddy [Leigh Fermor] on Idhra for a week. I hope he and I will get each other's books from our kind publisher!

Love dear Jock,

FREYA

JOHN GREY MURRAY

Idhra. 27 September 1958

Dearest Jock,

If ever you came to Idhra you would not only never be surprised at Paddy's delays, but be surprised at ever getting anything out of him at all: one steps out onto a whitewashed stone-flagged terrace, all yellow sun and blue pearl shadow, with a huge deep triangle of sea and the white houses scattering down to it at all angles round the corner of the town. Two little hills against the sea have cactus and prickly pear up rocky sides and a ruined windmill that looks like a watchtower on top; and on the other side of the house is a hillside of brown terraces and olives, where a goatherd talks to his flocks. There is no car on the island. Apart from the steamer and some frigidaires one is living the classic life and finding it very good.

I am in the middle of Paddy's book[2] and think it first rate. I think he

1 *Alexander's Path* by FS.
2 *Mani*.

writes better than I do – more consciously and with a fine choice of words. It is just the right length and should have a great success. He gives wonderful descriptions of rock and sky and the gauntness and *intensity* of this land – I do hope it will be liked as it deserves.

Tomorrow or Monday I go back to Athens (Embassy). It is very exciting to think of finding my book and I suppose it will be out this week or next? If possible, do you think one could hint to some reviewer – possibly *T.L.S.* – to notice *Xenophon* in my chapter 15? I am so anxious that my little *new* discovery should be introduced into the stream of Alexander.

Hope for letters soon.

Love,
FREYA

JOHN GREY MURRAY
Asolo. 11 October 1958

Dearest Jock,

I was glad to get your comforting letter as the zero hour draws near for *Alexander*: I hope he may be liked. I have a strange feeling that I would not like to let so fine a subject down and have no idea whether or not I have done so.

It is nice to be home. I feel as if I never want to leave, and it is good to be welcomed. Asolo is a *decent* little place, where we seem to be kind to each other, and go and see the old and the sick, and the young are not angry with us, and there is a peaceful orderly progress of the generations.

The *Christian Science Monitor* has written for a short article, beginning its letter with 'You may have noticed from our reviews that we are rather in love with you'. So of course I wrote it at once. Now the *T.L.S.* has asked me for a review of Fuller's *Alexander* and I will do that and yours which I fear I had quite forgotten. And then I think of writing an account of the Hakkiari, just plain travel, either for a long article or *very* short book to be written by Christmas. What do you think? Then I will get down to the autobiography.

Lots of love dear Jock,

FREYA

VICTOR CUNARD
Uckfield House, Sussex. 18 January 1959

Dearest Victor,

I was glad to find a letter from you when I got to London a few days ago after my tour round Oxfordshire. There was talk of you here and there, beginning at Cliveden where I lunched to see Nancy, whom I found full of sparkle. She forgets everything (but I *nearly* do so); still I feel that her age has much more life in it than lots of people's youth, and there is something very touching in an ardent spirit where the body gets so frail.

Paddy Leigh Fermor's book is spoken of well and selling not better, Jock tells me, but as well as *Alexander*. I went in to see old Mr Wilson at Bumpus's new shop and he told me that their first customer there was the Duchess of Kent and *Alexander* the first book ordered, which naturally pleased me.

After Christmas I was driven down to the Osbert Lancasters' and couldn't remember the house till I saw two poodly stone lions at the door which could *only* be Osbert, and were. Icy weather, but warm inside in every way. Went up to John Piper's and bought a lovely sketch of the Brenta country, all little puffs of trees and houses set in pale green distances. We drove next day to the John Millers' at Headley who have built the latest sort of house with lop-sided ceiling and one wall left brick indoors; you would *hate* it. It is all built for people who have no servants and seems to me a return to the cave age, every family for itself, an idea which met with scorn when I suggested it.

We drove over icy downs far more solitary than Alps to Woolston where the Seton Lloyds have found a village practically unaltered since the fifteenth century and then I relaxed in the wadded luxurious comfort of All Souls and Magdalen.

John Betjeman is piling up laurels, more copies sold than anyone since Byron. Jock quite worn and pale with success.

Love,
FREYA

It had been ten years of remarkably hard work: seven books, three of them volumes of autobiography, four of travel and history. It was now, as she neared seventy, that Freya discovered an intense new pleasure: taking young friends, godchildren and their friends, on some of her journeys. It was not altogether new of course; in wartime Cairo, Baghdad and Delhi she had been much fêted by young soldiers on leave from the front. But this was something rather different, and her own.

Molyvos, Mytilene. 23 August 1959

Darling Sydney,

I must write to you from this beautiful island clothed in olives and full of gently pointed hills. A Genoese castle has its battlements (touched up by the Turks) on the acropolis of the vanished Methymna. No one has dug it, so there may be temples and all sorts of things under the brown slope. On its other side there is Molyvos, a pretty small town with cobbled market-street climbing under vines and piled up with huge watermelons or eggplants like purple marble. From balconies one looks down on a tiny but snug and safe port filled with masts and the bulging blue or red sides of caiques. We drove here across the island (forty miles) from Mytilene after a very cold deck passage from Athens.

I have a godson (Simon Lennox-Boyd), a godson's brother (Lord Gowrie), a friend of theirs, Henry Berens, all going up to Oxford in October, a pretty and nice Irish girl with blue eyes and gold curls, and Barclay Sanders and Commander Beebe.[1] The four young ones have never been east of Italy and it makes me happy to see how this East is ravishing them. To come here with the Classics fresh inside one, at the age of nineteen, one cannot tell where a thing may lead one!

Dearest Sydney, I think of you often and with love always.

FREYA

MRS DEREK COOPER

Molyvos. 30 August 1959

Darling Pam,

Only three more days, and then we spend a night above the quays of Lesbos in a new hotel and sail to Athens on the night of the 4th to part on our separate ways. It has all gone in a flash: I can't tell you darling Pam what happiness it is giving me to have been able to open this Greek world to these four young pairs of eyes and to think that *something* I have been able to give will go on spreading and unfolding in their lives, Grey's [Gowrie] especially, for he and Skimper are my two dearest children and still play on the Asolo grass in my heart. He looks so much better and spends hours and hours bathing in the sun. The other two are both devoted to him. You must let us do another island next year and come with Derek too. The only thing I have missed this year is someone for me to pair off with and discuss the gossip of the day in cosy private and it would have been perfect with you and Derek there. We sleep under pines

1 Meyrick Beebe, a friend of Barclay Sanders.

where the scents and the sun have got inextricably mixed and from my bed I saw the loveliest sky this morning – Pleiades, Taurus, and Orion one below the other, and Capella (my small favourite constellation) shining softly on one side and a little old crescent of moon making the sky luminous around them and caught in the branches of the trees.

Love to all dear Pam,

Your
FREYA

JOHN GREY MURRAY

Asolo. 19 February 1960

Dearest Jock,

How wonderfully good you are to go so carefully over and over this typescript.[1] I have taken all your deletions except I think two. With all this docility, however, I have one uneasiness and that is that I hope you are remembering that our ideas on *modesty* differ slightly (or perhaps even a lot). It seems to me that the suppression of the nice things that people say to one is a mere passing fashion (just as when I was a child no one admitted going to the loo, and a little earlier one had to hide the legs of pianos): it isn't basic because it isn't truthful. The truth is that I was liked and encouraged in the Middle East, that I was continually told so, and that it gave me immense pleasure. If I now keep on suppressing this, it is like taking all the sunshine out of a picture. I don't think it shows a want of modesty to recognise the fact; it was, and always remains, a delightful surprise and a thing for which I am ever so grateful – and what I think I would do is to say this more or less, in the foreword or somewhere else, and that might make it all right? What prompts me to write this is what you say about the putting in of letters as illustrations being 'pretentious'. The point is that they are interesting in themselves and in fifty years' time people will like to see Lord Wavell's handwriting when that of Mr Snooks would leave them cold: it seems to me all wrong to suppress it merely because someone might think I do it for reasons that are quite foreign to me (Harold incidentally says he always likes to put in handwriting if he can).

What do you say to John Sparrow to read it over? And to MacMichael for the foreword?

Apart from the book, and the garden, there are labyrinths of plans for summer and autumn – the autumn trying to unravel the complication of

---

1 *Dust in the Lion's Paw*, the fourth volume of autobiography.

getting from Bokhara to Peking. Bokhara is quite near (as Asiatic things go) to Tabriz where I hope still to go once or twice, so it may be simpler to make it a separate journey another year. (I talk as if I had eternity before me, but I hope for a *few* seasons yet.) Peking I think of definitely for October.

Lots of love dear Jock,

FREYA

JOHN GREY MURRAY

Hotel Principe, Chianciano. 8 October 1960

Dearest Jock,

Of all dreary things to be alone at, a 'cure' is one of the dreariest – like a hen at the end of a string, always being given a tug to drink those waters whenever it wants to stray. But it is of course a very good place to work in and the last (I do hope) look over the typescript should be done by tomorrow. It would be most beautiful country, too, if left to itself and yesterday I wandered away from it all and found natural little paths in a tangle of limestone, oak, juniper and chestnut, and ended with two tough old women looking for mushrooms who, far from knowing a path, led straight down the roughest of hillsides saying that all ways were alike to them. One was a white-haired old toothless crone of sixty-one, so I was rather pleased to tell her I was six years older when we got safe to the bottom.

I have just been reading *Prospero's Cell*[1] which the *New York Times* want reviewed, and see how very poor mine is by comparison, but I don't think I can do much more to it and shall just go on feeling dispirited about it till it is out and can be forgotten.

Why should one envy the young? You say one should try not to – but I can't imagine doing so. It would be so *awful* to go back when one is so much nearer to the goal. I think you have got it wrong, Jock: one is old in this world, but young oneself for the next step. I feel about it as about the first ball, or the first meet of hounds, anxious as to whether one will get it right, and timid and inexperienced – all the feelings of youth; and for that one needs the comfort and companionship of one's own generation.

Love,

FREYA

---

1 By Lawrence Durrell.

MRS DAVID PAWSON

London. 4 March 1961

Dearest Pam,

I am still here and enjoying my 'season' after a bad start, three weeks in bed with bronchitis, but all well now and I am slimming, which is good for one I feel sure. Only now I am so broken in to fatless foods that Turkey is bound to *kill* me! On the 20th I fly to Angkor from Rome, to Hong Kong at end of month and trust to luck and Michael Stewart[1] to let me find a visa there for China. My only real preparation is a super summer suit woven in a mixture of linen–silk–wool which seems to be as creaseless and resilient as one would like to be oneself.

Lots of love, dear Pam, to you both. Hope to have lots to tell you in June.

FREYA

MRS T DEUCHAR

Angkor. 27 March 1961

Dearest Dulcie,

I wonder if I can keep this letter dry enough to be legible – water runs off as if one were a fountain and alas! there is no slimming about it. One drinks all the time. But I shall have been here a week tomorrow and feel that the things I have seen are with me forever. No Gothic cathedral, none of our monuments, was ever more noble than this central creation; in its broad basin of water, brown–gold, whose steps have crumbled, with the forest (immense trees) beyond; and the building itself rising from enclosure to enclosure, the outer wall with splendid gates, the balustrade and causeway, and the temple itself from terrace to terrace enclosed in cloisters carved and mellowed with grey lichen or dark with time. The last terrace is a bit of mountaineering up steep steps, and there you are with the five towers and the serene Buddha at the centre, and the roofs graded below. Not a wall or step is left undecorated, but it is done with great restraint.

One can never forget that it is *great* architecture, as great I almost think as the Parthenon. The whole base is carved with a tumult of battle scenes and I was thinking, as I was walking along, of the Elgin marbles and the difference. The *adventurousness* of the Greek makes him supreme, every movement, every flexibility of muscle in horse or man is experimented with. Here the liveliness is the same but it seems as if, when the right

---

1 Chargé d'affaires in Peking 1959–62.

formula was found, the sculptors were satisfied and continued to repeat it. But in architecture, which gains by symmetry and repetition, they seem to me to be on a par. The serene, mounting to a climax, was never better felt in any place of worship. It is already there in the early temples which I have been visiting (in one of the bright little motor-cycle-rickshaws that run about these flat forest roads). But the greatest later temple, carved with elusive faces in all its towers, is the decadence; and then the forest came gradually and ate the cities, and nothing but the stone-built temples are left. How mysterious it is. The people are the same, one can recognise the faces. But *something* – what? – has gone.

One has to have something very worth looking at to linger in this heat and today the clouds are massing as if the rain were to begin. What I have enjoyed most were three quiet mornings with my sewing in a court of Angkor and in one of the forest temples where the roots sprawl among the ruins, and only a few birds far away in sunlit tops were talking to each other. Sudden crowds of butterflies appeared, flying with slow heavy wings dark-brown or black, or flickering gay and light yellow, as if the souls of the old city were about.

I wish you could see it all, dear Dulcie, but I didn't wish for you for I believe you would pass out in the heat. I am just beginning to feel normal in it, and get up with the sunrise when the forests are delicious.

Dear love,

FREYA

MRS T DEUCHAR

Hong Kong. 2 April 1961

Darling Dulcie,

I sailed in a Comet to this most exciting city, where the climate is normal and delicious after the equatorial heat. It is so beautiful, the curving shallow beaches and retreating bays, the blue distances of peninsulas and islands, the domestic look of the smooth waters with crowds of sampans or junks dusky and slow, built out of the vast planks of the forest trees.

Michael Stewart is due down tomorrow and he and a secretary and I all go up together, D.V., on Thursday. I am now being transferred to Government House, and the Pink, beautifully pressed and not yet *froissé* by a camel, will be inaugurated for the occasion.

Meanwhile you will perhaps not be surprised to hear that I have gone quite mad, sables and pearls: years to recover, but how well worth it. How I wish you were here to enjoy it. To shop in these streets full of colour, crowded with their lovely Chinese letters on strips of red or blue or yellow, where you never see anything ugly except some European advertisement intruding (and very few of them), and to find people all eager to *make things*, enjoying the use of their craft. If you admire anything, they say 'Thank you'. I believe it is all very different as one goes north, but here one can see the old fashion of China and I can't understand how people can find Hong Kong uninspiring or insipid. For one thing, it gives me a feeling of terrific danger, as if on the edge of a volcano that at any moment might pour down. Long jerry-built houses are built for the refugees in rows and the whole thing has a pre-Deluge flavour.

Love to you, both, dearest Dulcie.

FREYA

JOHN GREY MURRAY

Siusi. 15 August 1961

Dearest Jock,

The reading party is going along nice and quiet and harmonious. Brought face to face with nineteen and twenty-one years, one is staggered to realise what an immense number of things one had to make up one's own mind about: how did we do it? Skimper is a very nice godson and, slowly gathering his tools, will be a good life-builder; Grey may take *any* turn. It will so much depend on whom he follows, and he follows only by opposing if you know what I mean. What distresses me is how this generation has to get along with no steady belief to help it. I have been reading *Le Milieu Divin* by Chardin and leaving it around in their hands hoping that one of its many sparks may light a candle. Have you got it? It is I think the most helpful book I have found since meeting Socrates in my youth. I am enjoying the revival of things long forgotten, talks about *Beowulf* and Middle English Sagas, and Pope and Dryden: not so much the New World – Graham Greenes and Joyces and a welter of present poets mostly it seems to me extremely fourth-rate.

I am walking and can (just) do four hours but something is still wrong and I can't quite think what. Hope it is not the poor old brain which Polizzi[1] says needs a rest. So I am doing no work at all though I would dearly love to write my first chapter of 'Rome on the Euphrates'. (Do you like the title?)

Love,
FREYA

1 FS's doctor in Asolo.

12

Building Montoria, rafting down the Euphrates, climbing the Himalayas, 'a quest of one's own'

Despite her lack of sympathy with the Romans and disapproval of their policies in Asia, Freya was now at work on her last major book, *Rome on the Euphrates*. She continued to make other journeys – to see friends, or with friends, revisiting the places of her first travels or in order to explore new ones – and to enjoy London seasons. Her father had been an imaginative designer of gardens and houses, and many of his skills and enthusiasms had been transmitted to Freya. Having spent a lifetime redesigning the interiors of the houses she lived in, she now embarked on a great and exhausting enterprise entirely her own: the building of a new house on the top of a small hill in the foothills of the Dolomites. It was called Montoria. On a stone lintel above the door she had carved the words 'Noi siam pellegrini, come voi altri' – we are pilgrims, as you are.

JOHN GREY MURRAY

Near Diyarbakir. 22 October 1961

Dearest Jock,

Such agreeable things fall out of the blue. A Mr Wigginston met me in Diyarbakir this morning and brought me out here,[1] along a desert road plastered with crude black oil for asphalt, to their camp on a high place in the middle of air and emptiness – a breadth and peace that seemed to feed one's soul. (Most of them don't feel it that way.) They have a dozen or so exquisitely sophisticated caravans and have given me one of them and are keeping me for a week to look at the battlefields of Lucullus. Electric light, frigidaire, bath, lots of cupboards, everything one can want is in the caravan – perhaps one day, when too clogged with possessions, I shall give up Asolo and *live* in one! The windows are netted and open so that one can always get a breeze and look out to sunset at night and sunrise in the morning. The wide Assyrian downs are all around below, clothed now in pale stubble and the bright poison-green of the fan-shaped euphorbias that spring up in the dark patches of the ploughed land. How I love this deserty spaciousness and the thin dry fineness of the

1 To an oil drilling company.

365

air. Even the pain that has been pursuing me so tiresomely seems to be going. It took me twenty-nine hours to come by train from Ankara – very leisurely and pleasant, and I was able to realise and I hope photograph the great bend of the Halys river inside which we travelled all yesterday, and woke this a.m. in time for the Euphrates (the sudden vividness it brings to its landscapes, and wild strength) and was really able to disentangle a lot of the strategy of Lucullus' day and Nero's by looking carefully out of the window. There is a strategic height between three rivers – Euphrates, Tigris and Murat – which a Roman should have held and didn't, and the railway crawls up and round it with ample time to size it up.

25 October 1961

It is most fortunate that the rig which actually drills is out of work till mid-November so that a Land Rover and a charming elderly mechanic engineer from Texas have given me two long days – first to look at two passes northward (where Xenophon, incidentally, went up). There is a bit of a wall across one of these gaps – possibly Urartian, made of great blocks; and beyond is a natural tunnel which for centuries was thought to be the source of Tigris and has inscriptions (we looked for in vain) of Assyrian kings. But the landscape was very great and has made one or two campaigns much clearer to me than they were.

Yesterday we went south and found the Tigris running by a wall of cliffs sliced smooth as if they were butter – and there, with hundreds of rock-scooped houses, is a town now half deserted and ruined but once the great bridge and crossing of the stream. They are building a new bridge of three great cement arches so that it may once more revive – but is now a sort of cave-dwellers' version of Les Baux. There is here so often this fierce mixture of beauty and hideousness which makes one have to be strong to take the East: this nakedness and poverty and beauty in spite of all. An ex-cook of the camp here appeared in the ruinous street and insisted on inviting us to food – stew, grapes and watermelon – and made it a thirteen-hour day, so that I am resting today. It makes a great difference to come back to the comfort of a caravan, heating, bath, light, Dunlopillo bed – all turned on by a switch or two, windows netted for flies, easy to open – and light woods pretty and shiny, so that everything is here except the 'patina' of life. Breakfast 6.30; lunch 11.30; supper 5.30 – and the eleven inmates (with two wives and four children) are pleasant and simple and easy and read awful novels and go shooting partridges or pigeons on Sundays. The villagers make holes under their roofs for the pigeons' nests and they go about the stubble in wide droves, turning with wings *blue* when the sun catches them, so that it looks as if a shred of the blue distance had come near.

The 'rig' has been so very kind to me and have I think enjoyed a whiff of Antiquity amid the oil. They take me to Urfa tomorrow, where Austerity begins (and oh dear, I have a tummy starting too!).

Love,

FREYA

JOHN GREY MURRAY

Mersin. 8 November 1961

Dearest Jock,

The adventure is over and tomorrow I should be in Beirut relaxing with nothing more than a bad cold and a few spasms of sciatica to pay for the last three weeks. The oil drillers at first and the Bank Managers from point to point of the Roman road this end helped me along with no permit and a *few* anxious moments, and I was able to do all I wanted except the scaling of a most remarkable and unexpected castle on a bend of the Euphrates (it was pouring with rain and the *kaimakan* who two days later was inspecting the bridge was washed off – no doubt in his city shoes – and rescued by his soldiers). I was prudent and also renounced the walls of Antioch, but climbed to a medium height and scanned them through my glasses. I went down to the old Hellenistic harbour, filled with water-flags and marsh and held in the decay of crumbled quays, and I have now followed the Roman way in the South from the sea to the Tigris, and should need only one more journey to where under Ararat Euphrates is born. I am glad to think of this, for I don't think I can do this travel much longer: the fact of being always in and out of some physical disaster, and the *moral* strain of nine, ten, twelve and thirteen hours either jolting in a jeep or talking – Turkish often – to strangers is much more than it used to be, so many years ago. Thirty-four years ago I was tossing off Mersin shore too rough to land: now there is a harbour, and a huge grain elevator (but no grain for export) and a white ship very spick and span, with apparently no passengers but myself inside it.

I came away sad however, for there is a dreadful feeling of failure all about. Everything they do seems just not good enough, and the old world is not entire in its aloofness and the new one too clogged to proceed. There is discouragement, and no visible prospect of a government that can function. And the very fact of this lavish kindness and hospitality is I suppose financially ruinous: the Turk is just *too nice* for the modern world. They took me to a French film last night so strident in its

367

depravity in contrast to this decent conventional people that I could hardly bear to sit it out.

Love,
FREYA

JOHN GREY MURRAY

Asolo. 30 January 1962

Dearest Jock,

How can I spend my birthday eve better than by neglecting my work and writing to you? So pleased I was to get two letters and hear your news – though it must be a very worrying life just now to be a publisher and watch all our standards of literature (it seems to me) going downhill at a terrific speed – or is this the natural reaction of sixty-nine? I am hoping for you that John junior's entry into the firm will not be too long delayed: one does need to have someone with the sense of *continuity*. I wrote to him a day or two ago by the way suggesting he might like to come out for his vac to work.

I am in the first chapter for better or worse. I hope to make the picture come humanly alive, but I myself shall be out of it, as it is essential for the history itself to speak. The plan so far is a series of separate chapters: the Battle of Magnesia (entry of Rome in Asia); the Wars of Mithridates (Lucullus and Pompey); the policy of Nero (fascinating on Euphrates and Armenia); Trajan's dream; Diocletian and the system of the border, etc., etc., down to the entry of the Arabs. The chapters are not continuous in time, but the theme of the frontier is continuous. As the book is meant to deal with only one point – the preferability of a peaceful to a warlike frontier – I think it should not be a long book. It means a lot of reading. I have just dropped a line to John Sparrow to ask him if he can find out how I may get by without reading the *whole* of Seneca and Cicero and to tell me which bits are necessary.

The Kuwait album looks very well and I am going today to start the work of Iraq. It strikes me that a series of picture books might be done on the Middle East as I knew it, with quotations – a sort of illustrated anthology? A nice little event was Malcolm MacDonald's[1] arrival with a Government Chauffeuress, a wonderfully unkempt but endearing private secretary, and a little Indian girl called Tuki, for two nights, and a day in Venice. They were lucky in icy but brilliant sun and it was very enjoyable. What an agreeable person he is, with the zest of a boy and a

1 An old friend. A former Cabinet Minister, High Commissioner in Canada in the war (when FS had stayed with him), and High Commissioner in India 1955–60.

very gay Bangkok tie, orange, yellow and vermilion crossed with black.
     Much love dear Jock,

FREYA

CHRISTÒPHER SCAIFE

Asolo. 8 February 1962

Dearest Christopher,
     I was so glad to get your letter, and now the photographer sends me this rather jaunty production, you and I looking like two old cronies that successfully let the world go by – and so we are. The sun seems to catch my bosom in rather a *protuberant* way; it surely isn't as extrovert as that? What is perfectly obvious is that all the party has enjoyed a very good lunch, and so I remember it.
     I have started chapter 1 of the Romans, the miserable tearing up of the Middle East by those brutal fascists. I must try and find a few nice ones to keep me going, Pliny so boring, Cicero insufferable, Julian, I discover on reading his letters, an appalling prig. Even Catullus jeers at a man for *being poor*! What a relief to turn to Polybius who was Greek. I would have liked to marry him. What a *decent* person. By the time you come next year the MS should be ready to be read.

Yours always affectionately
FREYA

JOHN GREY MURRAY

Asolo. 29 April 1962

Dearest Jock,
     I was glad to get your letter, cheerful and warming as the sun. Now I must tell you a rather sumptuous bit of news. I have sold my fourteen Prendergast sketches for £5,000! This relieves me of a sort of angst to which I am unreasonably liable (early poverty no doubt), feeling that if the day came when no one wants my books or I can't write, I should be unable to live here (and it is getting very expensive). I have told Mr Punchard[1] that I mean to spend them slowly over the next twelve years, and by then I will be eighty-two and Allah will provide. It is a great relief to feel this little margin – and I shall travel to England first class and buy *three* hats in Paris.

Love,
FREYA

---

1 Alan Punchard, FS's accountant and adviser.

369

Asolo. 3 May 1963

Darling Dulcie,

There is a lot of news. First of all, Larry Durrell is going to write a short foreword for *your* book (what news of it, by the way?).[1]

Secondly, I have had two sets of visitors and each has been trying to buy a house. One has succeeded, and the other is still in process.

Thirdly, I have bought a miniature mountain! While looking for the Hodgkins,[2] who preferred a lower little hillock, I discovered this stupendous view and got carried away and bought it with partly the money from those little pictures and partly (I hope and trust) an advance from Jock. It is ten acres and rises in a steep grassy slope with a church and cypresses on one side on another little hill, and all the Venetian foothills spreading to the plain below. Jock has seen and will tell you. I do so long to show it you! Now that this house is rather insecure[3] (three people show interest in the reversion plan) it gives me a delightful feeling to have this, like an animal with a bolt-hole. It has no noise, and no one can spoil the view, and two lost little country roads, and water and electricity, pass by at its feet.

The only other piece of news is that I dined with Stewart in Venice, cordial and casual and left me very sad.

Dearest love,

FREYA

Asolo. 19 May 1963

Dearest Jock,

Here is the agreement signed and I am sure you have done all that can be done for my income and hope there may be huge sales. Another title has suggested itself to me: 'Darkling I Listen'. 'Traveller's Joy' is anyway *too sentimental*, like little things about gardens in *Home Chat*! Joy is a tricky word isn't it?

Rather distracted not only by my own mountain but everyone else's, I am yet plodding on and just reaching Zenobia. Fascinating new lights keep on appearing. The Christian revolution for instance – it was not Christianity pulling the underdog out of the mire, but coming in in a military-cum-proletariat revolution on the *winning side*, and getting a bit tarnished in the process. I have just read the letters of Jerome, and don't

---

1 Dulcie Deuchar was editing an anthology of FS's writing.
2 Teddy and Nancy Hodgkin, friends from Baghdad days.
3 FS was trying to find friends to share Villa Freia.

like him; but the Greek Fathers, Basil, and two Gregorys, and John Chrysostom and Origen, all superb and sane. None however better than Plotinus.

Pam and Derek are dubious about taking on Asolo: I think it is a rooted reluctance to decide to leave Ireland. Meanwhile I might build a *little* house and let for a few years and then think again? I went yesterday with the owner to see the actual boundaries.

Lots of love,

FREYA

JOHN GREY MURRAY

Asolo. 1 February 1964

Dearest Jock,

What a month! I feel I need quite another one to digest it and think over all the days – Houghton and Cornwall and Lancaster and Sussex, and friends in London, and plays and Callas, and that memorable evening: who ever had such a birthday at seventy-one? Thank you, by the way, for the telegram. The birthday in fact has made me feel younger rather than older.

As for the mountain, a lovely white stone cornice is being put round it by way of eaves and the roof goes on as soon as nights stop freezing – and you want to hear its story from the beginning. Looking back over the last two or three years I can see that I had a feeling of constriction in Asolo, apart from the fact of its being too expensive. That could have been got over by sharing, but it is no home for young people to share as there is nothing to do or make, and if it were old people, I would still be housekeeping to my ninetieth year if spared. Even more so, though I realise it only now, was the spread of the *asphalt*: every road is being smoothed with it and even now I often renounce a walk because of that preliminary dullness. In a few years I would be like dear old Herbert Young, a prisoner in my garden: it is so beautiful and old now – even the rose bushes are like small houses and the trees are closing it all in, mercifully, from noise, or sight of other houses: the views are becoming vistas that one has to pick out between them – in fact one is enclosed. One of the great divisions of the human race is between those who like enclosure and those who need openness – and I believe I am very strongly one of the latter.

I hadn't thought about it however, and the mountain came by accident – by those £5,000 from the sale of my fourteen little Prendergast sketches. They were waiting to be prudently invested when the Hodgkins came here on a visit, fell in love with the countryside, and planned to

371

buy a bit of land and build a cottage. We sent for the agent and he took us to my mountain and to theirs, which is half the size and has a lovely but less generous view. I urged my mountain, but they wanted something small and easy and bought the other and it was only in a day or so that I felt that such a view *must* be bought; and 'Just as good an investment as an annuity'. I said to myself in that hypocritical way in which one deals with one's subconscious, knowing of course that one would never sell. The little hill was all green then, full of wild orchids in its summer, and nothing up it but a grassy path: always a little breeze, and noises of farms, sharpening of scythes of haymakers, geese cackling and cocks crowing, creaking of ox-carts, all faint and drenched by the sun.

There was the shell of a cottage that had been ruined in the war and I thought – and so did the masons, optimistically – that one could use it and build on a room or two and enjoy it meanwhile and in a day the whole thing was done.

Must stop this, dear Jock, as I have a *pile* of jobs waiting, but will go on if this is what you want to hear? Love and thanks for all,

FREYA

JOHN GREY MURRAY

Asolo. 2 February 1964

Dearest Jock,

One day after the other sunny and frosty; the tiles are going on but can't be fastened with cement till the weather gets warmer – but in a few days it should all be rainproof. The tying on of a roof looks very fragile to me and I can see how a tile dropped down and ruined the family of Ben Hur – but they say it is always tied up with bits of wire.

I left off when the hill was bought and the old owner took me over its ten-acre boundaries – a little wood at the bottom by a stream, and a round woodlet on the southern spur that was once the decoy place for birds – a labyrinth of hornbeam with box hedges and a tower to shoot from. All is overgrown and Derek has now cut paths through the thicket and we have planted two glades of hydrangea and peonies (they are budding already). On the north the hill slopes more gradually and there is a circle like a druid circle on Dartmoor, only of trees, not stones; all the rest is grassy terraces, with one smooth bit where one could put a cottage if necessary. When all was settled I left for Istanbul last July and was away for two months, rather shattered when I came back to find that the old cottage had been pulled down and new foundations laid without a word to me. Drama was here and there: the Italians suddenly realised that their lira was unsafe and sent all spare cash to Switzerland (priests took notes under their cassocks and made large profits I heard); so it suddenly became much more difficult to sell Asolo and months went by without an offer and everyone began to say how silly I was to have rejected £42,000 for it. Now the spring is round the corner and we look like a steady government, and all seems hopeful again. That Kipling poem 'If' is full of good advice and I clung to the first verse, and decided not to build gradually but do it all and finish it before the prices rose: they have now gone up to nearly half as much again as the contracts I made three months ago.

The walls were above the first storey before I left for England. They are made of old bricks and irregular stones that melt into a gentle colour of warmed earth like the peasant houses. Only the young peasant boys who do their own building still know how to do this work, and it is about three times as slow to build as the modern wall; but it is nearly twice as thick, warm in winter and cool in summer, and the portico melts into it with brick arches – quite plain without capital or keystone and no rigid line but the bricks irregularly drafted in among the stones. Austen Harrison had told me that it is vital for the vertical line to go up beyond the capital even for an inch only before the spring of the arch begins; but when we tried, the portico looked better with no capitals at all, and the only decoration of the façade will be a balcony now being cut in stone.

The autumn went by with all its little dramas and events: driving to where the stone quarries are, near Grappa, to choose slabs of marbly stone for the window sills, floors and stairs and swimming pool border; driving to Bassano for a modern kitchen to dangle before Emma's eyes. Emma has sparks of adventure though she is now round as a barrel, and is delighted with the prospects; Checchi wants to stay in Asolo with his garden (near the pubs I suspect) and work for the unknown buyers. One waits to see whether it will end in compromise or divorce.

We then had our major drama of burglary. This has been growing in Asolo over the last three years or so – beginning with cigarettes or food, and then a few trifles, and now 100,000 lire from the Mother Superior of the Infants' Asilo (knowing when the nuns were at mass and the one at home in bed with cold), and at last masked men with a tommy-gun rifled 300,000 lire and all the tobacco from a tobacconist in Casella. Between these two raids they came into this house from the garden (Emma *can't* have locked the door), and took away two teaspoons, two cigarette boxes and a watch, and 2,000 lire from Emma: and Bernardi came round the day after with a charming sheepdog called Zeno to guard us. He has straw-coloured eyes with pink veins, and a long coat smooth to the waist and then bagging out very shaggy and full like a pantomime clown – and sits like one too, with his toes turned out and his head on the side – and I walk him through Asolo on a leash so that everyone can see how well we are guarded. I also remembered a revolver given me by the A.M.G. after the war, when bandits were about, and found it – filled with live cartridges – in a cupboard and asked Bernardi to get a permit from his friend the 'Maresciallo'. That, the 'Maresciallo' said, was impossible, as I would get into trouble by declaring a revolver only after seventeen years; 'but tell the Signora not to worry,' he said: 'she can freely (*liberamente*) use the revolver and we will not incommode her.' We now carry the silver up every night in a basket and hope that one of these days the burglars may be found and removed.

Love dear Jock,

FREYA

EDWARD HODGKIN

Asolo. 27 January 1965

Dearest Teddy,

I am delighted to hear of your passing through, though April seems quite a way off still. If too early or for too short a time for your villa, do come here, *or* to Montoria if by any lucky chance this were sold.

What a sunset our Era is having, comfortless rather. We were lucky to live in an age which allowed for greatness. Of all the full-sized human figures I suppose Tito is almost the only survivor? Mao?

I have just finished Patrick's[1] *Ataturk*: they were giants, weren't they, good and bad?

My Romans are done and gone to be vetted. I have an enjoyable bit of leisure, but it does give one more time for one's *troubles* which is not so good.

Love to you all 3 from
FREYA

We sleep now and then at Montoria. Heavenly peace.

MRS DAVID PAWSON

Montoria. 13 January 1966

Dearest Pam,

The house is sold! Also paid for! And though there doesn't seem to be much left by way of income, I am free of all my debts! After all the strain I feel a bit battered, but like a ship in harbour, a very restful feeling. I don't

1 Kinross.

374

think I shall be up to Samarkand (though I hope for next year), but I do plan to reach Turkey and to linger in Greece on the way and perhaps go and bathe off an island? Would you be about in June? – and ready for what? I think I shall be rich enough to travel in comfort and leave the Istanbul bus for strong godchildren.

My book, too, is in proof and should be out in April,[1] and I plan to be in England for six weeks or so. So you see, life is getting into gear again and those moments when I thought *why* the devil did I ever think of building a house are quite forgotten and disowned.

Much love, dear Pam,

FREYA

MRS T DEUCHAR

Montoria. 7 June 1966

Dearest Dulcie,

You and Tommy still seem to be hovering here in some strange way, though it is a week since you left. It has been very quiet, just the sun going over our heads and the misty heat on the plain. I have trotted down the hill two or three times a day to watch the Angel's shrine. It is built now and looks very right, between a baby cypress and magnolia; and the long Sisyphus job with Caroly has finally ended with her accepting the slice of the hillside. (You would think my property was medicine, it is so hard to make anyone want it!)

8 June 1966

I have been thinking how unfair I was in complaining of women's jealousy; it is quite true that I have suffered, but only from the very second-rate, and such splendid charming women have been and are my friends. I think of you, dear Dulcie, and Sybil and Diana and Joan Aly Khan, and Pam, all noble creatures who like me as I am; it would be such ingratitude not to be thankful for such affection. Caroly too is true as steel (though extremely unpunctual).

Thanks and love to both of you,

FREYA

MAXWELL ARMFIELD[2]

Montoria. 28 June 1966

Dear Maxwell,

I have been struggling with a whole lot of tiresome things and never

---

1 *Rome on the Euphrates.*
2 An artist whose acquaintance FS had made when she bought one of his pictures exhibited at the Royal Academy in 1953.

got to my letters, which now look like a small mountain. The nicest thing however I have done is to build a little wayside shrine at the bottom of my hill. I promised this to my 'Guardian Angel' when my debts were paid, and now this has happened, leaving me poor but honest. The shrine is there with a whitewashed niche for the Angel's portrait. Would you like to paint him? – with big wings and holding the house in his hand like a Byzantine? If you felt like doing this I could let you have this house till the 25th of July (it is let for August) – and you would be very comfortable with a rather exuberant young housemaid to cook and look after you (and a swimming pool). I alas shall be away – but very nice neighbours are building a house and will be in and out. The cook is having her holiday, but the little maid is quite able to manage one person, and I do think you would like it. The Angel should be in tempera? Very straight and simple as he is to be looked at by the country people, and a nice Latin inscription must be thought of. I wish I could be here but I have to go to a niece. I hope you can come.

Yours ever
FREYA

JOHN GREY MURRAY

Montoria. 29 March 1967

Dearest Jock,

   Yesterday was full of tragedy: the Madonna on her hill had her *festa* and Henry's little hill was crawling with young girls supervised by two nuns; and Emma and I – alone in the house – came out to see them taking half my white narcissi up the opposite hill (there was a beautiful *lake* of them between the ilex, about 700 all in flower). I rushed up but it takes twenty minutes. However, I found those two monster nuns ready to lie themselves black as their robes: they hadn't *seen* a narcissus, and only later was I told of the whole bus filled with armfuls. I came down the hill and saw the remaining flowers being feverishly gathered (Emma left to guard was *sewing* indoors) and when I got back not one was left. Franco and Francesca returned from their day off and he was just in time to get the last culprits – a band of about six whom he brought up to me after a hand to hand show. They were frightened by then and said they would all *kneel* to me if I forgave what they called 'una distrazione' (absentmindedness). They came from Castelfranco so we sent them off uncomforted but are not pursuing either them or the nuns, but the three smallest culprits from S. Zenone were recognised and are being visited (but not further damaged) by the police tomorrow. I wept over my narcissi and the general depressingness of mankind – and am making a fence though I can't afford it.

Love,

FREYA

PAMELA COOPER

On the Bosphorus. 8 September 1967

Darling Pam,

I got here day before yesterday and walked into a dinner party with Diana and John Julius – now for another day with my Turkish friends in the old wooden house, the Bosphorus gnawing under one's bed at night and sending ripples of morning light across the nice old painted ceiling. A bath in the morning in huge stone-flagged bathroom with marble basin on its floor and the charming blue-eyed village maid from the north to soap and scrub one down: I can't think why it is so much more refreshing than any bath in Europe. We then sit on the garden terrace and drink coffee at intervals while Bosphorus glides by, full of things always coming round a corner like one's Life! It is this *movement* that makes it different from any other stream: the banks mean nothing, the things going to and fro are all that matter.

I wonder what the year will bring. There is a vast feeling of uncertainty and doom and no very clear road. What has happened to the England we knew?

One *can't* be defeated can one? Only oneself defeats oneself.

Love to you all,

FREYA

JOHN GREY MURRAY

Samarkand. 19 September 1967

Dearest Jock,

It seems strange, but here I am. We got into a very excellent aeroplane yesterday and breathed again as we got out in the Oriental atmosphere, the desert-ringed, earth-brick-built oasis, full of trees and waters, surrounded by heaped mounds of Samarkands destroyed and forgotten – the citadel of Alexander's Maracanda, the desperate heaps of misery left by Genghis and Tamerlane. It has been a wonderful day. The artisans who were separated and survived the awful depopulations were kept to rebuild Samarkand and here are their lovely works, the oldest the most beautiful, most delicate fancies, more perfect even than Isfahan. There is a street of tombs, daughter and wife of Tamerlane and others unknown,

377

a sort of Via Appia between sun-baked walls, melting with turquoise domes and walls, traceries cut deep in the earth-baked medium, every device and pattern of delightful fancy worked by these people whose homes and generations were destroyed. With what sad hearts they must have done these lovely things for the usurper, the last sunset of their civilisation. The oldest of these tombs are the most beautiful – but when one comes to the other wonder, the great centre of Samarkand called the Registan, there are three great façades of colleges on a rectangle, and Tamerlane's grandson built the earliest of them, and the next – soon after – is even more beautiful, with two of the loveliest ridged turquoise domes imaginable. The whole square is one of the world's wonders and a reward for all pains of travel. It comes like the cry of a civilisation across these wastes of space and time and I keep on thinking of Flecker's poem of the Saracens and the statue that survived.

The Russians are doing very careful restoration and preserving and the museum here is beautifully shown. The whole of their achievement is prodigious and Tashkent is coming along to be another in the chain of these great Central Asian civilisations. It is already a comfortable, clean, tidy town spread with many trees and gardens over a huge space, and will soon be a town of gardens too. Here, with fewer earthquakes to contend with, the old character has kept itself. The Uzbeks have charming peaceful faces, quite resolute but friendly. My little bits of Russian are welcomed in the flood of foreigners they have to deal with.

Love,
FREYA

LADY HUXLEY

Spinzar Hotel, Kabul. 1 October 1967

Dearest Juliette,

Are you surprised to see where your letter finds me? Just arrived from Samarkand. I spent a fortnight in that part of Russia and it has opened such a window: the Timurid buildings beautiful beyond dreams; and Bukhara still a pleasant Oriental town. But I don't want to go again and was glad to fly away this morning. It is the knowledge of *fear* always round the corner: one feels it so strongly. And the people look full of purpose, and never loiter about, but don't look happy – no *radiance* as in our untidy Mediterranean lands.

Darling Juliette, what a good person you are, and what an uphill it is. I am seventy-four, and what I feel is that I too would be drowned in depression if I thought of old age as an end and not a beginning. As it is, I find myself wondering with a feeling of timidity but also delight as to what is round the corner. Julian has not got this happiness. Don't you think that is enough to explain everything? How can one feel happy if one is riding downhill with a blank wall at the end? An old woman in the hotel near the Oxus came to my room and said, 'We have everything but we have not God'; and it must have been a comfort to her to say it for she disappeared and came back with a pot of tea and two precious chocolates to give me. Over and over one finds it – this Goodness which doesn't live by bread alone. It is said that it will inherit the earth, and I believe this in spite of all the babels we build.

Dear love to you both,

FREYA

MRS DEREK COOPER

Kabul. 2 October 1967

Darling Pam,

This is where I found your p.c. yesterday on emerging from Russia. So glad to get it and also to feel myself in the free wild air of this splendid country – still the East I knew forty years ago in spite of motor cars and tourists.

I went to another, modern, town just opened and took a silly photograph of a refinery in the distance: within three hours the poor Director of Tourism had been reprimanded and my film was asked for and kept overnight to be developed. I got I think the worst fright of my life thinking of what my Polish friends had warned me and realising that nothing could be done if they wanted to hold me. All night I lay in waves of panic, only soothed by a complete acceptance: if it has to be, I thought, I will accept it and think of the past and its happiness and hope to die soon. Then in the morning, at six o'clock, there was my little film, luckily producing a hideous picture of new workmen's dwellings as well as old touristy ruins – and the refinery cut out. I have never I think been afraid of a human being – but this cold machine terrified me as it does the people who work for it.

Love,
FREYA

JOHN GREY MURRAY

Kabul. 9 October 1967

Dearest Jock,

Back, over the Khyber and up the terrific Kabul gorge. What a citadel this country is between the northern high road (Russia) and the southern

379

(U.S.A. – Kandahar); inside those it is mountains as close folded as a concertina. I found, being brought up on Kipling, that the whole of Khyber was Romance, with the names of its regiments and their dates – Sikhs, Khyber Rifles, Punjabis – sculptured and coloured on the rocks and the little forts still sitting on every hill, and a notice to tell travellers they must be out of the pass before sunset.

I take a day off in between trips and clean up and read in my room and have just finished Evelyn Waugh's *Officers and Gentlemen*: it is a true picture, it seems to me, and makes me like Waugh better. If I were dealing in criticism I would put him in the family of Petronius – a voice of decadence but, here and there one feels it, a regretful voice. He will live no doubt but I think, like *Euphues* or other passing fashions, appealing to a small sealed company in their time: it isn't like Hardy (whom I was also reading), the *English* voice along its major stream. Here and there, almost unnoticeable, one can tell that he heard and felt that major voice, but he only lets it be inferred and is explicit only for failure – (same as Osbert really) the inferior alone is to be spoken. Ever so long ago W.P. wrote to me when we did not yet know each other well, and signed 'Yours affectionately'; then he added a P.S. – 'No! Affection is a poor word, and love is strong.' It was an equally reserved, but a more manly generation? This here is a manly people too: one feels happy and free among them though almost certainly it cannot last. My Persian is beginning to come back – words dropping from nowhere – and I would like to return among them. The months given to Russian were not wasted; I was able to talk and quite a number reverted to human beings – but I shall let it drop now: it isn't the air one wants to breathe in one's last years. It will be, if anything, my early loves, Persian and Arabic, and Turkish, and the only Eastern journey I should still like to make beyond is Kashmir and Nepal. I have a feeling that a huge *geographic* change is taking place here, the return of supremacy to land transport as against sea – it would tilt the whole balance of civilisation East again.

Love,
FREYA

PAMELA COOPER

Montoria. 14 March 1968

Darling Pam,

Your little cards are very welcome though they don't satisfy one's hunger and I hope so much to see you now that I am home again. It is always a tremendous stirring-up to go to England: friends with such *various* periods of one's life attached to them, all coming with the old memories and so many now drifting away as old age comes after us all. I lured Skimper and Ianthe (*not* Tiggy) to lunch with Dulcie to get my young Arabists to meet – two such charming ones, Francis Witt (wintered in Hadhramaut) and Colin Thubron (wrote a first rate book on Damascus). When I talk to them I feel life has not been quite wasted, and they are great dears and come and see me. Mark [Lennox-Boyd] is coming out, too – now working at law after the Yemen. He too met Skimper: it is all a little band and the M.E. will be their affair! It has all come back to me as I read H. Nicolson's last volume – *couldn't* read the 1940 for tears, that cataclysm we all seem rushing towards for the *third* time! It is like an infatuation with Juggernaut!

The swing back towards the Arab is I believe on its way. One has to give Israel a bit of time to damn herself – not a *glimmer* of generosity or understanding. I will try and write, but not just yet. My feeling is that before we can do any good we have to outlive the colonial–imperialist reputation: then the young can begin in a free field, and as *individuals* and not parts of a government: but till the prejudice has gone, it shackles every effort and spoils it. Anyway it is on its way out. When that chapter is sealed, the Empire will show for what it was – a stupendous miracle of an adventure which held the world in the hands of a tiny nation, in comparative peace.

Love,
FREYA

MRS T DEUCHAR

Montoria. 20 May 1968

Darling Dulcie,

Tomorrow the Gowries arrive, and meanwhile here are the Huxleys. He is eighty-two and with an old, old trace of brilliance like one of those musical boxes that make cracked tunes – not wisdom nor goodness which are the only vintages that last. Poor Juliette continues to be bright, devoted and unreconciled inside. Sad beyond words.

It fits into that awful world of Lytton Strachey I have nearly finished.[1] I will keep the book for you to take, as I shall not want to read it again. All through those years while that little group were trying to be clever (and succeeding one must say), I kept on thinking of the long lines of steel helmets plodding here up to the mountain passes to keep the world for them intact. There might have been no war as one reads, except for the inconvenience of a board meeting now and then to see whether the future

---

1 Biography by Michael Holroyd.

of the world could be saved without Lytton's help! Rather surprisingly, I seem to have met most of those people – Virginia Woolf, Duncan Grant, Vanessa and Clive Bell, Lady Ottoline, James Stephens, etc. . . . The book has strengthened my feeling that the Twenties was the time of our decay though it has taken that seed another two generations to develop fully. Lytton has the blindness to pity Keats for dying 'without copulating', a man whose horizon went beyond the universe and had all beauty in his heart. Miserable people!

Bless you and Tommy, dear Dulcie.

Your
FREYA

PAMELA COOPER
Island of Euboea. 18 September 1968

Dearest Pam,

I have been meaning to write ever since your letter came, and carrying it about from island to island. So worried about Derek and hope you can induce him to knock off. Do you remember Archie Wavell saying: 'Whenever one of my generals thinks himself indispensable I send him on leave.'? I know that when I got home in '45 and the war ended, everyone who had been working with us either got a good let-up (as I did) or went in for a nervous breakdown. One's body is the *instrument* we have to work with, and needs as much care as a soldier's gun! Mine is getting rather a poor old gun as it nears 80 – it can still *swim* beautifully but is sadly *deaf*, and not able to work as it used to. I hope however to induce it to do a little book on Afghanistan and the virtues of *Tradition*. I think that I can do whatever good I can do by writing and must try to go on as long as I can find readers (have had such touchingly welcoming reviews).

I think one can inspire (if one is lucky), but not *guide* over 70!! Skimper can work in Cairo and Mark wherever he may go, and there are others young and keen: it comforts me so much to think that I may have done something to set them first on the way, and it is wonderful when they come and tell me about it.

'As an old craftsman smiles to hear
His name remembered in the schools,
And sees the dust upon his tools.'

I get back next week to Montoria: rather a sad time as I have had to send away Emma (making life impossible and unable to live with *any* maid or the indispensable gardener). It means paying her £1,000 and so awful that one should be willing to pay that to *get rid* of someone. All very unhappy. Must send this with dear love and please, news of D.

Love,

FREYA

Florence. 27 May 1969

Dearest Mark,

My plan has more or less got settled for Istanbul about September 3rd and then three or four weeks into October in the South. It will make no difference if you suddenly find yourself free and send a telegram and join – except to make it much pleasanter.

What, however, would be even more exciting (though possibly just as difficult) is if you could think of spending part of *February next* in Nepal. Such an amusing thing has happened. I heard of an ex-Colonel of Ghurkhas who continues to live in his adored mountains and organises expeditions for people who want to walk about there. He takes them right in among the giants, round the skirts of Everest or Annapurna. I am no good for walking (thinking of the wind on Taurus) but I wrote and asked if he could arrange a fortnight's riding, although I am six years beyond his age limit. He sounds quite pleased and has written an excellent letter of suggestions, and says that though walking is the only way of getting near Everest, there is an even more beautiful bit of wandering round Annapurna, the most impressive of all these ranges, that can be done on ponies. He suggests about three weeks, half getting acclimatised or resting (lovely lakes), and half actual trekking. Very few people I would ask to join on such a jaunt so I hope you feel it as a traveller's tribute as well as love and affection, dear Mark. I shall try and do it myself just to 'raise my eyes to the hills'.

Love,

FREYA

Grappa. 12 August 1969

Dearest Jock,

This is to tell you that the *Minaret of Djam*[1] is packed and ready to be taken to you by one of the Stewart guests on the 20th: it is a wonderful opening of prison doors when a book finally gets off. This one is very small, but it has taken a lot of writing with rather feeble powers. When Ernest Barker produced a historical volume at eighty-one I remember

---

1 *The Minaret of Djam*, last of the travel books.

thinking it strange that his wife made such a fuss over it – but I now understand perfectly. The remarkable thing is what Dr Johnson said of the dog standing on two legs (was it?) – that he should do it at all. If it isn't good, I will stop writing; but I hope it *is* good.

As for title, I think just (Afghanistan) in brackets would be best? One only wants to give the information and not to take the accent off the Minaret. Also I don't think this deserves to be called a *journey*; if anything an excursion, but I think just Afghanistan either added or under the title would sound best. There is also an uncertainty in my mind about the chapter headings. I feel that I want to emphasize the abstract bits of philosophy (if that is what it is) and not to add more emphasis to the travel, which will already have the pictures and anyway is more obvious. With this in mind, will you give the headings a thought as you go? The little book is in your hands, dear Jock – may it not disgrace its foster-parents!

This has been a very good experiment for work: no other temptation except walking, and that has been an excellent combination. Three various parties have come up to lunch with me: it is a Babel at meal times, but in between one can step away into woods or grassy slopes, all dotted with peasant houses whence the cows are pastured – all to be spoilt soon but not just yet.

The travel book is at least a year away, but I have been wondering if you would like it dedicated to you? John has *Perseus*, but I don't believe you have one (though I may have forgotten) and surely that is wrong. A nice book of travel essays, with the portrait as frontispiece and little bits of poetry between?

Love,
FREYA

SIR MICHAEL STEWART

Montoria. 3 October 1969

Dearest Michael,

I had been thinking that it was a long time since I had news of you or had written, and sure enough here was a nice letter waiting for me. I got back yesterday, not from Turkey but London, where I ended up so as to go to Charles Lambe's commemoratory (nice word?) luncheon. Mount-batten made a speech, not inspired, and rather disinterested like that beautiful profile of his, *ahimé*. But I had a very happy time sitting next to Sir Francis Chichester.[1] We *both* exclaimed joyfully at sitting next to each

---

1 The well-known yachtsman. He had made his solo one-stop circumnavigation of the world at record speed in 1966–7.

other and had a splendid talk of deserts and seas, like tumbling suddenly into the Elizabethan Age. He has a charming face with that delicate, clean-cut *neatness* of the Elizabethans, those little wisps over the ears looking clean-cut and close-shaven and grey.

Did I tell you how glad I was about Ditchley?[1] It was arranged by Nancy Lancaster with exquisite taste and fine bits of Kent's original furniture, I do hope still there. I stayed a weekend with the Ronnie Trees, and hope to spend more. A lovely job, dear Michael, and will let you come here, too.

Lots of love to you both,

FREYA

In 1970, Freya was seventy-seven. The year marked another turn in her life: a journey to the Himalayas, where she had long wanted to go, with Mark Lennox-Boyd, and the start of a new and very different literary project, the collecting together of fifty-five years of letters. It also saw her relinquish her dreams for Montoria, and move back to Asolo. The house, in the end, had brought incessant worry: too big, too expensive, too lonely, and no one willing, as she had so hoped, to share it. In the decade that followed came more journeys, more honours, and more writing, essays now taking the place of history and travel. In the New Year Honours List of 1972 she was made a Dame; she found the title, she told friends, a little austere: in Italy she would stick to Donna. Most important, perhaps, remained her attachment to her friends; to them, every day, she continued to write.

MRS T DEUCHAR

Montoria. 24 September 1970

Dearest Dulcie,

My Guardian Angel has sent me what I hope may prove a godsend, a young secretary-couple who are typing out my letters from 1912 to now. It means reading them all and I have been all this time at it, 1912–27 so far. It is a strange labour, coming upon a stranger who is yet oneself and watching life hammering her out. It takes one's mind off present squalor and lets one see those of the past in a mild perspective. And even so I have nothing to complain of, and friends truly kind. What I should have done without Caroly through this lonely year I don't know. As it is I shall try to remain here when I get settled after Nepal, and pull the garden through the summer. When that ends I rather hope to have sold the house and then think again. I would not mind selling it outright and building *one room*, with small one for maid, and kitchen, close by with

1 Sir Michael Stewart had been appointed Warden of the Ditchley Foundation.

the same view. The view is the one thing that has given steadfast joy, ever changing and yet ever the same, and I should be sad to leave it.

Very dear love,

FREYA

MRS T DEUCHAR

At the crossing of the Himalayan range, between Annapurna and Daulaghiri. 17 November 1970

Darling Dulcie,

This letter will reach you after I do, but not many letters are sent from this apex of the world and I think it must please you to know that you are thought of as near Heaven as I am. *Warmly* thought of every night as I wrap myself in your woollies or wander out (boots and your Burberry) to find some little privacy among rocks under the moon.

This is now my highest point. The others, Mark and a nice young man who has more or less joined us as our journeys are the same, have made one day farther north where the flat begins and our tumultuous river runs smooth, and the frontier of Tibet is near. But I have come to the end of my *breath* and nearly suffocated the night before last until I thought of opening the tent and the oxygen in that icy air revived me. The same last night: I keep it closed for a few hours for warmth and then open. So I am here in absolute quiet till I meet them again tomorrow. It is a wide gap with two of the great summits, one on either hand, a little to the south. It is the main chain and Everest a little to the east and nothing I can ever tell you will describe the awe and the majesty of this approach, the last terrestrial footsteps to infinity. I sit here and look for hours, the look of Ondine as she ages, do you remember? with all one has to give in one's eyes. The three visible peaks of Annapurna are melting in their snow into the sky, the shoulders of great brown hills support them, and then the rounder curves and spearheads of the pines. We are 9,000 feet up, but they are still 18,000 feet above us. But it is not height, which we somehow share, but the feeling of *amplitude*, the manifold ranges so rising that the whole world seems to be a part of their adoration. I cannot express it, dear Dulcie, but tears are in my eyes.

Luckily I had no idea of how difficult the Himalayas are for riding, because I would not have dared it and would have missed it all. But I have got here and the good Angel will take me back I hope; if not, one must not wait till asked, but *give*, and I will not grudge even the fall down a precipice (of which there is such a variety round about here), if it is required. But these little ponies are like cats, and wherever the paths are steep their immense ups and downs are managed by slabs of stone arranged in stairs; and we, pony and I, climbed 2,000 feet up stairs in one afternoon. We have been nine days, six or seven hours a day with one day's rest. Mark walks and is getting very tough. So am I, though with blue bruises all over my thighs from holding on.

Love to you both,

FREYA

MRS ALAN MOOREHEAD

Montoria. 16 January 1972

Dearest Lucy,

Don't worry over which letters[1] come first till you have the whole vast lot in your mind. I am quite open to persuasion, only find it difficult to believe that my own life is more interesting than the war! The First World War surely was the climax for *my* generation; and the Second – a cry of protest broke from me when I read that 'so many issues have been overtaken by larger events'; you might, you know, say the same of Thermopylae? The point of my generation was, I think, that we were pushed by fate into a form of life that was *heroic*, whatever the dimness may be that has come over this word; but this is the one fact, the piece of information, that I would like to leave behind me. I would like still to write some little thing about it, but I think that the letters should make it unobtrusively evident, for it was the *climate* of our time, and anyway it is I think the only 'message' that my generation can still leave behind it? I agree that it is not being consciously sought after today, but I think it will be very soon, and the fact remains, I most deeply believe, that true and conscious heroism is a necessary ingredient for happiness – not that it always provides it, but there can be no perfect content without it. I hope the letters will bring this out, and so will those written to me. Oh dear, poor Lucy, what an awful lot of reading lies before you! And the little typist, extremely slow, is nearly through 1967 here.

Dear love,

FREYA

JOHN GREY MURRAY

Asolo. 1 February 1974

Dearest Jock,

A little flock of telegrams came pouring in and yours most welcome among them, like little rays of sunlight into this bleak year. I think of you and wonder which of all my friends is warm, and apart from that (which

1 FS had asked Lucy Moorehead to make a selection of her letters for publication.

anyway is helping the Arabs), there is great grief in thinking of what is happening to England itself. Now that I have a little leisure and lie nursing my sciatica, I think and look back and wonder where the deviation started between growth and ruin. In the country life of my childhood we were one nation, rich and poor leading the same life in spite of all difference: was it the motor car that brought the change? Was it that we stopped reading anything but documentaries of one sort or another and the guidance of life was left to advertisement? I can't help feeling that a great deal of the blame rests with writers, journalists and publishers too – with two generations spent knocking down old gods and placing the Second Rate in their place. People will go hungry for the First, but not for the Second-rate for long. Anyway, *ichabad*, here we are and I am rather glad to be 81.

I have just been accepting a charming dinner invitation for July 4 in London: a club that has never had a woman guest of honour so they suggest that I may take a friend to support: the Paiforce and Mesopotamia dining club: they meet once a year to reminisce and enjoy themselves without their wives, and I hope to see a lot of friends, Paiforce was our little spurt from Iraq into Persia in 1942 when we were great. They joined up with the Russians at a banquet and being asked to contribute a song could think of nothing but the Eton boating song.

We too have primroses, and hepaticas, and no rain for summer water. If one could forget Imperial America and its madness one could be happy. I am reading an old book: Seeley's *Expansion of England*: it was lent me at 18 by the first young man I fell (slightly) in love with and made a very deep impression at the time, and I still find it wonderfully good.

All love dear Jock from
FREYA

MRS T DEUCHAR

Asolo. 1 February 1974

Dearest Dulcie,

Thank you for the dear telegram, punctual yesterday. You would have enjoyed my little party – Caroly and the whole Berardocco family, a huge cake with eight candles for tens, and one in middle for the first step on the slippery ninety slope; and a little present for everyone on his or her plate. Dear Caroly, thinking of my solitude, wanted to come with a television set but I have explained that, while still able to write, I must have time to think and television is an Enemy. As it is, I tried to circumvent the doctor by suggesting a stick, a useful present that wouldn't ruin him – and this he brought, but also a radio, and was so happy to have spent so much more than he should on his friend. I was so touched, because he has so many debts and four sisters as well as his own family to look after, and arthritis as bad as mine and forty years more of life than me to carry it along. I love, as you know, to have the things as presents that are always about me, so I cherish the radio and am enjoying two concerts a day – lovely classical music morning and evening. One has to tame these little mechanical monsters as if they were wild animals and learn their ways and hours.

You would laugh: I have just discovered that I can, more or less, read Lucretius and have this wonderful excitement in the watches of the night. He is a most thrilling person to meet and sees and makes one see the world's wonder. I have also done another short essay on death (part of Old Age) and will send it if you like: I don't think sadly of it and so it should not depress. Two more are in my mind – they come flitting around me like kind and healing sprites.

All love to you and Tommy. Is he well? I long to see you both.

FREYA

SYBIL, LADY CHOLMONDELEY

Achentoul, Kinbrace. 26 August 1975

Dearest Sybil,

The days have rushed by and I meant to write before, but then waited to be able to tell you about our visit to the Queen Mother. It was in her castle by the sea[1] and more like a fairy tale than real life – the castle so right, with its pinnacles and towers and flag with many quarterings, and the gates open and none but one old retainer at the door. And herself so simple and royal in her welcome, so that one felt the genuineness of everything about her; it was a wonderful atmosphere of true and basic things. There were only two other charming people – Lady Mulholland and Sir Martin Gilliat – and they made us (Nuttings and young Nicholas stepson,[2] and Henrietta FitzRoy[3]) feel happy at once, and took the young up to the highest tower while the Queen showed me her garden and then took me down to the beach where she has a little seat that looks over the sea. The tide was out and the long ribs of shore lay below in slices of stone as if they were the good beef we had at luncheon on the way. The Orkneys were far away, but just visible in a silvery mist, and this delicate northern light lay on everything – the long low green headlands of our island, and the far outlines, and the changing iridescence of the sea. I

1 The Castle of Mey in Caithness.
2 Beatty. Diana Nutting had been previously married to 2nd Earl Beatty.
3 The Duke and Duchess of Grafton's daughter.

forgot it was the Queen as we sat there, two old women with most of our world behind us but happy in what we remember and what remains. She told me how she found this castle, falling into ruin, and on a sudden impulse decided to save it, and made it the quiet remote treasure it now is. How much you must have understood this, dear Sybil, and how I understand your love and regard for someone so true and so *human*. We all came away with this *human* feeling about us, after tea at a long white table out of our childhood. It was a great day anyway, and that sight of our northern frontier, the long green headlands with their small groups of houses and cattle browsing, and the feeling of remoteness and the long hard winters all about them, and our history so wrapped between south and north and so visible here – it left me very happy to have seen it all.

Dear love,

FREYA

JOHN GREY MURRAY

Asolo. 30 January 1976

Dearest Jock,

Thanks for the kind winged words: how many birthdays you have sent to! On the eve of this one the essay proofs have gone to you, my last book I truly think.

Your rigidity over punctuation reminded me of a dinner where you put Max Beerbohm and me together and we had such a happy time over punctuation lasting to the dessert. We agreed in being unorthodox. I keep semi-colons and colons like a jerk of a stop to ask for attention, and he graded, ; : according to the length of pause he required, and we came to the conclusion that our use of these signals was really the same. It is one of my regrets that I never got to know him better with Rapallo so near – he did of course have a very tiresome wife to begin with.

I hear you are back at work and in great form, but I am anxious, dear Jock: please don't forget my letter – one is given such short little runs as time goes by; and John must be thirty-three – the climax of Alexander. The timetables do keep us very humble. What I find rather sad is the forgetting of every language I have ever learnt.

Love,
FREYA

JOHN GREY MURRAY

Asolo. 5 October 1976

Dearest Jock,

Sue Pugh, whom I insist on calling Susie, spent a very cheerful weekend to discuss our possible programme for the B.B.C.'s 'The World About Us' – with Venice and the opening of its new (regional) university, and a Sunday here with the really so charming talk of Anthony Hobson,[1] wife, and daughter. He told us the *dreadful* story of Evelyn Waugh's review copy (I think) of Cyril Connolly's book – *The Unquiet Grave* was it? – and Connolly finding the most hideous things referring to himself inside it – thinking too that it came from a friend. I wonder if Evelyn W. ever thought he had a friend?

I gave Susie six countries to choose from and our common choice is the raft down the Euphrates (easiest too for me) and possibly with Mark and wife to join. It is up to her to solidify this vision, and I will be seeing how I get on along the edge of things in Yemen in November. The young are always ready and their risk is a lifetime; after eighty it isn't much more than a year or two anyway. Why should *anyone* hesitate? I am thinking of it with pleasure and hope it comes off.

Awful weather here and a little tremor they call mere 'assessment' now and then.

Love, dear Jock,

FREYA

JANE BOULENGER[2]

Asolo. 8 February 1977

Dearest Jane,

I will be very sad if you come in *May* because this river-scheme looks like coming off and May is the month when the Euphrates is just right. Its old rafts have drifted down it since Noah no doubt and B.B.C. is doing me on a journey down (April and May alas) from the Turk to the Iraq border, across Syria. Fun to see the modern world at work on my so ancient ways!

I ought not to be doing this at 84, but the Yemen trip was perfect, and wonderful to be in the open again, looking up from my little bed with those unbelievable starry heavens.

Even if I am not here my tower would welcome you, but I hate to think of that.

Love from
FREYA

1 Bibliophile and a director of Sotheby's.
2 Editor at Murray's.

Asolo. 28 February 1977

My dear Susie,

I am really very troubled about your programme, because it is something quite different from what I had understood and something I am not able to do except with many weeks' preparation (and wouldn't do anyway). What I had understood was: the raft expedition with *conversation* as the landscape went by, pointing out this or that as it caught our eye – but not a sort of Baedeker which requires condensed and accurate information in a rather boring form. I take it the film is for an hour; and with fourteen places to film it is roughly four minutes for each place – some more, some less.

What I had thought is that we would start from Birecik and go along talking of the *theory* of the Romans' wars of Mesopotamia. Have you got my *Rome on the Euphrates*? It contains all I know about this country, and I could read bits or mug them up – to accentuate the main events (the Battle of Carrhae and desert war; the descent of Trajan to his crossing from Euphrates to Tigris, and description of his boats, etc., and the main theme – the Emperor Julian, slipping down to defeat and death). Small details, like Zenobia founding Halebiya, or Risafe in the desert (I see you have not included), or the Greek civilisation in Doura, could all be slipped in casually as the landscape went by; but the main line would be a half-hour talk on what Rome felt she was doing there, while the visual details of the landscape would go by unexplained.

What I had been thinking of as a plan was to open on Asolo and its landscape and close that preface with me walking down our old street and opening my front door ('Nothing like home,' I could say to the audience); and then have either my terrace or sitting room and us over our drinks discussing the place. You would give the programme, and I would say that what I had thought and prepared was slightly different and more of a conversation, with the landscape slipping by but not (except once or twice) specifically referred to. I would say that the spectator must be trusted to enjoy the landscape, and the producer must enhance it with a living interest, and I had thought of five human beings (if we go to Carrhae) to make this river and Palmyra *live*: (1) the first, Alexander, whose ghost hangs there like a shadow, crossing at Zeugma; (2) Carrhae and the story of the battle (my book, p. 114); I have been told it is the best description of the tragedy and I might read it out? – it has I think the feeling of that desert edge; (3) Trajan taking his fleet down the stream to the crossing for Ctesiphon and the breaking up of his dream – dreamed no doubt when he stood in the room where Alexander died (we could discuss why one succeeded and the other failed?); and (4) our last of Euphrates – the Emperor Julian, his strange sad character and defeated death; and (5) when we come to Palmyra, the portrait, fascinating, of Zenobia.

Love,
FREYA

JOHN GREY MURRAY

Jerablus on the Euphrates. 30 April 1977

Dearest Jock,

Such a sad story. The raft too beautiful and a wonderful welcome when we drove up by the little sandy hills which surround it, and found a huge crowd massed on all their summits, clapping their hands as they saw us. The raft looked very cosy and just like its picture, opening over rush matting and a layer of dry hay, with my little raised apartment (one room with a loo) at the back and three armchairs in front. We decided to sleep there and the sun went and the crowd dispersed and we were really rather happy and slept wrapped in sleeping bags and warm, while the great river tossed its waves past us at great speed, pushing us more and more into our little inlet and rising round us as the clouds massed up in the direction of Iraq. At about 5 a.m. I woke up and thought the pleasant clucking notes of the waves much louder, and looking out, saw the hay and matting on our north-west corner submerged and a lisping of water all over it. I waited to finish doing my hair and then thought better to call to Arabella and Mark and we watched the little corner getting slowly more submerged. The details of this squalid story are too long to tell you, but anyway by that evening we decided to sleep here in the hotel (very clean and amiable and kept by a Circassian). The raft was stripped and we went down next morning across a subsidiary stream where a small crowd and three cars were gathered. The stream covered an asphalt road which had come to grief and split the rubber wheel of the last car across it (with a bit of iron girder) and the governor's order had come to suspend all traffic. The governor himself arrived, a plain but kindly elderly man, and listened unconvinced while one very nice A.D.C. explained the necessity for reaching the raft; and we were rather despondent when he seized my arm and said, 'Come, let *us* cross' – and so we did, shoes, stockings and all, the water not more than knee-deep and not too cold. Just over the hillock, with its crowd gathering, the poor raft lay with all the baggage on the bank beside it, a rather soppy wetness over everything and the rest of the morning spent stacking our woeful household into a police hut nearby. An old Russian launch and a little one beside it were there ready for anything, but the fact is that the river is more or less at its height and this is the third morning that begins bright and drifts into an evening storm. We spent the afternoon visiting a village on the bank of another subsidiary stream to look at the *shahtur*, the ferry-boats used to cross the river, and think of taking two of these and forgetting the raft which is obviously very shaky. (How often did I beg them to have some Western overseer at its construction?) It floats but tilts one end up if the current catches it.

Dear love,

FREYA

SYBIL, LADY CHOLMONDELEY

Asolo. 20 November 1978

Dearest Sybil,

I came back four days ago and was happy to find your letter, but not so over the news of your wrist. We are all getting on, darling Sybil; but what good lives we have had – something Homeric about them. I am reading the *Iliad* (for the fourth time) and carried away as ever by that continuous excitement, that greatness of the stage which is ever there, dominating and inspiring the greatness of its people and power of its incorrigible gods. I weep over Andromache and Hector as I did when I was fourteen, galloping about in those chariots quite independent of roads, with eternity round every corner and here and there friendly voices of the gods who happened to like you. With fifty years of writing behind me, I can be fascinated by looking into the *structure*, which draws itself up out of life's very depth – and does it so unerringly out of its crude materials, not trying to disguise them. What a poor world it becomes when people only try to be clever.

Love always,

FREYA

MR AND MRS FRANK HOLT

Asolo. 15 May 1979

Dear Anne and Frank,

How good to get your letter, and just as my mind too was beginning to wander off on journeys so that it seemed to meet you on the way! I was in fact wandering with you in spirit led by the magic word Afghanistan. Do you think one could ever get a visa for it now? Together with one for Russia next door and already unpopular? (I am so glad!) I have been reading *The Gilgit Game* by John Keay and a great longing comes over me for another glimpse of that roof of the world (but to me more like an *altar*). I would like to meet the Indus where I once crossed it below Peshawar, and go up to where (I take it) no road goes on beyond Hunza, but I like to imagine that those little ponies get across from where one leaves the Indus, and reaches Oxus by passes (Baroghil) to what look like villages (Sarhad-i-Wakhan and Bouzai Gumbad), and goes down into Badakhshan. If I could do it I don't believe I should at all mind dying on the way because after all one can't complain of departing from this world at eighty. Can one deal with height by taking oxygen? I am going to enquire into these things but not really with any solid hope, chiefly because of those two little bits of frontier paper. I have done no proper travelling now for years and can't tell you with what admiration and vicarious pleasure I read your itinerary. If there were to be a road for Bistritza over the Pamirs would you not come? I wish there were, just for such a chance!

I was so glad to get your letter and send love as always.

FREYA

JOHN GREY MURRAY

Asolo. 16 June 1979

Dearest Jock,

Your letter has come, most welcome, though I would like better news of your health. What a lot of letters we have written each other since first I stepped full of awe into that Byron room! Two wars have passed over it and ever so many journeys; and now we needn't worry much over what happens to us, for no one can take from us 86 years (a few less for you) of a very interesting life. People forget this *permanence* of the good times. It makes one remarkably free.

I wish I could give this freedom to Costanza.[1] There seems to be no sign of a cure, and I am sad not only for her but for Paolo and would gladly go to her in Turin but she is being kept strictly quiet with no emotion, and can neither read nor move. Surely one should be allowed a little pill and freedom?

Dear love dearest Jock. I think of you all so often. And so grateful for the books coming towards me. Have got a little pony-riding meanwhile.

Love from
FREYA

1 Freya's niece, Cici.

Asolo. 21 September 1979

Dear Mr Magyar,

I have just come back from a holiday in Greece and find your kind letter on my desk. I have not much time to answer all, but am much touched by your kind words. I must tell you that I am eighty-six years old, and have now stopped writing, and am enjoying these last years by reading. When I look back I see that my real and deep interest in travel was not so much geographic as human: what I have been and still am interested in is the development of the human creature and one can watch this through the centuries and look with deep interest at its geographic varieties which are yet so deeply the same.

Yours sincerely,

FREYA STARK

MISS MARLOW

Asolo. 23 April 1980

Dear Miss Marlow,

I am always interested to hear from someone who wishes to find out more about this strange world we live in, and you seem to me to have discovered the sort of way to set about it. You are a little younger than I was when I first took to Arabic and spent a winter in the Lebanon hills, and so got more and more drawn to the surrounding lands. I don't think you need worry about safety: the Arab feeling for women's propriety is so strong that you need only be careful to *show* that you are a modest creature by covering up to the neck, down more or less to ankles and wrists, and the hair (I used to wear woollen stockings – to protect myself against the sun); a skirt *over* my riding breeches; long sleeves and riding shirt buttoned to the neck – and got no suggestions other than quite numerous proposals of marriage, which I countered by explaining that my mother would not like me to settle so far away. This careful dressing, and the fact that one is genuinely interested in Learning, was quite enough for Arab or Persian: one should be a little older in Turkey, but even there the secret is clothes. I used to cover up my hair with a kerchief and only let it loose across mountain passes in Persia where (in a revolution very like the present) there was a probability of robbers in ambush who might shoot believing one to be a man.

As for funds, that is a general, and lasting, difficulty. I came at last to realise that, so long as one does not really mind about being comfortable, one can live on as little abroad as at home. This has seen me through many situations.

I would add one thing you may or may not find useful, but I think of as important: that one should have a quest of one's own – history, literature, photography, anything like a pursuit to give an added reason and interest for travel.

I do wish you all good luck and as much interest in it all as I have enjoyed.

Yours sincerely,
FREYA STARK

Index